C000226082

FOOD FUTURE AND SOCIETY

This book brings together a unique collection of chapters to facilitate a broad discussion on food education that will stimulate readers to think about key policies, recent research, curriculum positions and how to engage with key stakeholders about the future of food.

Food education has gained much attention because the challenges that influence food availability and eating in schools also extend beyond the school gate. Accordingly, this book establishes evidence-based arguments that recognise the many facets of food education, and reveal how learning through a future's lens and joined-up thinking is critical for shaping intergenerational fairness concerning food futures in education and society. This book is distinctive through its multidisciplinary collection of chapters on food education with a particular focus on the Global North, with case studies from England, Australia, the Republic of Ireland, the United States of America, Canada and Germany. With a focus on three key themes and a rigorous food futures framework, the book is structured into three sections: (i) food education, pedagogy and curriculum, (ii) knowledge and skill diversity associated with food and health learning and (iii) food education inclusivity, culture and agency. Overall, this volume extends and challenges current research and theory in the area of food education and food pedagogy and offers insight and tangible benefits for the future development of food education policies and curricula.

This book will be of great interest to students, scholars, policymakers and education leaders working on food education and pedagogy, food policy, health and diet and the sociology of food.

Gurpinder Singh Lalli is Reader in Education for Social Justice and Inclusion at the University of Wolverhampton, UK. He is sole author of *Schools, Food and*

Social Learning (Routledge, 2019), co-editor of *School Farms: Feeding and Educating Children* (Routledge, 2021) and sole author of *Schools, Space and Culinary Capital* (Routledge, 2023).

Angela Turner is an adjunct senior lecturer in Design and Technology in the Faculty of Education at Southern Cross University, Australia. She is the co-editor of *International Perspectives of Food Education in the School Curriculum* (2020).

Marion Rutland is an honorary research fellow at the University of Roehampton, UK. She is the co-editor of *International Perspectives of Food Education in the School Curriculum* (2020).

Routledge Studies in Food, Society and the Environment

For more information about this series, please visit: www.routledge.com/books/series/RSFSE

FOOD FUTURES IN EDUCATION AND SOCIETY

Edited by
Gurpinder Singh Lalli, Angela Turner,
and Marion Rutland

LONDON AND NEW YORK

Designed cover image: © Getty Images

First published 2024
by Routledge
4 Park Square, Milton Park, Abingdon, Oxon OX14 4RN

and by Routledge
605 Third Avenue, New York, NY 10158

Routledge is an imprint of the Taylor & Francis Group, an informa business

British Library Cataloguing-in-Publication Data
A catalogue record for this book is available from the British Library

Library of Congress Cataloging-in-Publication Data
Names: Lalli, Gurpinder Singh, editor. | Turner, Angela, editor. |
Rutland, Marion, editor.
Title: Food futures in education and society / edited by Gurpinder Singh
Lalli, Angela Turner, and Marion Rutland.
Description: New York, NY : Routledge, 2023. | Includes bibliographical
references and index.
Identifiers: LCCN 2022061011 (print) | LCCN 2022061012 (ebook) |
ISBN 9781032280219 (hardback) | ISBN 9781032280196 (paperback) |
ISBN 9781003294962 (ebook)
Subjects: LCSH: Food—Moral and ethical aspects. | Food habits—Study and
teaching. | Children—Nutrition—Study and teaching. | School
children—Nutrition—Study and teaching.
Classification: LCC RJ206 .F658 2023 (print) | LCC RJ206 (ebook) |
DDC 613.2083—dc23/eng/20230210
LC record available at https://lccn.loc.gov/2022061011
LC ebook record available at https://lccn.loc.gov/2022061012

ISBN: 978-1-032-28021-9 (hbk)
ISBN: 978-1-032-28019-6 (pbk)
ISBN: 978-1-003-29496-2 (ebk)

DOI: 10.4324/9781003294962

Typeset in Bembo
by codeMantra

CONTENTS

FIGURES

TABLES

ACKNOWLEDGEMENTS

We acknowledge the willingness and hard work of our authors in contributing to the aims and objectives of this book. They come from a wide range of international colleagues and professionals with an interest and belief in food futures in education.

We would like to acknowledge the reviewers for providing critical feedback and their valuable time in developing this edited collection.

CONTRIBUTORS

Kelly-Ann Allen, PhD FAPS, FCEDP is an educational and developmental psychologist, a senior lecturer in the Faculty of Education, Monash University, and an honorary senior fellow at the Centre for Wellbeing Science, University of Melbourne. She is also the co-director and founder of the Global Belonging Collaborative and editor-in-chief for the *Educational and Developmental Psychologist* and co-editor-in-chief of the *Journal of Belonging and Human Connection*.

Dr Tina Bartelmeß is Junior Professor of Food Sociology at the University of Bayreuth at the Faculty of Life Sciences: Food, Nutrition and Health. She studied Ecotrophology (BSc) and Food Economics (MSc) at Justus Liebig University Giessen and completed her doctorate on the topic of food communication. In her research, she deals with the importance of social media food communication for everyday nutritional actions, as well as with the role of food communication in promoting sustainability and climate awareness, and with the topic of food poverty.

Christopher Boyle, PhD, FBPsS is a professor of Inclusive Education and Educational Psychology in the School of Education at the University of Adelaide, Australia. He is a fellow of the British Psychological Society and a senior fellow of the Higher Education Academy. He was previously Editor-in-Chief of *The Educational and Developmental Psychologist* and is currently the co-inaugural founding editor of the new journal *Belonging and Human Connection* (with Kelly-Ann Allen) launched in 2022 and published by Brill. He is an internationally recognised and respected academic and author on the subjects of inclusive education and psychology. He is a registered psychologist in the UK and Australia.

Claire Bristow, PhD Candidate is a lecturer in Public Health and Health Promotion in the School of Public Health and Preventive Medicine, Faculty of Medicine, Nursing and Health Sciences, Monash University. Her research explores the multitude of factors influencing eating disorders and their many risk factors from a public health perspective.

Martin Caraher, PhD and MSc is Emeritus Professor of food and health policy at the Centre for Food Policy at City University London. He has published extensively on issues of food and public health policy. He has a particular interest in food literacy, food inequalities, food welfare and food charity. Recent work has included research on the European Most Deprived Persons Programme; a review of food taxation schemes; the UK sugar tax; a critique of the English Responsibility Deal and reviews of charity food provision in times of crises. He has published over 200 articles, 20 book chapters and 5 books.

Emily Elenio is a graduate of the University of Pennsylvania with a bachelor's degree in Anthropology and is currently a master's student in Public Health at Brown University. She also works as an engagement manager for Acsel Health, a life-science consulting firm where she performs quantitative and qualitative research projects across a wide variety of health-related topics. Emily plans to pursue a graduate education as she is interested in using ethnographic research methods to better inform nutrition and food policy.

Suzanne Gomersall is a senior lecturer at the Nottingham Institute of Education, part of Nottingham Trent University (NTU), in teacher education and specialises in primary Design and Technology. In 2019 she began her PhD, focusing on child-hood obesity. Her PhD is the evaluation of the Healthy Lifestyles Project (HLSP), which aims to develop children's practical skills, knowledge and understanding to choose, prepare and cook healthy ingredients to feed themselves and their families, helping to change their attitudes and perceptions towards choosing a healthier life-style. Suzanne is an active member of the All-Party Parliamentary Group on School Food and the Design & Technology Association's Subject Consultation Group.

Morgan K. Hoke is an assistant professor of Anthropology at the University of North Carolina. She studies growth and development, nutrition, health and most recently impact of eviction on people from a biocultural perspective. She was at the University of Pennsylvania as an assistant professor of Anthropology and served as an Axilrod faculty fellow and research associate at Population Studies Center at the University of Pennsylvania. She received her PhD and master's degree in Public Health (MPH) from Northwestern University.

Kristiina Janhonen is a docent in Home Economics Science, with exten-sive experience in education, food studies and school meals. Her research has included work on food education and learning at the intersection of formal and informal contexts, such as schools and homes. She has used both qualitative and quantitative methods in her work. In addition to studying food practices and participation of youth, her research includes explorations of informal food education and learning in the context of families with children, as well as school-based action research to design tools for evaluation and to support multi-professional collaboration between teachers and school food personnel.

Lynda M. Korimboccus has been Lecturer in Sociology at West Lothian College, Scotland, for over 15 years. She is an associate fellow of the Higher Education Academy and an independent scholar in the field of Critical Animal Studies and Vegan Sociology. A PhD sociology researcher, Lynda is documenting the experiences of vegan children in the education system with a view to making recommendations to expand its inclusivity. Lynda also writes for Faunalytics and is Editor-in-Chief of the *Student Journal of Vegan Sociology*.

Neha K. Lalchandani has a background in Food Science and Nutrition and is currently in her final year of studying for the Doctor of Philosophy (Public Health) at the University of Adelaide, Australia. She is working on a research project that explores the potential to improve schoolchildren's dietary habits while impacting the environment positively (through reduced waste and packaging) by assessing school lunchbox contents and packing practices, in order to inform future policies and practices in this area. Neha is interested in the socio-ecological influences on children's dietary and pro-environmental behaviours. She is also passionate about school food environments and the convergence of public and planetary wellbeing in this context.

Gurpinder Singh Lalli is a reader in Education for Social Justice and Inclusion at the School of Education, University of Wolverhampton. Trained as a sociologist, he has a vested interest in the sociology of education, social justice, inclusion and inequity. He is author of *Schools, Food and Social Learning* (2019) for which the book won the best newcomer by the Society of Educational Studies in 2022. He is co-lead editor of *School Farms: Feeding and educating children* published in 2021 and published a second monograph titled *Schools, Space and Culinary Capital (2023)*. He teaches on the Doctoral Programme in Education and is a trustee of the food education charity, TastEd. He is outgoing Editor-in-Chief of *Educational Research and Evaluation* (2021–2023) and incoming Editor-in-Chief of *European Journal of Education* (2023–2026). His work on the school meals service has been funded by the ESRC and he continues to produce work on this topic.

Deana Leahy, PhD is an associate professor in the Faculty of Education at Monash University, Australia. Her research draws on interdisciplinary perspectives to critically study health education – from policy formations to their translations into everyday pedagogies. Whilst her work has a strong school focus, she has recently begun to explore the possibilities of other pedagogical spaces and approaches that seek to teach us something about health including museums/ exhibits, festivals, kitchen gardens and various digital technology platforms.

Amanda McCloat is President of St Angela's College, Sligo, and prior to this she was Head of the School of Home Economics and Senior Lecturer in Home Economics. Amanda has wide-ranging experience teaching, lecturing and researching in the field of Home Economics and Home Economics teacher education at secondary and third level. She is the president-elect (2022–2024) of the International Federation for Home Economics (IFHE) and vice-president of the European Association Home Economics (EAHE). Dr McCloat was appointed to the inaugural Healthy Ireland Council in May 2014 and was a member of the Food in Schools (Ireland) steering committee (June 2021). She is Chair of the Steering Group of the National Centre of Excellence for Home Economics based at St Angela's College. Her research interests are Home Economics education, food education, food literacy, cooking skills and Education for Sustainable and Responsible Living.

Caomhan McGlinchey is an educational psychologist. He studied for a doctorate in Educational, Child and Community Psychology at the University of Exeter, UK. He is a chartered member of the British Psychological Society

Kyoko Murakami is a teaching fellow and an honorary research fellow in the Department of Education at the University of Bath. Previously she worked as an associate professor of psychology at the University of Copenhagen, Denmark. Her research focuses on aspects of cognition such as learning, identity and memory, examining language use and social relations in practices of education and discourses of remembering, drawing on discursive psychology, cultural psychology, discourse analysis and other qualitative approaches including ethnography. Since 1998 she has been researching on international reconciliation practices such as war grave pilgrimages by British veterans (e.g., 2012, 2014), family reminiscence as memory practice (2017), materiality of memory (2017) and ageing (2021, in press).

Marie Murphy is a research fellow at the University of Birmingham. With a background in Public Health Nutrition, Marie has worked in community nutrition roles as well as holding research positions exploring child and adolescent dietary behaviours and obesity prevention. Marie has a particular interest in addressing inequalities in health and investigating ways in which the school environment can support healthy eating. Her current research focuses on national school food policy and its implementation and impact in secondary schools.

Rounaq Nayak, PhD is an academic at Bournemouth University. He is a fellow of the Royal Society of Public Health (RSPH) and the Royal Geographical Society (RGS). Dr Nayak's expertise and research is within the field of social sustainability particularly as it relates to food security and social justice in the global agri-food system. His research emphasises a *systems thinking* approach into practice in a new and unique way and provides simple strategies for building healthier communities.

Marianne O'Kane Boal, PhD is candidate at Atlantic Technological University in Sligo researching the school-based food practices of children in contemporary Irish society. She has presented at the IRSCL International Conference in Chile, Oct 2021, BSA Annual Conference 2021 and BSA Food Studies Conference 2021. She has written for *Sociology*, *Irish Journal of Sociology* and published 'Small Existential Fractures and an interrogative relationship with the world: An existentialist reading of Frances Hardinge's *A Face like Glass* (2012)', in *IRCL* 15.2, 2022. She is a member of the SAI Sociological Association of Ireland, BSA British Sociological Association and BPSA British Philosophical Association.

Donna Owen is a secondary teacher currently working in a Sydney High School in New South Wales, Australia. She is also an academic researcher looking to continually expand her knowledge to better understand current food issues and trends. Donna's former background as a food technologist and interest in this area has contributed to her motivation to inspire the next generation of students. As a food educator, Donna encourages a growth mindset in her students to remain open and flexible when reflecting on food issues and trends, which is a critical lifelong skill to adapt to the ever-changing needs of the time.

Miranda Pallan is a consultant in Public Health and Reader in Public Health and Epidemiology. Her research is in the field of health improvement in children and adolescents, with a focus on healthy eating, physical activity and obesity prevention. She has a particular interest in improving these factors in children with socioeconomic disadvantage. Her current research focuses on national school food policy and its implementation and impact in secondary schools.

Lefteris Patlamazoglou, PhD is a counselling psychologist and lecturer in the School of Educational Psychology and Counselling, Faculty of Education at Monash University, Australia. His research and teaching focus on the well-being of young people and adults of diverse genders, sexes and sexualities, belonging, migration and grief. In his counselling practice, Lefteris works with clients with a variety of mental health issues, court-ordered parents and their children and individuals and couples pursuing artificial reproductive treatment.

Yiannis Polychronakis (PhD) is the head of Supply Chains, Procurement and Project Management at the Business School, University of Salford, Manchester. He has published several articles in international journals (the *International*

Journal of Production Economics, the *International Journal of Forecasting,* the *Journal of Manufacturing and Technology Management,* etc.) in the areas of Forecasting, Procurement, and Optimisation. Yiannis has a number of papers included in refereed International Conference Proceedings. He has also assisted a number of organisations in developing and implementing best practices for process management, optimisation, procurement and project management.

Danielle Proud is a public health dietitian who uses a systems approach working with organisations, across sectors and through policy, to enhance the health and wellbeing of individuals. She has worked for over 15 years in community and statewide initiative prevention roles as well as clinical mental health. She currently works across policy, program and learning in the education sector. She hopes to see young people lead the way in designing future food systems that can nurture the environment as well as a healthy population. This is made possible by breaking down current food system complexity and creating connection to the food we eat and how it is made. You will find her outside in the vegetable patch.

HildaRuth Beaumont is an honorary senior research associate at The Institute of Education, University College London. She, her and hers, has worked in education for some 50 years and for most of that time was known as David Barlex. David became an acknowledged leader in design and technology education, curriculum design and curriculum materials development. He taught science and technology in comprehensive schools for 15 years before becoming a teacher educator. He directed the Nuffield Design and Technology Project, which produced an extensive range of curriculum materials widely used in primary and secondary schools in the UK and adapted for use in Australia, New Zealand, Canada, Sweden, South Africa and Russia. He was Educational Manager of Young Foresight, an initiative that has developed approaches to teaching and learning that enhance students' ability to respond creatively to design and technology activities. In 2002 he won the DATA Outstanding Contribution to Design and Technology Education award. David's research activity stemmed from his conviction that there should be a dynamic and synergic relationship between curriculum development and academic research. His research interests included pedagogy that develops design ability and creativity, young peoples' perceptions of technology and the professional development of teachers.

Marion Rutland (PhD) is an honorary research fellow and a former principal lecturer in Design and Technology in the School of Education, University of Roehampton, London. Her roles at the University have included Design and Technology Curriculum Area Coordinator, Course Leader for the Secondary PGCE Design and Technology Secondary Programme, Curriculum Leader for the Primary Design and Technology, Design and Technology Pathway Leader and Tutor for the MA Education (Design and Technology) Programme, PhD

Supervisor and External Examiner. Prior to this, she taught food-related subjects for 22 years in a range of secondary schools in the UK and Australia, and was a president of the Association of Home Economics Teachers and Technology (NATHE) and an advisory teacher for Information Communication Technology (ICT) in London. Her research and publication interests include food education in schools, curriculum development, ICT, teaching and learning in design and technology, creativity and food technology.

Ruth Seabrook is currently the head of Secondary Initial Teacher Education (ITE) at the University of Roehampton, London. She has been a Design and Technology (D&T) teacher and lecturer for 23 years. Ruth was awarded a senior fellowship of the Higher Education Academy and principal teaching fellow in 2015. Ruth has provided expertise as an external examiner and worked with a number of other universities delivering subject expertise. She is also a trustee of Esher 6th Form College Board of Trustees. Ruth works as a health and safety consultant with the Design and Technology Association and an associate of the Chartered Institute of Environmental Health and works within the group of D&T ITE tutors and collaborated on chapters for several books.

Mark Stein (PhD) is an associate member of staff at Salford Business School and is writing up research results and co-editing a book about Sustainable Public Food Procurement in Europe. He grew up in South Africa and studied history at Witwatersrand University. His working life was mainly with Tameside Council in North West England, where he supported small business development, promoted e-commerce, secured external funding and developed sustainable procurement policies. After retirement he returned to university and has recently completed a PhD thesis at the Business School, University of Salford, Manchester, comparing sustainable food procurement for public kitchens in the UK with Denmark and Sweden.

Samantha Stone is a senior research associate in Ethnography in Bristol Medical School, University of Bristol. She is currently researching social aspects of living with long-term chronic pain, based within the Consortium to Research Individual, Interpersonal and Social Influences in Pain (CRIISP). Her PhD (2020, University of Bath) and MRes (2015, University of Bath) were both in Education and funded by the Economic Social Research Council (ESRC), exploring children's school mealtime socialisation from a child-centred perspective. She has taught in Education and Social Policy and has worked with Bristol charities to empower vulnerable women and children.

Suzanne Suggs, PhD, MS, BBA, CHES is a full professor of Social Marketing at the University of Lugano in the Institute of Public Health and the Institute of Communication and Public Policy, Faculty of Communication, Culture and Society and is Vice President of the Swiss School of Public Health. Her research focuses on understanding determinants of health behaviours and developing and testing strategies to modify health-related behaviours. She has led studies on understanding and promoting healthy diet among children and youth, measuring eating behaviour in children, perceptions of healthy foods, food policies, sustainable and healthy diets, and is a co-investigator of the Swiss national nutrition survey for youth (menu.ch kids).

Deborah Trevallion (PhD) has worked for 20 years at the University of Newcastle, NSW, Australia. Deborah is an honorary professor who specialises in Technology and STEM Education. She teaches design from a holistic approach using problem solving with authentic problems, critical thinking, research, experiential learning and ongoing evaluation that promotes lifelong learning. She has taught Technology in secondary schools for over 20 years and has a doctorate from Griffith University, Queensland, Australia. Deborah is a proud recipient of the prestigious Australian, King and Amy O'Malley postgraduate award. She is an international academic journal editor, is internationally published in journals and books and is an international consultant in secondary and tertiary Technology curriculum development.

Angela Turner (PhD) is an adjunct senior lecturer in Design and Technology (Secondary Initial Teacher Education) and research scholar (Southern Cross University) with 20 years higher education experience. She has actively formed university-school community engagement with rural primary and secondary school communities to advance teaching, learning and assessment in food settings that are project based and inquiry driven. Angela's research examines the symbiotic relationship between humans, technology and the environment. Core to this includes cross-cultural and ontological meaning making of food systems in relation to the sustainability and productivity of edible landscapes to feed growing populations in the face of climate change. Her publishing track record includes books, journal articles, food industry reports and conference papers. Angela has received peer recognition for integrating the domains of teaching and research awarded through a Southern Cross University Vice Chancellor's Teaching Citation (2018); School of Education Recognition Award (2018); Australian College of Educators Award (2017). She is currently a New South Wales Education Standards Authority (NESA) Curriculum Advisor for the Technical Advisory Group for Technologies seven to ten syllabus development.

FOREWORD

I have been involved in school food and nutrition education for 30 years, and while positive changes have been made in the UK, there are still societal issues related to malnutrition, education and wealth inequalities, social justice and political change. Often policy appears to be made based on ideology, rather than evidence, and school programmes are often short term. In addition, there is a need to look at bigger issues, such as climate change and sustainability, technological innovation, and education opportunity and mobility for all, a better understanding of the mental health of our young people alongside societal changes and new social norms. School food never looked so complex.

What is needed is a modern paradigm for food in school, a drive for something more inclusive, diverse and modern – for pupils now and in the future. For example, *does what pupils experience now set them up for life? Are we linking the food that is served to what is taught, and including pupil and parent voice in decision making? How do we know? What do we want for the future?* We need to stop, pause and review the evidence, consider what we do and why and decide what action might need to be taken. Together, we need to decide on new food futures in education and society.

This book brings a fresh perspective to the 'school food' debate – using the themes of policy and pedagogy, psychology and sociology to link together valuable and interdisciplinary areas of study. The 18 chapters in the edited book look at the evidence around school food, highlighting research and case studies of practice, with recommendations. This has been brought together by 33 distinguished, international contributors from universities, teacher training institutes, schools and consultancies, each experienced in different fields, sharing their insight and valuable expertise. Some I have met personally, others I have only followed, but together this collection provides an up-to-date snapshot of evidence from around the world.

As highlighted, this book provides insight, evidence and inspiration to make changes for the better, starting conversations for change through a holistic lens. It combines areas of policy, pedagogy, psychology and sociology, all of which are important in schools – the intrinsic requirement to give our young people broad experiences that will provide opportunities for healthy lives in an evolving technological society. For pupils it is about safe, healthy spaces and behaviours that reflect their cultural norms and feelings of inclusion. We owe it to them to facilitate this, including their parents and community.

This book has a broad audience including policy makers and researchers, teacher trainers and teachers, and it enables them to review the current status-quo and look at policy, procedural and/or practical changes for better learning and food experiences for pupils now and in future. It may also help set research agendas, based on the recommendations made. Policy changes could include curriculum design and school food standards, operations and service guidance (including eating together), and in schools it could address practical issues of management systems and structures (such as removing stigma and addressing inclusivity), teaching and learning styles and whole school food approaches. Though whole school food approaches have been discussed for decades, there is still much to be done to ensure consistency of approach, joined-up food experiences (eating, drinking and cooking) and community engagement. An evidence approach is required for change, with champions in schools leading the way such as senior staff, teachers, parents and pupils. Taking inspiration from this book, schools can start their journey to better food futures, and policy makers and researchers can better understand the impact of decisions made.

While reading through the chapters, thought provoking sub-themes emerged which will have relevance to the reader. Our societal context is important, and these interrelated sub-themes should be considered when piloting and/or making decisions about whole school food approaches. The sub-themes include inequalities (interrelationships of poverty, health and wellbeing); climate change and sustainability (from global issues to local action, and how we can all make a difference); pedagogy and attainment for positive life changes and mobility (especially around 'learning from doing' and eating together); social justice; inclusivity and equality of access for all (which includes culture and ethics) and the importance of ensuring pupil and parent voice in decision making. The book pulls these sub-themes together, with their specific foci, for more rounded, holistic approaches to school food – it is not just about what food is served or what is taught, it is more than the sum of its parts. It is about our society, communities and people, and what we want for a better future.

There is much to get excited about concerning school food, for example, whether it is what is served, how and when pupils eat together or what is taught and how. Critically, we need to ensure that all children and young people have consistent experiences to enable them to have happy and healthier lives, including their friends and families. The diverse nature of the book inspires us to look at what is currently happening through an evidence approach, consider the contextual sub-themes woven throughout its chapters and help define what changes could and should be made for good. It is about ensuring children and young people receive experiences which they can relate to throughout their lives. Food deserves respect, an understanding of its importance to life and the impact it can have on individuals and society.

This book demonstrates that a holistic approach to school food is required, not just in the traditional sense of canteen and curriculum. It is far wider, taking a worldview, reflecting personal cultures and values, being inclusive and modern and demonstrating diversity and inclusivity. Now is the time for school food – let's all be part of it for everyone's food futures.

Roy Ballam
School food and nutrition education consultant
Formerly Managing Director and Head of Education,
British Nutrition Foundation

PART I

Overview

1

INTRODUCTION

Food futures in education

Gurpinder Singh Lalli, Angela Turner and Marion Rutland

This book introduces new perspectives into the literature through an edited collection of texts with a focus on three key themes and a rigorous food futures frame from which the book is structured through (i) policy, curriculum and pedagogy, (ii) psychology of food and (iii) sociology of food. These themes aim to orient the reader to the mutually reliant relationships between people, technical processes and devices and ecology (our ultimate food source), brought together into an application context that involves why and how we teach food futures and the relationship with society. The novelty of the book stems from its variation in ideas from different subjects that draw on a common set of ideas in order to create more equitable food futures. While each chapter may appear as separate milieux, they are intricately interconnected as entangled concepts.

The value and importance of good nutrition for health and wellbeing underpin the context of food policy, curriculum and pedagogy that traverse cross-curricula and cross-cultural contexts in food education, health and physical education, science, design and technology syllabi. Moreover, eating is our most common behaviour and to understand why we choose certain foods, we must first understand the psychology of food concerning the brain behavioural system that influences our food choices and eating behaviours. Comparatively, the sociology of food enables us to develop different understandings of the world in terms of society, structure and its power relations.

The book consists of 20 chapters that include an introduction and a conclusion. A chapter-by-chapter synopsis of the project's planned content and main argument(s) follows in the next section.

DOI: 10.4324/9781003294962-2

Chapter overviews

To align to the themes of the book the chapter overviews are organised into three sections which include (i) policy, curriculum and pedagogy, (ii) psychology of food and (iii) sociology of food. These three themes are interrelated and bring together key debates on food in society.

Policy, curriculum and pedagogy

Chapter 2: School mealtime as a pedagogical event

This chapter is a very interesting and very currently relevant review of research into the provision of Finnish and UK school meals based on three complementary perspectives (1) institutional arrangements, (2) multisensory experiences and (3) commensality and interaction.

It explores the concept of school meals outside the view of being perceived as a way of feeding children when they are at school, to building an overarching conceptualisation of school mealtimes as an event that strengthens the pedagogical activities of a school. It is suggested that the framework can be used as a tool for further research into building a more overarching conceptualisation of school mealtimes as an event that supports children's learning.

The authors suggest that for this to be successful, there is a need for human and physical resources, support from senior leadership and the training of teachers and school service staff. In addition, to strengthen the educational potential of school mealtimes the frequently contesting social aspirations of children and adults need to be acknowledged. They propose, very effectively, that further collaboration with classroom-based teaching as well as homes and families, would provide additional pathways for strengthening the learning outcomes connected to, and collaborating with school mealtimes. This would provide a positive impact on students' view and understanding of the importance of food as an aspect of their everyday life now and in the future.

Chapter 3: Healthy lifestyles project: a practical food programme for primary schools

This chapter provides a summary of the Health Lifestyles Project (HLSP), based in Nottinghamshire, UK to support children's practical cooking and nutritional skills, knowledge and understanding. This six-year longitudinal study draws on the experiences of multiple stakeholders. The chapter unfolds by highlighting key evaluative summaries across five aspects of work which are underpinned by the socio-ecological model, which include (i) individual, (ii) interpersonal, (iii) organisational, (iv) community and policies and (v) laws and other cultures. This review of the HLSP shows that multipronged SEM approaches that draw strength from the community working together can impact children and their families' attitudes, behaviours and choices to healthy eating and other lifestyle choices. Ultimately, this helps provide children with the tools, skills, knowledge and understanding around nutrition and the ability and desire to choose, prepare and cook healthy meals.

Chapter 4: Food technology as a subject to be taught in secondary schools – a discussion of content, relevance and pedagogy

This chapter will be of relevance to those training to become food teachers, those training such teachers, those teaching food and those carrying out curriculum development in food. In the chapter, HildaRuth Beaumont begins by considering the narrative of food in the contexts of rich and poor countries as a sequence involving production and harvesting, storage, preservation and processing, sale and distribution and preparation and consumption in terms of the technologies deployed. Some are directly concerned with the intrinsic nature of food as a material and the way it behaves. Others have a more tangential, but no less significant, part to play within the narrative. The chapter then uses the lenses of social justice and stewardship to consider malnutrition and sustainable food production. How to engage learners in secondary school with each stage of the narrative is described in terms of a range of teaching possibilities. Future scenarios for the narrative of food are considered in the light of the conflicting requirements of feeding an increasing population and combating global warming. The chapter concludes with a proposal to engage stakeholders in further curriculum development.

Chapter 5: Learning from the true school food experts: an ethnographic investigation of middle school students during school lunch

This chapter presents an ethnographic study of American children during school lunch to offer a different perspective on how school food is actually consumed and shared. The analyses show how these actions illustrate the ways in which children demonstrate food agency and also agency through school food. Since children are the ultimate decision makers of what food they choose to eat, throw away, trade, or share, we argue that children's perspectives should be considered and analysed when policymakers are deciding upon school food policies. Often, we hear about how children are not consulted in decision making so this chapter shines a light on such narratives and how research can be guided to incorporate their voices.

Chapter 6: The role of schools in supporting healthy eating in children and young people

In this chapter on the role of schools in supporting healthy eating in children and young people, international school policies and interventions in place to promote healthy eating are reviewed, incorporating feeding programmes for addressing food insecurity, quality standards for provision and behavioural, environmental and whole school interventions. The chapter highlights the purpose of such initiatives and considers their impact upon schoolchildren. It describes some of the challenges faced by schools in supporting healthy eating and the requirements for successful implementation. Finally, key discussions are developed on the role of schools as part of a wider food system to benefit children and communities.

Chapter 7: Home economics curriculum policy in the Republic of Ireland: lessons for policy development

This chapter focuses on food education within home economics in the context of the Republic of Ireland. The teaching of food has seen many changes in countries across the world. It was first introduced in the UK as 'cookery' in the early 19th century to teach girls how to cook and manage their homes, followed by domestic science in the early 20th century with a focus on food and nutrition and home economics in the latter part of the 20th century. This was followed by food technology, based on a branch of food science that deals with production, preservation, quality control and research and the development of food products, alongside hospitality. Similar patterns can be found in other countries including Australia and New Zealand; however, countries such as Southern Ireland have evolved a different pathway based on the concept of home economics.

The Republic of Ireland has retained the term home economics as defined by the 1908 Lake Plaid Conference, focusing on the quality of family life by developing everyday skills and the responsible management of resources within the home. Home economics in Southern Ireland is the only subject on the curriculum directly concerned with teaching students theoretical and practical food skills in a holistic and integrated manner, although there are other inputs from the health sector and non-profit organisations related to healthy living.

Home economics is an optional subject for pupils aged 12–15 years and 16–18 years, though there have been recent calls to reintroduce home economics into the curriculum to cultivate essential culinary food skills, that many considered have been lost and deal with the increase in diet-related non-communicable diseases (DRNCDs). This has led recently to significant curriculum reform, developing and repositioning food education, based on Bernstein's Theory of the Pedagogic Device as a theoretical framework within the Home Economics Education Policy, as is presented in this chapter.

Chapter 8: Food technology and 21st century learning

This chapter presents a very interesting and valuable overview of the Food Technology Curriculum in New South Wales, Australia. It is well researched and explores the strengths and the weaknesses of the Stage 6 Food Technology syllabus studied by students in their final two years of study at school, which they complete at approximately 17 years. It includes an analysis and a justification for Food Technology to be made mandatory in the secondary school examination system, highlighting its links with students' lifelong learning and providing progression, through a range of pathways into the home, the workplace and technical, further, and higher education.

Food technology in New South Wales is based on problem solving, critical thinking, higher order skills and experimental activities and addresses the 'why' rather than the 'how to do'. It is certainly not only 'skills based'. There are connections with other syllabi subjects and includes issues such as the environment, sustainability, food processing and the food industry. It is emphasised that practical experiences in developing, preparing, experimenting and presenting food are integral throughout the course.

It is argued that food technology is based essentially on a technological viewpoint, with design and creativity centrally based, alongside extensive knowledge of nutrition and scientific understanding. It is acknowledged that there are differences between teaching food technology and hospitality in that they complement each other but have very different contents. The chapter emphasises the need to continuously revise the food technology curriculum due to the changing influences of socio-economies, political and education issues in the 21st century.

It is very encouraging to read how New South Wales has developed and reviewed their food technology syllabus over the years by considering the needs of the students and changes in society. It has resulted in a course based on a deep understanding of the key issues and the learning of high-order thinking skills that will contribute to the students' future lives in their social, economic and ecological future.

Psychology of food

Chapter 9: Food waste issues of universal infant free school meals in south-east England schools: a cautionary tale

The precautionary tale is this: the challenge to produce enough food will be greater over the next 50 years than in all human history and yet food waste continues to escalate across various domains from our homes, restaurants, cafes and schools. Research undertaken in this chapter exposed significant levels of food waste in schools where Universal Infant Free School Meals were served in east England. The research found that in most cases the discarded food from many schools was of excellent quality yet there was no thought given to reducing the waste nor any consideration to restructure the menu in consultation with pupils and parents. Given increasing consumption as population growth increases, and energy demands driving land, water and biomass diversions to bio-energy and high food wastage rates, it makes sense that schools should educate and promote food stewardship because we need to feed people rather than landfills and the best place to educate that is in the school dining rooms.

Chapter 10: Belonging, identity, inclusion and togetherness: the lesser-known social benefits of food for children and young people

This chapter explores the many changes that have taken place in society in recent years including, how young people connect, socialise and come together with each other and with their families. Changes resulting from shifts in families' working patterns, reductions in multi-generational families living together or near each other and technology have all been blamed for rising patterns of loneliness, mental health concerns and other negative outcomes. Although, research has not pinpointed the exact outcome of these socio-cultural shifts there remains a compelling and significant body of research around the importance of belonging and the role food plays in meeting this fundamental human need, particularly in the school setting.

A sense of belonging is defined as feeling that one is an integral part of one's surrounding systems, including family, friends, school, work environment, community and physical places. The role of food in fostering a feeling of belonging is well established but viewed differently by various disciplines. Research suggests there are certain situations where food can disrupt a student's feeling of belonging.

This chapter highlights the importance of food for fostering 'belonging' in a school setting through several perspectives. It explores implications for specific populations, particularly during a time of crisis (recent Covid outbreak), when families were not able to meet but instead organised remote lunches and parties on Zoom. Food has the potential to unite and bond people through routine, ritual and habit. It is highlighted that food is particularly appealing to children and young people in the school setting, especially at lunch time or during a break from classroom learning. Breakfast programs, recipe clubs, community/school cookbooks and kitchen garden programs all play an important role in the relationship between food and children providing physiological benefits and social bonding.

While this chapter highlights very relevant issues concerning the important role that food can play in the welfare of children across cultures and societies, students with special needs and disabilities (SEND), including autistic needs, also need to feel they belong. The inclusion of mental health under SEND suggests that some foods will become 'comforting' because they become associated with positive emotional and social interactions.

Chapter 11: Is the ability to cook enough to foster good eating habits in the future? Investigating how schools can empower positive food choices in adolescents

'Is the ability to cook enough to foster good eating habits?' is a very good question and one that is discussed and answered in this chapter because the need to develop and instil a critical mindset for making wise food decisions by young people flows into meal preparation. Just learning to cook is very clearly not the answer to fostering good eating habits.

The chapter explores key influences that impact adolescents and the need for them to make critical and sensible decisions about their food choices to ensure future healthy eating strategies, now and in later adulthood. The overarching goal of this research examines and highlights strategies that can be used to empower adolescents to make critical and important food base decisions. The role of schools is discussed, the influences that permeate food decisions, geographic locations and cultural and socio-economics reasons why adolescents choose to eat certain foods are put forward.

Food literacy is defined and described as 'the range of skills, knowledge and choices required each day when striving to achieve dietary recommendations that support good health'. It is highlighted that the crucial food elements are the *food skills combined with high order and critical thinking*. The author emphasises that schools can play a role in improving children's food knowledge in 'cooking' classes as well in the school canteen. Student voices and peers are identified as having an active role in this process, which is further enhanced when preparing a meal together. Learning to cook is important but it is not enough on its own and there is much more that they need to know and are able to do. Students should become more aware of how to prepare healthy meals and make better choices about their health. They will benefit considerably from 'doing' rather than just 'listening', so that they can make better life choices.

It is very important that adolescents take responsibility for their health and their food choices, and the research recommends a shift in mindset from the adolescents just 'needing' food to choosing and 'consuming food for personal health'. An important life skill that they will need throughout their life and one that schools have a responsibility to encourage and develop.

Sociology of food

Chapter 12: Social media platforms and adolescents' nutritional careers: upcoming development tasks and required literacies

Technological developments leading to the present day began in the early days of the industrial revolution. Fast forward to today, interconnected social media platforms are an important community for many people because it provides an emancipatory space for socially connecting to other people as a learner. In the context of food futures, different actors have divergent ideas about what should be included in a healthy diet, and how these ideas may be improved. Taking into account adolescents' developmental challenges, this chapter explores different social media practices related to food. In order to ensure healthy and sustainable careers in nutrition, the study referred to in this chapter highlights food, health and media literacy as critical elements for engaging with social media content.

Chapter 13: Food poverty and how it affects UK children in the long term

We may think of some schools as a type of unexamined ontological privilege that favours academic excellence over the health and wellbeing of their students, but in England, vouchers are provided to 'at risk' students who have poor access to quality food or restricted range of foods, and often suffer from hunger. This in turn affects their academic abilities due to a lack of essential nutrients that causes fatigue and resultant lack of concentration. In this chapter, historical, socio-economic, political and contemporary issues of child food poverty are explored through desktop research literature. The historical developments over time provide a snapshot about the reasons for implementing free school meals and the role of charity-based organisations such as 'food banks' in providing food for children. The chapter expands to discuss the relationship between nutritional food, and the important cognitive and physical growth and development of children and young people.

Chapter 14: School food lifeworlds: children's relational experience of school food and its importance in their early primary school years

In this chapter, the dualism automatically established between a child's interpersonal relationships and friendships is explored through food practices in an Irish primary school.

Concepts that illustrate the fluid and inter-relational characteristic of growing friendships and learning through food provide a 'blueprint' for a child's transition from pre-school to school, which can be an enduring tension for some children. This is an important aspect of this chapter because, in the past, only friendships were considered essential for a successful school environment. This body of work draws on a study undertaken by the author with 4–7 year old children, that document how they express friendships and family through food as manipulated objects and illustrations by the children.

Chapter 15: 'I like it when I can sit with my best friends': exploration of children's agency to achieve commensality in school mealtimes

Mealtimes are considered as complex socialising situations that transmit important sociocultural norms imposed by adult authorities. In this chapter, we argue that children act agentically, using non-verbal communication to socially and spatially organise and negotiate material and moral complexities to achieve commensality during school mealtimes. Commensality is the act of eating together and is often considered important for social communion. It underpins the core value of mealtime practices. To illustrate our argument, we draw on empirical material taken from the first author's doctoral research of children's school mealtime socialisation from a child-centred perspective. The data featured in this chapter originates from one of several semi-structured group interviews with children who regularly ate together during the school mealtime. The thematic analysis of the interview extract addresses how children worked around the mealtime structure and rules; how they relate to one another and negotiate seating arrangement for achieving commensality. School mealtimes are an important context in which we, researchers alike, learn something new about children's socialisation in the commensality practice and employ children's disruptions as a source of critical examination of our normative understanding of the children's socialisation process.

Chapter 16: Friends, not food: how inclusive is education for young vegans in Scotland?

This is a powerful chapter that explores a conundrum in Scottish schools concerning a school system that supports 'inclusivity' on paper but not necessarily in practice. Even though some people may feel that vegan diets are dangerous to children, a growing number of families are opening their minds to vegan diets for their children as research increasingly supports the nutritional and health benefits. Moreover, raising a child as a vegan can also create an ethical tension surrounding 'inclusivity' in an education system where meals are supplied by the school. Given the expectations by a parent or caregiver about the quality of the meals for their vegan children, it is crucial to dissemble meat-eating dominance in schools that provide free school meals by dwelling in these tensions and spaces in order to create a level playing field for food choices and preferences, and in doing so promote 'inclusivity'.

Chapter 17: Food pathways to community success

Even though we share a complicated tapestry of gender, age, race, religion and class, it is important to realise that not everyone has access to adequate food so that they can live active and healthy lives. Food assistance programs are becoming the 'new norm' in the UK as a result of food and fuel poverty issues. Creating sustainable and resilient local food systems through community and private-sponsored endeavours are discussed in this chapter that range from food banks to community kitchens, hubs and social supermarkets. Collectively these aim to support mental health and wellbeing for those who are in need of access to nutrient-rich rather than energy-dense food.

Chapter 18: A renewed pedagogy for health co-benefit: combining nutrition and sustainability education in school food learnings and practices

Schools are an important setting for learning and development. We describe how nutrition and sustainability concepts are edified in schools and recommend transformative education in these discourses. Refreshed and re-imagined perspectives are discussed in this chapter, moving away from conservative approaches of healthism, recognising educators' needs and perspectives in pedagogical stances and supercharging children's agency in school learning and participation. A bifocal lens encompassing both nutritional and environmental agendas is a step in the right direction to realise the health co-benefits of children making environmentally friendly food. Key considerations include valuing and encouraging children's autonomy, providing teachers with adequate pedagogic training for this topic, driving conceptual shifts in the food and sustainability literacy context and incorporating creativity and pragmatism in school-based learnings. Instead of nutritional policing, this text promotes positive relationships with nutritious and sustainable foods, so school stakeholders can understand and embrace the importance and connections of both.

Chapter 19: Exploring intersectional feminist food pedagogies through the recipe exchange project

This chapter highlights the impact of food on the everyday and contributes to the discussion on eating being a pedagogical act. The chapter explores community-based teaching and integrated experiential learning through intersectional feminist food pedagogy. It does so through critical reflections of two post-secondary courses, a third-year undergraduate class and a graduate-level seminar course, both of which focus on gender, health and food justice. Through the Recipe Exchange Project, students were encouraged to think about home in any way that fits their experience. Through an intersectional feminist food pedagogy, students considered the relationality of their own social positionalities as these are constructed through food practices that are shaped by wider food systems, which arguably, is social justice in the classroom.

PART II

Policy, curriculum, and pedagogy

2

SCHOOL MEALTIME AS A PEDAGOGICAL EVENT

Kristiina Janhonen and Gurpinder Singh Lalli

Introduction

Education and learning during school mealtimes have previously been examined, for example, from the viewpoint of students, teachers, headmasters and/or school food service staff (Berggren 2020; Lintukangas 2009; Waling and Olsson 2017) respectively bringing forth the importance of acknowledging the roles and viewpoints of these actors. However, limited research exists that would bring all these different viewpoints together and provide an overarching conceptualisation of the school mealtime as a pedagogical event. In this chapter, we take on this challenge and explore school mealtime as both an institutional context that promotes learning, as well as a routinised event that might not always be consciously reflected upon from a pedagogical point of view.

By this approach, we seek to acknowledge that school mealtimes can be assigned both formal (i.e. structured and organised; typically assessed and certified) and non-formal (i.e. planned; yet not always formally assessed or certified) learning aims in schools, but that they also contain features of informal learning (or in the terms of social sciences: socialisation), which by definition refers to learning achieved from often unplanned events in daily life (Laal et al., 2014; Oosi et al. 2019). These informal learning events might not always be understood as learning by the people involved, and they might, therefore, also include unreflexive, accidental and haphazard characteristics (Janhonen et al. 2018). Drawing inspiration from pragmatist learning theory (Dewey 1896 [1996], p.100, 1916 [1996], p.147, 1938 [1996], p.25), we approach learning as situated (i.e. context bound) and continuous transactions among people and their surrounding worlds. Our thinking has previously also drawn influences from social constructionist philosophy and childhood sociology (Christensen and James 2000; Corsaro 2005, tracing back to Berger and Luckmann 1966; Blumer 1969; Burr 2015; Mead

DOI: 10.4324/9781003294962-4

1934), which can be seen, for example, in our tendency to approach children and young people as active agents and contributors to social change, also in institutionalised and formal learning environments (e.g., Janhonen and Mäkelä 2021). Our approach and emphasis on social learning through school mealtimes have leant particularly on the works of Bandura and Walters (1963), who refer to social learning as being observational learning which occurs through symbolic processes and focuses specifically on questions in relation to how human beings learn behaviour patterns and, in this case, how children interact in the school dining hall, as introduced by Lalli (2019).

As a general starting point, we define education (or educational activities) as aspirations to change and influence people's behaviour (Janhonen and Rautavirta 2022; Torkkeli and Janhonen, 2022) and school mealtimes as one context and event in which such educational aspirations can be enacted. Notably, our definition of education includes not only interaction between older people (more experienced) and younger people (often less experienced), but also interaction between members of the same generation (between adults or between students), as well as situations in which a child or a young person guides the adult (Torkkeli and Janhonen 2022). This aligns with the idea of the transactional nature of learning in pragmatist learning theory, as well as reciprocal definitions of socialisation in recent social scientific literature (*Ibid.*)

By pedagogy, then, we refer to the study of principles of education and the means through which these principles are pursued; with our key contributions in this chapter being the exploration of how notions of education and learning could be more comprehensively than before understood in the context of school mealtimes.

Overall, our aim has been to advance conceptualisations of education and learning that can take place during school mealtimes, as well as to explore opportunities and boundaries for learning in relation to this complex and mundane event. As summarised in Figure 2.1, our examination is structured according to the following three perspectives: (1) institutional arrangements, (2) multisensory experiences and (3) commensality and interaction.

Firstly, we have chosen here to delineate our examination to the timeframe during which the mealtime takes place (i.e. the lunch break). From this starting point, we will also consider other school-level practices and routines that we understand as setting significant contextual boundaries for activities that take place in the dining hall. Based on our own respective backgrounds, practical examples in this chapter are provided with a focus on the Finnish and UK contexts, and thus, the lunch meal as delivered by outsourced school food service providers. We return to suggestions for further comparisons among different countries and school meal systems in the discussion section of our chapter.

Secondly, we have rooted our exploration to the physical space in which the meal is eaten (e.g., the dining hall); while acknowledging also other experiential and sensory-based aspects that can be considered as affecting what and how is learned during the mealtime. This decision is based on the notion of the

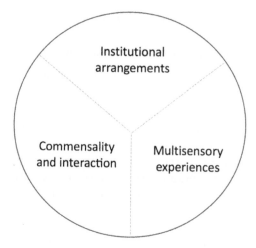

FIGURE 2.1 Three perspectives to pedagogy of school mealtimes

importance of aesthetic aspects in experiential learning processes (Dewey 1916, 1958), as well as recent highlights of taste-based perspectives in children's food education (Ciren 2021; Kähkönen et al. 2018). In this chapter, we have sought to integrate these viewpoints together, with the aspiration of contributing to a more comprehensive understanding of experiential learning in the school dining hall.

Finally, we have recognised the perspective of social learning to be a rising theme within research on school mealtimes, and accordingly, explore how commensality and interaction among different members of the school community can support learning in the dining hall. To advance critical discussion and development work in this area, we discuss and problematise the roles of those adults that are currently often assigned as central actors for providing education and guidance to students during the mealtime (i.e. teachers and school food service staff), as well as bring forth the importance of paying attention to contesting social agendas when developing school mealtimes as a pedagogical event.

In all, we see Figure 2.1 as complementary to such previous school meal models that have included some aspects of education or learning into their presentations, but have not approached school mealtimes with the aim of mapping different aspects of the lunch break particularly from the viewpoint of education and learning (Ciren 2021; Persson Osowski and Fjellström 2019). Below, we test our conceptualisation as a tool for structuring opportunities and boundaries for education and learning during school mealtimes. We acknowledge that the three perspectives might include overlapping areas that cut across one another. We will return to the discussion of these inter-relationships at the end of this chapter.

Three perspectives to pedagogy of school mealtimes

Institutional arrangements of school mealtimes

As a part of the formal schooling system, school mealtimes are embedded in practices and routines of the surrounding school community. These include the institutional arrangements that support school food provision, such as the scheduling of the mealtime, formal seating arrangements and rules regarding proper ways to behave in the dining hall (table manners) (Janhonen and Mäkelä 2021). However, in addition to functioning as a structure that potentially supports food-related learning, the institutional arrangements can place boundaries and practical constraints, such as time limits, for the enactment of educational activities during the mealtime (Berggren et al. 2020).

To exemplify, in the UK, such timings have changed within a defined period, from 65 minutes (including playtime) during the late 1990s (Blatchford and Sumpner 1998). By 2005, lunchtimes in primary schools in England ranged from 30 to 105 minutes (including playtime) in a UK context (Nelson et al. 2006). The trend that has seen lunch breaks reduced in time is partly due to a concern about conflicts, aggressive behaviour and bullying in schools (Baines and Blatchford 2019). Variation among countries suggests that contexts may differ, as can priorities of the surrounding wider school meal systems and time allocated for eating in schools. Importantly, as brought out in a recent Swedish study, school mealtimes might not always be integrated as a part of other activities in the school community that are assigned with educational and learning aims (Berggren et al. 2020). This affects the ways in which school mealtimes as opportunities for learning are interpreted and enacted in schools. Previous studies also show that school mealtimes might not presently be a part of the school's quality management (i.e., internal assessment of how a school succeeds in meeting government advisory guidelines regarding school meals); which has been shown to follow with in a lower tendency to interpret and include school mealtimes as part of the school's educational activities (Olsson and Waling 2016). The lack of systematic organisation and implementation on the school level might present a risk in terms of continuity and coherence of school meal related learning activities in schools. From this perspective, headmasters as school leaders can have a decisive role in recognising and supporting school-level initiatives, as well as aim setting, communication and allocation of resources within the school community (Berggren 2020; O'Rourke 2021). These are particularly significant points for development, if forms of formal (structured and organised; typically assessed and certified) and non-formal (planned; yet not always formally assessed and certified) forms of learning in relation to school mealtimes are to be strengthened.

From the perspective of outsourced food service providers, legislation and guidelines for school food procurement typically set institutional aims and boundaries to what is expected of the end food product (i.e. the school meal), as well as other professional activities of school food service staff in schools.

On the other hand, details in contracts of delivery of food services concerning budgeting, menu planning and human resourcing can also significantly affect the school-level work profiles of food service professionals, including the depth in which responsibilities concerning education (non-formal support, guidance and supervision of students) during the mealtime is expected of them. Where details of these contracts for food service providers can be influenced at the school level and by the headmaster, school leadership possesses great power and responsibility in shaping the expectations, resources and opportunities for school food service personnel to function as food educators. In line with these notions, further research is needed on how schools organise and assess educational and learning activities in relation to school mealtimes; how school meal related institutional arrangements are led and put into practice in schools; and to what extent different members of the school community are taken as active partners in this work.

The mealtime as a multisensory experience

Our definition of the school mealtime as a multisensory experience, then, seeks to bring together the physical, auditive, visual, tactile and other sensory-based aspects (e.g., taste) that affect learning during the mealtime. We include in this definition all educational materials placed within the dining hall (posters on the wall or on tables, a model of a proper serving placed at the beginning of the food line etc.), as well as the menu, the meal composition and all served food items as sources for learning. Our definition also includes the way in which the food service line is built and structured as a part of the physical space of the dining hall, as well as the strategic placement of items in a specific order in this line to promote particular kinds of food choices. For example, placing vegetables first to support vegetable intake, sometimes referred to also as 'nudging' (Metcalfe et al. 2020). Notably, if students are not involved in decision making, if justifications of decisions are not explained to the students, or if learning aims are not specifically communicated to and reflected upon with the students, emphasis is placed on the mediated educational effects of the food, the meal and the eating environment. This, in turn, might underline the unreflected, haphazard and unplanned characteristics of informal learning, as defined above. Of course, the institutionalised school meal system, including the meal product and the eating environment, can potentially already in itself provide a powerful pathway to education and change (Mäkelä and Rautavirta 2018; Risku-Norja et al. 2010), not the least through long-term exposure (repetitive nature) and broad coverage (reaching a large number of students). To exemplify, in Finland approximately 900 000 students eat the school meal on every school day.

The influence of the physical environment, then, has been previously examined from both positivist and interpretivist paradigms (Frerichs et al. 2015). Nevertheless, the physical design of the school dining hall has been largely under-researched, and interdisciplinary research has only recently started to consider the potential of the whole school building design and its impact on the daily lives of students (*Ibid.*). Overall, the physical environments have become known for influencing eating behaviours and the social cognitive theory supports this relationship between the individual and their environment in how it might affect behaviour (Bandura 1986). To provide an example from the UK context, physical environments have typically been identified as secondary objectives within strategic rebuilding programmes (Department for Education 2006), until more recently where they have been given more recognition (Department for Education 2013).

The other multisensory elements, such as the sound of the lunch bells at school or atmospheric characteristics such as lighting and odour, all contribute to creating a more or less desirable consumption experience (Neeley 2011). For example, previous studies have found that the noise level produced by a large number of people eating in the same dining space can follow with an experience of discomfort (Berggren et al. 2019; Hoppu et al. 2017). On the other hand, the visual presentation of foods can affect not only food selection but also evoke positive feelings and enjoyment during mealtimes (Paakki et al. 2015; Puurtinen et al. 2021). The study of Hoppu et al. (2017) further demonstrated how the preferred auditory and visual environment of lunch customers can differ according to what foods are available to choose from. Previous studies of public dining have also pointed out to the significance of taste to the overall eating experience, the construction of what food means to us (Aaltojärvi et al. 2016) and the acceptance of foods (Hoppu et al. 2017). In addition, the freshness of the food served in a food service context has been shown to increase customers' experience of the sensory quality of the meal (Kumpulainen et al. 2016). Taste is also to a growing degree emphasised particularly in the context of young children's food education (Ciren 2021; Kähkönen et al. 2018). Together, these studies provide reason to suggest that perhaps multisensory aspects should be taken more seriously than before also in the context of school mealtimes, including more thorough examination of the effects that these have for learning. This could mean, for example, designing the dining spaces more effectively by co-constructing with a range of groups including teachers, students and school food service staff in this crucial design work (Hansen et al. 2020).

Commensality and interaction in the dining hall

Constituting our third and final perspective in this chapter; sociality, sociability and social learning are terms which are to a growing degree used to connect with dining spaces in schools and in fostering good relationships (Lalli 2021; Murray and Wills 2020). Social factors are powerful in the development of food choices, preferences and role modelling by peers (Andersen et al. 2016; Hendy 2002) and teachers (Hendy and Raudenbush 2000), thus, affording acknowledgement also from the perspective of education and learning through school mealtimes. Despite its crucial importance, the influence of social factors on behaviour might be overlooked in the context of school mealtimes if the focus is merely on nutrition and its health consequences (Lalli 2019; Pike 2008). Below, we consider these social factors first from the viewpoint of commensality, followed by exploration of social interaction in the dining hall from the perspectives of food service staff, teachers and students.

The sharing of meals, in terms of the social construction and rules which govern behaviour, is considered to be part of the essence of our sociality (Morrison 1996). The term *commensality* refers to the practice of eating together which signifies unity and sharing in a given cultural context (Sobal and Nelsson 2003; Tuomainen 2014; Warde 1995). The study by Andersen et al. (2015) involved discussing commensality through the examination and comparison of lunchtime interactions within the same group of children in two contrasting meal situations. For example, the children ate together, but had individualised meals and therefore ate individualised food. According to Fischler (2015), commensality may be communal (eating the same food) or contractual (individualised meals), and what we learn from the meal may vary depending on what type of commensality occurs. However, the results failed to confirm the conventional notion that shared meals have great social impacts and benefits compared to eating individually. Although very little work has been done in this area and wider literature suggests how commensal eating strengthens social bonds, it does so through fundamentally excluding others (Grignon 2001). In light of these critiques of commensality, we also note the unseen benefits of interaction during mealtime, such as learning social skills for later professional and personal life and the role of citizenship (making informed decisions about food consumption) as what we observe is the social good (being able to lead a life of choice) that can come as a learning outcome through school mealtimes (Earl and Lalli 2020).

Also eating the same meal at school, rather than bringing lunch from home, is often discussed as enhancing aspects of commensality. A qualitative study conducted in Copenhagen, Denmark in 2016, illuminated such discourses in relation to four 'food schools' (Hansen et al. 2020). The most important aspect of the study revealed how each school operated differently in 'doing food', which included consideration of role division and expectations of different groups of actors in schools (teachers, students and school food service staff). Connected with this discussion, Lintukangas (2009) has proposed that school food service staff have great potential to function as food educators, for example, through (informal, non-formal) interaction with students during the mealtime. However, it is noteworthy that this professional group might also have reservations for providing guidance (non-formal education) for students, since their professional training rarely includes pedagogical studies. In line with this, Lintukangas (2009) has called for the importance of such training for school food service staff. A recent Finnish study (Janhonen and Elkjaer 2022) also found that the distant role of school food service staff in the school community, as well as different employers of teachers and food service staff, can function as experienced hindrances for collaboration to promote learning through school meals, which are important notions to consider in further initiatives.

From the viewpoint of teachers and of supporting interaction and learning in the dining hall, a Swedish study of Persson Osowski et al. (2013) found three different kinds of teacher roles ranging from adult- to child-oriented, and including differing levels of interaction (i.e. sociable, educative and evasive). The study emphasised the importance of teachers becoming aware of the effects of their actions in the dining hall and the cruciality of providing teachers professional training in how they could actively work towards reaching the aims for school mealtimes, as stated in official policy documents (*Ibid.*). Accordingly, supporting teachers' awareness, skills and active contributions to reaching (formal or non-formal) learning aims for school mealtimes can be seen as a way to support the achievement of these aims. However, it is important to note that previous studies also show how students often interpret the lunch break as their free time (as an informal social event), with peer interaction experienced as particularly important (Berggren et al. 2019; Neely et al. 2014; Stone and Murakami 2021). This illustrates how school mealtimes can include both formal and informal aims that might sometimes be in tension with one another (Janhonen and Mäkelä 2021; Punch et al. 2011). When school mealtimes are developed as social events for education and learning, it is important to carefully evaluate these contesting aspirations to avoid unwanted consequences, such as descending participation rates or disengagement of students.

Discussion and conclusions

This chapter has explored school mealtimes as a pedagogical event through the following three perspectives: (1) institutional arrangements, (2) multisensory experiences and (3) commensality and interaction. We acknowledge that some of these dimensions might cut across several perspectives presented in Figure 2.1. This can be exemplified, for example, through earlier theorisations and conceptualisations in relation to definitions of a social environment. One such example is the model of Denman (1999, p.400), which differentiates between the physical (places, objects), temporal (time periods, events) and social (actors, activities, goals and feelings) perspectives. Recognising the inter-relatedness of these perspectives is crucial, as they are said to influence one another (*Ibid.*). In addition, although we have reviewed research across disciplines and geographical areas, our practical examples have drawn particularly from the Finnish and UK contexts. Consequently, further research needs to address a greater variety of comparative perspectives across countries, as well as more in-depth explorations of such societies that rely on the responsibility of parents to compile packed lunches for children and young people. We acknowledge that different societal systems might need different kinds of solutions, which highlights the need for continuous discussions that include perspectives across the globe.

To summarise across the three perspectives (Figure 2.1), our exploration brought light to the importance of sufficient allocation of resources (time; human resources); systematic organisation, implementation, and assessment on the school level (as supported by school leadership); adequate training of professionals (e.g., teachers and school food service staff); and acknowledgement of contesting social aspirations (e.g., between adults and children). These can all be taken as both potential boundaries, as well as suggestions for development points in efforts to strengthen the educational potential of school mealtimes. Accordingly, we suggest further research on the aims, role division and processes of enacting and assessing pedagogy through school mealtimes (i.e. pedagogy for *what, by whom* and *how*). Our conceptualisation brought out how school dining rooms can be understood as versatile learning environments, including routinised, multisensorial and social aspects, which can support students' learning in a variety of ways. We propose that further collaboration with classroom-based teaching, as well as homes and families, could provide additional routes for strengthening the learning outcomes connected with school mealtimes. Finally, particularly from the perspective of assessment of learning outcomes, it is important to note that there exists no uniform definition of what constitutes (high quality or good) pedagogy, education, teaching, or learning. In line with Damsa and others (2020), we underline that it cannot be taken for granted that by talking about learning (or pedagogy or education or teaching), we always talk about the same thing, which highlights the need for advancing conceptual work on school meal pedagogy also in the future. We hope that this chapter will inspire further research in this area.

Acknowledgements

This chapter has been written as a part of the FOODSENSE research project funded by the Academy of Finland (funding reference no. 322598) and University of Helsinki.

References

Aaltojärvi, I., Kontukoski, M., and Hopia, A., 2016. Framing the local food experience: a case study of a Finnish pop-up restaurant. *British Food Journal* [online], 120 (1). Available from: https://doi.org/10.1108/BFJ-12-2016-0613.

Andersen, S. S., Holm, L., and Baarts, C., 2015. School meal sociality or lunch pack individualism? using an intervention study to compare the social impacts of school meals and packed lunches from home. *Social Science Information* [online], 54 (3). Available from: https://doi.org/10.1177/0539018415584697.

Andersen, S., Vassard, D., Havn, L. N., Damsgaard, C. T., Biltoft-Jensen, A., and Holm, L., 2016. Measuring the impact of classmates on children's liking of school meals. *Food Quality and Preference* [online], 52, 87. Available from: https://doi.org/10.1016/j.foodqual.2016.03.018.

Baines, E., and Blatchford, P., 2019. *School break and lunch times and young people's social lives: a follow-up national study.* Final report, Nuffield Foundation, Institute of Education: UCL [online]. Available from: https://www. nuffieldfoundation.org/wp-content/uploads/2019/05/Final-report-School-break-and-lunch-times-and-young-peoples-lives-A-follow-up-national-study.pdf.

Bandura, A., 1986. *Social foundations of thought and action*. Englewood Cliffs, NJ: Prentice-Hall.

Bandura, A., and Walters, R. H., 1963. *Social learning and personality development*. New York: Holt Rinehart and Winston.

Berger, P., and Luckmann, T., 1966. *The social construction of reality: a treatise in the sociology of knowledge*. New York: Doubleday.

Berggren, L., 2020. *It's not really about the food, it's about everything else: pupil, teacher and head teacher experiences of school lunch in Swede*n. Unpublished thesis. University of Umeå.

Berggren, L., Olsson, C., Rönnlund, M., and Waling, M., 2020. Between good intentions and practical constraints: Swedish teachers' perceptions of school lunch. *Cambridge Journal of Education* [online], 51 (2). Available from: https://doi.org/10.1080/03057 64X.2020.1826406.

Berggren, L., Olsson, C., Talvia, S., Hörnell, A., Rönnlund, M., and Waling, M., 2019. The lived experiences of school lunch: an empathy-based study with children in Sweden. *Children's Geographies* [online], 18 (3). Available from: https://doi.org/10.1080/14733 285.2019.1642447.

Blatchford, P., and Sumpner, C., 1998. What do we know about breaktime? Results from a national survey of breaktime and lunchtime in primary and secondary schools. *British Educational Research Journal*, 24 (1), 79–94.

Blumer, H., 1969. *Symbolic interactionism: perspective and method*. Edward Cliffs, NJ: Prentice-Hall.

Burr, V., 2015. *Social constructionism*. 3rd ed. London, UK: Routledge.

Christensen, P. H., and James, A., 2000. Research with children: perspectives and practices. *British Journal of Educational Studies*, 48 (3), pp. 344–345.

Ciren, B., 2021. Food and meal policies and guidelines in kindergartens in Norway and China: A comparative analysis. *European Early Childhood Education Research Journal*, 29 (4), 601–616.

Corsaro, W., 2005. *The Sociology of Childhood*. London/Thousand Oaks/New Delhi: Sage Publications.

Damsa, C. and Muukkonen, H., 2018. Conceptualising pedagogical designs for learning through object-oriented collaboration in higher education. *Research Papers in Education*, 35 (1), 82–104.

Daniel, P., and Gustafsson, U., 2011. School lunches: children's services or children's spaces? *Children's Geographies* [online], 8 (3). Available from: https://doi.org/10.1080/147332 85.2010.494865.

Denman, S., 1999. Health promoting schools in England – a way forward in development. *Journal of Public Health Medicine*, 21 (2), 215–220.

Department for Education, 2006. Every child matters: primary capital programme, DfES Publications, Nottingham [online]. Available from: https://dera.ioe.ac.uk/6022/.

Department for Education, 2013. The school food plan: how to improve school food and schoolchildren's diets [Online]. Available from: https://www.gov.uk/government/publications/the-school-food-plan [Accessed 28 June 2021].

Dewey, J., 1896 [1996]. The reflex arc concept in psychology. *In:* J. A. Boydston and L. Hickman, eds. *The collected works of John Dewey* (2nd Release). Electronic Edition. *The early works of John Dewey, 1882–1898* (Vol. 5: 1895–1898), Essays, Early Essays. Charlottesville, VA: InteLex Corporation.

Dewey, J., 1916 [1996]. Democracy and Education. *In:* J. A. Boydston and L. Hickman, eds. *The collected works of John Dewey, 1882–1953* (2nd Release). Electronic Edition. *The Middle Works of John Dewey, 1899–1924* (Vol. 9: 1916, ss. 1–370), *Democracy and education. An introduction to the philosophy of education.* Charlottesville, VA: InteLex Corporation.

Dewey, J., 1938 [1996]. Experience and education. *In:* J. A. Boydston and L. Hickman, eds. *The collected works of John Dewey, 1882–1953* (2nd Release). Electronic Edition. *The later works of John Dewey* (Vol. 13, ss. 1938–1939), *Essays, experience and education, freedom and culture, and theory of valuation.* Charlottesville, VA: InteLex Corporation.

Dewey, J., 1958. *Experience and nature.* New York: Dover Publications, Inc.

Earl, L., and Lalli, G., 2020. Healthy meals, better learners: debating the focus of school food policy in England. *British Journal of Sociology of Education* [online], 41 (4). Available from: https://doi.org/10.1080/01425692.2020.1735999.

Fischler, C., 2015. Introduction. *In:* C. Fischler, ed. *Selective eating: the rise, meaning and sense of personal dietary requirements.* Paris: Odile Jacob, 15–35.

Frerichs, L., Brittin, J., Sorensen, D., Trowbridge, M. J., Yarochm, A. L., Siahpush, M., Tibbits, M., and Huang, T. T., 2015. Influence of school architecture and design on healthy eating: a review of the evidence. *American Journal of Public Health* [online], 105 (4). Available from: https://doi.org/10.2105/AJPH.2014.302453.

Grignon, C., 2001. *Commensality and social morphology: An essay of typology.* National Institute of Agronomic Research.

Hansen, M. W., Hansen, S. R., Dal, J. K., and Kristensen, N. H., 2020. Taste, education, and commensality in Copenhagen food schools. *Food and Foodways* [online], 28 (3). Available from: https://doi.org/10.1080/07409710.2020.1783817.

Hendy, H. M., 2002. Effectiveness of trained peer models to encourage food acceptance in pre-school children. *Appetite*, 39 (3). Available from: https://doi.org/10.1006/appe.2002.0510.

Hendy, H. M., and Raudenbush, B., 2000. Effectiveness of teacher modelling to encourage food acceptance in preschool children. *Appetite*, 34 (1). Available from: https://doi.org/10.1006/appe.1999.0286.

Hoppu, U., Hopia, A., Pohjanheimo, T., Rotola-Pukkila, M., Mäkinen, S., Pihlanto, A., and Sandell, M., 2017. Effect of salt reduction on consumer acceptance and sensory quality of food. *Foods*, 6, 103. Available from: https://doi.org/10.3390/foods6120103.

Janhonen, K., and Elkjaer, B., 2022. Exploring Sustainable Food Education as Multi-professional Collaboration between Home Economics and School Food Catering. *Journal of Education for Sustainable Development*, 16 (1–2), 19–41. Available from: https://doi.org/10.1177/09734082221120101.

Janhonen, K., and Mäkelä, J., 2021. To connect and be heard: informal dimension of school mealtimes represented by students' self-initiated YouTube videos. *Young* [online], 30 (1). Available from: https://doi.org/10.1177/11033088211015802.

Janhonen, K., and Rautavirta, K., 2022. Muuttuva toimintakenttä, muuttuvaasiantuntijuus: Toimijoiden näkemyksiä ravitsemus- ja ruokakasvatuksesta 1990–2010-luvuilla [Changing field of activity, changing expertise: practitioners' views on nutrition and food education in the 1990s–2010s.], *Ainedidaktiikka*, 5 (3), 113–135. Available from: https://doi.org/10.23988/ad.111239.

Janhonen, K., Torkkeli, K., and Mäkelä, J., 2018. Informal learning and food sense in home cooking. *Appetite*, 130. Available from: https://doi.org/10.1016/j.appet.2018.08.019.

Kähkönen, K., Rönkä, A., Hujo, M., Lyytikäinen, A., and Nuutinen, O., 2018. Sensory-based food education in early childhood education and care, willingness to choose and eat fruit and vegetables, and the moderating role of maternal education and food neophobia. *Public Health Nutrition* [online], 21 (13). Available from: https://doi.org/10.1017/S1368980018001106.

Kumpulainen, T., Sandella, M., Junell, P., and Hopia, A., 2016. The effect of freshness in a foodservice context. *Journal of Culinary Science and Technology* [online], 14 (2). Available from: https://doi.org/10.1080/15428052.2015.1102783.

Laal, M., Laal, A. & Aliramaei, A., 2014. Continuing education; lifelong learning. *Procedia – Social and Behavioral Sciences*, 116 (21), 4052–4056.

Lalli, G., 2019. School mealtime and social learning in England. *Cambridge Journal of Education* [online], 50 (1). Available from: https://doi.org/10.1080/0305764X.2019.1630367.

Lalli, G., 2021. A modern take on school dining consumption: critical food design for education. *In:* S. Massari, ed. *Transdisciplinary case studies on design for food and sustainability.* Amsterdam, The Netherlands: Elsevier, 185–194.

Lintukangas, S., 2009. *School catering staff on the way to becoming educators.* Helsinki, Finland: University of Helsinki.

Mäkelä, J., and Rautavirta, K., 2018. Food, nutrition, and health in Finland. *In:* V. Andersen, E. Bar and G. Wirtanen, eds. *Nutritional and health aspects of food in Nordic countries* [online]. Available from: https://doi.org/10.1016/b978-0-12-809416-7.00005-6.

Mead, G. H., 1934. *Mind, self and society.* Chicago, IL: University of Chicago Press.

Metcalfe, J. J., Ellison, B., Hamdi, N., Richardson, R., and Prescott, M. P., 2020. A systematic review of school meal nudge interventions to improve youth food behaviors. *International Journal of Behavioural Nutrition and Physical Activity* [online], 17 (77). Available from: https://doi.org/10.1186/s12966-020-00983-y.

Morrison, M., 1996. Sharing food at home and school: perspectives on commensality. *Sociological Review* [online], 44 (4). Available from: https://doi.org/10.1111/j.1467-954X.1996.tb00441.x.

Murray, S., and Wills, W., 2020. Institutional spaces and sociable eating: young people, food and expressions of care. *Journal of Youth Studies*, 24 (5). Available from: https://doi.org/10.1080/13676261.2020.1748182.

Neeley, S. M., 2011. The influence of school eating environment on children's eating behaviour: an examination of the SNDA-III. Unpublished MA thesis, Wright State University, Dayton, OH.

Neely, E., Walton, M., and Stephens, C., 2014. Young people's food practices and social relationships. A thematic synthesis. *Appetite*, 82 (1), 50–60.Nelson, M., Nicolas, J., Suleiman, S., Davies, O., Prior, G., Hall, L., Wreford, S., and Poulter, J., 2006. *School meals in primary schools in England.* Nottingham, UK: DfES Publications.

Olsson, C., & Waling, M., 2016. School meals do not have a given place in Swedish school's quality management. *Health Education Journal*, 75 (8), 961–971. https://doi.org/10.1177/0017896916644000.

Oosi, O., Koramo, M., Korhonen, N., Järvelin A. M., Luukkonen, T., Tirronen, J., and Jauhola, L., 2019. A Study on Structures to support Continuous Learning – International Benchmarking. Government's analysis, assessment and research activities 18/2019. Available from: https://julkaisut.valtioneuvosto.fi/handle/10024/161392.

O'Rourke, J., 2021. *Food education in schools: why do some headteachers make this a priority?* Unpublished thesis. Sheffield, South Yorkshire, England: Sheffield Hallam University.

Paakki, M., Sandell, M., Hopia, A. (2015) Consumer's reactions to natural, atypically colored foods: An investigation using blue potatoes, Journal of Sensory Studies, 31(1), pp. 78-89.

Persson Osowski, C., and Fjellström, C., 2019. Understanding the ideology of the Swedish tax-paid school meal. *Health Education* [online], 78 (4). Available from: https://doi.org/10.1177/00178969187984.

Persson Osowski, C., Göranzon, H., and Fjellström, C., 2013. Teachers' interaction with children in the school meal situation. The example of pedagogic meals in Sweden. *Journal of Nutrition Education and Behavior* [online], 45 (5). Available from: https://doi.org/10.1016/j.jneb.2013.02.008.

Pike, J., 2008. Foucault, space and primary school dining rooms. *Children's Geographies* [online], 6 (4). Available from: https://doi.org/10.1080/14733280802338114.Punch, S., McIntosh, I., and Emond, R., eds., 2011. *Children's food practices in families and institutions*. New York: Routledge.

Puurtinen, M., Puputti, S., Mattila, S., and Sandell, M., 2021. Investigating visual attention toward foods in a salad buffet with mobile eye tracking. *Food, Quality and Preference* [online], 19. Available from: https://doi.org/10.1016/j.foodqual.2021.104290.

Risku-Norja, H., Kurppa, S., Silvennoinen, K., Nuoranne, A., and Skinnari, J., 2010. *Public food service and food education: through daily practices to sustainable food procurement.* Sweden: MTT Kasvu.

Sobal, J., and Nelson, M. K., 2003. Commensal eating patterns: a community study. *Appetite* [online], 41 (2). Available from: https://doi.org/10.1016/s0195-6663(03)00078-3.

Stone, S., and Murakami, K., 2021. Children's humour and the grotesque pleasures in school mealtime socialisation. *Children and Society* [online]. Available from: https://doi.org/10.1111/chso.12451.

Torkkeli, K., and Janhonen, K., 2022. Informaali ruokakasvatus ja jaettu ruokataju osana ruokatyötä – Analyysi kasvisruokaan liittyvistä kompromisseista [Informal food education and shared food sense as a part of foodwork - An analysis of compromises about vegetable-based foods in the daily life of families with children]. *Ainedidaktiikka*, 5 (3), 90–112. https://doi.org/10.23988/ad.103223.

Tuomainen, H., 2014. Eating alone or together? commensality among Ghanaians in London. *Anthropology of Food* [online], 14 (10), 1–17. Available from: https://doi.org/10.4000/aof.7718.

Waling, M., and Olsson, C., 2017. School lunch as a break or an educational activity: a quantitative study of Swedish teacher perspectives. *Health Education*, 117 (6), 540–550.

Warde, A., 1995. Consumption and theories of practice. *Journal of Consumer Culture* [online], 5 (2). Available from: http://umu.diva-portal.org/smash/get/diva2:952574/FULLTEXT01.pdf.

3

HEALTHY LIFESTYLES PROJECT

A practical food programme for primary schools

Suzanne Gomersall

Introduction

Childhood obesity has reached epidemic levels in developed countries, with those who live in lower socio-economic groups twice as likely to be obese (Davies 2019). Research has shown that obese children are more likely to become obese adults, with serious health consequences linked to obesity (World Health Organisation [WHO] 2018), such as heart disease and diabetes. Worryingly, the UK's childhood obesity rates are ranked amongst the worst in Western Europe and Public Health England (PHE) (2017) estimates that over 30,000 deaths are linked to obesity each year, meaning that obesity is now the biggest cause of preventable death rather than smoking. The UK Government has been tracking levels of childhood obesity since 2014 through its National Child Measurement Programme (NCMP) by weighing and measuring over 1 million children in mainstream state-maintained schools, in their first and final years of primary school (NCMP 2021). Current statistics show that 9.9% of reception children are obese, doubling to 21% by the time children reach the end of year 6.

The British government has been trying to tackle this issue for decades, and in the last 20 years alone we have seen the reintroduction of standards for all food and drink served in schools, the publication of the School Food Plan (Dimbleby and Vincent 2013) and most recently, the National Food Strategy (Dimbleby 2021). As a result of the 2013 School Food Plan, cooking and nutrition became a key focus of the primary design and technology curriculum in the English national curriculum (Department for Education 2013). In addition, in 2016 the government doubled the School Sports Premium from £160 million to £320 million, funded by the soft-drinks industry levy, or 'sugar tax' and launched the Healthy Schools rating scheme in 2019. However, despite these interventions, childhood obesity continues to rise (NCMP 2021).

DOI: 10.4324/9781003294962-5

Internationally, many interventions have been created and implemented to attempt to address this global issue, from Move and Munch in Australia to The Daily Mile in Scotland, with little success. Surprisingly, in all the research explored, none of the interventions have focused on teaching the children how to choose, prepare and cook healthy food from a young age.

Justifying the programme design

In order to attempt to tackle childhood obesity, it was important to get an understanding of what the possible causes could be behind such an increase in the prevalence of childhood obesity over the last 30 years. For the majority of people, an 'energy imbalance' is suggested as the main cause (Van Sluijs and McMinn 2010), caused by an increase in the availability of high-calorific foods, higher reliance on processed foods, people's working and home lives becoming less active due to technological advances, coupled with an increase in sedentary behaviour due to a greater reliance on electronic entertainment. The Department of Health and Social Care (2018) identified further causes, such as the consumption of energy drinks, food labelling, product placement, pester power and advertising. All of these factors link to learnt behaviour or one of the following three characteristics: physiological, environmental and social.

The authors behind The School Food Plan (Dimbleby and Vincent 2013) identify another possible cause of the obesity epidemic as the decrease in the number of adults who have the knowledge and understanding of healthy eating and how to cook healthy dishes. They are concerned that if we continue to marginalise cooking in schools, we "run the risk of another generation being unable to pass on these essential life skills to their own children" (p.32). This lack of importance given to teaching and learning practical cooking skills was evident in the wide range of childhood obesity interventions explored as part of this study, as this key element was absent in all the interventions researched. Instead, most school-based interventions designed to tackle childhood obesity focused on one or more of the following: change in diet, decrease in sedentary behaviour, increase in physical activity and behaviour modification. These interventions were mostly delivered through encouraging children to reduce their screen time and move more, adapting school food, introducing Physical Activity programmes and delivering nutrition education, rather than through a regular practical cooking and nutrition programme over a sustained period of time. Therefore, the Healthy Lifestyles Project (HLSP) approach will be an empirical study with practical cooking and nutrition teaching and learning at its heart.

Theory and research suggest that when looking at changing behaviour, interventions that have several aims and approaches are more successful. Therefore, when designing the HLSP, a multi-pronged approach was required to address attitudes and behaviours by tackling some of the physiological, environmental and social issues behind childhood obesity. One theoretical framework that the HLSP aligns to closely is the Social-Ecological Model (SEM) (Figure 3.1).

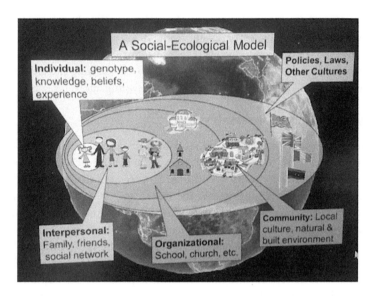

FIGURE 3.1 The Social-Ecological Model (Sammons and Bowler 2020)

The SEM focuses around behavioural changes of self, interpersonal, organisational, community and public policy. Working with the school (organisation), parents (community) and the children individually and as a group (individual/interpersonal) gives the project a strong theoretical framework to influence public policy around cooking and nutrition teaching in primary schools.

This is not to say that there haven't been any successes in reducing childhood obesity. Three international programmes that have been successful are: EPODE in France (Ensemble Prevenons l'Obesite Des Enfants), JOGG in Holland (Jongeren op Gezond Gewicht) and TCOCT in Denmark (The Children's Obesity Clinic Protocol) follow this multi-pronged SEM approach, with the House of Commons Health Committee crediting the levels of success down to the fact that all "these successful initiatives has adopted a sustained, systematic, joined up approach, rather than separate ad hoc initiatives, either in a community setting (EPODE and JOGG) or a clinical setting (TCOCT)" (House of Commons Health Committee 2018, p.9).

There have been successes in the UK too, with Leeds City Council adopting a citywide child obesity strategy in 2008 which looked to tackle the physiological, environmental and social factors linked to childhood obesity from including healthier snacks in leisure centre vending machines, providing training programmes for parents, promoting Active Travel campaigns, to providing better school food. As a result, the city's obesity levels dropped by around 0.6% (Lockyer and Spiro 2019).

All of the HLSP sessions and teaching and learning resources have been carefully designed in consultation with class teachers, a garden educator, a chef and a nutritionist, to ensure they are appropriate, progressive, high quality and provide accurate health advice. Regular data is collected from the children, parents and teachers through various data collection methods such as food diaries, questionnaires, skill audits and group activities. By reviewing the data collected after each cycle, adaptations that may support and refine the HLSP have been made, increasing its impact. As most changes in behaviour are incremental and that a continued and focused effort will be required to keep this 'lifestyle change' occurring, the HLSP was designed to consist of six intervention cycles over the six years children spend at primary school, targeting the participating children, parents and teachers.

The HLSP programme

In September 2018 the six-year HLSP longitudinal study began, exploring the impact of the project, to see if providing children practical cooking and nutrition sessions would change their attitudes and behaviours towards healthy eating and ultimately, reduce the number of children who became overweight or obese. The HLSP, which aims to make a positive contribution to tackling children's health in the UK and beyond, draws on design and technology (D and T) pedagogy, alongside the theoretical SEM framework to provide the following multi-pronged approach (see Figure 3.2).

Practical Sessions: The Design and Technology Association (DATA) recommends a minimum of one cooking and nutrition unit per year. The HLSP provides a choice of 2 units per year group, giving class teachers variety, the opportunity to teach more than 1 unit per year if desired and offers flexibility around mixed year groups. In addition, individual lessons are suggested for the other two terms to ensure children are receiving practical cooking and nutrition

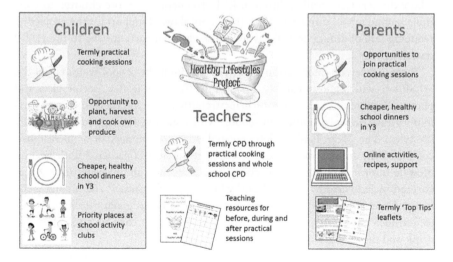

FIGURE 3.2 The many aspects included within the HLSP multi-pronged approach

opportunities every term. These sessions teach children the basics of food preparation and cooking in a standard primary classroom, without the need for cooking facilities, as these are uncommon in most primary schools. These practical sessions follow best practice in D and T, by using a sequence of Investigative and Evaluative Activities (IEAs), Focused Tasks (FTs) and Design, Make and Evaluate Assignments (DMEAs). These hands-on sessions are also opportunities to provide support, guidance and training for parents and teachers so that they can learn the correct food preparation techniques to enable them to encourage their children to prepare and cook healthy meals at home.

A progressive termly sequence of practical cooking and nutrition lessons has been co-created with Idris Caldora, the head chef at the Adopt a School Programme, founded in 1990 by the Royal Academy for the Culinary Arts, whose vision is that every child learns about food in a holistic sense at an early age and has the confidence to eat well, be healthy and happy.

Gardening: Alongside this, the children get the opportunity to understand where their food comes from by working with the garden educator, Anna Bond from Allotment Education. Each year the children get to plant, tend and harvest their own produce. They then prepare, cook and eat the food they have grown in the practical cooking sessions, such as herbs, tomatoes and potatoes. Connecting children with the food on their plate is extremely powerful and research shows that children are more likely to eat fruit and vegetables if they have grown them themselves (Green and Duhn 2015). To develop the HLSP's interpersonal and community approach, parents are encouraged to volunteer and support Anna as the school food gardens become more and more established and cover a greater proportion of the school grounds.

School Dinners: Research shows that school dinners are more healthy than packed lunches (School Food Trust 2012) and as a result, the government made school dinners free to all children in KS1. To encourage more children to continue having school dinners in KS2, the school showed support for the project by reducing school dinner costs for when those children participating in the HLSP started in year 3.

Parents received information each term through the school website, via the HLSP tab, which allows parents to access the Top Tips leaflets, recipe ideas and photos of the children's work to help strengthen the interpersonal and community link between home and school, whilst sharing messages about healthy lifestyles. The 'Top Tips' leaflets, created with the support of a nutritionist, combined the annual findings of the HLSP research data gathered with healthy lifestyle information, suggested action, healthy recipes and website links. Areas covered include healthy snacks, healthy breakfasts, 'fakeaways' and mental well-being. Completing food diaries and surveys annually has given parents a chance to consider the behaviours and attitudes their families have towards food and drink and the changes they are making or need to take.

As well as gaining useful knowledge, skills and understanding during the termly practical sessions, whole school staff training has been provided to enable all teachers to understand the D and T approach the HLSP uses and the correct food preparation techniques, skills and equipment they will use with their pupils. The school has adopted the HLSP across their long-term planning so that each term an HLSP session or unit is included for all year groups. To enable teachers to deliver these sessions independently after the completion of

---

Case Study: an example of the programme from year 3

Overview

Autumn term: DMEA – to design and make a pizza that uses the Eatwell Guide to create a balanced meal.

Spring term: IEA: (Geography focus) – map work looking at contrasting locations. Tasting and evaluating food from around the world or a specific location.

Summer term: FT – introduce a sharp knife and a heat source – practice the bridge and claw cutting techniques, with adult supervision, to make vegetable soup.

Gardening: In year 2, children plant dwarf tomato plants, transfer into pots and take them home to look after over the summer holidays. The children will be asked to bring in some of the tomatoes they have grown to use in their pizza recipes at the start of year 3 (Figures 3.3 and 3.4).

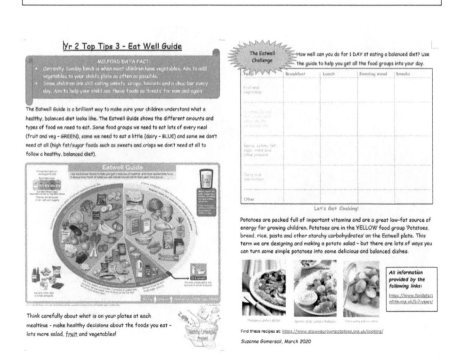

FIGURE 3.3   Top Tips leaflet: a focus on the Eatwell Guide

FIGURE 3.4 Parents supporting a practical session under the guidance of the Healthy Lifestyles team

FIGURE 3.5 Teachers were trained in the bridge and claw and a video of how to make the pizza was provided

---

D&T National Curriculum (KS2 Programmes of Study):

- understand and apply the principles of a healthy and varied diet
- prepare and cook a variety of predominantly savoury dishes using a range of cooking techniques
- design purposeful, functional, appealing products for themselves and other users based on design criteria
- generate, develop, model and communicate their ideas through discussion, annotated sketches, and exploded diagrams
- select from and use a wider range of materials and components, including ingredients, according to their functional properties and aesthetic qualities
- evaluate their ideas and products against their own design criteria and consider the views of others to improve their work

DMEA "To design and make a pizza that uses the Eatwell Guide to provide a balanced meal."
FT "Cutting and mixing skills, weighing ingredients and following a recipe"
IEA "Exploring different ingredients in different food groups, using the Eatwell Guide"
Design decisions – choosing pizza toppings based on food groups and quantities of each for a healthy diet

Cross-curricular opportunities:

Maths – choose and use appropriate standard units to estimate and measure mass (kg/g); to the nearest appropriate unit, using scales

English – describing food, labelling, giving reasons for choices, word categories - adjectives

Science
– identify that animals, including humans, need the right types and amount of nutrition, and that they cannot make their own food; they get nutrition from what they eat. (They might research different food groups and how they keep us healthy and design meals based on what they find out).
-Use their senses to compare different textures, sounds and smells

Art - to improve their mastery of art and design techniques, including drawing

---

FIGURE 3.6 Teacher's Toolbox: Y3 Autumn term planning overview

the study, a 'Teacher's Toolkit' has been created based on the English national curriculum, with activities and resources tried and tested by the children, parents and teachers.

Parents were invited to the practical food session to learn how to make pizza dough and a simple tomato sauce, in addition to being introduced to the Eatwell Guide to create healthy balanced meals (Figures 3.5 and 3.6).

This unit consisted of five sessions, ranging from introducing the Eatwell Guide to then using this information to design, make, test and evaluate their pizza.

How will the HLSP be evaluated?

The success of the HLSP is measured in a range of ways. To identify any changes in attitudes and behaviours, the following data collection tools were utilised, enabling the data to be triangulated, to ensure a more robust measure: food diaries, parent surveys, children's surveys and teacher interviews. This ensured that certain questions, for example around breakfast, were included in both surveys and captured in the food diaries. Before the HLSP, the school believed many children were not eating breakfast so provided biscuits and milk each morning. However, the evidence collected showed that over 95% of children were eating breakfast every day. This resulted in a change of school policy and the end of the supplementary morning snack. Fruit at breaktime was still provided and it could be argued, more likely to be eaten as the children had not filled up earlier on biscuits.

To find out about the development of the children's skills, knowledge and understanding, observations were made during the taught sessions each term and a group activity and discussion were undertaken once a year. In the practical cooking sessions, children were able to demonstrate their knowledge, skills and understanding through discussion and skill demonstration when preparing food. The British Nutrition Foundation's (BNF) core skills for Key Stage 1 and 2 were used as a measure for this.

Two physical measurements were taken annually as part of the HLSP, children's Body Mass Index (BMI) and their Waist to Height Ratio (WtHC). This is because in addition to having a positive impact on children's behaviours around healthy lifestyles, the HLSP aims to positively affect the number of children who are deemed to be a healthy weight by the end of year 6, when compared to children in Nottingham and the whole of England through the NCMP.

The decision to use the BMI measure was not only to enable the HLSP data to be directly comparable to the NCMP data, but also because in a meta-analysis on school-based interventions on childhood obesity by Gonzalez-Suarez et al. (2009), BMI was the measure used in all papers included. However, some researchers oppose the accuracy of BMI (Yangbo et al. 2019) as it does not distinguish between fat and muscle, in particular, in relation to children (Evans 2007), so a second measure of obesity was taken. Using various waist measurements such as waist circumference (WC), waist-to-hip (WHR) and waist-to-height (WHtR) have been recognised as useful measures of obesity as "they all, in various ways, try to compensate for the shortcomings of BMI" (Fredriksen et al. 2018, p.12).

Initial findings (2021)

Since March 2020, Coronavirus has impacted people's weight due to physical activity restrictions during lockdowns, lack of daily physical activity at school due to closures, and food choices being greatly reduced due to food shortages. The delivery and data collection of the HLSP in the second, third and fourth years of the project were greatly affected, due to a move to online learning and social distancing when back in the classroom. The impact of the pandemic on the school's ability to deliver the HLSP over this time was described by the school's D and T leader Tracy Haslam, as 'massive'. However, having analysed and triangulated the data at this halfway stage, the following initial findings can be shared:

- Parent's awareness of choosing healthy foods has increased by 19% from **75%** to **94%**. This, in turn, influenced the food choices they make 'a lot' or 'all of the time', up 18% from **47%** to **65%**.
- The number of meals being cooked from scratch most days has increased, from **38%** to **57%**. The food diaries show that children are eating a wider range of healthy main meals at home most days.
- The number of children cooking at home has doubled with **29%** of parents encouraging their children to help at least three times a week.
- Children have *developed confidence* in their own cookery skills across the BNF Core Competencies, many of which the children feel they can do independently. By the end of year 3, they are able to measure, mix and knead ingredients, as well as use a sharp knife and a heat source correctly with adult supervision.
- **100%** of children were able to design a healthy meal including key food groups – fruit/vegetables, carbohydrates and protein.
- Every day children are eating on average 3–4 of their 5 a day.
- Children were *more willing to try* different foods.
- Out of school, children are *active*, on average, for over 4 ½ hours a week. The Chief Medical Officer's recommendations are for children to do a daily average of 1 hour's physical activity, with 30 minutes being during the school day.

The children's measurement data shows a mixed picture (see Figure 3.7).

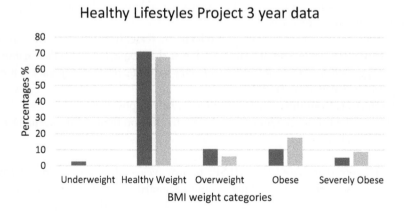

FIGURE 3.7   BMI comparing start data and current data

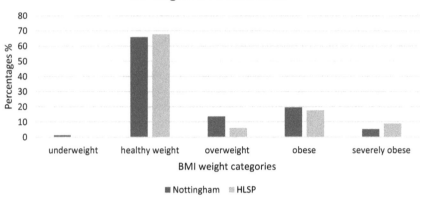

FIGURE 3.8 Current HLSP year 3 children against 'predicted' Nottingham year 3 cohort

Positively, 0% of the children are in the underweight category, the number of overweight children has halved and the number of children at a healthy weight has only slightly dropped. However, the number of children who have been categorised as obese or severely obese has increased from 16% at the beginning of year 1 to 27% in year 3 (Figure 3.8).

However, we get a different picture if we compare the HLSP data to the NCMP data collected from reception-aged children and year 6 children in Nottingham and create predicted year 3 results for this cohort (Figure 7). Using the national statistics that the number of children that are overweight and obese doubles between reception and Year 6, we are able to predict levels for year 3 children in Nottingham as 39.3%.

For my cohort, there has been a moderate increase, from 26.2% at the start of year 1 to 32.3% at the end of year 3, 7% lower than expected. *From these statistics, we can suggest that more children will be a healthy weight by the time they reach year 6 if they have been part of the HLSP.*

Comments from the participants were equally as positive:

When asked about the impact the HLSP has had on their children, the D and T leader explained:

> I know that before the (HLSP) project, vegetable soup would not have been something the children would necessarily.....have wanted to try, but because they cooked it themselves .....everyone tried the soup and I don't think that would have happened before...... But more than that, a lot of the pupils really loved it and had seconds! I think the willingness to try healthier options, the confidence to cook healthier options is all there. It's all in place and the enthusiasm to go home and then bring that to their

families.....it's because it's the whole community involved. It's through school, through the pupils, then going home and it's that whole four-way process, isn't it?

When asked how the project was impacting on family choices, she explained:

I think....parents having to help us with [the food diaries] what they're having as a family....is having a big impact because the parents are the ones making the choices on the meals and the children can influence parents, but the parents ultimately are the ones that are going to make those choices.

Through discussions, children showed they had a good knowledge and understanding around the importance of leading a healthy lifestyle, with comments such as:

If you eat stuff that's unhealthy it is not good for your body
    Too much sugar rots your teeth.

One child showed an awareness of the impact it may have on his life expectancy:

If we eat too much food with lots of sugar and fat in when we get older, we will die a little bit earlier but if you are healthy you will die a little bit later.

Another child talked about the traffic light system on food packaging:

I've been checking (with my mum) how much stuff are (on the wrappers) and I've been eating more healthy stuff. If it's green its good, if it's amber it's not as good and if its red it's not good for you.

Through the annual survey, many parents say the project is a great idea and comment on the change in their children's willingness to try and eat more healthily, such as:

It's made X much more likely to try new foods. He is more interested in preparing food and thinks at times about his choices
    My child used to be a very fussy eater. And this year he has tried a lot of new foods at school and continues to eat them at home. This has made his diet far healthier and less repetitive.

Other parents commented on the change in awareness and behaviour in their children, such as:

I think it's been fantastic. P takes note of what he eats more now and uses the traffic light labelling when out shopping. It's helped me have more confidence in him helping in the kitchen.

In some cases, the HLSP was reported to be having a positive impact on the whole family, with comments such as:

> Healthy lifestyle is definitely important to us however it means giving up a lot of things e.g. junk food....and it's a challenge but more exciting is receiving guidance from your child of what's better, due to school practice, it gives us a better grounds to carry on.

Conclusion

Over six years, the HLSP aims to impact change to the lifestyle choices made by the children and their families, by supporting the individual, interpersonal, organisational and community, with the ultimate aim of changing public policy, so that funding and expectation increase for children to be taught regular cooking and nutrition lessons as part of the statutory curriculum. Although cooking and nutrition are already part of the English national curriculum (DfE 2013), Ofsted reported that 75% of schools are not providing them. Likewise, awards such as the government's 'Healthy School Rating scheme' (DfE 2019) need to require schools to provide both practical cooking and nutrition lessons and a minimum of two hours of sport per week to be awarded the Gold rating, which is currently not the case. I believe that by giving both diet and exercise equal status, renaming the School Sports Premium to the 'Healthy Lifestyles Premium' and making this a priority area for Ofsted inspections, schools will begin to recognise the key organisational part they have to play in tackling childhood obesity (Gomersall 2018).

After three years, this review of the HLSP shows that multi-pronged SEM approaches that draw strength from the community working together can impact children and their families' attitudes, behaviours and choices to healthy eating and other lifestyle choices. This in turn, equips children with the skills, knowledge and understanding around nutrition and the ability and desire to choose, prepare and cook healthy meals now and for the rest of their lives.

References

Davies, S., 2019. Time to solve childhood obesity: an independent report by the chief medical officer [online]. Department of Health and Social Care. Available from: https://www.actiononsalt.org.uk/media/action-on-salt/CMO-Special-Obesity-Report.pdf [Accessed 22 August 2021].

Department for Education, 2013. *The national curriculum in England: primary curriculum* [online]. Available from: https://www.gov.uk/government/publications/national-curriculum-in-england-primary-curriculum [Accessed 22 August 2021].

Department for Education, 2019. *Healthy school rating scheme* [online]. Guidance for schools. Available from: https://assets.publishing.service.gov.uk/government/uploads/system/uploads/attachment_data/file/1112071/Final_Healthy_schools_rating_scheme.pdf [Accessed 22 August 2021].

Department of Health and Social Care: Global Public Health Directorate: Obesity, Food and Nutrition, 2018. *Childhood obesity: a plan for action, Chapter 2* [online]. Available from: https://assets.publishing.service.gov.uk/government/uploads/system/uploads/attachment_data/file/718903/childhood-obesity-a-plan-for-action-chapter-2.pdf [Accessed 22 August 2021].

Dimbleby, H. and Vincent, J. 2013. *The school food plan* [online]. Available from: The School Food Plan_2315_11JULY.docx.

Dimbleby, 2021. The National Food Strategy. *The plan* [online]. Available from: https://assets.publishing.service.gov.uk/government/uploads/system/uploads/attachment_data/file/718903/childhood-obesity-a-plan-for-action-chapter-2.pdf [Accessed 22 August 2021].

Evans, J., 2007. Health education or weight management in schools? *Cardiometabolic Risk and Weight Management*, 2 (2), 12–16.

Fredriksen, P. M., Skår. A., and Mame, A., 2018. Waist circumference in 6–12-year-old children: the health oriented pedagogical project (HOPP). *Scandinavian Journal of Public Health*, 46 (21), 12–20. Available from: https://doi.org/10.1177/1403494818767790.

Gomersall, S., 2018. *Schools key to obesity response*. Available from: www.cypnow.co.uk/analysis/article/schools-key-to-obesity-response [Accessed 22 August 2021].

Gonzalez-Suarez, C., et al., 2009. School-based interventions on childhood obesity: a meta-analysis. *American Journal of Preventive Medicine*, 37 (5), 418–427.

Green, M., and Duhn, I., 2015. The force of gardening: investigating children's learning in a food garden. *Australian Journal of Environmental Education*, 31 (1), 60–73.

House of Commons Health Committee, 2018. *Childhood obesity: time for action. Eighth Report of Session 2017–19*. Available from: https://www.parliament.uk/globalassets/documents/commons-committees/Health/Correspondence/2017-19/Childhood-obesity-Government-Response-to-eighth-report-17-19.pdf [Accessed 22 August 2021].

Lockyer, S., and Spiro, A., 2019. Socio-economic inequalities in childhood obesity: can community level interventions help reduce the gap? *British Nutrition Foundation*, 44, 381–393.

National Child Measurement Programme, 2021. Official statistics, National statistics, 2021. *England 2020/21 School Year, 2021* [online]. Available from: https://digital.nhs.uk/data-and-information/publications/statistical/national-child-measurement-programme/2020-21-school-year#:~:text=This%20report%20presents%20findings%20from, state%2Dmaintained%20schools%20in%20England [Accessed 22 August 2021].

Public Health England, 2017. *Health matters: obesity and the food environment* [online]. Available from: https://www.gov.uk/government/publications/health-matters-obesity-and-the-food-environment/health-matters-obesity-and-the-food-environment--2 [Accessed 22 August 2021].

Sammons, P., and Bowler, M., 2020. Introducing a new pedagogical model from health-based PE. Available from: https://www.afpe.org.uk/physical-education/wp-content/uploads/afPE-webinar-1-Introducing-HBPE.pdf [Accessed 22 August 2021].

School Food Trust, 2012. Primary school food survey: school lunches vs. packed lunches [online]. Available from: http://cft-staging-cdn.core-clients.co.uk.s3-eu-west-1.amazonaws.com/2015/06/primary_school_lunches_v_packed_lunches_revised2012.pdf [Accessed 22 August 2021].

Van Sluijs, E., and McMinn, A., 2010. Preventing obesity in primary school children. *British Medical Journal* [online], 340. Available from: https://doi.org/10.1136/bmj.c819.

World Health Organisation, 2018. *Taking action on childhood obesity* [online]. Available from: https://apps.who.int/iris/bitstream/handle/10665/274792/WHO-NMH-PND-ECHO-18.1-eng.pdf [Accessed 22 August 2021].

Yangbo, S., et al., 2019. Association of normal-weight central obesity with all-cause and cause-specific mortality among postmenopausal women. *Journal American Medical Association* [online]. Available from: https://doi.org/10.1001/jamanetworkopen.2019.7337.

4

FOOD TECHNOLOGY AS A SUBJECT TO BE TAUGHT IN SECONDARY SCHOOLS

A discussion of content, relevance, and pedagogy

HildaRuth Beaumont

Introduction

The narrative of food in the world starts with its production mainly through agriculture and moves on to include storage, preservation and processing, sales and distribution at different levels of scale, complexity and sophistication depending on context. This narrative concludes with food preparation and consumption. It is important that young people at school learn about this in order to understand that the place of food in society is dependent on the way in which various technologies are deployed throughout this narrative and how these may or may not help in our responses to the two great challenges confronting humanity today: social justice for all and the stewardship of Planet Earth in the face of climate change. It will be important to consider how the knowledge and understanding of the relevant technologies and these challenges might be taught. And finally it will be important to speculate about the way the narrative of food might develop in the future. Hence this chapter will consist of the following five parts.

Part 1 The Narrative of Food in the light of underpinning technologies
Part 2 The Narrative of Food through the lenses of social justice and stewardship of Planet Earth
Part 3 Pedagogy for the Narrative of Food in secondary school
Part 4 Future scenarios within the Narrative of Food
Part 5 Concluding remarks

It is also important to note that the technologies deployed in the narrative of food vary in the extent to which they are food specific in their original intention. Some are directly concerned with the intrinsic nature of food as a material and the way it behaves. Plant breeding to increase crop yields is an example. Others will have

DOI: 10.4324/9781003294962-6

a more tangential, but no less significant, relationship within the narrative. The development of particular tools to aid harvesting is an example. Both sorts of technology will be considered here in order to achieve a holistic view.

Part 1: The narrative of food in the light of underpinning technologies

Food production and harvesting

Preamble

According to Yuval Harari (2011) humans stopped feeding themselves as hunter-gatherers some 10,000 years ago and made the transition to farming which changed their lives in many ways, some for the worse including:

- Being less healthy as their diet became much more limited
- Suffering from a variety of physical ailments such as slipped discs, arthritis and hernias, due to the requirements of tilling the soil, planting and reaping crops, weeding and protecting the crops from pests
- Lives become much more monotonous with much less variety of physical activity as farming for food requires more time than hunter-gathering.

So, why make the change? According to Harari the main reason is that the concentration of food production through farming enabled a section of land to support far more people than the same section of land used for hunter-gathering, about ten times more. Living in the resultant larger communities accompanied by the building of shelters offered protection from the elements and wild animals but also resulted in an increase in communicable diseases. From an evolutionary point of view, Harari argues, moving from hunter-gathering to farming enabled more people to survive but under worse conditions. In its most basic form this farming is subsistence farming by which a family or community grows just enough food for them to be able to eat with little if any surplus. Any disruption of this endeavour quickly leads to hunger and starvation. In 2015, about 2 billion people (slightly more than 25% of the world's population) in 500 million households living in rural areas of developing nations survived as 'smallholder' farmers, working less than 2 hectares (5 acres) of land (Rapsomanikis 2015) i.e., as subsistence farmers.

The tasks facing early humans as they moved away from hunter-gathering are those facing any subsistence farmer: clearing some land to allow planting, tilling the soil, planting the crops, tending the crops, and harvesting the crops. A different but related set of tasks face subsistence farmers who wish to rear livestock: providing grazing land, preventing the livestock from wandering off and protecting them from predators, milking, shearing, and butchering. It is important not to denigrate the achievements or scientific understanding of these early subsistence farmers with regard to their developing understanding of the biology of plants and utilising this understanding. For example, in 2006, remains of figs were discovered in a house in Jericho dated to 9400 BC. The figs are of a mutant variety that cannot be pollinated by insects, and therefore the trees can only reproduce from cuttings. This evidence suggests that figs were the first cultivated crop and marks the invention of the technology of farming. This occurred centuries before the first cultivation of grains (Kislev et al. 2006). So, we have to ask what tools were available to early humans to enable these tasks and to what extent have they changed with regard to subsistence farmers today?

From the humble sickle to the autonomous tractor

The sickle has been used since pre-Neolithic times and had a profound impact on the ability to farm. A curved blade mounted on a handle provided the means to harvest seeds from initially wild, and subsequently domesticated grasses. Initially made from bone embedded with flint flakes the design remained essentially unchanged as it embraced other materials, first bronze and then iron and steel. The addition of a long handle to the sickle gave rise to the scythe which enabled more efficient use without bending and grasping the crop. Different sorts of blade were developed for particular tasks: a long, thin blade 90–100 centimetres (35–39 in) for mowing grass or wheat, while a shorter, more robust scythe 60–70 centimetres (24–28 in) is more appropriate for clearing weeds, cutting reed or sedge, and can be used with the blade under water for clearing ditches and waterways. The sickle and scythe have only relatively recently been superseded by mechanisation in modern farming and they, and their equivalents (e.g., machetes), are still widely used by subsistence farmers. The addition of a long handle to reduce the need to bend led to the development of the hoe which was, and still is, used to shape soil, remove weeds, clear soil, and harvest root crops.

In order to grow crops, it is necessary to turn over the soil to form a furrow to take the plant or seed. This is an arduous and tedious task when undertaken with a hoe and this problem was addressed by the development of the plough, initially pushed through the topsoil by hand but then with the aid of animals – oxen or horses. There is archaeological evidence of the use of ploughs dating back to the Han Dynasty in China (202 BC–220 AD). Its use in mediaeval Europe was widespread and its use throughout the world in modern farming has become mechanised using first steam power and then tractors powered by the internal combustion engine. (For a more detailed description of the development of the plough, see, https://www.ploughmen.co.uk/about-us/history-of-the-plough on the website of The Society of Ploughmen.) This mechanisation has been extended to the task of harvesting leading to the development of the combine harvester. This versatile machine combines four separate harvesting operations: reaping, threshing, gathering and winnowing into a single process. Among the crops that can be harvested include wheat, rice, oats, rye, barley, corn (maize), sorghum, soybeans, flax, sunflowers, and rapeseed. The separated straw, left lying on the field, comprises the stems and any remaining leaves of the crop with limited nutrients left in it: the straw is then either chopped, spread on the field and ploughed back in or baled for bedding and limited-feed for livestock. John Deere, a UK manufacturer, produces state of the art combine harvesters incorporating the latest conformation and communication technology. Details are available at https://www.deere.co.uk/assets/publications/index.html?id=4dea4966#1.

The Food and Agriculture Organisation of the United Nations (2009) warns that the world population will have reached over 9 billion by 2050, from its current population of some 7.4 billion. This will place a significant burden on food production. For example, the report warns that it is estimated that by 2050 developing countries' net imports of cereals will more than double from 135 million metric tonnes in 2008/2009 to 300 million in 2050. The technological response of modern farming has been ever more mechanisation to increase both capacity and efficiency. Hence the tools available to modern farming now incorporate satellite navigation and robotics into both planting and harvesting. Drones with sensors capture real-time data about soil conditions on farms, satellites are used to accurately predict weather conditions and pest migrations and autonomous vehicles can now plant and harvest on very large scales with only minimal human oversight. What a paradox – in many parts of the world we have millions of subsistence farmers using indigenous knowledge with tools and methods developed in the distant past to literally scrape a living for themselves and their families whilst at the same time we have modern farming practices elsewhere producing and harvesting vast amounts of crops, informed by sophisticated technology, and implemented through automation requiring minimal human involvement in the activity.

Modern farming methods to support subsistence farmers

In his provocative book, *What technology wants* Kevin Kelly (2010) lists a range of trajectories that influence the ways technology plays out in society. One of these is 'ubiquity' and he argues that just as living things spread from their point of origin so do technologies. Kelly mounts an interesting discussion about the haves and have-nots of technology as technology spreads. He argues that it is better to consider this as haves and have-laters and that in most situations the have-laters will catch up and probably get a technology that is better than that used by first adopters where there were still 'bugs' of various sorts to be ironed out. I wonder if this thinking might be applied to some extent, to subsistence farming. If data relevant to particular subsistence farming situations could be made available to the farmers and aid agencies there is every possibility that the farmers could modify their practice in response and avoid the many uncertainties which render their existence so precarious. This might lead to a step change in their farming enabling the production of sufficient food for the farmers to have enough for their own needs and a surplus which they can sell to others through local markets. A further increase in the scale of food production would enable these farmers to produce food for sale only and use their earnings to buy food from other food producers or from shops and businesses that sell food. This sort of farming can feed into regional, national, and global markets and make a significant contribution to global food production.

Food storage

As hunter-gatherers there was no need for humans to store their food. In the main it was readily available in daylight hours as they moved through the countryside. Different fruits, nuts, and berries become available at different times throughout the year. However, all this changes once humans settle into small communities and become farmers. The limited numbers of crops now grown have a particular harvest time and once these crops are gathered in it will be some time before there is another harvest. This can of course be mitigated to some extent by growing a range of crops but archaeological evidence points to these early communities growing only a few staple foods. This Agricultural Revolution (Harari 2011) had a profound effect on the way humans lived: in one place, as opposed to being nomadic, in shelters they built for themselves as opposed to taking shelter where available and developing technologies that could be used to keep harvested crops and domesticated animals safe from harm. If allowed to roam free livestock may wander off or may be stolen by rival tribes. If left out in the open, harvested crops may become damaged by the weather, food for a variety of insects, birds, and small mammals, and spoiled by bacterial and fungal infestation. Hence the construction of barriers to act as pens for livestock and barns to keep harvested crops safe and within these barns pottery and fabric artefacts for storage and transport. Without the availability of these storage and protection technologies the move from hunter-gatherer to farmer would not have been able to take place. These technologies also found application in other areas of living; cooking, artistry, and clothing for example such that they permeated many other aspects of the lives of early subsistence farmers.

So again, it is worth asking to what extent are the technologies for storage of crops and safekeeping of livestock available to subsistence farmers today significantly different from those available to early humans. The answer is that with regard to the safekeeping of livestock there are instances in which they are almost identical. Cows and sheep need land on which to graze and, given similar pasture the time taken to fatten up has not changed significantly and the need to protect livestock from theft or predators remains the same. In developed nations the only significant difference is that of scale. In the UK for example a commercial livestock enterprise is defined as rearing more than 10 cows, or 50 pigs, or 20 sheep (Office of National Statistics 2020). In some developed countries the number of livestock reared on a single enterprise is huge. For instance, the largest sheep farm in Australia covers over 10,000 square kilometres and stocks approximately 60,000 sheep.

The rearing of pigs is interesting in that unlike sheep and cows it lends itself to intensive farming methods. Many of these are allowed in the US and Canada but are banned in the UK and EU. Such intensive farming is undoubtedly more efficient than the historical methods used by subsistence farmers but raises serious concern with regard to animal welfare (Compassion in world farming 2013) and is seen by some as facilitating the corporatisation of the traditional rural lifestyle. With the storage of crops farmers in developed countries are again operating on a much larger scale with the use of structures called silos which vary in size from 3 to 27 m in diameter and 10 to 90 m in height. (International Silo Association 2020) Silo storage keeps crops such as grain safe from harm and in that sense, it may be seen as preserving the grain. However, food preservation usually involves some form of processing in addition to safe storage so it is to food preservation and processing that we now turn.

Food preservation and processing

Food preservation

Once early humans became farmers and settled to living in communities based in particular places, they were faced with the problem of preserving their hard-won food supplies. Keeping crops and livestock safe from pests, predators and rival communities was relatively straightforward but protection from spoiling through microbial attack was a different matter. Many methods of preservation were developed long before there was much in the way of scientific knowledge and understanding of the role of bacteria in the spoiling of foodstuffs. Some of these 'traditional' methods of preservations are summarised in Table 4.1 with a brief explanation as to why they are effective. This table finishes with the development of pasteurisation, a process named after its inventor Louise Pasteur. His work during the second half of the 19th century disproved the theory of spontaneous generation and established the germ theory of diseases and explained the role of bacteria is causing food to spoil. At the same, developments in the understanding of thermodynamics and the behaviour of volatile liquids in high- and low-pressure environments lead to the availability of refrigerators for both commercial and domestic use. Some of the modern means of food preservation developed in the 20th century are summarised in Table 4.2.

Food processing

Carlos Monteiro and colleagues (2019) have provided a useful classification of food processing in a scheme called NOVA and is now recognised as a valid tool for nutrition and public health research, policy, and action, in reports from the Food and Agriculture Organisation of the United Nations and the Pan American Health Organisation. It categorises foods according to the extent and purpose of food processing, rather than in terms of nutrients and has four categories:

- Unprocessed or minimally processed foods
- Processed culinary ingredients

TABLE 4.1 Development of food preservation techniques from ancient times until 19th century

Method	Date
Fire Cooking Cooking food over a fire kills bacteria in meat, improved taste, and breaks down the protein and muscle fibre within the meat enabling it to be digested more efficiently.	~500,000 BC
Sun drying The heat from the sun heats and causes the water within the food to evaporate. Without the presence of water, the growth of bacteria on food is greatly inhibited.	~12,000 BC
Pickling Vinegar and brine are used in a process called pickling, in which food items are submerged in these liquids which begin to replace the water within vegetables or eggs with the vinegar or brine. This creates a harsh environment for bacteria to grow and effectively sterilises the product.	~2000 BC
Jam making The rotting of fruit can be prevented by the process of pulverising and then extract the juice from fruits (oranges, limes, lemons) and boiling down the juice/pulp mixture. After a period of boiling and adding sugar, the pectin present in the fruit juice becomes viscous and jelly-like, which results in a spreadable fruit concoction.	600 AD
Curing If meat is left out, it begins to oxidise, causing it to become rancid and inedible. Surrounding cuts of meat in salt (sodium chloride) dries out the meat by extracting water from the meat and any bacteria or microorganisms within it, effectively sterilising the meat. The salt also acts to slow the oxidation process, preventing the meat from going rancid.	1400 AD
Refrigeration Early forms of refrigeration included the creation of small sheds or holes in the ground. Butchers or residents would wrap cuts of meat and bury or surround them in ice and snow. This froze the meat and inhibited the growth of organisms and prevented the meat from turning rancid.	1784 AD–
Canning Food is added to a small container and heated to high temperatures expelling most of the air in the container, and the lid is quickly added to seal the container. When the container has cooled to room temperature the food is now in an air depleted environment lacking the oxygen required for bacteria to grow.	1809 AD–
Pasteurisation This process involves rapidly heating and cooling food to destroy most of the bacteria present and keeping the resultant food in a relatively sterile environment which stunts the growth of harmful bacteria. Pasteurisation is not commonly used outside of dairy products as it often mars the taste and quality of the food.	1871 AD–

TABLE 4.2 Modern food preservation methods

Method
Vacuum Packaging Vacuum-packing stores food in a vacuum environment, usually in an air-tight bag or bottle. The vacuum environment strips bacteria of oxygen needed for survival.
Irradiation Multiple types of ionising radiation can be used, including beta particles (high-energy electrons) and gamma rays (emitted from radioactive sources such as cobalt-60 or cesium-137). Irradiation can kill bacteria, moulds, and insect pests, reduce the ripening and spoiling of fruits, and at higher doses induce sterility.
Modified atmosphere (MA) Packaging Many products such as red meat, seafood, minimally processed fruits and vegetables, salads, pasta, cheese, bakery goods, poultry, cooked and cured meats, ready meals and dried foods are packaged under MA. The packaging is sealed from the atmosphere and within the packaging the atmosphere has been modified to in order to improve shelf life. This 'in-package' atmosphere usually contains a smaller percentage of oxygen and includes other gases such as nitrogen or carbon dioxide. This reduces or delays oxidation reactions and prevents the growth of bacteria.
Artificial food additives Preservative food additives can be antimicrobial which inhibit the growth of bacteria or fungi, including mould; or antioxidant such as oxygen absorbers, which inhibit the oxidation of food constituents.

- Processed foods
- Ultra-processed food and drink products

The definitions of these groupings are summarised in Table 4.3.

Monteiro and colleagues argue that since the 1980s a monolithic global industrial food system has emerged and that the food supplies of high-income countries with less strong culinary traditions, such as the US, Canada, the UK, and Australia, have become dominated by packaged, ready-to- consumer products. They also argue that in other high-income countries and settings, and in middle- and low-income countries, these products are rapidly displacing traditional dietary patterns based on minimally processed foods and freshly prepared dishes and meals. The result is that rates of obesity and diabetes have correspondingly risen very rapidly as indicated in Part 2 of this chapter. There is little doubt that the formulation and the ingredients of these products make them highly convenient (ready-to-consume), highly attractive (hyper-palatable), highly profitable (low-cost ingredients), and – of great importance – highly competitive with foods that are naturally ready to consume and freshly prepared dishes and meals. As a result of their formulation, products belonging to this food group are intrinsically nutrient-unbalanced and tend to be consumed in great amounts.

TABLE 4.3 The NOVA classification of foods according to processing

---

Unprocessed or minimally processed foods

Unprocessed (or natural) foods are edible parts of plants (seeds, fruits, leaves, stems, roots) or of animals (muscle, offal, eggs, milk), and fungi, algae, and water, after separation from nature.

Minimally processed foods are natural foods altered by processes such as removal of inedible or unwanted parts, drying, crushing, grinding, fractioning, filtering, roasting, boiling, pasteurisation, refrigeration, freezing, placing in containers, vacuum packaging, or non-alcoholic fermentation. None of these processes adds substances such as salt, sugar, oils, or fats to the original food.

Processed culinary ingredients

The second NOVA group is of processed culinary ingredients. These are substances obtained directly from group 1 foods or from nature by processes such as pressing, refining, grinding, milling, and spray drying. The purpose of processing here is to make products used in home and restaurant kitchens to prepare, season and cook group 1 foods and to make with them varied and enjoyable hand-made dishes, soups and broths, breads, preserves, salads, drinks, desserts, and other culinary preparations.

Processed foods

These are relatively simple products made by adding sugar, oil, salt, or other group 2 substances to group 1 foods. Most processed foods have two or three ingredients. Processes include various preservation or cooking methods, and, in the case of breads and cheese, non-alcoholic fermentation. The main purpose of the manufacture of processed foods is to increase the durability of group 1 foods, or to modify or enhance their sensory qualities. Typical examples of processed foods are canned or bottled vegetables, fruits, and legumes; salted or sugared nuts and seeds; salted, cured, or smoked meats; canned fish; fruits in syrup; cheeses and unpackaged freshly made bread.

Ultra-processed food and drink products

These are industrial formulations typically with five or more and usually many ingredients. Such ingredients often include those also used in processed foods, such as sugar, oils, fats, salt, antioxidants, stabilisers, and preservatives. Ingredients only found in ultra-processed products include substances not commonly used in culinary preparations, and additives whose purpose is to imitate sensory qualities of group 1 foods or of culinary preparations of these foods, or to disguise undesirable sensory qualities of the final product. Group 1 foods are a small proportion of or are even absent from ultra-processed products.

Source: Extracted from Monteiro et al. (2019)

The narrative of food by its very nature is not static, but fluid with different features emerging over time at different rates and in different places. The narrative is evolving and the emergence and continued operation of a global food industry producing vast quantities of ultra-processed food and drink products must be a cause of concern. The extent to which the production of such food and drink products can be scaled back with attendant health benefits is open to question but some countries are attempting to do this. The Brazilian Ministry of Health (2015) has produced dietary guidelines with the golden rule, "Always prefer natural or minimally processed foods and freshly made dishes and meals to ultra-processed products". There is an irony here in that the Amazon RainForest is being subject to deforestation at an alarming rate to facilitate the production of beef much of which will end in ultra-processed foods. In England The National Food Strategy (2022) has as one of its main recommendations, to escape the junk food cycle and protect the National Health System.

Food sale and distribution

Food sale and distribution depend on supply chains. For the subsistence farmer there is no supply chain as all that is produced is used by the farmers and their families. As soon as there is a surplus produced there is the opportunity for these farmers to form an agribusiness and take the surplus produce to local markets where they can be sold. Hence the food produced becomes part of a short food supply chain. Such supply chains are characterised by short physical distance between the producers and consumers with few if any intermediaries. These are not restricted to developing countries and are a feature in many countries where towns are close to countryside in which farming takes place. They may take the form of farm shops, farmers markets, collective farmers shops and community-supported agriculture in which consumers subscribe to the harvest of a certain farm or group of farms. Originally seen as farmers resisting the modernisation of the food system which is characterised by the development of supply chains based on long-distance trade this view has changed with the realisation that short food supply chains are a boon to rural development (EU 2016).

At the other end of the spectrum there are supermarkets. Most urban households in the UK buy their groceries from supermarkets which offer a wide range of food, beverages and household products organised into sections from which customers collect their purchases prior to paying for them through check out systems which increasingly are operated by the customers themselves. Supermarkets pay great attention to the layout of their stores to maximise purchasing. The supply chains that support supermarkets are long with foods and food products coming from different parts of the country and other countries in different parts of the world. Most of the goods are transported to central distribution centres in refrigerated containers and from there are transported to individual supermarkets in refrigerated lorries. Hence the carbon footprint of many of the goods sold in supermarkets is high. Recently UK supermarkets have developed their online order services giving customers the option of home delivery during a specified time slot or 'click and collect' in which customers can collect their order from a designated store. In order to maintain food stocks and meet both in-store and online sales supermarkets need a robust inventory management system to ensure that they do not run out of or over stock particular food items. Perishable goods pose the problem that some of the inventory may spoil while sitting in the store. Tracking exactly what is bought both across a store and at individual customer level provides the information needed for the necessary inventory control. The checkout is a key component of this system as the scanning of the bar codes of items purchased provides the information needed for robust inventory management.

Supermarkets are criticised on the grounds that they place significant economic pressure on suppliers and smaller shopkeepers (EESC 2013) and also that they often generate considerable food waste although modern technologies such as biomethanation units may be able to process the waste into an economical source of energy. Also, purchase tracking is helping supermarkets become better able to size their stock of perishable goods, reducing food spoilage.

The Plan of the National Food Strategy (2022) acknowledges the significance of supermarkets in the purchase of food noting that supermarkets (and the hospitality sector) are extremely adept at nudging consumers towards certain products and behaviours. With this in mind Recommendation 2 of the Plan suggests that there should be a statutory duty for all food companies with more than 250 employees – including retailers, restaurant and quick service companies, contract caterers, wholesalers, manufacturers and online ordering platforms – to publish an annual report on the following set of metrics:

- Sales of food and drink high in fat, sugar or salt (HFSS) excluding alcohol
- Sales of protein by type (of meat, dairy, fish, plant, or alternative protein) and origin
- Sales of vegetables
- Sales of fruit
- Sales of major nutrients: fibre, saturated fat, sugar and salt
- Food waste
- Total food and drink sales.

The recommendation argues that publishing these numbers will allow investors, Government, and others to track the direction in which businesses are heading with a view to enabling better scrutiny and maintaining public pressure on companies "to do the right thing".

Food preparation and consumption

For those living in poor countries having ingredients with which to cook meals is literally a matter of life and death. The impact of malnutrition in these situations is considered in more detail in Part 2 of this chapter. Sufficient to write here that the WHO Malnutrition Fact Sheet (World Health Organisation 2021) paints a bleak picture; with undernutrition, in 2014, leading to approximately 462 million adults world-wide being underweight and, in 2016, an estimated

155 million children under the age of 5 suffering from stunting. For those living in wealthy countries or the wealthier parts of poor countries overnutrition is the problem and the WHO factsheet is equally damning reporting that world-wide 1.9 billion adults are overweight or obese.

But there is more to eating than simply staying alive. Meals shared with other people have significance. Sometimes such meals are associated with rites of passage; birth, attaining adulthood, marriage, death. Sometimes they are related to religious belief such as Passover for Jews, Christmas for Christians, Eid for Muslims, and Diwali for Hindus. In some of these cases external caterers are used to cook and provide the food but in many members of the communities taking part cook food items which they bring to the occasion for all to share. Families eating together is generally seen as beneficial and there is evidence for this. A systematic review of the literature (Harrison et al. 2015) found that eating frequent family meals was associated with better psychosocial outcomes for children and adolescents. Frequent family meals were inversely associated with disordered eating, alcohol and substance use, violent behaviour, and feelings of depression or thoughts of suicide. There was a positive relationship between frequent family meals and increased self-esteem and commitment to learning or a higher grade point average. Hence it is worrying to find that research carried out by Sainsbury's in the UK points to a significant decline in the number of families that do eat together (Sainsbury 2021). The poll of 2,000 UK respondents reveals that just 28% of households are sharing the same meal in the evening, with an even lower 12% sharing breakfast. The research found that a busy schedule is the most common reason families don't dine together, with 55% of the sample admitting to struggling to find the time. Nearly one in five (19%) aged 25–34 said they often eat a totally different meal to the rest of the family due to working late. Almost a quarter (23%) of parents in this age group admitted that their children eat meals in front of the TV or games console. It is possible to relate this decline in family eating to the availability of ready meals at supermarkets which facilitate individual family members having their meals at different times as they can usually be prepared by a few minutes heating in a microwave oven. This eliminates the preparation of ingredients and reduces cooking time significantly. It is worth putting this family experience of eating into the wider context of how we are all being encouraged to eat through the advertising that is currently taking place. (See for example https://www.just-eat.co.uk/blog/inspiration/magic-is-real and https://www.youtube.com/watch?v=dvRrh8NOTbM.) Underlying these adverts is the message that time spent preparing your own food is time wasted when you could be doing other things. So, people are encouraged to dial up fast food for home delivery so that they can get on with much more exciting activities. At the time of writing in the town where I live, the 'Just Eat' website (https://www.youtube.com/watch?v=dvRrh8NOTbM) identified 186 different restaurants from which I could order takeaway meals to be delivered to my door.

Part 2: The Narrative of Food through the lenses of social justice and stewardship of Planet Earth

Introduction

For the purposes of this chapter social justice concerns the relationship between the individual and society as measured by the distribution of wealth, opportunities for personal development and social privileges. In a just world, all people should be able to live in freedom from hunger and fear and have shelter from harm. They should have opportunities to pursue happiness and make the best of their lives. The plight of subsistence farmers in developing countries is a particular cause for concern, families and communities are growing just enough food for them to be able to eat with little if any surplus. The precarious nature of this existence often leads to under nutrition which severely affects the quality of their lives and limits their aspirations. Ironically it is over nutrition among the poor in the developed nations that affects the quality of life and limits aspirations.

In considering stewardship it is important to move beyond the standard evaluation of conventional practices which usually limits itself to answering the question, "Do they achieve what they are supposed to achieve?" Particular practices might well achieve what they were supposed to achieve, but this interrogation must be extended to include the following questions:

Is what was supposed to be achieved worth achieving?

To what extent do they contribute to a future worth wanting?

What might be the unintended consequences of wide-scale practice?

To what extent will these consequences compromise the wellbeing of Planet Earth and its ability to support life?

Malnutrition, its causes, and effects

Over nutrition in developed nations

Being overweight or obese is a major form of malnutrition in developed countries. A key indicator of this form of malnutrition is the Body Mass Index (BMI). The BMI is a value derived from the mass and height of a person. It is defined as the body mass divided by the square of the body height and is expressed in units of kg/m^2, resulting from mass in kilograms and height in metres. Table 4.4 shows a range of values.

The government in England, along with those of many other countries in the developed world, is seriously concerned about the nation's health with particular regard to the impact of poor dietary choices on the cost of the National Health Service (NHS). As early as 2007, Foresight reported that the predicted increase in obesity was a ticking time bomb as far as health service costs were concerned (Department for Innovation, Universities and Skills [DIUS] 2007a) This extract

TABLE 4.4 Variation in Body Mass Index (BMI)

Category	BMI (kg/m^2)[c]
Underweight (Severe thinness)	<16.0
Underweight (Moderate thinness)	16.0–16.9
Underweight (Mild thinness)	17.0–18.4
Normal range	18.5–24.9
Overweight (Pre-obese)	25.0–29.9
Obese (Class I)	30.0–34.9
Obese (Class II)	35.0–39.9
Obese (Class III)	≥40.0

from the summary of key messages (DIUS 2007b) indicate the seriousness of the situation:

- By 2050, Foresight modelling indicates that 60% of adult men, 50% of adult women and about 25% of all children under 16 could be obese. Obesity increases the risk of a range of chronic diseases; particularly type 2 diabetes, stroke, and coronary heart disease and also cancer and arthritis. The NHS costs attributable to overweight and obesity are projected to double to £10 billion per year by 2050. The wider costs to society and business are estimated to reach £49.9 billion per year (at today's prices).

Written just over 15 years ago this provided a stark warning and now prescriptions for Type 2 Diabetes caused to a large extent by lifestyle choices leading to being overweight and obese are costing the NHS in England more than £1 billion a year (Ives 2018).

The latest data from the Health Survey for England (2019) paints a similarly bleak picture with these headlines:

- Among adults 16 and over, 68% of men and 60% 0f women were overweight or obese.
- Among children, 18% of boys and 13% of girls were obese.
- Children with obese parents were more likely to be obese.
- Adults living in the most deprived areas were the most likely to be obese. This difference was particularly pronounced for women, where 39% of women in the most deprived areas were obese, compared with 22% in the least deprived areas.

One of the contributory causes of poor dietary choice is the ready availability of inexpensive, prepared food that is high in fat, sugar, and salt. At a time when many families are struggling financially, ready meals from the supermarket or from a fast-food outlet provide an affordable, if unhealthy, source of food.

Research has indicated that the numbers of fast-food outlets can double the chances of becoming obese (Briggs 2014) and UK high streets currently have the highest concentration of fast-food outlets since 2010 (Homer 2018). Data from the National Office of Statistics reported by Homer is also worrying:

- The UK has seen a 34% increase in fast food outlets from 2010 to 2018.
- In 2010, the average number of fast-food outlets per 100,000 people was 47. It had risen to 61 by 2018.
- In nearly every area (204 out of 215) the rate of takeaways per 100,000 people was higher in 2018 than 2010.

Hence those who are poor in developed countries find themselves in a situation in which they appear to have little choice but to adopt an unhealthy diet in which there is an overabundance of calories combined with ingredients that are intrinsically unhealthy. It is clearly unjust that the poor in such countries find themselves in this situation. Governments have been using a variety of strategies to rectify the situation, but it has to be admitted, without much in the way of success. If one looks at such diets through the lens of stewardship of Planet Earth many of the ingredients used to produce and deliver such food carry a heavy carbon footprint and also deplete the Planet's ability to absorb carbon dioxide. As Foresight acknowledged, confronting this issue is a major challenge requiring a coordinated partnership between government, science, business and civil society and it is interwoven with our efforts to combat climate change.

Under nutrition in developing nations

Under nutrition makes children in particular much more vulnerable to disease and death. According to the WHO (World Health Organisation 2021) around 45% of deaths among children under 5 years of age are linked to undernutrition. These mostly occur in low- and middle-income countries. Women, infants, children, and adolescents are at particular risk of malnutrition. Optimising nutrition early in life – including the 1,000 days from conception to a child's second birthday – ensures the best possible start in life, with long-term benefits.

The WHO (ibid) has identified four broad sub-forms of undernutrition:

- Wasting
  - Low weight-for-height usually indicates recent and severe weight loss because a person has not had enough food to eat and/or they have had an infectious disease, such as diarrhoea, which has caused them to lose weight. A young child who is moderately or severely wasted has an increased risk of death, but treatment is possible.
- Stunting,
  - Low height-for-age and is the result of chronic or recurrent under nutrition, usually associated with poor socioeconomic conditions, poor

maternal health and nutrition, frequent illness, and/or inappropriate infant and young child feeding and care in early life. Stunting holds children back from reaching their physical and cognitive potential. In 2016, an estimated 155 million children under the age of 5 years were suffering from stunting.

- Being underweight
  - A child who is underweight may be stunted, wasted, or both. In 2014, approximately 462 million adults worldwide were underweight.
- Deficiencies in vitamins and minerals.
  - Inadequacies in the intake of vitamins and minerals often referred to as micronutrients can also be grouped together. Micronutrients enable the body to produce enzymes, hormones, and other substances that are essential for proper growth and development. Iodine, vitamin A, and iron are the most important in global public health terms; their deficiency represents a major threat to the health and development of populations worldwide, particularly children and pregnant women in low-income countries.

Poverty, in both developed and developing nations, amplifies the risk of, and risks from, malnutrition. People who are poor are more likely to be affected by different forms of malnutrition. In addition to lessening opportunities and aspirations, malnutrition increases health care costs, reduces productivity, and slows economic growth, which can perpetuate a cycle of poverty and ill-health. The impact of global warming is intertwined with the impact of poverty and exacerbates the already deleterious effects of malnutrition. Steps taken to limit greenhouse gas (GHG) emission and enhance carbon capture from the atmosphere will influence the narrative of food and it is a consideration of sustainable food production that we now turn to.

Sustainable food production

Climate change and the way we produce and consume food are intertwined and the situation is stark. At COP26 Agnes Kalibata, UN Food Systems Summit Special Envoy, warned, "We cannot fix climate change unless we fix our food systems".

The World Resources Institute's Report (2019) Creating a Sustainable Food Future identifies three important 'gaps' that need to be bridged by 2050. These are

The Food Gap

- The difference between the amount of food produced in 2010 and the amount necessary to meet likely demand in 2050; 56% more crop calories will be needed compared to that produced in 2010.

The Land Gap

- The difference between global agricultural land area in 2010 and the area that will be required in 2050 – even if crop and pasture yields continue to grow at rates achieved in the past. 593 million hectares of extra land will be needed, an area nearly twice the size of India.

The GHG mitigation Gap

- The difference between the level of annual GHG emissions from agriculture and land-use change in 2050, which we estimate to be 15 gigatons (Gt), and a target of 4 Gt that represents agriculture's proportional contribution to holding global warming below 2°C above pre-industrial temperatures. Holding warming below a 1.5°C increase would require meeting this 4 Gt target *plus* freeing up hundreds of millions of hectares for reforestation.

The report identifies five courses of action that together could close these gaps.

1. Reduce growth in demand for food and agricultural products.
2. Increase food production without expanding agricultural land.
3. Protect and restore natural ecosystems.
4. Increase fish supply (through improved wild fisheries management and aquaculture).
5. Reduce GHG emissions from agricultural production.

Carrying out these courses of action will require coordinated efforts by many millions of farmers, businesses, consumers, and all governments. Within these five courses of action eight themes stand out. These are

1. Raising productivity
2. Managing demand
3. Linking agricultural intensificationwith natural ecosystems protection
4. Moderating ruminant meat consumption
5. Targeting reforestation and peat land restoration
6. Requiring production-related climate mitigation
7. Spurring technological innovation

The final item is of particular interest in the consideration of a food technology course. Opportunities for innovation include developing crop traits or additives that reduce methane emissions from rice and cattle, improved fertiliser forms and crop properties that reduce nitrogen runoff, solar-based processes for making fertilisers, organic sprays that preserve fresh food for longer periods, and plant-based beef substitutes. A revolution in molecular biology opens up new opportunities for crop breeding. Progress at the necessary scale requires large increases in R&D funding, and flexible regulations that encourage private industry to develop and market new technologies. Some of these technological developments will be considered in Part 4 Future scenarios for the narrative of food.

Part 3: Pedagogy for the narrative of food in secondary school

Growing food

What experiences of food production might we wish young people to have? Is it unrealistic to expect young people to have the experience of growing and harvesting food for themselves? Perhaps schools that teach food technology should have one or more allotments on which young people can grow and harvest a variety of crops according to the season. For the moment I am ruling out rearing and subsequent slaughter of livestock although I could certainly make a case for keeping chickens and harvesting eggs and goats for milk which could be used to produce cheese and yoghurt. There could be arrangements for some of their produce to be sold at a local market or a school shop. Some of the produce could be used in cooking lessons and some could be further processed through preservation, e.g., jam or pickle making or in the case of wheat-producing flour which might be used for simple baking. This is in no sense a trivial endeavour. It would require funding, organisation and commitment but its educational potential is high. The activities of planting, growing, tending, and harvesting are underpinned by an understanding of the following Big Ideas concerning the needs of plants:

• Fertile soil in which to grow, for some soils fertilisers might be needed.
• Appropriate weather conditions to supply sunlight and water at temperatures that do not harm the plants. In adverse conditions additional water, protection from sunlight and cold might be required.
• Protective measures against pests and disease which effect yields.
• Drainage to prevent the soil becoming waterlogged and preventing growth.
• Appropriate planting to maximise yields and enable harvesting.

None of these ideas are particularly difficult to understand but unless each is considered in the teaching and the way the allotment is managed then the learning achieved by the young people and their appreciation of these in the light of the narrative of food will be limited.

The learning associated with school-based food production can act as a springboard for considering food production in the world outside the confines of the school allotment with particular reference to the way technologies, particularly new and emerging technologies are being utilised. Barlex (2020) gives examples of this with regard to the cultivation of leafy greens in a school allotment and the use of vertical farming.

Cooking food

There appears to have been agreement across successive governments in England that it is important to teach young people to cook as part of educational initiatives to encourage healthy lifestyles and develop self-reliance as they enter the adult world. Whether this has been successful is to some extent doubtful (Barlex 2020). Whilst few would argue against teaching young people to cook, in this chapter we are considering the nature of food technology as a subject to be taught in secondary schools in the light of the entire narrative of food. So, it has to be decided how significant teaching cooking should be within this endeavour. Given all else there is to teach about food technology and the time it takes for young people to learn how to cook well I think a strong case can be made for teaching cookery outside food technology courses. This in no way denigrates the importance of teaching young people to cook, quite the reverse. Shoe-horning teaching cookery into a food technology course will do little justice to the teaching of cooking as the content will be minimal and the time taken to acquire the necessary skills insufficient. I think it is far preferable to teach cookery from within a PSHE curriculum where it is much more likely to get the time it needs to be effective. This of course does not mean that students should not have hands-on experience of food materials in a food technology course; quite the opposite but the focus of the interaction with food should be investigation as opposed to cooking simple meals. Hence it is to investigate food we know in turn.

Investigating food

Some teachers are resistant to the idea of investigating food as an activity in its own right. They contend that this is a 'waste' of food. They argue that students should use food to develop and cook products and/or meals that they can take home and use to feed themselves, their friends and family. The fact that in many secondary schools students' families have to supply the ingredients or are charged for them strengthens this position. This is a strong argument in the context of teaching young people to cook and I agree that it is important to develop the idea that food is a precious resource and should not be wasted. However, in the context of a food technology course in which teaching to cook is not a priority then I think it loses its strength. It is of course important that only small quantities of food are used for investigations and that any that remains that is uncontaminated is put to good use, such as composting. Possible areas for investigating food are as follows:

- Exploring the composition of food
- Measuring the energy content of food
- Exploring ways to control the flavour and odour of food
- Exploring ways to control the texture of food
- Exploring ways to control the colour of food
- Exploring the influence of flavour, odour, texture, and colour on food preferences

Each of these will be considered briefly. Developing knowledge and understanding from these activities needs to be underpinned by the following important scientific ideas:

- All matter is composed of particles – atoms, ions and molecules and in many cases, food contains molecules in the form of polymers.
- All materials, including food, have properties according to their composition and the way the atoms, molecules or ions are arranged and interact with one another.
- The properties of food materials can be modified through the application of heat and combination with other materials and may involve the formation of colloids and emulsions.

Exploring the composition of food

Food and food products are complex combinations of different materials but there are three fundamentals that, in varying amounts, constitute food. These are fats, carbohydrates, and proteins. It is possible to test for these and it is instructive for students to learn to carry out these tests and apply them to a variety of food stuffs in order to explore their composition. Instructions on how to carry out these tests are available free to download at the author's website (Beaumont 1996).

Measuring the energy content of food

Burning a weighed sample of food material and measuring the heat produced is the conventional method. This is usually achieved by transferring the heat from the burning reaction to a known amount of water and measuring the resultant temperature rise. The problem of over nutrition in developed countries (discussed in Part 2 of this chapter) is to some extent due to the excessive consumption of inexpensive energy-dense foods. Hence the idea that the energy content of foods can be measured, and the resulting information used in deciding what and how much of various foods we should eat is potentially a powerful one. Also, students may well be familiar with the idea of the energy content of foods through the labelling on food packaging. However, this is conceptually challenging for secondary school students. Firstly, they are being asked to believe that the energy released by the burning reaction taking place at several hundred Celsius will be the same as the energy released when the food is digested which takes place at body temperature – 37 Celsius. Secondly the calculation which translates the temperature change in Celsius to an energy change in either calories or joules is arithmetically complex and involves compound units which students are known to find difficult. The considerable demands both conceptual and practical, are discussed further in Banks and Barlex (2021). Here it is worth noting that unless sufficient time is given to the activity to enable students to get to grips with the inherent difficulties, they are more likely to become confused than gain understanding.

Exploring ways to control the flavour and odour of food

Ingredients have their own unique flavour and odour. The extent to which an ingredient contributes to the overall flavour and odour of food will depend on the following:

- The amount used
- The exact type of a particular ingredient
- Whether the ingredient has been subject to any preservation technique
- Whether the ingredient has been treated before use as in marinating for instance
- The cooking technique used

Exploring ways to control the texture of food

Ingredients have their own unique texture. The extent to which an ingredient contributes to the overall texture of food will depend on the following:

- The amount used
- The age of the ingredient
- Mechanical treatment of the ingredient (pounding, chopping, grating, pureeing for example)
- Chemical treatment of the ingredient (tenderising by marinating; foaming through release of carbon dioxide, setting by use of pectin or gelatin, for example)
- The cooking technique (frying giving crispness and boiling giving softness to vegetables for example)

Exploring ways to control the colour of food

- The colour of food may be controlled in the following ways:
- Adding coloured ingredients
- Adding food colouring
- The choice of ingredients
- The method of cooking
- The temperature at which the food is cooked
- The length of time cooked

It is relatively straightforward for students to explore these different ways to control flavour, odour, texture, and colour of food and they provide opportunities for different small groups of students to carry out different explorations and share their findings.

Exploring the influence of flavour, odour, texture,
and colour on consumer food preferences

There is a wide range of different and well-established testing procedures that can be used to explore these influences such as ranking tests, difference tests, preference tests, and attribute profiling. It is worth noting that students can use commercially available food items for these explorations which will reduce the time taken as they are not required to make the food items under investigation. However, care must be taken in choosing these items such that there is likely to be significant differences between them with regard to the features being explored.

Exploring the narrative of food

If students are to understand the narrative of food, then it is important to provide them with the 'Big Picture' so that they can relate the various stages to their own lives. This will increase their ownership of the material to be learned as well as give relevance to the learning. This immediately raises the question, "How might teachers provide the Big Picture?" A useful place to start is with the possibility of using Dual Coding (Caviglioli 2019). In this approach to teaching and learning material to be learned is presented in the form of pictures (often diagrams) AND commentary. In this way students are able to use two senses (sight and hearing) simultaneously which has significant benefits for enabling the information to become part of their long-term memory. The approach to the narrative of food taken in this chapter is to see it as a linear sequence involving five stages; starting with (a) food production mainly through agriculture and moving on to include (b) storage, (c) preservation and processing, (d) sales and distribution at different levels of scale, complexity and sophistication dependant on context and concluding with (e) preparation and consumption. Presenting this sequence all at once, even by means of a mix of diagrams and comments, is likely to overwhelm students so it will be important to build up the sequence a stage at a time until the entire sequence is complete. In addition to avoiding overloading the students with information this has the following advantages:

- The teacher can ask the students about each stage, so he has some sense of their existing knowledge and understanding.
- The class can build up a shared appreciation of what they, as a learning community, already know and believe (some of which may well be erroneous).
- The teacher can use this to inform his dual coding presentation as he teaches the class about each stage.
- He can also ask questions that provoke the students to re-evaluate their knowledge and the place of that stage in the sequence in their lives.

In responding to the students' comments, it is essential to treat their answers with respect, especially those answers that reveal misapprehensions. Many students, especially those living in cities have little contact with farming and the origins of their food and their ideas will often be incorrect. Only the students themselves can correct these misconceptions in the light of the information the teacher presents. If they are made to feel foolish it is highly likely they will become resentful and cease paying attention.

Figures 4.1–4.5 show possible presentation slides, along with possible questions, that might be used to build up a big picture of the narrative of food.

Once the narrative of food has been established as a sequence of stages to which the students can relate then each stage may be re-visited in greater depth as the students develop a more sophisticated and nuanced understanding of the issues pertinent to that stage.

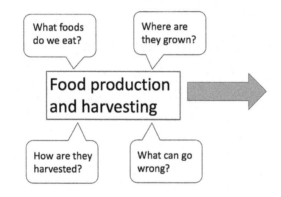

FIGURE 4.1 The narrative of food part 1

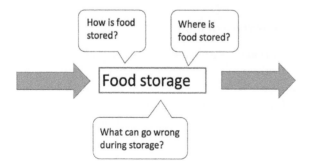

FIGURE 4.2 The narrative of food part 2

The Narrative of Food Part 3 of 5

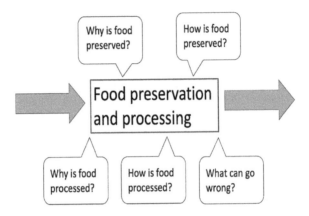

FIGURE 4.3 The narrative of food part 3

The Narrative of Food Part 4 of 5

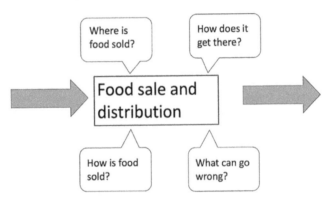

FIGURE 4.4 The narrative of food part 4

Critiquing the narrative of food

For learners to critique the narrative of food they need to stand back and consider the various stages in the narrative through the lenses of social justice and
stewardship of Planet Earth. One way to do this is to use a winners and losers
analysis tool. This involves using the target chart shown in Figure 4.6. An activity in a stage of the narrative of food is placed in the centre of the chart. Two
charts are required, one to consider through the lens of social justice and one to
consider through the lens of stewardship for Planet Earth. With regard to considering social justice those groups and individuals who are directly involved in
the activity being considered are written in the inner circle. Those groups and

The Narrative of Food Part 5 of 5

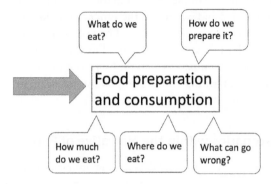

FIGURE 4.5 The narrative of food part 5

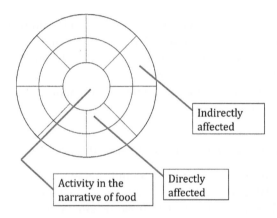

FIGURE 4.6 A winners and losers target chart

individuals indirectly affected are listed in the outer circle. Then these entries are classified as either winners (those who benefit from the activity) or losers (those who suffer some form of detriment). Giving one colour to the winner segments and a different colour to the loser segments gives an immediate visual picture of the winner–loser balance although care must be taken in the interpretation of this as it does not, of itself, give any indication of the size of the groups involved or the severity or otherwise of any impact. An effective way to stimulate discussion around a completed chart is to assign some learners the role of 'winners' and other learners the role of 'losers'. The task then facing the learners is for the winners to justify why it is permissible for them to win at the losers' expense and the losers to argue for some form of recompense from the winners. As an example, the use of robot crop pickers might be placed in the centre and the implications of their use considered in terms of winners and losers with regard to social justice.

With regard to the stewardship of Planet Earth an activity from a particular stage in the narrative is placed in the centre and the direct impacts of the activity on the planet are identified and written in the inner circle. Any indirect impacts on the planet are written in the outer circle. The task then facing learners is to decide whether for each of these impacts Planet Earth is a winner or a loser. As an example, the use of vertical farming might be placed in the centre. Whether the use of this method of farming constitutes good stewardship or not may then be discussed (Figure 4.6).

Part 4: Future scenarios within the Narrative of Food

The contribution of farming to global warming juxtaposed to the need for greater food production in the light of population increase creates a situation in which there are conflicting requirements. This section will consider the following six ways in which these conflicts might be addressed

- Increasing food production without expanding agricultural land
- Developing crops that are resistant to climate extremes
- Growing food in ways that do not contribute to climate change
- Utilising foods from unusual sources
- Providing alternatives to ruminant meat consumption
- Preventing spoilage

Increasing food production without expanding agricultural land

The Netherlands provides a unique example because as a country it has very little land available for agriculture yet is the second largest global exporter of food by dollar value after the US. It has invested heavily in 'smart' greenhouses which allow farmers to closely control growing conditions and use fewer resources like water and fertiliser. Over the period 2003–2014 vegetable production increased by 28% whilst energy consumption decreased by 6%, pesticide use by 9% and fertiliser use by 29%. The farming of tomatoes provides a compelling example. The area devoted to growing this crop is only 6.9 square miles but has a yield of 144,352 tons per square mile (greater than anywhere else in the world) with a water footprint 25 times less than the global average. This is achieved through large-scale greenhouse cultivation growing plants without soil in nutrient-rich solutions (Viviano and Locatelli 2017).

The Nemo Garden is located in the sea off the Italian Riviera. It consists of six large underwater domes which are used to grow plants using hydroponics. This is still in a small-scale experimental stage investigating which plants will grow best inside the domes but if successful it might provide the basis for farming without dry land (Li 2022).

Developing crops that are resistant to climate extremes

Some see the genetic modification of both plants and animals as an important, indeed necessary, approach to combating world food shortages. However, others argue that the risks of this approach are not justified. In England there was a backlash against genetically modified (GM) crops, fuelled by the popular press with the strapline "Frankenfoods" leading to supermarkets withdrawing such products from their shelves (Banks and Barlex 2021). Genetic modification involves the introduction of genes from one organism into another in the expectation that this new genetic material will confer benefits on the host organism. Gene technology has now moved on and there is the possibility of altering the genetic material of an organism in ways that do not require the introduction of genes from a different organism. Hence, we are now in a situation in which a new wave of gene-edited crops is becoming available. Through such gene editing it is possible to rapidly create plants that are drought resistant, immune to disease and improved in flavour. And importantly, they need not be labelled as GM crops and may thus escape the notice of supermarket customers, hence avoiding the backlash suffered by GM crops earlier. This is because the various food regulation authorities do not classify them as GM crops and insist that they are labelled as such which would then severely limit their commercial viability and use in combating world hunger. At the time of writing this is in the balance (Regalado 2017).

Growing food in ways that do not contribute to climate change

It is widely acknowledged that the production of meat, particularly beef, is bad for the planet and a very inefficient process. Hence the idea that we might be able to simply grow meat in bioreactors, using our knowledge of biotechnology is very appealing. This is not a new idea, Winston Churchill wrote about it in 1931, (Kleeman 2020) and in principle it is simple. Staring with a small sample of cells from an animal the cells are grown in a bioreactor such that they cling to an edible scaffold to create 3D tissue i.e., meat. This meat is then harvested and turned into food products without the need to clear forests for grazing, raise herds of cattle on the cleared land, slaughtering and butchering their carcasses etc. with the attendant environmental damage. This might be described as 'cellular agriculture' (Lawton 2020). The similarity of the products to conventional meat and public acceptance will play a large part in whether these endeavours are commercially successful but one considerable advantage of cultured meat is that it is free from antibiotics. Worldwide, 80% of antibiotics are used in agriculture although this may be a mixed blessing in that conventional meat contains bacteria that may protect us against food poisoning. (ibid).

Precision fermentation is the use of genetically engineered microorganisms to produce animal products and this process is being used to produce milk; hence, in addition to milk itself it is possible to develop a range of dairy-free milk-based products – ice cream, yoghurt, cheese. Initially these are likely to appeal to those who wish to adopt a diet that does not include food derived from animals but as the prices become more competitive such products will move into the mainstream (Lawton 2021).

Utilising foods from unusual sources

Eating insects is perfectly acceptable in some cultures, e.g., Thailand and Mexico, but faces considerable consumer resistance in other countries. However, they are finding a market in the United States as high protein animal feed or ingredients for processed foods, writes Tracie McMillan (2018). Crickets in particular appeal as a food material in that they offer more protein and micronutrients per pound than beef, thrive in dark densely crowded conditions, allowing for factory-scale production on a tiny footprint and produce relatively little waste unlike some large hog and cattle farms with their manure lagoons. The Aspire Food Group in Austin, Texas (see https://aspirefg.com) provides an interesting example of the growth of insect farming. Formed in 2013 with a staff of seven the company had grown to a staff of 60 in 2018, began constructing the world's largest cricket farm in 2020 and was awarded $16.8 million Canadian from Next Generation Advanced Manufacturing Supercluster for building the world's smartest insect production facility.

As with insects, seaweed is an acceptable food in some parts of the world; particularly Asia but is less so in other jurisdictions. However, this may change as there is a burgeoning kelp industry off the coast in Scotland (Shaw 2021). Kelp is high in vitamins and minerals and there are now many ways to introduce it into our food (Sea Food Nutrition Partnership 2021).

Palm oil is an edible vegetable oil derived from the mesocarp (reddish pulp) of the fruit of the oil palms. The oil is used in food manufacturing, in beauty products, and as biofuel (Immerzeel et al. 2013). The use of palm oil has attracted the concern of environmental groups due to deforestation in the tropics where palms are grown and has been cited as a factor in social problems due to allegations of human rights violations among growers (AP News 2020). Hence, finding an alternative to palm oil that can be grown without deforestation or human rights violations would be beneficial. Preliminary work at the Nanyang Technological University, Singapore has explored the use of microalgae to produce edible oils with superior properties to palm oil. To produce the oils, pyruvic acid – an organic acid that occurs in all living cells – is added to a solution with the algae *Chromochloris zofingiensis* and exposed to ultraviolet light to stimulate photosynthesis. After 14 days, the microalgae is washed, dried, and treated with methanol to break the bonds between the oils and the algae protein so that the oils can be extracted. If this process can be scaled up and use natural sunlight as opposed to ultraviolet light then the use of microalgae to produce a substitute for palm oil could become commercially viable (The Engineer 2022).

Providing alternatives to ruminant meat consumption

Niall Firth (2018) cites the advantages of plant-based meat substitutes for the planet; carbon footprint 0.6 (kg CO_2 equivalent), water consumption 17 litres and Land use 0.31 square metre for an 85 g plant-based burger compared with a carbon footprint of 2.4 (kg CO_2 equivalent), water consumption 68 litres and 6.2 square metres for an 85 g beef burger. This is no flash in the pan development. Macdonald's now has on its standard menu in the UK a vegan burger made with a plant-based patty co-developed with Beyond Meat® featuring vegan sandwich sauce, ketchup, mustard, onion, pickles, lettuce, tomato, and a vegan alternative to cheese in a sesame seed bun (McDonalds 2022).

Preventing spoilage and food poisoning

Michael Le Page (2022) describes the use of bacteria-killing viruses, called bacteriophages, to destroy harmful microbes during food processing, to stop food rotting, to prevent food poisoning and to treat plant and animal diseases on farms. One difficulty with this approach is that phages are bacteria specific so a mixture of phages is required to kill all the strains of different bacteria that might be present. And because bacteria are always evolving the effectiveness of each phage needs to be constantly monitored and the mixture adjusted as necessary. Tobi Nagel of the organisation Phages for Global Health (see https://www.phagesforglobalhealth.org) argues that the use of phages is an important addition to the methods already in use and has considerable potential to reduce the use of antibiotics.

Part 5: Concluding remarks

This chapter has been a preliminary consideration of some factors relevant to developing a food technology course to be taught in secondary school. Part 1 developed a 'narrative of food' as a starting point in the light of underpinning technologies, some directly concerning food itself and some more tangential but highly relevant. Part 2 considered this narrative through the lenses of social justice and stewardship of Planet Earth. Part 3 discussed the way different aspects of the narrative might be taught. Part 4 described some future scenarios within this narrative in the light of the apparent conflict between feeding a growing world population and the need to combat global warming. This chapter is inevitably limited and to some extent naïve in that the influence of global and national politics and warfare on food poverty has not been discussed. Writing about the global food crisis in the London Review of Books Tom Stevenson (2022) identifies multiple instances of extreme food poverty in situations where civil war and machinations by those in power: military juntas, politicians, and financial institutions, contribute significantly to the continued hunger of the poorest in the world. George Monbiot (2022) calls for a revolution in the way we farm, to radically change the narrative of food. He creates a manifesto as follows:

To allow human beings and the rest of life on earth to flourish, we should:

- Become food-numerate
- Change the stories we tell ourselves
- Limit the land area we use to feed the world
- Minimise the use of water and farm chemicals
- Launch an Earthroamer Programme to finely map the world's soil
- Enhance fertility with the small possible organic interventions
- Research and develop a high-yield agroecology
- Stop farming animals
- Replace the protein and fat from animals with precision fermentation
- Break global corporations' grip on the food chain
- Diversify the global food system
- Use our understanding of complex systems to trigger cascading change
- Rewild the land released from farming (Page 129)

It is reassuring to see that some of the actions in the manifesto are identified in this chapter as relevant to the development of food technology as a subject to be taught in secondary schools. As far as the UK is concerned the recent publication of the National Food Strategy (2022) suggests important curriculum changes that should be made. These include reinstating the food A level, prioritising the teaching of cookery such that it becomes a high-status subject inspected with the same rigour as maths and English lessons and schools working with accreditation schemes such as Food for Life (2022) to improve food and food education. The underpinning emphasis on teaching young people to cook and understand nutrition is understandable and laudable but I think this approach risks missing out teaching the 'Big Picture' of the narrative of food and understanding how technologies of various sorts may be developed and used to improve how food moves from farm to table in ways that can feed the world without compromising the well-being of the Planet and life on Earth. The National Food Strategy also suggests that Ofsted should set up a team to create and publish a food and nutrition "research review", as it has started doing with other subjects. If such a research review is set up, I hope (a) that its terms of reference are wide enough to consider developing a curriculum that teaches across the narrative of food as outlined in this chapter and (b) the contributors include stakeholders from academia, education, industry and government.

References

AP News, 2020. *Child labor in palm oil industry tied to Girl Scout cookies* [online]. Available from: https://apnews.com/article/palm-oil-forests-indonesia-scouts-83b01f2789e9489569960da63b2741c4 [Accessed 19 May 2022].

Banks, F., and Barlex, D., 2021. *Teaching STEM in the secondary school.* 2nd ed. Oxon, UK: Routledge.

Barlex, D., 2020. A curriculum developer's perspective on the place of food in the secondary school. *In:* M. Rutland and A. Turner, eds. *Food education and food technology in school curricula: international perspectives.* Cham, Switzerland: Springer, 243–260.

Beaumont, H. R., 1996. *Food tests* [online]. Available from: https://dandtfordandt.files.word-press.com/2013/08/ks4-food-products-fcrt01-food-tests.pdf [Accessed 18 May 2022].

Brazilian Ministry of Health, 2015. *Brazilian Ministry of Health dietary guidelines for the Brazilian population* [online]. Available from: https://bvsms.saude.gov.br/bvs/publicacoes/dietary_guidelines_brazilian_population.pdf.

Briggs, H., 2014. *Takeaway clampdowns 'may combat obesity epidemic'* [online]. Available from: https://www.bbc.co.uk/news/health-26546863 [Accessed 18 May 2022].

Caviglioli, O., 2019. *Dual coding with teachers.* Woodbridge, UK: John Catt Educational.

Compassion in World Farming, 2013. *Welfare sheet - pigs* [online]. Available from: https://www.ciwf.org.uk/media/5235121/Welfare-sheet-Pigs.pdf [Accessed 18 May 2022].

Department for Environment Food and Rural Affairs, 2020. *Farming statistics - livestock populations at 1 December 2020, UK* [online]. Available from: https://assets.publishing.service.gov.uk/government/uploads/system/uploads/attachment_data/file/973322/structure-dec20-ukseries-25mar21i.pdf [Accessed 18 May 2022].

Department for Innovation, Universities and Skills, 2007a. *Tackling obesities: future choices – project report.* Available from: https://assets.publishing.service.gov.uk/government/uploads/system/uploads/attachment_data/file/287937/07-1184x-tackling-obesities-future-choices-report.pdf [Accessed 18 May 2022].

Department for Innovation, Universities and Skills, 2007b. *Tackling obesities: future choices – summary of key messages* [online]. Available from: https://assets.publishing.service.gov.uk/government/uploads/system/uploads/attachment_data/file/287943/07-1469x-tack-ling-obesities-future-choices-summary.pdf [Accessed 18 May 2022].

European Economic and Social Committee, 2013. *Unfair trading practices/supply chain* [online]. Available from: https://www.eesc.europa.eu/our-work/opinions-informa-tion-reports/opinions/unfair-trading-practices-supply-chain [Accessed 30 May 2022].

European Union, 2016. Smart and Competitive food and drink supply chains-EU Rural Review No 22 [online]. Available from: https://enrd.ec.europa.eu/sites/default/files/publi-enrd-rr-22-2016-en.pdf [Accessed 30 May 2022].

Firth, N., 2018. *The fake burger test: could meat made of plants ever fool you?* [online]. Available from: https://www.newscientist.com/article/mg23831761-800-the-fake-burger-test-could-meat-made-of-plants-ever-fool-you/ [Accessed 19 May 20].

Food and Agriculture Organisation of the United Nations, 2009. *How to feed the world in 2050* [online]. Available from: http://www.fao.org/fileadmin/templates/wsfs/docs/expert_paper/How_to_Feed_the_World_in_2050.pdf [Accessed 19 May 2022].

Food for Life, 2022. Feed the future food for life supports Free School Meal extension [online]. Available from: https://www.foodforlife.org.uk [Accessed 30 May 2022].

Harari, Y. N., 2011. *Sapiens a brief history of humankind.* New York: HarperCollins.

Harrison, M. E., Norris, M. L., Obeid, N., Fu, M., Weinstangel, H., and Sampson, M., 2015. Systematic review of the effects of family meal frequency on psychosocial out-comes in youth. *Canadian family physician Le Médecin de famille canadien* [online], 61 (2). Available from: https://www.ncbi.nlm.nih.gov/pmc/articles/PMC4325878/.

Health Survey for England, 2019. *National Statistics Survey 2020.* Available from: https://digital.nhs.uk/data-and-information/publications/statistical/health-survey-for-england/2019/main-findings [Accessed 18 May 2022].

Homer, A., 2018. *More takeaways on high street despite anti-obesity push* [online]. Available from: https://www.bbc.co.uk/news/uk-45875294 [Accessed 18 May 2022].

Immerzeel, D. J., Verweil, P. A., van der Hilst, F., and Faail, A. P., 2013. Biodiversity impacts of bioenergy crop production: a state of the art review. *GCB Bioenergy*, 6 (3). Available from: https://doi.org/10.1111/gcbb.12067.

International Silo Association, 2020. *History of the silo* [online]. Available from: https://silo.org/about-us/history/history-of-tower-silo/ [Accessed 18 May 2022].

Ives, L., 2018. *Diabetes prescriptions now cost NHS £1bn* [online]. Available from: https://www.bbc.co.uk/news/health-46139595 [Accessed 30 May 2022].

Kelly, K., 2010. *What technology wants*. London, England. Penguin Books.

Kislev, M. E., Hartmann, A., and BarYosef, O., 2006. Early domesticated fig in the Jordan Valley. *Science* [online], 312 (5778). Available from: https://doi.org/10.1126/science.1125910.

Kleeman, J., 2020. *Sex robots and vegan meat: adventures at the frontier of birth, food, sex, and death*. New York: Pegasus Books.

Lawton, G., 2020. *Forget exercise and diet fads – this is the secret of a healthy life* [online]. Available from: https://www.newscientist.com/article/mg24532652-800-forget-exercise-and-diet-fads-this-is-the-secret-of-a-healthy-life/ [Accessed 18 May 2022].

Lawton, G., 2021. *Real milk, no cows needed: lab-made dairy products are now a reality* [online]. Available from: https://www.newscientist.com/article/mg25133470-900-real-milk-no-cows-needed-lab-made-dairy-products-are-now-a-reality/ [Accessed 18 May 2022].

Le Page, M., 2022. *How bacteria-killing viruses are being used to keep food safe* [online]. Available from: https://www.newscientist.com/article/mg25333694-200-how-bacteria-killing-viruses-are-being-used-to-keep-food-safe/ [Accessed 18 May 2022].

Li, G., 2022. *Undersea beds: Nemo's garden takes terrestrial farming to new depths* [online]. Available from: https://www.newscientist.com/article/2310333-undersea-beds-nemos-garden-takes-terrestrial-farming-to-new-depths/ [Accessed 18 May 2022].

McDonalds., 2022. McPlant[TM]. [online]. Available from: https://www.mcdonalds.com/gb/en-gb/product/vegan-mcplant.html [Accessed 19 May 2022].

Mcmillan, T., 2018. *Menu of the future: insects, weeds, and bleeding veggie burgers* [online]. Available from: https://traciemcmillan.com/articles/menu-of-the-future-insects-weeds-and-bleeding-veggie-burgers/.

Monbiot, G., 2022. *Regenesis: feeding the world without devouring the planet*. London, UK: Allen Lane.

Monteiro, C. A., Cannon, G., Lawrence, M., Costa Louzada, M. L., and Pereira Machado, P., 2019. *Ultra-processed foods, diet quality, and health using the NOVA classification system* [online]. Available from: https://www.fao.org/3/ca5644en/ca5644en.pdf.

Office of National Statistics 2020. Farming Statistics - Livestock Populations at 1 December 2020, UK.

Rapsomanikis, G., 2015. *The economic lives of smallholder farmers: an analysis based on household data from nine countries* [online]. Available from: http://www.fao.org/3/a-i5251e.pdf [Accessed 19 May 2022].

Regalado, A., 2017. *These are not your father's GMOS* [online]. Available from: https://www.technologyreview.com/2017/12/19/146805/these-are-not-your-fathers-gmos/.

Sainsbury, 2021. *New research reveals family dinnertime is on the decline with only 28% of households sharing the same meal* [online]. Available from: https://www.about.sainsburys.co.uk/news/latest-news/2021/12-01-21-new-research-reveals-family-dinnertime [Accessed 27 May 2022].

Sea Food Nutrition Partnership, 2021. What is kelp and why should I eat it? [online]. Available from: https://www.seafoodnutrition.org/seafood-101/recipe-roundup/what-is-kelp-and-why-should-i-eat-it/ [Accessed 18 May 2022].

Shaw, J., 2021. *The seaweed farmers with high hopes for their harvest* [online]. Available from: https://www.bbc.co.uk/news/uk-scotland-57996627 [Accessed 18 May 2022].

Stevenson, T., 2022. Not war alone: Tom Stevenson on the global food crisis. *London Review of Books* [online], 44 (9). Available from: https://www.lrb.co.uk/the-paper/v44/n09/tom-stevenson/not-war-alone [Accessed 12 May 2022].

The Engineer, 2022. *Microalgae produces alternative to palm oil* [online]. Available from: https://www.theengineer.co.uk/content/news/microalgae-produces-alternative-to-palm-oil [Accessed 19 May 2022].

The National Food Strategy, 2022. *National Food Strategy* [online]. Available from: https://www.nationalfoodstrategy.org [Accessed 19 May 2022].

Viviano, F., and Locatelli, L., 2017. *How the Neverlands feeds the world* [online]. Available from: https://www.nationalgeographic.com/magazine/article/holland-agriculture-sustainable-farming [Accessed 18 May 2022].

World Health Organisation, 2021. *Malnutrition factsheet* [online]. Available from: https://www.who.int/news-room/fact-sheets/detail/malnutrition.

World Resources Institute, 2019. *World resources report: Creating a sustainable food future* [online]. Available from: https://research.wri.org/sites/default/files/2019-07/WRR_Food_Full_Report_0.pdf [Accessed 18 May 2022].

5

LEARNING FROM THE TRUE SCHOOL FOOD EXPERTS

An ethnographic investigation of middle school students during school lunch

Emily Elenio and Morgan K. Hoke

Introduction

School lunch is an integral part of a child's school and eating experience. In the United States, school lunch is primarily assessed using large data sets and quantitative methods which typically evaluate what foods are served and offered, rather than what is actually eaten (Fox and Condon 2012). There is a dearth of high-quality ethnographic research of school lunch in the United States. As a result, policymakers often merely speculate about what occurs at the school lunch table. By examining children's interactions during school lunch, this study serves to help fill the aforementioned gap. This chapter focuses on ethnographic data of school lunch, using observations and semi-structured interviews with children and educators to examine how childhood food agency is enacted during school meals. Following a brief review of the literature, we present ethnographic findings from school lunches that describe examples of sharing and trading food. While we acknowledge how external forces can influence children during school lunch, observing students without their guardians provides an opportunity to witness food agency and socialization mechanisms. We discuss how children exhibit agency during school mealtimes and how exchanging food can support collective agency among peers.

Background

The decision to share food or engage in commensality has been studied extensively, especially within anthropology (Ochs and Shohet 2006; Riley and Paugh 2019). However, there is far less anthropological research conducted within American school lunchrooms. Food exchange among children is important, with prior anthropological and sociological research showing how commensality

DOI: 10.4324/9781003294962-7

can encourage feelings of belonging within social groups (Husby et al. 2009). Examinations of commensality at the school lunch table have yielded divergent findings. Some ethnographic studies support the notion that sharing food is a positive action that fosters and promotes social connections (Berggren et al. 2020; Morrison 1996; Neely et al. 2015; Nukaga 2008). Other studies have contested the conventional opinion that sharing food strengthens social ties and instead argue for a more complex view that encompasses negative consequences of commensality including social exclusion and marginalization (Andersen et al. 2015; Gotthelf and Tempestti 2017). Nukaga (2008) argues that commensality occurs among students with stronger social bonds and can reinforce friendships, while trading is characteristic of weaker relationships. Commensality at the school lunch table may represent children's social bonds, or the lack thereof.

The topic of agency is broad and spans many fields, but a brief discussion is useful when thinking about children's food agency. Within education pedagogy, the concept of 'popular education' considers a child's agency in the context of the institution and centers the student as an agent by acknowledging that children must actually consume food to participate in school food curricula (Rud and Gleason 2018). Although this pedagogy exists and agency is a broad topic, there is limited literature investigating children's agency during mealtimes and during school lunch (Dotson et al. 2015). Qualitative studies of European school children suggest that as children age, they prefer and exert greater agency over their dietary choices (Fitzgerald et al. 2010; Warren et al. 2008). Yet, American preschool children were found to demonstrate agency during school meals to educators through verbal and non-verbal actions by verbally denying teachers' requests to eat certain foods and pretending or refusing to eat (Dotson et al. 2015). Nukaga (2008) maintains that when children exchange food, they are exerting control over their relationships and thus intertwine elements of agency and commensality.

School lunch is a frequently discussed and politicized topic in the United States, and elements of agency have emerged in these discussions. Former First Lady Michelle Obama is considered a 'champion' of childhood nutrition due to her 'Let's Move' Campaign (Billings 2019). An analysis of Michelle Obama's 'Let's Move' speeches argues that she presented the obesity crisis by emphasizing parents' agency over children (Backstrom 2020). Backstrom (2020) delineated the analysis by themes one of which, the 'Recalcitrant Children frame', portrayed children as having little to no agency. These words contradict the literature that supports children's agency during mealtimes. Michelle Obama's speeches, although well-intended, support the notion that discussions of children's agency are absent at the policymaker and advocate level.

Scholars have commented on the scarcity of ethnographic data of American children during school lunch and more broadly, how the field of education has largely ignored food and school lunch (Laird 2018; Poppendieck 2012; Rice and Rud 2018; Weaver-Hightower 2011). Globally, there is some literature that has examined children's commensality at the school table (Andersen et al. 2015;

Mason 2021; Morrison 1996; Nukaga 2008), but discussions of childhood agency are largely absent from these ethnographies with few exceptions (see Nukaga 2008). This study intends to add to the growing body of ethnographic literature of American children during school lunch and further hones in on agency.

Methods

This ethnographic study was performed at an American middle school, which we refer to as 'Lincoln Middle School' from November 2018 to February 2019. All participants' names were replaced with pseudonyms to ensure confidentiality. Informed consent was collected from all participants and their guardians.

Lincoln School was selected because it is the largest school in the district and services over 1,000 students. Students ranging from third to eighth grade were observed during school lunch sessions. During school visits, children were observed on initial days while selecting food from the lunch line, and then on subsequent days, while eating. Given the size of the school, lunch periods are spread across four sessions by grade; the method of observation varied by the age of the students and capacity of the lunchroom. When space was available, and especially with older students, observations were collected while directly participating during lunch.

Semi-structured interviews were conducted with eight Lincoln students at their respective homes and all discussions began with 'What is your favorite food?'. All interviews were recorded and transcribed with permission and were accompanied by field notes detailing non-verbal actions. Lincoln staff members including educators, school nurse, food service workers, principal, assistant principal, and teachers' aides, were also interviewed with permission. Interviews ranged from unprompted conversations where employees provided their perspectives on school lunch to more-structured interviews, particularly with the school nurse and principal.

Following prior ethnographic studies with children and frameworks from Vasquez (2013), Ruckenstein (2012), and Konstantoni and Kustatscher (2016), we consider children to be active and crucial agents in the ethnography. This approach reflects the shift from some of the foundational ethnographies of children by Mead (1928/1933) and even Malinowski (1921/1992) where children were initially considered 'objects of study' and instead we consider that children are 'subjects in the research process' (Konstantoni and Kustatscher 2016, p.225). Further, 'child-centered approaches', which can encompass the method of directly eating lunch and interacting with students, have been shown to ameliorate some of the power dynamics between the observer and children, which can improve not only the quality of research, but also empower participants (Leibel and Fenton 2016; Nukaga 2008; Rey Vasequez 2013). This ethnography is rooted in anthropology, but as school lunch is interdisciplinary by nature, frameworks, and insights from other fields including education, sociology, and public health, were considered and incorporated.

Results: case studies

Sharing game

During all site visits, a group of eight sixth-grade girls (aged 11 to 12 years) were observed during school lunch as they engaged in a unique sharing game. All eight children considered each other friends and discussed their plans to see each other outside of school at playdates and extracurricular activities. One of the participants, Rebecca, was also interviewed at her home on a separate evening. Below are summaries of the field notes collected, supplemented with excerpts and findings from Rebecca's interview.

REBECCA: We have this game that we play that it's a game, that one person brings food and we just put it on the table. We lay it out and then we put our hands behind our back and then we say three, two, one and then we rush to get it. And yeah, I mean my day is Monday. I usually bring jumbo marshmallows and it's the best.

ETHNOGRAPHER: So, one person brings food and you put it in the middle?

REBECCA: Yeah, I mean we take turns Monday through Friday. I mean Friday's 'Freedom Friday'…Yeah, Friday's 'Freedom Friday'. Wednesday is like chips, Mondays, 'Marshmallow Monday' or 'Mushroom Monday', like chocolate mushrooms. We assign one person to bring something in, but I mean I usually bring marshmallows.

The sharing game occurred every day after the girls had finished their main lunch. For each day of the week, one girl is assigned to bring a shareable portion of food which is then placed in the center of the table. Rebecca explained during the interview that the game was only played with 'junk food' noting that 'no one would want to play if it was a carrot'. The game was observed with the following types of snacks: chips, CheetzIts, cookie dough, and marshmallows. After the snacks are placed in the center, the group chants in unison 'one, two, three, go' and then each person races to collect as many pieces of the snack as possible. The winner is determined by the person with the greatest number of pieces. There is no prize and the students share the snack evenly. Redistribution depends on the snack. For 'Marshmallow Monday' which includes jumbo marshmallows, the bag is divided evenly with one or two marshmallows per person. For smaller-sized snacks, such as chips, the girls recollect the pieces and leave the pile in the center to share.

When asked why the snacks are ultimately spread equally, Rebecca was unsure. The game is explicitly not an opportunity to trade food. While other boys and girls were observed trading for food on multiple occasions with the expectation of receiving a snack, or a better seat at the lunch table, the sharing game occurs without expectations of a formal exchange. There are agreed-upon rules and assignments embedded with the sharing game. The rules of the game are fluid, as on one special 'Marshmallow Monday', the girls chose to consume marshmallows before playing the game because one participant asked, 'can I have one?'. The girl who brought the marshmallows instantly replied, 'okay everyone will have one to start off'. The game then proceeded as normal.

Each individual participant at the table is tasked with certain responsibilities and decisions. On the most basic level, the girls must decide each day whether or not to participate. For their assigned day, they must communicate with their guardians to ask for a shareable portion of food that is amenable to them and their friends. On one occurrence, a student forgot their snack, so they purchased two bags of chips from the school snack line. As a group, they are responsible for determining the rules through consensus. The rules of the game are clearly flexible as the participants can ask for amendments as long as the group agrees.

Another notable component of the game is the selection of food. Prior to the commencement of the game, this group of students elects to consume their 'main' lunch without exchange, and then plays the sharing game with so-called 'junk foods'. This sharing structure differed from other observed students who either reported or were observed trading and sharing core parts of their lunch (e.g., part of a sandwich, a piece of kimbap, etc.).

Trading food

Although trading and sharing food are officially discouraged at Lincoln School due to concerns regarding food allergies, children were observed both trading and sharing food on all observation days and across all lunch periods. For this study, trading is considered providing a piece of food explicitly in exchange for something else; children were observed trading food for different food options and also for favors, such as saving a seat at the table.

Interview participants distinguished between trading and sharing food, delineating them as different acts. Some noted that they may share food, but may not trade food. However, observations indicate that the two actions may be less distinct in the lunchroom. For instance, acts that interview participants defined as sharing often occur after another student asked for a piece of someone else's food rather than as a spontaneous, prosocial offering. Requests to share frequently instigated a cascade of exchange. The giving student would typically respond by providing the food while simultaneously asking for something in exchange from the asking child. There were no instances of the asking student denying the giving student's request, nor were there examples of spontaneous sharing without expectations of reciprocity.

The interviewed participants expressed different views on trading, even within the same family. Rebecca, a sixth-grade girl and participant of the sharing game, and Hugo, a seventh-grade boy, are siblings who both attend Lincoln school. Due to the school schedule, they have different lunch periods and therefore, do not interact with each other during lunch. Below is an excerpt of their conversation on trading:

ETHNOGRAPHER: But do you ever trade food?…

HUGO: Oh yeah.

ETHNOGRAPHER: What do you trade?

HUGO: We like something that I've missed. Like I'm full and I don't want to eat it [extra snack], [so I trade it] for like a drink, like a juice. We usually get water, or we bring our own water bottle.

REBECCA: I don't trade. I usually eat everything, or you just leave it. I mean I usually only bring healthy food because then when I say, hey, I have a carrot, they're like, oh no, it's okay, you can keep that.

Rebecca partially rationalized her decision not to trade by arguing that her chosen snacks are 'healthy' and thus, unappealing to her friends. She enjoys the food that she and her mom prepare, and therefore, sees little need to trade or share her lunch. Hugo, however, elects to trade away pieces of his meal or extra snacks in exchange for juice. His mother packs him water for lunch, yet Hugo prefers juice; thus, he sometimes chooses to prioritize his preference for juice when he wants it or if he is too 'full' to consume his snacks.

Discussion

Unlike the family dinner table, the school cafeteria presents the opportunity for children to consume food and socialize in the absence of their guardians. For this reason, we can view the lunchroom as a window through which to observe how food agency manifests and is further shaped by socialization. Although children are awarded a greater level of leniency and agency during school lunch, their actions are nonetheless influenced by external and internal forces. We analyze our ethnographic findings that demonstrate childhood food agency while considering these additional forces. In the lunchroom, children consider and abide by different sets of rules: official rules set by school administrators and social rules that are created and negotiated by children. We will discuss both forms in the context of a food agency. Although external forces, including school rules and cultural norms, impact children's decisions during lunch, we present and analyze examples where participants' actions deviate and further suggest their autonomy through school food.

First, we consider the more fluid 'social' rules which are enforced and reinforced by the students themselves. Lalli (2019) writes that 'pupils are negotiating the rules and regulations of the dining hall', but with the caveat that ultimately, it is teachers and educators who may have the final say (p.65). Although rules often imply the loss of agency, we can view the students' choices to enforce and create social rules as a form of control and in parallel, decision-making. The sharing game is a well-defined example of social rulemaking where the participants negotiate and decide upon the rules together. The renegotiation of rules was observed, when the cadence of the game deviated from the habitual structure. When a student asked to consume a marshmallow before playing the game, the provider of the marshmallows agreed to allow everyone to eat one marshmallow and then initiated the game. In this example, the student who brought the snack held the most social power and perhaps agency, but this was short-lived as her proposed solution was accepted by all participants ultimately demonstrating the role of group agreement and consensus building. As a close-knit group, they engage in collective decision-making and group agency.

Children's actions surrounding trading and sharing food also imply the presence of socially embedded rules and aspects of morality. Trading often occurs due to the expectation and perception of exchanging food of similar value. Through her ethnographic findings and linguistic analysis of Senegalese children sharing food, Yount-André (2016) contributes to the growing body of literature that sharing and trading food is intertwined with morality. Yount-André also observed how children's asymmetrical redistribution of food and semiotic practices contrasted with the adult Senegalese behaviors and ideologies. These dynamics of morality and deviation from individual cultural norms were also observed at the Lincoln school lunch tables. Prior to asking for a trade or to share food, children were often prepared and expected to be asked for something. Further, although the sharing game uses the word 'sharing' and there is no *formal* expectation of exchange, there are some informal expectations because each participant is responsible for providing food on a rotating basis. Thus, we may consider this arrangement to be a delayed and also attenuated form of trading or exchange, albeit with an element of sharing or at least equal redistribution of goods.

The 'sharing game' and observed trading instances indicate how external stakeholders, such as teachers and other authority figures, can support children's agency. While sharing and trading are explicitly prohibited at Lincoln School, it is unclear exactly how or when the restriction on sharing is enforced, if at all. Other ethnographies of American school children have observed trading even though sharing food violates school rules (Baxter et al. 2001; Mason 2021; Nukaga 2008). Baxter and Thomas (2001) suggested that younger students were more inclined to follow rules compared to older students. Yet in our study, children were observed trading and sharing food at all ages, suggesting that a different explanation is warranted. At Lincoln, there were no instances of teachers or administrators enforcing the no-sharing rule; rather, the principal was observed asking the sharing game participants what snack they had brought today. By not enforcing the rule, educators are allowing students to not only challenge school rules but also are providing an avenue for children to demonstrate agency by trading and sharing food during school lunch. If children were actively punished for exchanging food, it is likely that the sharing game and trading of food would be greatly reduced.

Ethnographic investigations of family discussions during mealtimes have shown that children are socialized into taste, gender, morality, and more (Ochs et al. 1996; Ochs and Shohet 2006; Paugh and Izquierdo 2009). It is logical to often assume that siblings may demonstrate the effects of mealtime socialization similarly compared to two non-related children. Yet, two interviewed siblings, Rebecca and Hugo expressed divergent opinions on trading food. Hugo electively trades away food in exchange for juice, while Rebecca does not trade food but participates in the sharing game with dessert and snack foods. Both children reported eating dinner together at home with their parents. Even though Rebecca and Hugo participate in dinner-time discussions and socialization mechanisms at home, their behavior regarding trading differs. School lunch provides a venue for children that have been socialized together at home to express their individual agency that manifests with divergent behaviors.

Trading food may represent the most explicit example of economic exchange within the school cafeteria. Observed examples of trading at Lincoln, for instance, a bag of chips in exchange for saving a friend's spot at the lunch table, were often easily negotiated and resulted in greater comradery; to the ethnographer, these interactions appear to be trades, but the easy-going exchanges could imply these interactions are more akin to sharing. This differs from Nukaga (2008) who observed that trading occurs among children with less meaningful social ties, while sharing is a characteristic of closer friendships. Chin (2001) describes the sharp divisiveness due to failed lunch trades and observed children throwing away unwanted food, even though others wanted it. Although observed instances of trading occurred without incident at Lincoln, it is a risker form of exchange (Nukaga 2008), as it requires negotiation and agreement between parties. Trading also enforces the theme of collective agency between peers. While not observed at Lincoln, trading among unequal peers with moderate social ties can provide certain students with greater social power that may impact less privileged students' agency (Nukaga 2008).

Limitations

While this work has shed important light on children's food agency at school, a limitation of this discussion is the focus on neurotypical students enrolled in the 'regular education' program of the school. Lincoln School does maintain a robust special education program and separate observations, conversations, and data on this program were collected (see Elenio 2019). Although the observations of special education students are not within the scope of this chapter, we feel it is important to echo Bashinski and Smilie's (2018) conclusion that special needs students are often ignored, marginalized, and excluded in the lunchroom and also in academic literature. We acknowledge their call to action and have documented some of the key findings in other work (Elenio 2019). We have observed how special needs students similarly exert agency during school lunch, however, some of the socialization tendencies differ by gender and compared to regular education students. Further, this work is limited to students between the third and eighth grades and thus does not encompass the perspectives of younger students. Future research could consider a longitudinal design across school years to capture how children's demonstration of agency evolves as they age.

Conclusion

Although other stakeholders including guardians, policymakers, and educators, may directly decide what ends up on a child's lunch plate, at the end of the day, children are the ultimate decision-makers about what goes in their mouths. School lunch represents one of the first times children are presented with this degree of agency regarding their dietary choices. We see that on an individual level, students choose what to put in their mouths and what to trade. These ethnographic findings also highlight that while these decisions occur in the absence of their guardians, there is a collective agency through socialization.

Although anthropology is rich in ethnography, thus far, few social scientists have studied American children during school lunch (Poppendieck 2012; Rud and Gleason 2018). These findings support the value of using qualitative methods to assess and evaluate school lunch in the United States. Other researchers have also encouraged both quantitative and qualitative methodologies to explore important concepts such as commensality (Scander et al. 2021). American researchers have previously documented the frequency of trading during school lunch through small-scale studies and concluded that trading food impacts the validity and findings of food recall surveys, and observational research can help correct these errors (Baxter et al. 2001, 2002). Ultimately, if children are deciding which foods they chose to eat or not to eat, researchers should consider directly interacting with and observing students using similar principles and frameworks to ensure the collection of high-quality data.

References

Andersen, S. S., Holm, L., and Baarts, C., 2015. School meal sociality or lunch pack individualism? Using an intervention study to compare the social impacts of school meals and packed lunches from home. *Social Science Information* [online], 54 (3). Available from: https://doi.org/10.1177/0539018415584697.

Backstrom, L., 2020. Shifting the blame frame: agency and the parent–child relationship in an anti-obesity campaign. *Childhood* [online], 27 (2), 203–219. Available from: https://doi.org/10.1177/0907568220902513.

Bashinski, S. M., and Smilie, K., 2018. Social consequences of school lunch for students who receive special education services: a critical outlook. *In:* S. Rice and A. G. Rud, eds. *Educational dimensions of school lunch: critical perspectives.* 1st ed. New York: Springer Science+Business Media, 135–155.

Baxter, S. D., Thompson, W. O., and Davis, H. C., 2001. Trading of food during school lunch by first- and fourth-grade children. *Nutrition Research* [online], 21 (3). Available from: https://doi.org/10.1016/S0271-5317(01)00273-1.

Baxter, S. D., Thompson, W. O., Litaker, M. S., Frye, F. H. A., and Guinn, C. H., 2002. Low accuracy and low consistency of fourth-graders' school breakfast and school lunch recalls. *Journal of the American Dietetic Association* [online], 102 (3). Available from: https://doi.org/10.1016/S0002-8223(02)90089-1.

Berggren, L., Olsson, C., Talvia, S., Hörnell, A., Rönnlund, M., and Waling, M., 2020. The lived experiences of school lunch: an empathy-based study with children in Sweden. *Children's Geographies* [online], 18 (3). Available from: https://doi.org/10.108 0/14733285.2019.1642447.

Billings, K. C., 2019. Child nutrition programs: issues in the 115th Congress. *CRS Report*, *R45486*, 23. Available from: https://crsreports.congress.gov/product/pdf/R/R45486.

Chin, E., 2001. *Purchasing power: black kids and American consumer culture* [online]. University of Minnesota Press. Available from: https://www.upress.umn.edu/book-division/books/purchasing-power.

Dotson, H. M., Vaquera, E., and Cunningham, S. A., 2015. Sandwiches and subversion: teachers' mealtime strategies and preschoolers' agency. *Childhood* [online]. Available from: https://doi.org/10.1177/0907568214539711.

Elenio, E., 2019. *I don't really get it: an ethnographic investigation of the national school lunch Program of middle school children in New Jersey* [University of Pennsylvnia]. Available from: https://repository.upenn.edu/anthro_seniortheses/192.

Fitzgerald, A., Heary, C., Nixon, E., and Kelly, C., 2010. Factors influencing the food choices of Irish children and adolescents: a qualitative investigation. *Health Promotion International* [online], 25 (3). Available from: https://doi.org/10.1093/heapro/daq021.

Fox, M. K., and Condon, E., 2012. school nutrition dietary assessment study-iv: summary of findings [online]. Available from: https://www.readkong.com/page/school-nutrition-dietary-assessment-study-iv-1716174.

Gotthelf, S. J., and Tempestti, C. P., 2017. Breakfast, nutritional status, and socioeconomic outcome measures among primary school students from the City of Salta: a cross-sectional study. *Archivos Argentinos De Pediatria* [online], 115 (5), 424–431. Available from: https://doi.org/10.5546/aap.2017.eng.424.

Husby, I., Heitmann, B. L., and O'Doherty Jensen, K., 2009. Meals and snacks from the child's perspective: the contribution of qualitative methods to the development of dietary interventions. *Public Health Nutrition* [online], 12 (6). Available from: https://doi.org/10.1017/S1368980008003248.

Konstantoni, K., and Kustatscher, M., 2016. conducting ethnographic research in early childhood research: questions of participation. *In:* A. Farrell, S. L. Kagan and E. K. M. Tisdall, eds. *The SAGE handbook of early childhood research*. Thousand Oaks, CA: Sage, 223–239.

Laird, S., 2018. Alice Waters and the edible schoolyard: rethinking school lunch as public education. *In:* S. Rice and A. G. Rud, eds. *Educational dimensions of school lunch: critical perspectives*. New York: Springer Science+Business Media, 11–33.

Lalli, G. S., 2019. School meal time and social learning in England. *Cambridge Journal of Education* [online], 50 (1), 57. Available from: https://doi.org/10.1080/0305764X.2019.1630367.

Leibel, S., and Fenton, N., 2016. Building trust: Children experiences with food allergies at summer camp. *Health* [online], 8 (14). Available from: https://doi.org/10.4236/health.2016.814143.

Malinowski, B., 1992. Ethnology and the study of society. *Economica*. Available from: https://doi.org/10.2307/2548314.

Mason, A. E., 2021. Children's perspectives on lunchtime practices: connecting with others. *Journal of Occupational Science* [online], 28 (3). Available from: https://doi.org/10.1080/14427591.2020.1771407.

Mead, M., 1933. *Coming of age in Samoa: a psychological study of primitive youth for western civilisation*. New York: Blue Ribbon Books.

Morrison, M., 1996. Sharing food at home and school: perspectives on commensality. *The Sociological Review* [online], 44 (4). Available from: https://doi.org/10.1111/j.1467-954X.1996.tb00441.x.

Neely, E., Walton, M., and Stephens, C., 2015. Building school connectedness through shared lunches. *Health Education* [online], 115 (6). Available from: https://doi.org/10.1108/HE-08-2014-0085.

Nukaga, M., 2008. The underlife of kids' school lunchtime: negotiating ethnic boundaries and identity in food exchange. *Journal of Contemporary Ethnography* [online], 37 (3). Available from: https://doi.org/10.1177/0891241607309770.

Ochs, E., Pontecorvo, C., and Fasulo., A., 1996. Socializing taste. *Ethnos*, 61 (1–2), 7–46.

Ochs, E., and Shohet, M. 2006. The cultural structuring of mealtime socialization. *In:* R. W. Larson, A. R. Wiley, and K. R. Branscomb, eds. *Family mealtime as a context of development and socialization.* Available from: https://www.academia.edu/1457070/The_cultural_structuring_of_mealtime_socialization [Accessed 22 February 2021].

Paugh, A. L., and Izquierdo, C., 2009. Why is this a battle every night?: negotiating food and eating in American dinner time interaction. *Journal of Linguistic Anthropology* [online], 19 (2). Available from: https://anthrosource.onlinelibrary.wiley.com/doi/abs/10.1111/j.1548-1395.2009.01030.x.

Poppendieck, J., 2012. School food. *In:* K. Albala, ed. *Routledge international handbook of food studies.* London, UK: Routledge, 329–341.

Rey Vasquez, C., 2013. Opening the lunchbox: what distinction looks like from the playground. *Global Ethnographic* [online], 1. Available from: https://oicd.net/ge/wp-content/uploads/2013/01/Vasquez-C.-Global-Ethnographic-2013-1.pdf.

Rice, S., and Rud, A. G., 2018. Introduction. *In:* S. Rice and A. G. Rud, eds. *Educational dimensions of school lunch: critical perspectives.* New York: Springer Science+Business Media, 1–10.

Riley, K. C., and Paugh, A. L., 2019. *Food and language: discourses and foodways across cultures.* London, UK: Routledge.

Ruckenstein, M., 2012. *Everyday ambiguities: food consumption in and out of schools* [online]. Available from: https://www.academia.edu/2921126/Everyday_ambiguities_Food_consumption_in_and_out_of_schools.

Rud, A. G., and Gleason, S., 2018. School lunch curriculum. *In:* S. Rice and A. G. Rud, eds. *Educational dimensions of school lunch: critical perspectives.* New York: Springer Science+Business Media, 173–187.

Scander, H., Yngve, A., and Lennernäs Wiklund, M., 2021. Assessing commensality in research. *International Journal of Environmental Research and Public Health*, 18 [online], (5). Available from: https://doi.org/10.3390/ijerph18052632.

Warren, E., Parry, O., Lynch, R., and Murphy, S., 2008. If I don't like it then I can choose what I want: Welsh school children's accounts of preference for and control over food choice. *Health Promotion International* [online], 23 (2). Available from: https://doi.org/10.1093/heapro/dam045.

Weaver-Hightower, M. B., 2011. Why Education researchers should take school food seriously. *Educational Researcher* [online], 40 (1). Available from: https://doi.org/10.3102/0013189X10397043.

Yount-André, C., 2016. Snack sharing and the moral metalanguage of exchange: children's reproduction of rank-based redistribution in Senegal. *Journal of Linguistic Anthropology* [online], 26 (1), 41–61. Available from: https://doi.org/10.1111/jola.12108.

6

THE ROLE OF SCHOOLS IN SUPPORTING HEALTHY EATING IN CHILDREN AND YOUNG PEOPLE

Marie Murphy and Miranda Pallan

Introduction

The role of schools in supporting adequate and healthy nutrition in children has a long history as a public health measure, particularly through the provision of school meals, dating back to the 1850s in some countries (Oostindjer et al. 2017). Until the latter part of the 20th century, the main aim of school meal provision was to ensure children were not prevented from engaging in education due to hunger and undernutrition. This remains a key aim in many lower-income countries, and there is also a renewed focus on food insecurity in higher-income countries such as the UK in recent times, particularly in light of the 2020 Coronavirus pandemic and resulting increase in food insecurity in lower-income families (Francis-Devine 2021). However, as a response to the rapid rise in childhood obesity in the late 20th century, the focus of school food programmes has expanded to the provision of meals of high nutritional quality and lower energy density as a way of addressing overnutrition and improving overall health in school-aged children.

School food provision is only one facet of the role of schools in supporting healthy eating in childhood. In the mid-1990s, the World Health Organization (WHO) launched the Health Promoting Schools (HPS) initiative, and continues to encourage all schools to use this approach (Sawyer 2021). The HPS approach recognises that schools allow an opportunity to provide a physical, social and emotional environment to promote health and wellbeing, healthy behaviours and engagement in education, which is itself a determinant of future health. In line with this approach, and driven by the global rising prevalence of childhood obesity, a broad range of school-based approaches to support healthy eating that go beyond school food provision have been developed and implemented.

DOI: 10.4324/9781003294962-8

School food and nutrition policy and intervention

School feeding programmes to address hunger and food insecurity

School feeding programmes form a key part of national school food policy across the globe (see Box 1 for examples). Key aims of these programmes are to alleviate hunger and food insecurity, thus improving attendance, engagement, cognition and academic achievement, which should contribute to economic growth in the longer term (World Food Programme 2021). However, measuring the impact of school feeding programmes on long-term economic growth is challenging and the relationship is not well-evidenced. At the start of 2020, the World Food Programme estimated that around half of the world's population of children were receiving daily meals at school. Over 90% of countries with school feeding programmes deliver these as part of a wider school health and nutrition package. School feeding programmes have physical, psychosocial and educational benefits in disadvantaged populations (Kristjansson et al. 2007), for example, improved linear growth in certain groups, higher achievement in core subjects and in low-income countries, increased enrolment and attendance.

School feeding programmes are not always provided universally free of charge, for example, in the UK universal provision of school meals is in place for children in the first three years of schooling, but in subsequent school years, only families on lower incomes are eligible for free school meals (Francis-Devine 2021). However, evidence suggests that universal free school meals have multiple benefits, including improved meal participation, food security, diet quality and academic achievement, although associations with improved attendance are mixed (Cohen et al. 2021).

School food provision policies to improve nutrition

School food policies have increasingly encompassed the quality and nutritional value of foods, particularly in high-income countries, where childhood obesity is a more prominent public health issue than undernutrition. Policy addressing nutrition falls into two categories, direct provision of healthy foods/drinks and quality standards for school food provision.

Direct provision of healthy foods or drinks

Several countries have introduced schemes to provide healthy food/drinks in addition to school meals. Since 2017, the European Union (EU) has had a school fruit, vegetables and milk scheme, aiming to encourage healthier diets in children and reduce obesity (European Commission 2022). The scheme funds the distribution of fruit, vegetables and milk to children from preschool to secondary school age across EU countries. In the UK the Milk in Schools Scheme was introduced in 1934, initially for economic reasons to support the dairy industry

(Atkins 2005), but it has been maintained as a key school policy to support welfare and address nutritional needs. Currently in England, schoolchildren up to the age of 5 years are entitled to free school milk with older school children eligible to receive subsidised milk (UK Government Rural Payments Agency 2017). England also has a national fruit and vegetable provision policy in place. Launched in 2004, the School Fruit and Vegetable Scheme entitles all children aged 4–6 years in state-funded schools to a piece of fruit or vegetable, outside of mealtimes, each school day (National Health Service 2017). The USA has a similar scheme which applies to elementary schools (age 5–10 years) where at least 50% of the pupils qualify for subsidised school meals, and funds them to provide free fresh fruit or vegetable snacks to pupils (Jamelske and Bica 2012). Evaluations of school provision of fruits and vegetables show that these policies have a positive short-term effect on fruit and vegetable consumption, particularly fruit intake (Micha et al. 2018a). However, studies exploring the longer-term impact of these policies suggest that their positive impact on consumption is not sustained once the fruit and vegetable provision has ceased. There is no clear evidence that overall energy intake is impacted (Micha et al. 2018a), suggesting that these policies are not effective in specifically addressing childhood obesity, but can improve dietary quality in the short-term, leading to health and educational benefits.

Quality standards for school food

Food quality standards in schools have been adopted in many high-income countries from the 1970s onwards, again, largely in response to the so-called obesity epidemic (Oostindjer et al. 2017). UK standards for school food have a longer history. Introduced in 1941 the first UK school food standards built on existing school food policy in place to address undernutrition. These were scrapped in 1980 as part of a wider move to reduce expenditure on state welfare provision, but were reintroduced again in 2001 following concerns about school meal quality (Evans and Harper 2009). Since then, the school food standards in England have undergone several iterations (latest in 2015), with the aim of ensuring balanced and nutritious provision of school food (The Independent School Food Plan 2014). The introduction of school food standards has been shown to have a positive impact on nutritional intake (Spence et al. 2013), influencing dietary elements such as sodium, fat, fruit and vegetables, but the impact has not been demonstrated on overall energy intake or body fat (Micha et al. 2018a; Valizadeh and Ng 2020). The latest school food standards in England differ from those previously in place, as they are based on foods, and not nutritional content, and have yet to be fully evaluated. Whilst there is evidence that healthier school meal composition positively influences educational attainment (Anderson et al. 2018), the direct impact of nutritional school food standards as a policy intervention on educational outcomes has not been evaluated.

Policies to support healthy eating in schoolchildren

As demonstrated in the examples in Box 6.1, school feeding programmes are often accompanied by additional policy interventions to support the development of healthy eating behaviours. These encompass a range of intervention approaches (discussed in the next section), including educational/behavioural, food/eating environment and whole-school interventions. England provides an example of national policy encompassing many of these approaches. In 2013 a national School Food Plan (SFP) was introduced. This is a plan of action for schools to help them transform the environment and culture relating to food, and how schoolchildren learn about food (Dimbleby and Vincent 2013). Actions set out in the SFP are wide-ranging but broadly relate to creating a positive and sociable eating environment; incentivising healthier choices; improving interaction with children and parents about school food; teaching cooking within the curriculum and running extracurricular cooking and gardening clubs; and developing a whole school approach to food and healthy eating. Although in place for several years, implementation of the SFP is voluntary and not monitored. Therefore, the degree to which the SFP has been embedded across primary and secondary schools in England, and its overall effect on children's nutrition, education and development is unknown.

BOX 6.1 EXAMPLES OF SCHOOL FEEDING PROGRAMMES

Brazil: Programa Nacional de Alimentacão Escolar (PNAE)

This national school feeding programme was implemented to support growth, development and academic productivity of school students, as well as instilling healthy eating habits. The programme ensures through federal law that subsidised school meals are universally provided to over 42 million school students attending more than 160,000 schools. The programme is planned by nutritionists and incorporates the promotion of healthy eating, as well as the provision of healthy, nutritionally balanced meals. The PNAE also has an important impact on the sustainable economic development of communities, as the law states that 30% of the food provided must be procured from smallholder farmers (World Food Programme 2021).

India: The Mid-Day Meal Scheme (MDMS)

This national scheme was introduced to address hunger and education and ensures that all children in primary education (up to age 14 years) attending publicly funded schools have a cooked midday meal. The scheme reaches over 90 million children attending 1.1 million schools. The meals provided have to meet specific energy and protein requirements, appropriate to the child's age group. The MDMS runs alongside a school health check-up scheme, which includes the provision of iron and folic acid supplements. Other policy initiatives to support the MDMS include guidelines for school vegetable gardens, cooking competitions and community participation (World Food Programme 2021).

Kenya: Home Grown School Meals Programme

The Kenyan Government launched the Home Grown School Meals Programme in 2009, taking over from the World Food Programme-supported school meals scheme. The programme provides a daily hot lunch to primary school children and reaches 1.6 million children in arid and semi-arid lands and unplanned urban settlements, where school enrolment and completion rates are lowest with high gender disparities (World Food Programme 2018). Guided by the School Meal and Nutrition Strategy, published in 2017 (Ministry of Education et al. 2017), the programme is expanding with the aim of providing one nutritious meal per school day to all pre-primary and primary school children. Other key aspects of the School Meal Strategy are nutrition and nutrition education as core components of school meal provision, and procurement of school food from smallholder farmers (Ministry of Education et al. 2017).

Finland: School Feeding System

A free-of-charge school feeding system has been in place in Finland since 1943 and around 830,000 nutritionally balanced school meals are provided to all children attending school daily. School meals have been within the national core curriculum since 2004, and as such school feeding is seen as an essential educational activity. Along with the provision of school meals, Finland's school feeding system incorporates education relating to food and eating, including food culture, nutrition, social aspects of eating and sustainability. Children are also encouraged to participate in school meal planning and implementation (Ministry for Foreign Affairs of Finland and Finnish National Agency for Education 2019).

England: Free School Meal Provision

Primary and secondary schools have had a duty to provide school meals to those who want them since 1944. Schools are able to charge families for school meals, but the government-funded Free School Meal (FSM) scheme exists for all schoolchildren of families with low incomes. In 2021 the proportion of school pupils eligible to receive FSM was 21% (1.74 million children); an increase of 3% since the onset of the COVID-19 pandemic (Francis-Devine 2021). In 2014, a universal FSM policy was introduced for children aged 4–7 years. The aim of this was to ensure a hot nutritious meal for all children of this age, and thus improve academic attainment, and followed pilot schemes of universal FSM provision that showed higher vegetable consumption and better academic attainment in those receiving universal FSM, compared with peers (Long et al. 2021).

Healthy eating interventions in school-settings

Schools are recognised as opportune settings in which to deliver interventions aiming to encourage healthy eating behaviours in children (O'Brien et al. 2021). However, evidence of the impact of healthy eating interventions in school settings is mixed. The most common healthy eating intervention types in schools can be categorised as educational and behavioural; food and eating environment; or whole-school approaches. We provide more detail on each category below, with example interventions provided in Box 6.2.

Educational and behavioural interventions

Educational interventions aim to increase pupils' healthy eating knowledge, literacy or food preparation/food growing skills and confidence. Examples include lesson plans, teaching resources and web-based/eHealth resources, implemented as standalone programmes or integrated into existing subjects. There is evidence that school-based nutrition education is effective in positively influencing some dietary elements (e.g. reducing fat intake), but not others (e.g. increasing vegetable intake) (O'Brien et al. 2021). A key critique of educational interventions is that improving knowledge and skills in isolation is unlikely to lead to the desired behaviour change. Behaviour change occurs as a result of having the capability, opportunity and motivation to change (Michie et al. 2014), therefore interventions designed to address all these elements may be more likely to have success.

Behavioural interventions attempt to address this critique to some extent by including components that motivate or support individuals to make behaviour changes. Within school-based healthy eating interventions, this typically includes components such as incentives, goal-setting, peer support or developing cognitive-behavioural skills. Nutrition education interventions that pay attention to behavioural influences are more likely to be successful in positively influencing healthy eating behaviours (Peters et al. 2009).

Food and eating environment interventions

Interventions operating at an environmental level have become more prominent in recent years, and have demonstrated more success in improving a range of dietary behaviours than nutrition education interventions (O'Brien et al. 2021).

Food environment interventions aim to change the food/drink offer available to children (including food quality standards) or restructure elements of the food environment. This latter approach is termed choice architecture and encompasses an array of strategies in which alterations are made to the immediate physical or social environments to influence automatic/non-conscious psychological processes and cue healthier behaviour (Hollands et al. 2013). A key benefit of this approach is that it requires little to no cognitive engagement on the part of the individual, so that even those who are not motivated to make a healthy choice will benefit. Such strategies typically alter the placement, convenience, marketing, promotion, variety or portions of healthy or unhealthy foods/drinks available (Metcalfe et al. 2020). Examples include increasing the number of water fountains; proactive offer of a vegetable side dish, having fruit in convenient locations for ease of access; and attractive posters featuring healthy foods to 'prime' individuals to make healthy selections.

Evaluation of choice architecture in school settings suggests that it is effective in increasing the selection of fruit, vegetables, milk, water and main meals, but it is less certain that this translates to increased *consumption* of such items (Metcalfe et al. 2020). A limitation of choice architecture is that it generally only impacts the immediate choices that an individual makes, and few studies demonstrate sustained improvements (Pineda et al. 2021).

An additional type of food and eating environment intervention relates to the school dining room as a social learning environment. 'Family style dining' is one example of this approach i.e. a replication of a sit-down shared meal that might typically be found in the home environment. School dining interventions have a range of potential benefits, including learning about food, social development and encouragement of healthier food consumption [1]. However, the potential impact of these interventions on nutritional and other outcomes has yet to be fully evaluated.

Whole school approaches

Whole school approaches align with the WHO HPS initiative and offer a wide-ranging programme of resources and activities to schools, often featuring components that have already been mentioned (e.g. educational, environmental), but also policy and partnership development, such as creating a school food policy and action plan; and parental and community engagement (e.g. cooking classes for parents). Such approaches also tend to target a broader suite of behavioural outcomes, often coupling dietary outcomes with efforts to increase physical activity levels, support food hygiene, or improve general health and wellbeing. Nutrition interventions that utilise whole school approaches are more effective at improving dietary outcomes and reducing BMI in children and adolescents (Langford 2014). However, the evaluation of whole school approaches is complex, partially due to the wide range of activities which typically make up such interventions, and there is a lack of core indicators upon which to base such evaluations (Mūkoma and Flisher 2004).

BOX 6.2 EXAMPLES OF SCHOOL-BASED HEALTHY EATING INTERVENTIONS

Food Dudes, UK and Ireland

Food Dudes is a curriculum-linked educational and behavioural intervention for children aged 4–13 years, to encourage increased fruit and vegetable intake, incorporating strategies such as repeated exposure (tastings), rewards and positive role models (Food Dudes 2022). Initially piloted in Wales, the programme has been implemented in over 3,300 schools across Ireland since 2007. An evaluation found a significant increase in fruit and vegetable consumption at 3 months for children in intervention schools, but only for those eating school-supplied lunches, and the changes weren't sustained at 12 months (Upton et al. 2013).

Smarter Lunchrooms Movement, US

The Smarter Lunchroom Movement is a choice architecture programme implemented in thousands of schools in the US since 2010 (California Department of Education 2022). The programme utilises evidence-based choice architecture strategies such as managing portion sizes, increase convenience, improved visibility, suggestive selling and pricing strategies to encourage the purchasing and consumption of target foods/drinks such as water, milk, fruits and vegetables. A pilot programme found that students were more likely to select a fruit or vegetable post-intervention versus pre-intervention (Hanks et al. 2013), but the programme has not yet been comprehensively evaluated.

APPLE Schools, Canada

APPLE Schools (A Project Promoting Healthy Living for Everyone in Schools) is a whole-school approach for improving healthy eating, physical activity and mental health habits in children, which has engaged over 87 schools in Canada (APPLE Schools 2022). The programme comprises a dedicated School Health Facilitator who supports student, parent, staff and community engagement to develop a tailored school action plan, which may include classroom gardens, after-school cooking classes and physical activity programs. An evaluation found that schools implementing APPLE showed a small but significant increase in daily fruit and vegetable consumption of 0.39 portions and reduction in total energy intake, whilst schools not implementing APPLE showed non-significant changes in these dietary outcomes (Fung et al. 2012).

It is worth highlighting that the impact of schools-based interventions on nutrition is likely to be relatively small. For example, it is estimated that the implementation of multi-component nutrition interventions will on average increase fruit and vegetable intake by a third of a portion per day (Evans et al. 2012). Although this small change carries a marginal health benefit, the impact of school-based healthy eating interventions on improving health outcomes and preventing ill health may be limited if introduced in isolation. This emphasises that schools need to be seen as one of a range of potential settings to target for healthy eating intervention, with consideration given to a broader socio ecological approach, incorporating socioeconomic, cultural and environmental conditions, social and community networks and individual and familial characteristics (Townsend and Foster 2013).

Challenges in supporting healthy eating in school settings

Despite the view of schools as an ideal setting in which to support healthy eating efforts, challenges to implementation exist.

A key challenge is the relative priority given to implementing healthy eating policies and interventions. Implementation may be hampered by pressures upon schools and staff to focus on academic attainment, a lack of time to accommodate intervention components and low levels of staff motivation, as well as school leaders' perceptions of the role of schools in health promotion (Day et al. 2019; Jessiman et al. 2019). It often falls to schools to address a broad range of complex social problems faced by children and adolescents, which can include safeguarding, student health and mental wellbeing, poverty and counterterrorism (Skovdal and Campbell 2015). The implementation of healthy eating policies and interventions are likely to put an additional strain on this overburdened system, especially if not appropriately resourced.

There are also setting-specific challenges – for example, the effective components of dietary interventions may differ in secondary schools where there is greater food choice, compared to primary schools (Capper et al. 2022). The effectiveness of school food policy and intervention on dietary intake in secondary school settings is underresearched compared to primary school settings (Micha et al. 2018b).

A further implementation challenge is the adaptability required of schools in navigating emerging evidence around healthy eating, and what works to support healthy eating. As more evidence becomes available, recommended policies and interventions change, requiring schools to adapt their approach. This adaptability also applies to changing political agendas and media narratives on school food, with schools often having to introduce or withdraw healthy eating policies or interventions intermittently. Coupled with this is a consideration of broader factors that accompany the issue of food and health, including concerns around planetary health. Schools have highlighted issues that put these two aims in conflict (e.g. increasing the availability of fruit and vegetables can lead to increased waste (Oostindjer et al. 2017)). However, school-based food policy and intervention also offer an opportunity to address public health and planetary health synergistically.

Measuring the impact of school food policies and interventions has been hampered by a lack of policy monitoring and programme evaluation. For example, in England, the implementation of the mandatory School Food Standards is not monitored, making it difficult to determine the level of implementation and the impact of such a policy of nutrition, health, educational and economic outcomes.

Schools as part of the food system

Schools play a key role in our wider food and agricultural systems. In addition to providing the opportunity for children to learn about food and nutrition, access nutritious food and develop healthy eating behaviours, they can contribute to local economies and the broader sustainability agenda. This can involve direct mechanisms, such as school food procurement from local farmers (Global Panel on Agriculture and Food Systems for Nutrition 2015), as well as education around food systems, sustainability and planetary health (dos Santos et al. 2022).

There are many examples of schemes that involve local school food procurement alongside educational and school-community partnership initiatives relating to food from countries across the income range. In addition to the examples of Brazil and Kenya given in Box 1, the USA has a Farm to School programme, in which 42% of public schools participate. The key components are procurement of local foods, engaging students in learning about food growing through school gardens and educational activities relating to food systems, health and nutrition (National Farm to School Network 2022). Farm to school programmes have been shown to positively influence healthy food consumption and knowledge relating to food, nutrition and agriculture (Prescott et al. 2019b).

School food procurement from local producers has also been shown to have beneficial economic impacts. The Food for Life Programme is a scheme for schools and other public sector settings in England, involving procurement of seasonal and preferably organic foods from local producers, along with food and healthy eating education, development of a healthy eating culture, and local community involvement (The Soil Association 2022). An economic evaluation of the programme estimated that for every £1 spent on seasonal local produce for school meals, there is approximately a £3 return in terms of local economic, social and environmental benefits (Kersley 2011). In lower-income settings, other benefits include improving smallholder farmers' access to markets and providing opportunities for growth, as well as diversification of food production and sustainable agricultural practices (Hunter et al. 2017).

The longer-term impact of schemes that link schools to local food systems has not been fully evaluated. There is limited knowledge of the impact of these schemes on educational outcomes, such as overall educational engagement and achievement. There may be positive influences on educational outcomes, which, together with benefits to local economies, would have an indirect impact on the long-term economic, social and health prospects of schoolchildren (Due et al. 2011; Vila 2000). Another potential longer-term outcome of these schemes is a more general societal shift towards sustainable food systems and improved planetary health through the provision of education to children relating to sustainable agricultural practices and food production, and reduction of food waste. There is already evidence for short-term benefits from food systems educational interventions, such as reduction of food waste in schools and improvement in dietary quality of schoolchildren (Prescott et al. 2019a). Overall, linking school food provision and educational activities to wider food systems can have a range of beneficial impacts at an individual, community and societal level.

Summary

Schools represent an important setting for supporting healthy eating in children and young people. Support can be provided through school feeding programmes to address hunger and food insecurity, and through policies and initiatives that aim to enhance the nutritional value of school food, in-turn improving the dietary intake of schoolchildren. Schools are also a setting in which children and young people can be equipped with the knowledge, practical skills and behavioural skills required to make healthy food and drink choices. The impact of healthy eating interventions is likely to be optimised when schools adopt multiple approaches, including improving the food and eating environment, and engagement with parents and communities. However, successful implementation of such interventions in schools is challenging and requires an enabling policy, legal and institutional environment, including appropriate support and resources. Increasingly, school food is being framed as one component in a broader food system that can contribute towards local economies and the broader sustainability agenda. However, it is important to conceptualise schools as just one potential setting amongst the many others influencing nutritional intake in children and young people.

References

Anderson, M. L., Gallagher, J., and Ritchie, E. R., 2018. School meal quality and academic performance. *Journal of Public Economics* [online], 168. Available from: https://doi.org/10.1016/j.jpubeco.2018.09.013.

Apple Schools, 2022. *About APPLE Schools* [Online]. Available from: https://www.apple-schools.ca/about [Accessed 24 February 2022].

Atkins, P., 2005. The milk in schools scheme 1934–45: nationalisation and resistance. *History of Education* [online], 34 (1). Available from: https://doi.org/10.1080/004676 0042000315291.

California Department of Education, 2022. *Smarter lunchrooms movement* [Online]. Available from: https://www.cde.ca.gov/ls/nu/he/smarterlunchrooms.asp [Accessed 24 February 2022].

Capper, T. E., Brennan, S. F., Woodside, J. V., and Mckinley, M. C., 2022. What makes interventions aimed at improving dietary behaviours successful in the secondary school environment? A systematic review of systematic reviews. *Public Health Nutrition* [online], 25 (9). Available from: https://doi.org/10.1017/S1368980022000829.

Cohen, J. F., Hecht, A. A., Mcloughlin, G. M., Turner, L., and Schwartz, M. B., 2021. Universal school meals and associations with student participation, attendance, academic performance, diet quality, food security, and body mass index: a systematic review. *Nutrients*, 13 (3). Available from: https://doi.org/10.3390/nu13030911.

Day, R. E., Sahota, P., and Christian, M. S., 2019. Effective implementation of primary school-based healthy lifestyle programmes: a qualitative study of views of school staff. *BMC Public Health* [online], 19. Available from: https://doi.org/10.1186/s12889-019-7550-2.

Dimbleby, H., and Vincent, J., 2013. *The school food plan* [Online]. Available from: http://www.schoolfoodplan.com/wp-content/uploads/2013/07/School_Food_Plan_2013.pdf [Accessed 1 May 2020].

dos Santos, E. B., da Costa Maynard, D., Zandonadi, R. P., Raposo, A., and Botelho, R. B. A., 2022. Sustainability recommendations and practices in school feeding: a systematic review. *Foods* [online], 11 (12), 176. Available from: https://doi.org/10.3390/foods11020176.

Due, P., Krølner, R., Rasmussen, M., Andersen, A., Damsgaard, M. T., Graham, H., and Holstein, B. E., 2011. Pathways and mechanisms in adolescence contribute to adult health inequalities. *Scandinavian Journal of Public Health* [online], 39 (6). Available from: https://doi.org/10.1177/1403494810395989.

European Commission, 2022. *School scheme explained* [Online]. Available from: https://ec.europa.eu/info/food-farming-fisheries/key-policies/common-agricultural-policy/market-measures/school-fruit-vegetables-and-milk-scheme/school-scheme-explained_en [Accessed 24 February 2022].

Evans, C., and Harper, C., 2009. A history and review of school meal standards in the UK. *Journal of Human Nutrition and Dietetics* [online], 22. Available from: https://doi.org/10.1111/j.1365-277X.2008.00941.x.

Evans, C. E. L., Christian, M. S., Cleghorn, C. L., Greenwood, D. C., and Cade, J. E., 2012. Systematic review and meta-analysis of school-based interventions to improve daily fruit and vegetable intake in children aged 5 to 12 years. *The American Journal of Clinical Nutrition* [online], 96. Available from: https://doi.org/10.3945/ajcn.111.030270.

Food Dudes, 2022. *What is food dudes?* [Online]. Available from: https://www.fooddudes.ie/ [Accessed 24 February 2022].

Francis-Devine, B., 2021. Food poverty: households, food banks and free school meals. Available from: https://dera.ioe.ac.uk/37861/1/CBP-9209%20%28redacted%29.pdf [Accessed 3 June 2021].

Fung, C., Kuhle, S., Lu, C., Purcell, M., Schwartz, M., Storey, K., and Veugelers, P. J., 2012. From "best practice" to "next practice": the effectiveness of school-based health promotion in improving healthy eating and physical activity and preventing childhood obesity. *International Journal of Behavioral Nutrition and Physical Activity* [online], 9 (27). Available from: https://doi.org/10.1186/1479-5868-9-27.

Global Panel on Agriculture and Food Systems for Nutrition, 2015. Healthy meals in schools: Policy innovations linking agriculture, food systems and nutrition. Available from: https://glopan.org/sites/default/files/HealthyMealsBrief.pdf [Accessed 16 May 2021].

Hanks, A. S., Just, D. R., and Wansink, B., 2013. Smarter lunchrooms can address new school lunchroom guidelines and childhood obesity. *Journal of Pediatrics*, 162 (4). Available from: https://doi.org/10.1016/j.jpeds.2012.12.031.

Hollands, G. J., Shemilt, I., Marteau, T. M., Jebb, S. A., Kelly, M. P., Nakamura, R., Suhrcke, M., and Ogilvie, D., 2013. Altering micro-environments to change population health behaviour: towards an evidence base for choice architecture interventions. *BMC Public Health* [online], 13. Available from: https://doi.org/10.1186/1471-2458-13-1218.

Hunter, D., Giyose, B., Pologalante, A., Tartanac, F., Bundy, D., Mitchell, A., Moleah, T., Friedrich, J., Alderman, A., and Drake, L., 2017. *Schools as a system to improve nutrition: a new statement for school-based food and nutrition interventions. UNSCN Discussion Paper.* [Online]. Available from: https://www.unscn.org/uploads/web/news/document/School-Paper-EN-WEB.pdf [Accessed 24 February 2022].

Jamelske, E. M., and Bica, L. A., 2012. Impact of the USDA Fresh Fruit and Vegetable Program on children's consumption. *Journal of Child Nutrition Management*, 36. Available from: https://www.researchgate.net/publication/282677233_Impact_of_the_USDA_Fresh_Fruit_and_Vegetable_Program_on_Children's_Consumption [Accessed 24 February 2022].

Jessiman, P. E., Campbell, R., Jago, R., Van Sluijs, E. M. F., and Newbury-Birch, D., 2019. A qualitative study of health promotion in academy schools in England. *BMC Public Health* [online], 19. Available from: https://doi.org/10.1186/s12889-019-7510-x.

Kersley, H., 2011. *The benefits of procuring school meals through the food for life partnership: an economic analysis* [Online]. Available from: https://neweconomics.org/uploads/files/8730d0b778c9021bab_cpm6b61os.pdf [Accessed 24 February 2022].

Kristjansson, E. A., Robinson, V., Petticrew, M., Macdonald, B., Krasevec, J., Janzen, L., Greenhalgh, T., Wells, G., Macgowan, J., Farmer, A., Shea, B. J., Mayhew, A., and Tugwell, P., 2007. School feeding for improving the physical and psychosocial health of disadvantaged elementary school children. *Cochrane Database of Systematic Review* [online], (1). Available from: https://doi.org/10.1002/14651858.CD004676.pub2.

Langford, R., Bonell, C. P., Jones, H. E., Pouliou, T., Murphy, S. M., Waters, E., Komro, K. A., Gibbs, L. F., Magnus, D., and Campbell, R., 2014. The WHO Health Promoting School framework for improving the health and well-being of students and their academic achievement. *Cochrane Database of Systematic Reviews* [online], 16 (4). Available from: https://doi.org/10.1002/14651858.CD008958.pub2.

Long, R., Danechi, S., and Roberts, N., 2021. *School meals and nutritional standards in England* [Online]. Available from: https://assets-learning.parliament.uk/uploads/2021/12/School-Meals-and-Nutritional-Standards-in-England.pdf [Accessed 24 February 2022].

Metcalfe, J. J., Ellison, B., Hamdi, N., Richardson, R., and Prescott, M. P., 2020. A systematic review of school meal nudge interventions to improve youth food behaviours. *International Journal of Behavioral Nutrition and Physical Activity* [online], 17. Available from: https://doi.org/10.1186/s12966-020-00983-y.

Micha, R., Karageorgou, D., Bakogianni, I., Trichia, E., Whitsel, L. P., Story, M., Penalvo, J. L., and Mozaffarian, D., 2018a. Effectiveness of school food environment policies on children's dietary behaviours: A systematic review and meta-analysis. *PloS One*, 13 (3). Available from: https://doi.org/10.1371/journal.pone.0194555.

Micha, R., Karageorgou, D., Bakogianni, I., Trichia, E., Whitsel, L. P., Story, M., Peñalvo, J. L., and Mozaffarian, D., 2018b. Effectiveness of school food environment policies on children's dietary behaviors: a systematic review and meta-analysis. *PLOS ONE* [online], 13. Available from: https://doi.org/10.1371/journal.pone.0194555.

Michie, S., Atkins, L., and West, R., 2014. *The behaviour change wheel: a guide to designing interventions.* London, UK: Silverback Publishing.

Ministry for Foreign Affairs of Finland and Finnish National Agency for Education, 2019. *School feeding: investment in effective learning – Case Finland* [Online]. Available from: https://www.oph.fi/sites/default/files/documents/um_casestudyfinland_schoolfeeding_june2019_netti.pdf [Accessed 26 May 2022].

Ministry of Education, Ministry of Health, Ministry of Agriculture, Livestock and Fisheries. 2017. *National school meals and nutrition strategy 2017–2022* [Online]. Available from: https://docs.wfp.org/api/documents/WFP-0000070917/download/?_ga=2.60932524.1867284158.1645650761-122132956.1645650761 [Accessed 24 February 2022].

Mūkoma, W., and Flisher, A. J., 2004. Evaluations of health promoting schools: a review of nine studies. *Health Promotion International* [online], 19 (3). Available from: https://doi.org/10.1093/heapro/dah309.

National Farm to School Network, 2022. *About farm to school* [Online]. Available from: https://www.farmtoschool.org/about/what-is-farm-to-school [Accessed 24 February 2022].

National Health Service, 2017. *School fruit and vegetable scheme* [Online]. Available from: https://assets.nhs.uk/prod/documents/SFVS-factfile-2017.pdf [Accessed 24 February 2022].

O'brien, K. M., Barnes, C., Yoong, S., Campbell, E., Wyse, R., Delaney, T., Brown, A., Stacey, F., Davies, L., Lorien, S., and Hodder, R. K., 2021. School-based nutrition interventions in children aged 6 to 18 years: an umbrella review of systematic reviews. *Nutrients*, 13 (11). Available from: https://doi.org/10.3390/nu13114113.

Oostindjer, M., Aschemann-witzel, J., Wang, Q., Skuland, S. E., Egelandsdal, B., Amdam, G. V., Schjøll, A., Pachucki, M. C., Rozin, P., Stein, J., Lengard Almli, V., and Van Kleef, E., 2017. Are school meals a viable and sustainable tool to improve the healthiness and sustainability of children's diet and food consumption? A cross-national comparative perspective. *Critical Reviews in Food Science and Nutrition*, 57 (18). Available from: https://doi.org/10.1080/10408398.2016.1197180.

Peters, L. W., Kok, G., Ten Dam, G. T. M., Buijs, G. J., and Paulussen, T. G. W. M., 2009. Effective elements of school health promotion across behavioral domains: a systematic review of reviews. *BMC Public Health*, 9 (182). Available from: https://doi.org/10.1186/1471-2458-9-182.

Pineda, E., Bascunan, J., and Sassi, F., 2021. Improving the school food environment for the prevention of childhood obesity: what works and what doesn't. *Obesity Reviews* [online], 22 (2). Available from: https://doi.org/10.1111/obr.13176.

Prescott, M. P., Burg, X., Metcalfe, J. J., Lipka, A. E., Herritt, C., and Cunningham-Sabo, L., 2019a. Healthy planet, healthy youth: a food systems education and promotion intervention to improve adolescent diet quality and reduce food waste. *Nutrients* [online], 11 (8). Available from: https://doi.org/10.3390/nu11081869.

Prescott, M. P., Cleary, R., Bonanno, A., Costanigro, M., Jablonski, B. B. R., and Long, A. B., 2019b. Farm to school activities and student outcomes: a systematic review. *Advances in Nutrition* [online], 11(2). Available from: https://doi.org/10.1093/advances/nmz094.

Sawyer, S., 2021. Making every school a health-promoting school. *Lancet Child Adolescent Health* [online], 5 (8). Available from: https://doi.org/10.1016/S2352-4642(21)00190-5.

Skovdal, M., and Campbell, L. C., 2015. Beyond education: what role can schools play in the support and protection of children in extreme settings? *International Journal of Educational Development* [online], 41. Available from: https://doi.org/10.1016/j.ijedudev.2015.02.005.

Spence, S., Delve, J., Stamp, E., Matthews, J. N. S., White, M., and Adamson, A. J., 2013. The impact of food and nutrient-based standards on primary school children's lunch and total dietary intake: a natural experimental evaluation of government policy in England. *PloS One* [online], 8. Available from: https://doi.org/10.1371/journal.pone.0078298.

The Independent School Food Plan, 2014. *Background to the new school food standards* [Online]. Available from: http://www.schoolfoodplan.com/background-to-the-new-school-food-standards/ [Accessed 24 February 2022].

The Soil Association, 2022. *Transforming food culture for all* [Online]. Available from: https://www.foodforlife.org.uk/about-us/our-partners/soil-association [Accessed 24 February 2022].

Townsend, N., and Foster, C., 2013. Developing and applying a socio-ecological model to the promotion of healthy eating in the school. *Public Health Nutrition* [online], 16 (6). Available from: https://doi.org/10.1017/S1368980011002655.

UK Government Rural Payments Agency, 2017. *Eligibility for the school milk subsidy scheme - milk consumed from 1 August 2017* [Online]. Available from: https://www.gov.uk/guidance/eligibility-for-the-school-milk-subsidy-scheme-milk-consumed-from-1-august-2017 [Accessed 24 February 2022].

Upton, D., Upton, P., and Taylor, C., 2013. Increasing children's lunchtime consumption of fruit and vegetables: an evaluation of the Food Dudes programme. *Public Health Nutrition* [online], 16 (6). Available from: https://doi.org/10.1017/S1368980012004612.

Valizadeh, P., and Ng, S. W., 2020. The New school food standards and nutrition of school children: direct and indirect effect analysis. *Economics & Human Biology* [online], 39. Available from: https://doi.org/10.1016/j.ehb.2020.100918.

Vila, L. E., 2000. The non-monetary benefits of education. *European Journal of Education* [online], 35 (1). Available from: https://doi.org/10.1111/1467-3435.00003.

World Food Programme, 2018. *School meals programme in Kenya* [Online]. Available from: https://docs.wfp.org/api/documents/WFP-0000102591/download/#:~:text=Kenya's%20national%20Home%20Grown%20School, farmers%20and%20local%20food%20suppliers [Accessed 2 March 2022].

World Food Programme, 2021. *State of school feeding worldwide 2020* [Online]. Available from: https://www.wfp.org/publications/state-school-feeding-worldwide-2020 [Accessed 24 February 2022].

7

HOME ECONOMICS CURRICULUM POLICY IN IRELAND

Lessons for policy development

Amanda McCloat and Martin Caraher

Introduction

Home Economics, as a recognised field of study, first emerged in 1908 at the Lake Placid conferences which took place to draw attention to the importance of educating women. The focus was on improving the quality of family life by developing everyday life skills and responsible management of resources within the home (Dreilinger 2021). Although the field is known today under many names across the world (e.g., Family and Consumer Sciences in the USA and Human Ecology in Canada), the nomenclature 'Home Economics' is used by the International Federation for Home Economics (IFHE) to recognise the origin of the field. Home Economics is also the name used to define the curriculum subject, mostly in secondary or post-primary school education, in many countries (Japan, South Korea, Finland, Norway, Germany, Ireland, Northern Ireland, Malta, Scotland, some states/provinces in Canada and Australia) (McCloat and Caraher, 2019). As a subject in the school setting, the aim of Home Economics is to "facilitate[s] students to discover and further develop their own resources and capabilities to be used in their personal life" (IFHE 2008, p.2). Home Economics is identified in educational policy as the subject area which teaches a holistic food education to young people encompassing practical and theoretical food skills.

However, the subject has often lost ground to the impact of curriculum reform and the consequence of a reorientation of curriculum policy towards industry interests and demands for a skilled hospitality workforce (Owen-Jackson and Rutland 2016; Ronto et al. 2017a; Rutland 2008, 2017; Stitt et al. 1997). In some countries this has resulted in the removal of Home Economics as a subject in its traditional format from the school curriculum (Sweden, England, Wales). During the reform, the subject was fragmented into associated discipline areas, e.g., food technology, health studies or nutrition or textiles with an

DOI: 10.4324/9781003294962-9

aim of preparing students for work as opposed to developing essential life skills. Furthermore, the subject is often offered as an optional subject on the curriculum which results in many students, predominantly males, not taking up the opportunity to study Home Economics. This chapter, using the theoretical lens of Basil Bernstein's Theory of the Pedagogic Device (Bernstein 1990, 2000) analyses the process of how the 2017 curriculum reform of Junior Cycle Home Economics in Ireland was undertaken; and examines the positioning of food education within the new Home Economics Specification.

Setting the context – Home Economics education in Ireland

In Ireland the curriculum subject 'Home Economics' is offered in secondary school at both Junior Cycle (12–15 years) and Senior Cycle (16–18 years) as an optional area of study. In the early 1800s, Home Economics was first introduced in Irish primary schools to address the concerns around the wellbeing and health of working and lower-class families, particularly when most children completed their formal education before the age of 11 (Coolahan 2017; Durcan 1972). Although it was once an established subject in primary school, this is no longer the case since the major reform of the primary curriculum in 1991. Establishing Home Economics, as a subject area under various name guises, to improve the quality of life for families was the genesis and rationale for Home Economics in Irish curriculum policy that is still reflected today (McCloat and Caraher 2018). The mission of Home Economics, as described by Engberg (1979), to give due priority to "the importance of the family and creating a better quality of life for all people" (p.36) was very much reflected in the orientation of Home Economics education in Ireland.

In secondary schools in Ireland, Home Economics remains a relatively popular choice of subject at Junior Cycle. In 2018, it was studied by 36% (n = 23,043) of the total cohort of students (n = 64,330) sitting the Junior Certificate examination in 2018 (State Examinations Commission, 2019). At Senior Cycle, in 2021, 22% (n = 12,594) of all students (n = 57,886) studied Home Economics (State Examinations Commission 2022a). However, uptake is gender biased at Junior Cycle with females being the significant majority (82%, n = 18,852) of those who study Home Economics. The Junior Certificate Home Economics curriculum, which is the focus of this chapter, was first introduced in 1991. No changes were made for over 25 years until the process of the Reform of Junior Cycle Home Economics (Department of Education and Skills [DES] 2015) was initiated in 2016 and a new Home Economics Specification was finalised in 2017 and introduced for the first year students in all schools in September 2018 (DES 2017).

Reforming Home Economics curriculum policy

Reforming national curriculum policy can be a long, complex and often arduous process (Priestley et al. 2014; Tikkanen et al. 2017). In Ireland, the National Council for Curriculum and Assessment (NCCA) manages the process of curriculum reform and advises the Minister for Education on all curriculum and assessment matters. A curriculum is developed and implemented, at a national level, across all schools in the country. In 2016, the NCCA initiated the reform of Junior Cycle Home Economics as part of a wider *Framework for Reform of Junior Cycle* (2015). What is interesting and pertinent to this chapter is the selecting and framing of the knowledge base for the Home Economics Specification (2017) at the macro policy level and how this was interpreted and enacted at the micro level of the classroom. Bernstein's 'pedagogic device' is used as a theoretical lens to analyse the reform of the Home Economics curriculum policy (1990, 2000) and facilitates the understanding of pedagogic discourse across curriculum, pedagogy and assessment (Apple 2002). The pedagogic device identifies the "rules of the policy process" (Singh et al. 2013, p.467) as it contributes to the regulation and "the production of the school curriculum and its transmission" (Apple 2002, p.613).

The classification and framing of Home Economics as a subject have belea-guered the field for many decades in many countries (Attar 1990; Cunningham-Sabo 2012; Dreilinger 2021). A strong classification, as outlined by Morais (2002), infers a subject has a strong identity and boundary of its knowledge and skills. Conversely, a weak classification is a more integrated approach to a curriculum which is easily permeated by other subjects (Sadovnik 2001). During the consultation stage of the development of the new curriculum, there were many calls with a passion for change from Home Economics professionals for the subject to be made compulsory. Research demonstrates that food education is often considered a lesser priority compared to subjects such as Mathematics or a Science subject or a Foreign Language choice (Ronto et al. 2017a, 2017b; Slater 2013). This can be attributed to these subjects having more strongly insu-lated 'esoteric' discourse and less 'common' discourse (Bernstein 2000; Sadovnik 2001); whereas the balance often shifts the other way in peoples' perception of Home Economics. This balance of common and esoteric discourse has a direct influence on the positioning of the subject in schools (Singh et al. 2013) and through the reform of the Junior Cycle, the new Specification aimed to move beyond a common discourse by "re-defining what constitutes legitimate knowl-edge and legitimate pedagogic practices" (Penney 2013, p.15). This sits within the larger context of work by Freidson of distinctions between the professions and the semi-professions (Freidson 2018). The old, and what are referred to as the 'true' professions, have their own body of knowledge and have traditionally been distinguished by a regulatory structure which excluded other professions or outsiders (Freidson 1988). Teaching generally is considered within this frame of reference as a semi-profession.

Reforming Home Economics curriculum policy within the field of recontextualisation

The field of recontextualisation comprises two levels: the official recontextu-alising field (ORF) at the macro level and the pedagogic recontextualisation field (PRF) at the meso level (Apple 2002). In the reform of Junior Cycle Home Economics, the ORF is completed by the NCCA who select and dislocate the knowledge from the production field (where the knowledge is generated) which can comprise universities, research centres or anywhere that involves the generation of expert knowledge (Bernstein 2000; Singh et al. 2013). The PRF primarily involves teacher associations and teacher educators and pertains to how they construct the non-official pedagogic discourse and influence the development of the curriculum policy through consultations and representation on behalf of members. This may also be influenced by school-based structural determinants such as facilities and costs, which can vary from school to school. As is detailed further in this section teacher unions and school management were also key stakeholders in the consultation process. The knowledge is then recontextualised to develop the new curriculum policy.

Developing curriculum policy is widely recognised as being complex and multifaceted resulting in much tension and challenges (Jephcote and Davies 2004; Penney 2013; Priestley et al. 2014). In Ireland, the NCCA is responsible for the development of curriculum policy on behalf of the Minister for Education who in turn is answerable to the Houses of the Oireachtas. In order to inform the new curriculum policy, the NCCA engaged in an extensive and iterative consultation process. Initially, a subject expert in Home Economics was engaged to prepare a draft Background Paper for Home Economics in 2016 which was disseminated for public consultation. Compared to other subject consultations, engagement was very high (244 individual responses to the online questionnaire and 2 written submissions) and involved stakeholders such as teachers, parents, student teachers, students, industry and school management (NCCA 2017a). The final published 'Background Paper for Home Economics' contained the feedback received from the public consultation (NCCA 2016). From a Bernstein perspective, in the field of recontextualisation, the published Background Paper selected and identified the most pertinent discourses and what was most relevant to inform the development of the new Home Economics Specification. Notably, the Paper identified four interconnected societal factors (changes to family and social systems; education for sustainable development and responsible living; food and health literacy; home and resource management) that were important to ensure Home Economics curriculum would remain current and relevant "in the lives of individuals, families, communities and society" (NCCA 2016, p.31).

The NCCA then set up a Home Economics Subject Development Group (SDG) comprising 12 members selected from the subject association: Irish Association Teachers Home Economics, Department Inspectorate, teacher unions, school management bodies, a subject expert and the State Examinations Commission. The role of the SDG was to guide and provide feedback on the curriculum development of Home Economics conducted by the NCCA. The development of a Draft Specification took place over a five-month period and was then released for public consultation. Engagement ensued resulting in 295 responses to the online survey, comprising 84% Home Economics teachers, eight written submissions and one focus group (NCCA 2017b). The iterative process engaged by the NCCA afforded all key stakeholders, in a very transparent manner, the opportunity to input into the development of the new Home Economics curriculum policy within the ORF and PRF. The final Junior Cycle Home Economics Specification, once approved by the Minister for Education, was published by the Department of Education in 2017 (DES 2017) and was enacted in schools in September 2018 for all first-year pupils. It is in the field of reproduction (Bernstein 1990, 2000) at the meso (school) and micro (classroom) level where the Home Economics teachers enact and reproduce the curriculum policy.

Positioning of food education in Home Economics curriculum policy in Ireland

In secondary education in Ireland, the subject Home Economics is the only subject on the curriculum directly concerned with teaching students theoretical and practical food skills in a holistic and integrated manner, although there are other inputs from the health sector and NGOs related to healthy living but not part of the formal curriculum and often delivered by non-teachers or those without pedagogical training. The Junior Cycle for Teachers (a professional development unit set up by the Department to support the roll out of the new Junior Cycle) launched a series of professional development seminars for teachers during the academic year 2017–2018 to support teachers to teach and assess the Junior Cycle Home Economics. The Home Economics Specification is set for 200 hours of timetabled student engagement over a three-year period. Home Economics, at Junior Cycle, aims to "develop students' knowledge, attitudes, understanding, skills and values to achieve optimal, healthy and sustainable living for every person as an individual, and as a member of families and society" (DES 2017, p.5).

The Specification comprises three interconnected strands: Food, Health and Culinary Skills; Responsible Family Living and Textiles and Craft underpinned by four cross-cutting elements (Figure 7.1) of Health and Wellbeing; Individual and Family Empowerment; Sustainable and Responsible Living; and Consumer Competence.

The Specification shifted the balance in Junior Cycle Home Economics towards a strongly insulated Home Economics discourse and beyond the common discourse of basic cooking skills. This was achieved through articulating the philosophical and pedagogic underpinnings, drawn from evidence-based research, of the subject in the Background Paper (NCCA 2016) which was then reflected in the final Specification. The research-informed Background Paper set out, for the first time in Ireland, the body of knowledge for Home Economics education which then informed the development of Home Economics curriculum policy.

Learning outcomes are set out under each of the three strands, with the largest number of learning outcomes weighted in the food, health and culinary skills strand. This chapter specifically focuses on the food, health and culinary skills

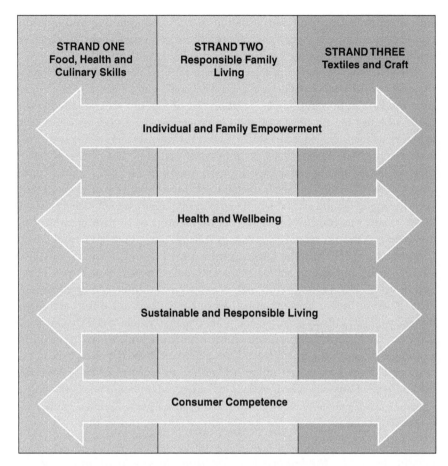

STRAND ONE Food, Health and Culinary Skills	STRAND TWO Responsible Family Living	STRAND THREE Textiles and Craft

Individual and Family Empowerment

Health and Wellbeing

Sustainable and Responsible Living

Consumer Competence

FIGURE 7.1   The elements of the contextual strands showing the integrated nature of the Home Economics specification (DES 2017, p.12)

strand as well as the four cross-cutting elements (individual and family empowerment; health and wellbeing; sustainable and responsible living and consumer competence as they pertain to food education). This balance in the number of learning outcomes in strand 1 of the Specification reflects the results of the extensive consultation to the policy development process where the potential for Home Economics to make a significant contribution to students' developing a positive relationship with food and practical food skills was identified (NCCA 2017a, 2017b). The strand food, health and culinary skills aim to enable students to "develop a healthy, sustainable attitude and positive relationship with food through practical experiential learning" so that they can "adopt a healthy lifestyle and make informed decisions that impact the health and wellbeing of themselves as individuals as well as within their families" (DES 2017, p.15). The learning outcomes for strand 1 reflect the emphasis on facilitating students to apply their knowledge and understanding of food, nutrition, diet and health in real-life situations so that they are equipped to make positive health choices now and in the future.

The practical application of learning these skills in the classroom underpins the experiential learning approach and is reflected in the balance of the assessment marks. The Specification has an allocation of 50% of the externally assessed marks allocated to a practical food skills examination where students are asked to apply their food knowledge and skills to meet the requirements of a specific brief issued by the State Examinations Commission each year. The brief may reflect topics of the Home Economics Specification including, for 2022, healthy family meals; sustainable food practices; diet-related diseases; nutritional requirements at each stage of the life cycle (State Examinations Commission 2022b). As Singh (2015) notes, the evaluative site, in education contexts, is often controlled by the State and this is certainly the case in Ireland, with the State Examinations Commission, specifically the Chief Examiner for Home Economics, responsible for setting and examining all of the externally assessed components of the Specification. Bernstein (1990, 2000) reflects on the influence of the assessment mode on how recontextualised discourse is transformed into pedagogic discourse. This influence was evident in research conducted (McCloat and Caraher 2020) which demonstrated Home Economics teachers, as agents of the pedagogic device at the micro level, having anxiety about the assessment of the new curriculum. Research (Penney 2013, 2020; Priestley et al. 2014) associates the enacting of any new curriculum with anxiety and tension and links this to a weaker classification of subject, which has been a legacy of Home Economics on the curriculum.

Lessons learned – the implications for future food education policy

The reform of Home Economics curriculum policy in Ireland has resulted in a broad-based Junior Cycle programme comprising food knowledge and practical skills underpinned by scientific theory and taught utilising an experiential pedagogical approach. It involved a move towards the inclusion of evidence-based research in the design and content of the new Specification, drawn during the field of recontextualisation (Bernstein 2000). Although the Home Economics curriculum in Ireland includes strands on sustainable and responsible living, and textiles, fashion and design; as well as food, health and culinary skills; the element health and wellbeing is a cross-cutting theme across all strands. Food, health and culinary skills, strand one, is reflective of a broad range of food knowledge and skills as it focuses on areas including menu planning; food choices; nutrition; dietary needs through the life cycle; food science; ethical and ecological factors; shopping and budgeting; food safety and hygiene and the practical food and cooking skills (DES 2017). It can be argued that it has a stronger insulated esoteric discourse now reflected in the Specification, although how this influences the positioning in schools remains to be seen as the rollout of the new curriculum is very much in its infancy. The breadth and comprehensiveness of the subject is a key facet of the reformed Home Economics curriculum policy. This reflects the strength of the multidisciplinary field of Home Economics and its capacity to draw expert content and knowledge from "multiple disciplines, synthesising these through interdisciplinary and transdisciplinary inquiry" (IFHE 2008, p.1; Pendergast 2015; Renwick 2016; Turkki 2012).

Research demonstrates the importance of food education programmes to be multifactorial and multidisciplinary, integrating a wide range of food knowledge and practical skills (Dean et al. 2022; McGowan et al. 2017; Renwick 2016). Lichtenstein and Ludwig (2010) note the importance of integrating practical food skills with the scientific and theoretical underpinnings as essential components of any comprehensive food curriculum so that young people can develop the confidence to prepare food for themselves and their families as a sustained public health measure. Home Economics curriculum policy in Ireland aims to develop student's knowledge and practical food skills in a sequential, comprehensive way over a three-year period. It is not a short-term, piecemeal intervention which are often not sustainable to implement nor effective in affecting change in behaviour over a period of time (Caraher and Seeley 2010; McCloat and Caraher 2016; McDowell et al. 2014; Reicks et al. 2018; Upton et al. 2015; Utter et al. 2018). Nanayakkara et al. (2017, 2018) reported the views of key stakeholders such as parents, young adults and food professionals, all of whom espoused a comprehensive food subject on the curriculum in schools that integrates knowledge and skills to establish healthy food behaviours; however, the majority of respondents were not in favour for it to be compulsory in schools. This is contrary to the many calls for Home Economics to be made compulsory in Ireland (Boland 2017; Donnelly 2022; Hickey 2018; Maguire 2017; Safefood 2018; St. Angela's College 2018). A challenge that faces the implementation of an integrated and comprehensive food education programme is the tendency to reduce food education to a technocratic and simplistic view of 'cooking skills' and this is somehow a magic bullet to solve the obesity crisis. As Smith (2016) identifies, this places an unwelcome association and reduces a broad-based food education to a simplistic narrative. Furthermore, it associates teaching people how to cook with solving the "dilemma of fatness and ill-health" (Earl 2018, p.48). By having an established subject on the curriculum, such as Home Economics, it facilitates a broad range of food-related knowledge, skills and behaviours to be taught sequentially and developmentally over a sustained period of time by subject and pedagogic expert Home Economics teachers. This was further supported, in November 2018, when the Irish Houses of the Oireachtas Join Committee on Children and Youth Affairs' Report on Tackling Childhood Obesity recommended that Home Economics be a compulsory subject in post-primary schools for all Junior Cycle students (Houses of the Oireachtas 2018).[1]

In a study conducted on Home Economics teachers and their perceptions of the reformed Specification, they identified teaching students' food-related life skills as having the potential to make a real difference in the lives of young people now and in the future (McCloat and Caraher 2020). Although there is no longitudinal research which investigates the impact of food education on health outcomes, there is research to support a positive correlation between those who have studied food education, or Home Economics, at a young age and their associated level cooking skills, healthy food practices, diet quality and food knowledge in later life (Begley et al. 2017; Burton et al. 2017; Lavelle et al. 2016; McDowell et al. 2014; Worsley et al. 2015; Wolfson et al. 2017; Wolfson and Bleich 2015). In the long term this relationship between cooking skills and culinary knowledge delivered by home economics and reduction in diet-related non-communicable diseases remains to be researched in more detail. If these links can be established it can help in support for home economics in the school setting from the area of public health (Lichtenstein and Ludwig 2010). The importance of having teachers who have the required pedagogical and subject expertise is recognised and Home Economics teachers can facilitate the empowerment of young people with the food knowledge and skills because they have this expertise (Boddy et al. 2019; Burton et al. 2017; Cunningham-Sabo and Simons 2012; Wolfson et al. 2017; Worsley et al. 2015). Undoubtedly, this is a major strength in Ireland, where there is a dedicated, and popular, Bachelor of Education (Home Economics) University programme, which is an undergraduate, honours teacher education degree in St Angela's College, Sligo. However, it is recognised that many countries (such as the UK) no longer educate specialist Home Economics teachers due to the demise of the subject in its traditional format on the curriculum (Owen-Jackson and Rutland 2016). More research continues to emerge on the role of Home Economics education and teachers and their contribution to developing essential food life skills (Boddy et al. 2019; Burton et al. 2021; Fordyce-Voorham 2018; Lavelle et al. 2022; Nanayakkara et al. 2018; Smith 2016). It is hoped that this will have a positive influence by providing evidence-based research for policy makers to make informed decisions relating to school curricula and the education of teachers.

Conclusion

This chapter, using Bernstein's Theory of the Pedagogic Device as a theoretical framework, has shown curriculum policy developments at the macro stage and in doing so provides insights into how food education is positioned within the curriculum.

There are some key learnings, at a macro level, for those hoping to influence policy development. The curriculum development process in Ireland was an iterative one, grounded in public consultation and engagement. However, in order to inform policy development, it is important that Home Economics professionals engage with the process at every available level through individual consultations, teacher unions, subject associations and group consultations. Having a consistent and coherent, research-informed discourse to present is required so that the subject content can be framed and classified accordingly. This process also demonstrates how presenting a strongly reasoned and evidence-based case to policy makers can result in positive outcomes.

The policy development process has resulted in an inherent focus on facilitating the empowerment of students so that they can have the knowledge and skills for a healthy and sustainable way of living now and in the future. Home Economics can provide the ideal framework through which comprehensive food education should be taught to young people. However, challenges exist, the subject is still very gendered bias as reflected in the gender breakdown of students taking the subject (SEC 2022a). It is not available in some single-sex male schools and in mixed schools, boys often do not choose the subject for a myriad of reasons including the availability of timetabled classes; resources in boys schools; and gendered connotations. From a policy perspective, the implementation of the recommendation of the Houses of Oireachtas (Irish Parliament) would go some way in addressing these issues; however, adequate resourcing of school facilities would need to be considered. Home Economics supports the development of comprehensive food education consisting of theoretical and practical food skills. As it is taught over a three-year period, teachers have the opportunity to develop skills in a sequential and holistic way.

Note

1 The Irish National Parliament or Oireachtas consists of the President and two Houses: Dáil Éireann (House of Representatives who are elected) and the Seanad Éireann (Senate who are indirectly elected).

References

Apple, M. W., 2002. Does education have independent power? Bernstein and the question of relative autonomy. *British Journal of Sociology of Education*, 23 (4), 607–616.

Attar, D., 1990. *Wasting girls' time*. London, UK: Virago Education Series.

Begley, A., Gallegos, D., and Vidgen, H., 2017. Effectiveness of Australian cooking skill interventions. *British Food Journal* [online], 119 (5), 973–991. Available from: doi:10.1108/BFJ-10-2016-0451.

Bernstein, B., 1990. *The structuring of pedagogic discourse*. 1st ed. London, UK: Routledge.

Bernstein, B., 2000. *Pedagogy, symbolic control and identity*. Revised ed. New York: Rowman and Littlefield Publishers.

Boddy, G., Booth, A., and Worsley, A., 2019. What does healthy eating mean? Australian teachers' perceptions of healthy eating in secondary school curricula. *Health Education*, 119 (4), 277–290.

Boland, R., 2017. Home Economics: no longer the 'wife material' course. *The Irish Times* [online], 20 November. Available from: https://www.irishtimes.com/news/education/home-economics-no-longer-the-wife-material-course-1.3291314.

Burton, M., Reid, M., Worsley, A., and Mavondo, F., 2017. Food skills, confidence and household gatekeepers' dietary practices. *Appetite*, 108, 183–190.

Burton, M., Riddell, L., and Worsley, A., 2021. Food literacy in Australian secondary schools—views of young adults, parents, and teachers. *International Journal of Home Economics*, 14 (2), 4–18.

Caraher, M., and Seeley, A., 2010. Cooking in schools: lessons from the UK. *Journal of Home Economics Institute of Australia*, 17 (1), 2–9.

Coolahan, J., 2017. *Towards the era of lifelong learning: a history of Irish Education 1800–2016*. Dublin, Ireland: Institute of Public Administration.

Cunningham-Sabo, L., 2012. Home Economics: an old-fashioned answer to a modern-day dilemma. *Nutrition Today*, 47 (3), 128–132.

Dean, M., O'Kane, C., Issartel, J., McCloat, A., Mooney, E., McKernan, C., Brooks, S., O'Kane, N., Crowe, W., Murphy, B., and Lavelle, F., 2022. Cook like a boss: an effective co-created multidisciplinary approach to improving children's cooking competence. *Appetite*, 168, 105727.

Department of Education and Skills [DES], 2015. *Framework for junior cycle 2015*. Dublin, Ireland: The Stationery Office.

Department of Education and Skills [DES], 2017. *Junior cycle home economics specification* [online]. Available from: http://www.curriculumonline.ie/Junior-cycle/Junior-Cycle-Subjects/Home-Economics.

Donnelly, M., 2022. Young people don't have the skills to cook a meal from scratch. *Farming Independent* [online], 1 June 2022. Available from: https://www.independent.ie/business/farming/agri-business/agri-food/young-people-dont-have-the-basic-skills-to-cook-a-meal-from-scratch-41710542.html.

Dreilinger, D., 2021. *The secret history of home economics: how trailblazing women harnessed the power of home and changed the way we live*. 1st ed. New York: W.W. Norton and Company.

Durcan, T., 1972. *History of Irish education from 1800*. North Wales, UK: Dragon Books.

Earl, L., 2018. *Schools and food education in the 21st Century*. London, UK: Routledge.

Engberg, L., 1979. Research in home economics. *In*: V. Hutchinson, ed. *New trends in home economics education*. Paris: UNESCO, 36–52.

Fordyce-Voorham, S., 2018. A food literacy model for food education program design and evaluation. *International Journal Home Economics*, 11 (2), 2–11.

Freidson, E., 1988. *Profession of medicine: a study of the sociology of applied knowledge*. Chicago, IL: University of Chicago Press.

Freidson, E., 2018. The futures of professionalisation. *In*: M. Stacey, M. Reid, C. Heath, and R. Dingwall, eds. *Health and the division of labour*. London: Routledge, 14–40.

Hickey, M., 2018. *World Home Economics day 2018 press release* [online]. Available from: https://www.athe-ireland.com/articles/world-home-economics-day-2018/41/.

Houses of the Oireachtas, 2018. *Joint committee on children and youth affairs report on tackling childhood obesity* [online]. Available from: https://data.oireachtas.ie/ie/oireachtas/committee/dail/32/select_committee_on_children_and_youth_affairs/reports/2018/2018-11-14_report-on-tackling-childhood-obesity_en.pdf.

International Federation for Home Economics [IFHE], 2008. *Introducing the IFHE position statement Home Economics in the 21st Century*. Available from: https://search.informit.org/doi/10.3316/INFORMIT.774193676335580 [Accessed 20 August 2021].

Jephcote, M., and Davies, B., 2004. Recontextualising discourse: an exploration of the workings of the meso level. *Journal of Education Policy* [online], 19 (5), 547–564.

Lavelle, F., McGowan, L., Spence, M., Caraher, M., Raats, M., Hollywood, L., McDowell, D., McCloat, A., Mooney, E., and Dean, M., 2016. Learning cooking skills at different ages: a cross sectional study. *International Journal of Behavioural Nutrition and Physical Activity* [online], 13, 119. Available from: https://doi.org/10.1186/s12966-016-0446-y.

Lichtenstein, A., and Ludwig, D., 2010. Bring back Home Economics education. *Journal American Medical Association* [online], 303 (18). Available from: https://doi.org/10.1001/jama.2010.592.

Maguire, N., 2017. Celeb chef Neven Maguire wants obligatory school cooking lessons. *Irish Examiner* [online], 29 September 2017. Available from: https://www.irishexaminer.com/ireland/celeb-chef-neven-maguire-wants-obligatory-school-cooking-lessons-459917.html.

McCloat, A., and Caraher, M., 2016. Home Economics as a food education intervention: lessons from the Irish secondary education context. *Education and Health* [online], 34 (4). Available from: http://sheu.org.uk/x/eh344finalam.pdf.
Here is the link copied from the website http://sheu.org.uk/sheux/EH/eh344finalam.pdf

McCloat, A., and Caraher, M., 2018. The evolution of Home Economics as a subject in Irish primary and post-primary education from the 1800s to the twenty-first century. *Irish Educational Studies* [online], 38 (3). Available from: https://doi.org/10.1080/03323315.2018.1552605.

McCloat, A., and Caraher, M., 2019. An international review of second-level food education curriculum policy. *Cambridge Journal of Education* [online] 50 (3). Available from: https://doi.org/10.1080/0305764X.2019.1694641

McCloat, A., and Caraher, M., 2020. Teachers' experiences of enacting curriculum policy at the micro level using Bernstein's theory of the pedagogic device. *Teachers and Teaching: Theory and Practice* [online], 26 (5). Available from: https://doi.org/10.1080/13540602.2020.1863210.

McDowell, D., McMahon-Beattie, U., and Burns, A., 2014. Schoolinary art: practical cooking skills issues for the future. *British Food Journal*, 117 (2), 629–650.

McGowan, L., Caraher, M., Raats, M., Lavelle, F., Hollywood, L., McDowell, D., Spence, M., McCloat, A., Mooney, E., and Dean, M., 2017. Domestic cooking and food skills: a review. *Critical Reviews in Food Science and Nutrition* [online], 57 (11). Available from: https://doi.org/10.1080/10408398.2015.1072495.

Morais, A. M., 2002. Basil Bernstein at the micro level of the classroom. *British Journal of Sociology of Education* [online], 23 (4). Available from: https://doi.org/10.1080/01425690220000841.

Nanayakkara, J., Margerison, C., and Worsley, A., 2017. Food professionals' opinions of the food studies curriculum in Australia. *British Food Journal*, 119 (12), 2945–2958.

Nanayakkara, J., Margerison, C., and Worsley, A., 2018. Senior secondary school food literacy education: importance, challenges, and ways of improving. *Nutrients* [online], 10 (9). Available from: https://doi.org/10.3390/nu10091316.

National Council for Curriculum and Assessment, 2016. *Background paper for Home Economics* [online]. Available from: https://ncca.ie/en/resources/home-economics-bp-final-may-2016 [Accessed 15 August 2021].

National Council for Curriculum and Assessment, 2017a. *Report on the consultation on the background paper for Home Economics* [online]. Available from: https://ncca.ie/en/resources/consultation-report-on-the-background-paper-for-junior-cycle-home-economics [Accessed 15 August 2021].

National Council for Curriculum and Assessment, 2017b. *Consultation report on the draft specification for Junior Cycle Home Economics* [online]. Available from: https://ncca.ie/media/3510/homeec_consultation_may2017_en.pdf.

Owen-Jackson, G., and Rutland, M., 2016. Food in the school curriculum in England: its development from cookery to cookery. *Design and Technology Education: An International Journal*, 21 (3), 63–75.

Pendergast, D., 2015. HELM – Home Economics Literacy Model – A vision for the field. *Victorian Journal of Home Economics* [online], 54 (1). Available from: https://www.homeeconomics.com.au/images/PDFs/VJHE_Vol54_No1.pdf.

Penney, D., 2013. Points of tension and possibility: boundaries in and of physical education. *Sport, Education and Society* [online], 18 (1). Available from: https://doi.org /10.1080/13573322.2012.713862.

Penney, D., 2020. Health education policy and curriculum. *In*: D. Leahy, K. Fitzpatrick, and K. J. Wright, eds. *Social theory and health education: forging new insights in research.* Oxfordshire, UK: Routledge, 114–123.

Priestley, M., Minty, S., and Eager, E., 2014. School-based curriculum development in Scotland: curriculum policy and enactment. *Pedagogy, Culture & Society*, 22 (2), 189–211.

Reicks, M., Kocher, M., and Reeder, J., 2018. Impact of cooking and home food preparation interventions among adults: a systematic review (2011–2016). *Journal of Nutrition Education and Behavior*, 50 (2), 148–172.

Renwick, K., 2016. Home Economics education in a time of schooling. *Victorian Journal of Home Economics*, 55 (1), 2–6.

Ronto, R., Ball, L., Pendergast, D. & Harris, N. 2017a, "Environmental factors of food literacy in Australian high schools: views of home economics teachers", *International Journal of Consumer Studies*, 41 (1), 19–27. https://doi.org/10.1111/ijcs.12309.

Ronto, R., Ball, L., Pendergast, D., and Harris, N., 2017b. What is the status of food literacy in Australian high schools? Perceptions of home economics teachers. *Appetite*, 108, 326–334. https://doi.org/10.1016/j.appet.2016.10.024.

Rutland, M., 2008. *Licence to cook: the death knell for food technology?* [online]. Available from: https://repository.lboro.ac.uk/articles/online_resource/Licence_to_Cook_the_ death_knell_for_food_technology_/9345773.

Rutland, M., 2017. Food in the school curriculum: a discussion of alternative approaches. *In*: M. J. de Vries, ed. *Handbook of technology education.* Manhattan, NY: Springer. Available from: https://doi. org/10.1007/978-3-319-38889-2_25-2.

Sadovnik, A. R., 2001. Basil Bernstein 1924–2000. *Prospects*, 314 (4), 607–620.

Safefood., 2018. *Submission to Joint Oireachtas Committee on Children and Youth Affairs. Tackling Childhood Obesity* [online]. Available from: https://data.oireachtas.ie/ie/ oireachtas/committee/dail/32/joint_committee_on_children_and_youth_affairs/ submissions/2018/2018-08-22_submission-safefood_en.pdf.

Singh, P., 2015. Performativity and pedagogising knowledge: globalising educational policy formation, dissemination and enactment. *Journal of Education Policy*, 30 (3), 363–384.

Singh, P., Thomas, S., and Harris, J., 2013. Recontextualising policy discourses: a Bernsteinian perspective on policy interpretation, translation, enactment. *Journal of Education Policy*, 28 (4), 465–480.

Slater, J., 2013. Is cooking dead? The state of home economics food and nutrition education in a Canadian province. *International Journal of Consumer Studies* [online], 37 (6), 617–624. Available from: https://doi. org/10.1111/ijcs.12042.

Smith, M. G., 2016. Bring back Home Economics? Challenging contested discourses on obesity. *Journal Family Consumer Sciences*, 108 (4), 7–12.

St. Angela's College, Sligo, 2018. *Submission to Joint Oireachtas committee on children and youth affairs. tackling childhood obesity.* Available from: https://data.oireachtas.ie/ie/ oireachtas/committee/dail/32/joint_committee_on_children_and_youth_affairs/ submissions/2018/2018-08-22_submission-st-angela-s-college-sligo_en.pdf.

State Examinations Commission [SEC], 2019. *Junior certificate statistics.* Available from: www.examinations.ie/statistics/ [Accessed 12 September 2021].

State Examinations Commission [SEC], 2022a. *Junior certificate statistics.* Available from: https://www.accs.ie/state-examinations-2022 [Accessed 12 September 2021].

State Examinations Commission [SEC], 2022b. *Junior cycle Home Economics: Food literacy skills examination 2022* [online]. Available from: https://www.examinations.ie/misc-doc/IR-EX-77447066.pdf [Accessed 12 September 2021].

Stitt, S., Jepson, M., Paulson-Box, E., and Prisk, E., 1997. Schooling for capitalism: cooking and the national curriculum. *In*: B. M. Köhler, E. Feichtinger, E. Barlösius, and E. Dowler, eds. *Poverty and food in welfare societies*. Berlin: WZB, 363–374.

Tikkanen, L., Pyhältö, K., Soini, T., and Pietarinen, J., 2017. Primary determinants of a large-scale curriculum reform National board administrators' perspectives. *Journal of Educational Administration*, 55 (6), 702–716.

Turkki, K., 2012. Home Economics: a forum for global learning and responsible living. *In*: D. Pendergast, S. McGregor, and K. Turkki. *Creating Home Economics futures: the next 100 years*. Brisbane: Australian Academic Press, 38–51.

Upton, P., Taylor, C., and Upton, D., 2015. The effects of the Food Dudes Programme on children's intake of unhealthy foods at lunchtime. *Perspect Public Health*, 135 (3), 152–159.

Utter, J., Larson, N., Laska, M. N., Winkler, M., and Neumark-Sztainer, D., 2018. Self-perceived cooking skills in emerging adulthood predict better dietary behaviors and intake 10 Years Later: a Longitudinal study. *Journal of Nutrition Education & Behavior*, 50 (5), 494–500.

Wolfson, J. A., and Bleich, S. N., 2015. Is cooking at home associated with better diet quality or weight-loss intention? *Public Health Nutrition* [online], 18 (8). Available from: doi:10.1017/S1368980014001943.

Wolfson, J. A., Frattaroli, S., Bleich, S. N., Smith, K. C., and Teret, S. P., 2017. Perspectives on learning to cook and public support for cooking education policies in the United States: a mixed methods study. *Appetite* [online], 108, 226–237. Available from: https://doi.org/10.1016/j.appet.2016.10.004.

Worsley, A., Wang, W. C., Yeatman, H., Byrne, S., and Wijayaratne, P., 2015. Does school health and home economics education influence adults' food knowledge? *Health Promotion International* [online], 31 (4). Available from: https://doi.org/10.1093/heapro/dav078.

8

FOOD TECHNOLOGY AND 21ST CENTURY LEARNING

Deborah Trevallion

Introduction

This chapter explores the strengths and weaknesses of teaching current Food Technology in Australian, specifically New South Wales (NSW), Stage 6 Food Technology (FT) 2021 syllabus which is offered for students to study in their final two years of senior schooling at age approximately 17 years and its applications for students' life after school. The analysis and a justification of Food Technology's mandatory inclusion in the secondary school curriculum and its inclusion in the Higher School Certificate (HSC) or the matriculation curriculum will be highlighted through its links to students' lifelong learning, whether that path be at university, Technical and Further Education (TAFE), in the workplace or in the home. An explanation of how its overlap and connections with other syllabus subjects strengthen and reinforce essential skills used in 21st century learning is included as well as a synthesis of suggestions for future directions of Food Technology in secondary education is discussed.

Historical development of Food Technology in Australia

The Food Technology curriculum has evolved over time to coincide with the world we live in and the needs of its people. In 1910, Food Technology was a part of a subject called Domestic Science, here the course reflected the society and cultural values of the time, with content such as how to be a good wife and mother, how to cook and sew (Suttor 1982, pp.12–14) being a major part of its focus. Every girl in school studied it as a mandatory subject that taught them how to be, what was seen as, a good wife and mother.

During the 1950s, the newly named, Home Economics syllabus was composed of Home Science and Textiles reflected a stronger science base that aimed to

DOI: 10.4324/9781003294962-10

question the 'why' rather than undertake the 'how to' undertake these processes. There was a minor move away from making and towards experimentation. This made the course more scientific and aimed at a move away from a sexist subject. It was hoped to making it acceptable for males. It was falsely believed that making it more scientific would increase the number of males who studied the subject. Whilst there was an increase in males studying the subject, even today it is rare to have a Food Technology class that is dominated by male students.

In 1991, the NSW Technology Education curriculum moved even further away from a skill-based, 'lockstep' curriculum to a technology curriculum focusing on problem solving and critical thinking (Howard and Mozejko 2015; Turner and Seemann 2006; Walmsley 2008). This focus on problem solving and critical thinking is what characterises the current Technology curriculum, including the current Stage 4 Technology Mandatory and the Stage 5 Food Technology 7–10 (2021) syllabi.

Stage 6 Food Technology syllabus, NSW, Australia

The 28-page Stage 6 Food Technology syllabus in NSW, Australia is an online document accessed by thousands of schools and their teachers. It is used to develop student understandings and assist them in preparation for their final matriculation exam called the HSC as well as the world around them. At first glance, this document can be quite confusing and overwhelming, but as you analyse it closer, you are able to discern that it is structured and organised in an orderly manner that allows the reader to easily locate information. This syllabus focuses on the provision and consumption of food are significant activities of human endeavour, with vast resources being expended across domestic, commercial and industrial settings.

The current (2021) Food Technology Stage 6 syllabus, the Year 11 Food Technology syllabus covers fundamental topics including core strands in the Preliminary Course titled 'Food Availability', 'Food Selection', 'Food Quality' and 'Nutrition' (Stage 6 Food Technology Syllabus NESA 2021).

> The Preliminary course will develop knowledge and understanding about food nutrients and diets for optimum nutrition, the functional properties of food, safe preparation, presentation and storage of food, sensory characteristics of food, the influences on food availability and factors affecting food selection. Practical skills in planning, preparing and presenting food are integrated throughout the content areas.
>
> *(Stage 6 Food Technology Syllabus, NESA 2021).*

Once students have reached their final year of school the students showcase some of their previously learnt topics into practice and go further in depth in topics including 'The Australian Food Industry', 'Food Product Development',

'Contemporary Nutrition Issues' and 'Food Manufacture' (Stage 6 Food Technology Syllabus 2021). These components aim to develop and enhance students' knowledge surrounding skills and abilities, regarding making informed decisions about food and food systems.

> The HSC course involves the study of: sectors, aspects, policies and legislations of the Australian Food Industry; production, processing, preserving, packaging, storage and distribution of food; factors impacting, reasons, types, steps and marketing of food product development; nutrition incorporating diet and health in Australia and influences on nutritional status.
>
> *(Stage 6 Food Technology Syllabus [NESA] 2021)*

Within the topic 'The Australian Food Industry', students develop an in-depth understanding about what goes on within the workings of the Australian food industry. Other parts of the syllabus, such as Food Product Development, enhance students' knowledge of the Australian food industry by assisting them in studying the market, as well as environmental, and technological aspects that the Food Technology syllabus can investigate. The practical skills that students will learn in the focus areas of planning, creating, testing and experimenting, manufacturing, packaging and labelling and evaluating food items that are incorporated throughout the course: *Practical experiences in developing, preparing, experimenting and presenting food are integrated throughout the course* (Stage 6 Food Technology Syllabus [NESA] 2021).

The current Stage 6 Syllabus, first published in 2003, was first modified in 2009, altered in 2013, and edited again in 2021 but only the assessments were altered. Further analysis of this syllabus shows that the syllabus requires major revision if it is to cater for 21st century learners.

Strengthening Food Technology for 21st century learners

This section of the paper will suggest improvements to make relevant the current Stage 6 syllabus to the 21st century learner. Perhaps it is time for change? Whilst the Stage 6 Syllabus covers a variety of food-related themes, it is a critical document for students to fully understand the depth of food technology and how it can be applied to their lives. However, like any evolving learning guide, it excels in studying certain topics but obvious flaws can be found in the syllabus.

The aim of all Food Technology syllabus is seen in the rationale (Board of Studies 2021). The rationale refers to the correlation between human endeavour, significant food knowledge and issues that are relevant to both an individual's professional and personal life (Owen 2020). It must justify each topic in the syllabus by explaining that food issues have a constant relevance to life. This concept underpins the subject and is reflected throughout the course where critical thinking and problem solving are used as the preferred pedagogy in the classroom.

The Food Technology syllabus rationale provides students with broad understandings related to Food Technology including:

> The factors that influence food availability and selection are examined and current food consumption patterns in Australia investigated. Food handling is addressed with emphasis on ensuring safety and managing the sensory characteristics and functional properties of food to produce a quality product. The role of nutrition in contributing to the health of the individual and the social and economic future of Australia is explored. The structure of the Australian food industry is outlined and the operations of one organisation investigated. Production and processing practices are examined and their impact evaluated. The activities that support food product development are identified and the process applied in the development of a food product. Contemporary nutrition issues are raised, investigated and debated.
>
> *(Stage 6 Food Technology Syllabus [NESA] 2021, p.8)*

This knowledge enables students to make informed responses to changes in the production-to-consumption continuum and exert an influence on future developments in the food industry as educated citizens and in their future careers. Opportunities exist for students to develop skills relating to food that are relevant and transferable to other settings. The strengths of the Stage 6 Food Technology deliver broad concepts with specific understandings and a wide and diverse range of practical skills, allowing students to gain confidence and skills in food handling, product design and production and transferable skills like communicating with colleagues and critical thinking. The strengths of the Stage 6 Food Technology syllabus are many and give students a broad understanding of food including but not limited to food relationships and the environment. It is these relationships between the syllabus topics that will build deep understandings and higher-order thinking skills. Spady (2005) reminds us that "Whatever one learns becomes a new resource for living".

Food relationships involve building understandings surrounding how students relate to food and this is supported by options for exploring food in relevant contexts such as trends, demand, sectors and global agriculture. This bodes well for students as they build more complex links, for example, when purchasing food, they can successfully evaluate its origins, sustainability, nutritional knowledge and societal influences which may develop in the individual an educated social understanding which may result in food choice interventions and a healthy choice of foods.

A topic covering 'current food trends' needs to be synthesised for inclusion. The topic, 'developing new food products' with enhanced health properties, is a suitable topic for 21st century learners because it is based on problem solving and builds creativity. It is imperative that modern biotechnological techniques be integrated into the syllabus as these techniques are used to improve traditional processing procedures to upgrade their production methods (Mishra et al. 2018). With the food industry constantly evolving, the teaching of Food Technology should be open enough to allow the inclusion of new content to better suit the world we live in today and better pedagogy that is based on problem solving and uses higher-order thinking skills.

The current Food Technology syllabus highlights extensive knowledge of nutrition and more specifically relating to Food Technology is how individuals can interpret and comprehend food labelling. Rutland (2020b) expresses the importance of teaching students useful information regarding nutrition, to ensure they can use those skills to make good choices surrounding food and allow them to live healthy lives. The Dietary Guidelines also promote the importance of Australia's youth knowing the correct information surrounding nutrition to allow them to make decisions about their own health (Health and Council 2013).

An understanding surrounding food industries and food processing applications will reduce the student risk of food poisoning, malnutrition and ingredient contamination as the mindfulness associated with consuming good choice, safe and healthy food creates student–buyer awareness and responsible consumer behaviour. Environmental considerations linked to contemporary nutrition build upon understandings supporting personal and societal health, which builds an awareness of the environmental effects on food products. This is important because, again, it allows individuals to make informed decisions about the food they consume. Justifying and understanding processes allow individuals to maintain food integrity when making decisions about food selection.

Developing an understanding of the Food Legislation together with government policies, marketing and food production development (NSW Education Standards Authority Food Technology 2021a) is important to know if students are to create new products for consumers. Food Technology itself is a creative and adaptive syllabus allowing teachers to add elements illustrated where the student is expected to emulate industry processes when creating and producing new food products for the food market. Here, students research syllabus ideas on legislation, manufacturing and nutrition (NSW Education Standards Authority Food Technology 2021a) which are foundations to build upon students' understandings of the Australian Food Industry.

Due to current changes in the Australian population and their social and cultural influences, Food Technology is ever-evolving and changing this is evident in syllabus updates which encompass the global migration of cultural groups and the use of foods native to Australia. Malakellis (2017) demonstrates that this shows a relationship in relevance to key learning aspects as the syllabus incorporates content such as influences on food availability and factors affecting food selection. Subsequently, allowing students to develop an understanding of the impact culture and socio-economic changes has on food selection.

Titus et al. (2020), convey the importance of students developing knowledge and understanding about the food they consume, its impact on the body for health purposes and its greater impact on society and the economy. A strength of the Stage 6 Food Technology syllabus is its ability to educate students on the importance of food availability. Currently the Australian Food and Grocery Council (2020) calculate that Australia is classed as a 'highly food secure' country; however, this can easily change depending on the economy, the impact of the pandemic or climate change. Continuing to educate students on food availability and how to maintain this is significantly important as this will ensure that the next generation of food consumers, will be educated with deep understandings and strong opinions which will allow them to problem solve ensuring Australian society maintains its 'highly food secure' due to the ongoing education of food availability (Rutland 2020c). This syllabus provides not only foundational learning, but also rigorous knowledge which can be applied to ongoing lifelong learning.

Suggested additions for 21st century learning

The opportunity exists to create improvements in Food Technology syllabi. With frequent changes occurring relating to eating habits, new dietary and nutritional understandings, malnutrition of the population, changing cultural impact, the use of food molecular gastronomy and the advancement of technologies used in the food and agricultural industries, there is a need to implement more frequent syllabus updates, pedagogical suggestions and provide teacher professional development opportunities in the areas related to food technological advancements.

Regular, relevant updates to the Food Technology syllabus can have a real impact on Australian society, combating the increasing case of adolescent obesity (Malakellis et al. 2017) by providing the latest knowledge on how students can change their diet for the better by making the healthiest food choices. If Food Technology was a mandatory secondary school subject to be studied by all children, it would impact the country's economy in a positive way. Food Technology was removed as a mandatory subject from the Australian curriculum in 1991. At that time the incidence of obesity in Australian teenagers increased. Whilst there are a number of factors that are associated with the increasing adolescent obesity rate such as the need for two parents to work if they wish to 'keep up with the Jones', additional money to spend on food, the marketing and distribution of quick take away and eat in food restaurants like MacDonald's and KFC, the increased consumption of sugar-laden sodas such as Coke and Pepsi and the sedentary lifestyle of the masses, one must wonder if it is time to educate our children on how to select, create and prepare, consume, problem solve and evaluate healthy diet choices and what the impact will be on their health and lifestyle choices and the Australian economy.

The entirety of the Food Technology syllabus is of great importance and covers a wide range of content relevant to contemporary learners; however, the method of delivery of the content often lacks problem solving and active learning time. Dr. Angela Turner's 2007 study aimed at clarifying what Food Technology is, examined two groups with different versions of it. The results clearly identified an issue within the syllabus, as it exhibited different interpretations of how an educator conducted their education, which ultimately lead to varying student levels of knowledge. The greater point of concern to take away from this study, however, "is that the subject has not evolved due to the curriculum writers and teacher's historically acculturated view of the subject" (Turner 2007).

The syllabus is inclusive of the needs, interests and aspirations of both genders and provides opportunities and challenges for students of all abilities to deal with food products and systems. In order to be a relevant and meaningful learning experience, which fully extends students' understanding and application of Food Technology, programs developed from this syllabus must take into consideration the life experiences, values, learning styles and characteristics of both male and female students. Sadly, in spite of many attempts to create a Food Technology syllabus that appeals to both male and female students, Food Technology remains a female-dominated subject choice. This is evident in the NSW HSC matriculation statics of completion which show that in 2020, 71% of students studying the Stage 6 Food Technology course are females (HSC Enrolment 2021; NSW Education Standards Authority 2021a). This demonstrates a significant gender dominance within the subject, therefore creating a gap between education and possibly eventually the health of females and males (Turner and Wilks 2018). This could be overcome if the subject was mandatory for all secondary school students with a STEM-based approach.

During the recommended updates to a mandatory Food Technology course, perhaps topics that appeals and is acceptable to both females and males could be included, a topic such as molecular gastronomy which science-driven, using role models such as Mr Heston Blumenthal with his lickable wallpaper and such make the success of males in the career field obvious. Adding food psychology as a topic would be a necessity as the latest weight-reducing programs, such as Noom, rely heavily on daily psychology readings and interactions to explain why people eat, for example, boredom, habit, guilt, emotional eating, sadness and then teach them with individual coaches and group sessions how to overcome their eating issues. Including food psychology as a topic to be covered in the mandatory course may also help in overcoming the number of male psychologists in Australia where, currently, only one in five practicing psychologists are male.

21st century learning with Food Technology pedagogues

The entirety of the Stage 6 Food Technology syllabus is of great importance and covers a wide range of content relevant to contemporary learners; however, the method of delivery of the content often lacks problem solving and active learning time. Dr Turner's 2007 study aimed at clarifying what Food Technology is, examined two groups with different versions of it. The results clearly identified an issue within the syllabus, as it exhibited different interpretations of how an educator conducted their education, which ultimately lead to varying student levels of knowledge. The greater point of concern to take away from this study, however, "is that the subject has not evolved due to the curriculum writers and teacher's historically acculturated view of the subject" (Turner 2007). Furthermore, as this study demonstrates, disparity amongst educators is prevalent and the students are left to suffer at the mercy of whomever the educator is that year, and their representation of the current syllabus. Thus, a call to restructure the Stage 6 Syllabus would not only benefit students, but also the educators. The move in content delivery away from a didactic approach to learning, to an active problem-solving approach that allows an appreciation of links between syllabus topics takes time to implement but is a must for 21st century learners.

It is suggested by Lopa et al. (2018) that increasing the active learning time within a food education classroom will enhance students' motivation and engagement surrounding food. This active learning does not simply involve cooking, it includes primary research, testing, experimentation, creation of new food products. Skills taught include the ability to research, analyse and communicate. Students also develop the capability and competence to experiment with and prepare food as well as design, implement and evaluate solutions to a range of food situations.

Dewey (1947), explains that 'personal growth occurs when people are confronted with substantive, real-world problems to solve' such as a global or the global use of genetically modified food sources. This is vital to ensure that students and more broadly the next generation maintain studying and critically thinking about food. The students studying the Food Technology syllabus must gain both practical or problem solving or active and theoretical knowledge and skills as the Stage 6 Food Technology syllabus covers food production, packaging and preparation. This is in addition to a practical investigation into a range of factors affecting the diet, nutrition and health of individuals or family members that make the syllabus relevant to students (NSW Education Standards Authority 2021b).

This active learning can be also increased in the Food Technology classroom by increasing students' physical interactions with food products and other areas such as food storage. Although the syllabus includes and makes relationships between relevant and important concepts, the way it is delivered in the classroom will contribute to a greater degree to the students' understanding. Their understandings are deeper through the promotion of active, problem-solving learning that builds connections between syllabus topics. This will better suit the learning style, the needs and future opportunities of 21st century, contemporary learners.

There are syllabus weaknesses, the extensive amount of content required for students to consume — it's too much for students to comprehend. The Food Technology syllabus needs to be rewritten to allow enough time for developing deep understandings in the appropriate learning environment. It should include field trips, adequate in-class experiences, testing, experimentation and problem-solving tasks rather than creating a theory-driven environment that is essentially unengaging. The syllabus must note that it is up to the teacher to make it relevant and relatable in a social real-life context (relatable to Goddard's social cognitive theory).

Relationships with other syllabi

The NSW Education Standards Authority syllabi evolve around ensuring students receive an adequate understanding of that specific subject and often this content can overlap. When analysing the Food Technology and other Stage 6 syllabi, one can identify that there are areas of overlap; this allows students to develop a deeper understanding of the topics in Food Technology through using repetition and application in new contexts and the forming of relationships and links to other subject areas will further develop and deepen skills and knowledge. The syllabus overlaps with other subjects and lends opportunities to create cross-curricular rich tasks. For example, Food Technology, Hospitality, PDHPE, Science and STEM build student confidence across curriculum syllabus (Malakellis et al. 2017).

The overlap with other subjects such as PDHPE, Science, STEM and Hospitality strengthens and reinforces the life skills and academic content of the FT subject. Below is an analysis of some current overlaps in HSC subjects. PDHPE focuses on a concept called nutrition whilst food service skills are taught in hospitality and science develops understandings in chemicals and toxicity in foods. Some of these concepts tend to overlap with Food Technology (NSW Education Standards Authority 2021b, 2021c). This could be used as an opportunity to promote an existing Food Technology syllabus which is derived from a technological focal point where design and creative thinking are at the forefront. The 21st century learner requires these skills to be successful within the current climate of the industry.

PDHPE and Food Technology allow teachers to possibly teach similar content at the same time via cross curricular applications. This is evident in overlapping and similar content. For example, Food Nutrition in Food Technology and explanations of how nutrition affects recovery in PDHPE along with Food Technology's contemporary nutrition issues and PDHPE improving health (NSW Education Authority Food Technology 2021b, 2021c) would allow the overlap to ensure deep cross curricular understandings. Another topic focused on during Year 11 in the PDHPE syllabus is 'Better Health for Individuals' this overlaps with a Food Technology topic 'Food Availability and Selection' which describes how a variety of factors influence an individual's health. This overlapping content would be a great opportunity for the two subjects to integrate and potentially allow students to strengthen and enhance their knowledge and understanding, while providing the perspective from each independent subject.

Hospitality and Food Technology are subjects that complement each other but have very different content. They also have syllabus overlap. In hospitality students must use the hygienic practices for food safety unit of competency overlaps with FT in Hazard analysis and critical control points (HACCAP) and basis of all food safety procedures (NSW Education Standards Authority 2019, 2021b). These common skills are important to HSC students as they enter the workforce during their final school years with the casual hospitality industry. Food Technology students are well equipped from a theoretical perspective, but when the discussion about preparing for the workplace starts, students frequently choose Hospitality (Turner 2007).

The distinguishable difference between the two subjects, if not chosen together, can leave student's with only 50% of the answer when it comes to pursuing a career within the industry. Food Technology offers a strong perspective into the science of food, nutrition, the Food Industry and issues whereas, Hospitality is gleaned from nationally accredited TAFE content with a practical skill-based focus (Trevallion 2020). Ultimately, Food Technology can provide after-school work and real-world opportunities, but that field is becoming narrow and specific to a theory-based environment. With greater application on combining the practicality of Hospitality, with Food Technology, or at least the encouragement to take up both, our students will be less limited to their field, and more diverse career opportunities will present themselves. This again affirms the necessary action of restructuring and/or potentially partnering these two subjects within the syllabus.

Within Science and Food Technology students must work within the 'working scientifically' framework, which has a technology-based learning practice. Working scientifically prepares students for problem solving and development of ideas and projects post-HSC. This knowledge and understanding is the basis of all technology subjects, and its links to planning, investigation, data, problem solving and communication all relate back to how Food Technology students design and develop projects and tasks.

Learning across the curriculum, including Science, technology, engineering and mathematics (STEM) education is something which is supported by the HSC and doesn't stop at those courses previously mentioned. Indigenous education in schools and appropriate pedagogy is also being taught cross curricular to enhance students' knowledge about indigenous ingredients and educate them on the food safety and customs which surround them in their local area (Gumbo 2020).

Students are given the opportunity to deepen their understanding within their chosen field if they are interested in a future in technology by utilising these cross-curricular subject areas. It also helps teachers in bridging the gap in their key subject areas and promotes teacher development and training (Saunders 2020). As with all project-based subjects, technology, and creativity and both essential skills in the 21st century, and enough time must be devoted to these subjects so the students' skills can evolve with the world (Cusanelli 2020).

Lifelong learning

As students enter senior school, selecting Stage 6 courses to study comes with the responsibility of choosing subjects that may shape their future careers and life after high school. Arguably, one of the greatest areas to develop adult knowledge revolves around food, however, few must consider how Food Technology prepares our students for when schooling is over. The knowledge, skills and attitudes gained during the course will have applications to, and provide benefits for, both vocational and general life experiences.

The inclusion of Food Technology in the NSW HSC, the matriculation certificate is important as is making it a mandatory subject for all students early in secondary school education. The focus on lifelong learning is gained through a knowledge of and understanding the importance of how food promotes health, safety and how the relationship we have with nutrition is essential to living (Slatter 2020). This vital knowledge and content need to be taught to students as it adequately prepares them for life beyond school.

Food technology Stage 6 syllabus is abundant in content which is relevant to contemporary learning and life after school with the content learnt (NSW Education Authority Food Technology 2021b). The Stage 6 Food Technology syllabus holds an abundance of vital information that will strengthen students' knowledge to allow them to extend careers into such sectors as food scientist and the ever-evolving technology surrounding food. Important strands that are directly related to these careers include food product development and food manufacture. Within these syllabus points students learn of the importance of how foods are developed and manufactured. Often advanced technologies are included to show how they are used within production. These provide an opportunity to gain employment outside school using some of the basic knowledge they have learnt (Gottfried and Sublett 2018). This is evident in many entry-level jobs within hospitality requiring a very basic knowledge of food quality in order to gain a position.

Food Technology has a long-term impact on students' after they graduate from high school, since it can help them choose a professional career route such as food manufacturing, food product development, or even the hospitality business. Unlike the commercial food industry on trade entry, a student who is interested in pursuing a career as a food technologist will need to have completed the HSC for entry requirements to university. This can lead to opportunities in University and TAFE such as becoming a Food Technology teacher, a nutritionist, or earning a degree in Food Science and Human Nutrition, which can lead to other opportunities such as Health Promotion Officer, Community Health, and many other exciting careers.

In addition to this many first-year nutrition courses offered at university too follow along with Stage 6 content therefore giving students background knowledge to succeed (Turner and Wilks 2018). Overall the syllabus provides students with skills that will benefit them not only in school but after school as well. Food Technology is a school subject that needs to be advocated for, as this subject can open up lifelong career options for students who are interested in taking their learning that one step further, and also in helping to educate students about the role that Food Technology plays in our daily life.

Stage 6 Food Technology adequately equips students with the skills to succeed in various paths they choose after school. This can include further tertiary studies,

TAFE, a cooking-related occupation, or just general life skills. The Stage 6 Food Technology outcomes are recognised by TAFE NSW and often see students' HSC results to be transferred directly as credits, into their chosen course. Recognition like this allows students to have even more to work for during their HSC, as they know the benefits of achieving high. Furthermore, many of the skills learnt within HSC Food Technology can be directly used in students' day-to-day lives. For instance, understanding the current contemporary food issues within society will allow students to make informative choices when purchasing and using food products. Another impact that Food Technology instils into students is their ability to understand and handle food quality. This is important in career paths in the hospitality industry as students enter the field with an established knowledge of this content.

With all things considered, this subject will generate a greater path in helping our students achieve success when their schooling finishes. "The great chefs of the world do not use their amazing skills to emulate food production, they research, test, experiment and use their highly developed skills to create products that distinguish them from the norm" (Trevallion 2020).

Future directions

Food Technology (FT) within the Stage 6 syllabus can be deeply debated with regard to its relevance and contribution to Stage 6 learning for students in their final years of schooling and the preparation it provides students for life after school. The syllabus needs to be continually updated as it has always been influenced by socio-economic, political and educational perspectives over the years. Therefore, it needs to be further updated to meet the demands of students and teachers so as to create better opportunities in prospective studies and careers.

The Food Technology (2019) syllabus needs to reflect the changing needs, technologies and lifestyle of the Australian people. While it prepares students for food-related workplaces, it doesn't achieve its title of being characterised by technology. Twenty-first century learners are immersed in and influenced by technology and social media, and within that, food trends, on-display body image, and nutrition have become a focus. This has resulted in a resurgence and a passion to attain knowledge surrounding food. The same nutritional content and issues are evident in the syllabus. There are career pathways as online nutrition coaches, food bloggers, influencers and web content creators that can be established using this syllabus knowledge.

The knowledge obtained from within the Food Technology syllabus paves the way for further education at university and tertiary institutions, by laying fundamental knowledge on the above-mentioned core strands. The continuum of learning for Food Technology students extends past the individual subject, reinforcing the core skills needed to be successful thinkers in the workforce today. The syllabus supports HSC students to become lifelong learners regardless of their post-school path, and the inclusion of overlaps in other subjects reinforces those skills.

Food Technology sits in a multifaceted position where it has a unique opportunity to deepen understanding by building links with other Stage 6 syllabi. This allows the syllabus to develop greater holistic technological understandings. Sitting under the umbrella of the Technology Education curriculum, this subject' should be characterised by the importance of technological activity, including problem solving, design thinking and volition in human development (McLain et al. 2019). Food Technology should still promote and allow the fundamental skills of experiential food practices to be developed, through problem solving and design thinking.

Morrison-Love (2017) explains that the heart of pedagogy and curriculum in Food Technology is the transformation of food resources into objects to shape our environment where conceptual and procedural knowledge are in a symbiotic, non-dualistic, relationship with thinking (head) and action (hand) work together – knowledge for action (Kimbell 1996). This symbiotic relationship surrounding Food Technology contributes to the building of passion, deep knowledge, deep understandings and real-world applications throughout individuals' life where lifelong learning becomes the norm rather than the exception.

In conclusion

The importance of studying Food Technology should not be underestimated. Studying Food Technology is of such importance to society that it should be a mandatory secondary school subject. If studied by all Australian children, it would have a strong impact on both the Australian people and the Australian economy in a positive way. It could improve the wellbeing of Australians in relation to food choices, body image, health and well-being as they select, create and prepare, consume and evaluate healthy food and exercise choices. As Australians move towards becoming a health-conscious nation, the number of diet-related diseases will decrease, reducing the health and medical costs that are a significant part of the Australian economy.

With the food industry constantly evolving, the Food Technology syllabus should be frequently revised to reflect the changing Australian culture, people, technology, needs and Trends. It must be kept open enough to allow the inclusion of new content to better suit the world we live in today. This way the Stage 6 Food Technology syllabus will remain highly appropriate and relevant for contemporary learners. The Food Technology syllabus provides students with relevant information and knowledge to take into the skills acquired during Stage 6 Food Technology significantly prepare students for life after school be that at TAFE, university, everyday living and life-long careers.

The Stage 6 Food Technology demonstrates appropriate content for contemporary learners but relationships between syllabus topics, to real-life applications and the links to other subjects and real life must be made clear using pedagogies that involve higher-order thinking, creativity, problem-based learning as this will promote critical thinking, an essential 21st century skill.

Food Technology is an ingredient to the creation of educated young adults who possess the essential basic knowledge required to enter the workforce and wisely choose a nutritional lifestyle. Succi and Canovi (2020) have found that students with previously developed skills are also more likely to gain employment after their completion of school, studying Stage 6 Food Technology significantly prepares contemporary learners for their lives after school.

The Stage 6 Food Technology strengths and applications for student life allow students to gain confidence, passion and skills related to a healthy life-style and transferrable lifelong skills like communication, problem solving and critical thinking. The Stage 6 Food Technology syllabus strengths are many and varied, they give students a broad understanding of food and its relation-ships. With the knowledge, skills and attitudes gained through the study of this syllabus, and an understanding of the relationships between the syllabus topics young men and women will have the potential to build deep understandings and higher-order thinking skills that are needed to contribute positively to their own future and to the social, economic and ecological future of Australia in the 21st century.

References

Australian Food and Grocery Council, 2020. *No need to panic, Australia produces enough food for 75 million* [online]. Available from: https://www.afgc.org.au/news-and-media/2020/06/no-need-to-panic-australia-produces-enough-food-for-75-million [Accessed 31 May 2022].

Australian Government. *Bullseye Career Information: School Subjects you like and jobs they can lead to* [online]. Available from: https://cica.org.au/wp-content/uploads/Bullseye-Career-Information-Booklet-2013.pdf [Accessed 31 May 2022].

Board of Studies NSW, 2021. *Personal development, health and physical education: stage 6 syllabus* [online]. Available from: https://educationstandards.nsw.edu.au/wps/portal/nesa/11-12/stage-6-learning-areas/pdhpe/pdhpe-syllabus [Accessed 31 May 2022].

Cusanelli, L. and Trevallion, D., 2020. Using technology for productive, creative pur-pose. *International Journal of Innovation, Creativity and Change* [online], 13 (1). Available from: https://www.ijicc.net/images/vol_13/13100_Cusanelli_2020_E_R.pdf.

Dewey, J., 1947. Some stages of logical growth. In: J. Boydston, 1976 ed. *The collected works of John Dewey: Vol 1. The middle works.* Carbondale: Southern Illinois University Press, 151–174.

Downs, S., Ahmed, S., Fanzo, J., and Herforth, A., 2020. Food environment typol-ogy: advancing an expended definition, framework, and methodological approach for improved characterization and wild, cultivated, and built food environments toward sustainable diets. *Foods* [online], 9 (4). Available from: https://www.mdpi.com/2304-8158/9/4/532.

Gottfried, M. A., and Sublett, C., 2018. Does applied STEM course taking link to STEM outcomes for high school students with learning disabilities? *Journal of Learning Disabilities* [online], 51 (3). Available from: https://doi.org/10.1177/0022219417690356.

Gumbo, M., 2020. Teaching food technology in a secondary technology education classroom: exploring ideas in Indigenous contexts. *In:* M. Rutland and A. Turner, eds. *Food education and food technology in school curricula: international perspectives.* Cham, Switzerland: Springer, 283–297.

Howard, S., Mozejko, A. 2015. *Teachers, technology, change and resistance.* Cambridge, UK: Cambridge University Press.

Kimbell, J., 1996, The APU design and technology model in Blomm, N., 2015. Extended Information Processing of technology education during the early phases of the design process. Thesis for masters on ResearchGate.net.

Lopa, J., Elsayed, Y., and Wray, M., 2018. The state of active learning in the hospitality classroom. *Journal of Hospitality and Tourism Education* [online], 30 (2). Available from: https://doi.org/10.1080/10963758.2018.1436971.

Malakellis, M., Hoare, E., Sanigorski, A., Crooks, N., Allender, S., Nichols, M., Swinburn, B., Chikwendu, C., Kelly, P. M., Petersen, S., and Millar, L., 2017. School-based systems change for obesity prevention in adolescents: outcomes of the Australian capital territory 'It's your move!'. *Australian and New Zealand Journal of Public Health*, 41 (5). Available from: https://doi.org/10.1111/1753-6405.12696.

McLain, M., Irving, D., Wooff, D., and Morrison-Love, D., 2019. Humanising the design and technology curriculum: why technology education makes us human. *Design and Technology Education: An International Journal* [online], 24 (2). Available from: https://ojs.lboro.ac.uk/DATE/article/view/2610/2806 [Accessed 31 May 2022].

Middleton, M., and Curwood, J. S., 2020. A brave new world: teachers' conception of the value of creativity in the new stage 6 English syllabus. *The Australian Journal of Language and Literacy* [online], 43 (2). Available from: http://www.jenscottcurwood.com/wp-content/uploads/2020/09/Middleton-and-Curwood-Teachers-Conceptions-of-the-Value-of-Creativity.pdf.

Mishra, P. M., Mishra, R. R., Yadava, A., and Mishra, R. S., eds., 2018. *Food technology: from health to wealth and future challenges.* New Delhi, India: Bharti Publications.

Morrison-Love, D., 2017. Towards a transformative epistemology of technology education. *Journal of Philosophy of Education*, 51 (1), 23–37.

National Health and Medical Research Council, 2013. *Australian Dietary Guidelines* [online]. Available from: https://www.eatforhealth.gov.au/sites/default/files/files/the_guidelines/n55_australian_dietary_guidelines.pdf.

NSW Education Standards Authority, 2021a. 2021 HSC enrolments by course. Available from: https://educationstandards.nsw.edu.au/wps/portal/nesa/11-12/hsc/about-HSC/HSC-facts-figures/HSC-course-enrolments.

NSW Education Standards Authority, 2021b. *Stage 6 Food Technology Syllabus (2013)* [online]. Available from: https://educationstandards.nsw.edu.au/wps/portal/nesa/11-12/stage-6-learning-areas/tas/food-technology-syllabus [Accessed 22 June 2022].

NSW Education Standards Authority, 2021c. *Personal development, health and physical education stage 6 syllabus (2012)* [online]. Available from: https://educationstandards.nsw.edu.au/wps/portal/nesa/11-12/stage-6-learning-areas/pdhpe/pdhpe-syllabus.

NSW Education Standards Authority, 2022. *Hospitality curriculum framework stage 6 syllabus based on the SIT tourism, travel and hospitality training package (version 1.3) for implementation from 2019 updated April 2022* [online]. Available from: https://educationstandards.nsw.edu.au/wps/wcm/connect/e5ae5c51-1ce5-4cd2-b3e4-53a9a39a863d/hospitality-11-12-syllabus-based-on-sitv-1-3.pdf?MOD=AJPERES&CVID=.

Owen, D., 2020. Positive ingredients to redefining food education in schools in Australia. *In:* M. Rutland and A. Turner, eds. *Food education and food technology in school curricula: international perspectives.* Cham, Switzerland: Springer Nature, 139–153.

Parasecoli, F., 2017. Food, research, design: what can food studies bring to food design education? *International Journal of Food Design*, 2 (1), 15–25.

Rutland, M., 2020a. Food teaching in upper secondary English schools: progression into food-related undergraduate courses in higher education. *In:* M. Rutland and A. Turner, eds. *Food education and food technology in school curricula: international perspectives.* Cham, Switzerland: Springer Nature, 209–225.

Rutland, M., 2020b. Positive ingredients to redefining food education in schools in Australia. *In:* M. Rutland and A. Turner, eds. *Food education and food technology in school curricula: international perspectives.* Cham, Switzerland: Springer Nature, 139–153.

Rutland, M., 2020c. Current research in nutrition in the school curriculum in England. *In:* M. Rutland and A. Turner, eds. *Food education and food technology in school curricula: international perspectives.* Cham, Switzerland: Springer Nature, 229–243.

Saunders, C., 2020. Continuing professional development for secondary Food Technology Teachers in Australia. *In:* M. Rutland and A. Turner, eds. *Food education and food technology in school curricula: international perspectives.* Cham, Switzerland: Springer Nature, 195–209.

Slatter, W., 2020. A Technological Approach to secondary food education in New Zealand. *In:* M. Rutland and A. Turner, eds. *Food education and food technology in school curricula: international perspectives.* Cham, Switzerland: Springer Nature, 63–81.

Spady, W., 2005. OBE: Reform in search of a definition. *In:* R. Killen, ed. *Programming and assessment for quality teaching and learning.* Cham, Switzerland: Springer Nature, 5.

SRCOE pune, 2016. *Why practical knowledge is more important than theoretical knowledge?* [online]. Available from: https://medium.com/@srespune/why-practical-knowledge-is-more-important-than-theoretical-knowledge-f0f94ad6d9c6 [Accessed 31 May 2022].

Succi, C., and Magali Canovi, M., 2020. Soft skills to enhance graduate employability: comparing students and employers' perceptions. *Studies in Higher Education*, 45 (90), 1834–1847.

Suttor, J., McClintock, J., 1982 Action for social progress: the responsibilities of government and voluntary organisations, *Australian National Report: International Conference on Social Welfare*, Brighton, UK, August 26-September 4, 1982.

Titus, D., James, J. J. E., and Mohana Roopan, S., 2018. Importance of food science and technology- way to future. *In:* S. Roopan, and G. Madhumitha, eds. *Bioorganic phase in natural food: an overview.* Cham, Switzerland: Springer. Available from: https://doi.org/10.1007/978-3-319-74210-6_2.

Trevallion, D., 2020. Changing the professional identity of food technology teachers in Australia. *In:* M. Rutland and A. Turner, eds. *Food education and food technology in school curricula: international perspectives.* Cham, Switzerland: Springer Nature, 167–183.

Turner, A., 2013. The utility of technacy genre theory in technology education: a case study into food technology teaching. *In:* J. Williams and D. Gedera, eds. *27th annual pupils attitude toward technology conference*, 2–6 December 2013. Christchurch, New Zealand: Technology Education for the Future: A Play on Sustainability, 482–490.

Turner, A., 2020. Learning cultural, ecological and food literacies through the Gumbaynggirr Pathway of Knowledge Project. *In:* M. Rutland and A. Turner, eds. *International perspectives of food education in the school curriculum.* Cham, The Netherlands: Springer Nature, 297–317.

Turner, A., and Seemann, K., 2006. It's time to study values at the core of food technology education. *In:* H. Middleton, ed. *4th Biennial international technology educational research conference*, 5–9 December 2006. Surfers Paradise, Australia: Values in Technology Education: Griffith University, 201–220.

Turner, A., and Wilks, J., 2018. A place for food in Australian schools: a socio- historical review of food education. *International Journal of Technology and Design Education* [online], 28 (1). Available from: /link.springer.com/article/10.1007/s10798-016-9377-9.

Walmsley, D. J., 2008. The Work life balance: Perspectives on Lifestyle and Leisure, *Address to the Institute of Australian Geographers' Conference*, Hobart, July 2008.

Zaglas, W., 2019. *Food education boosted by new online resources for teachers* [online]. Available from: https://www.educationreview.com.au/2019/05/food-education-boosted-by-new-online-resources-for-teachers/.

PART III

Psychology of food

9
FOOD WASTE ISSUES OF UNIVERSAL INFANT FREE SCHOOL MEALS IN SOUTH-EAST ENGLAND SCHOOLS

A cautionary tale

Mark Stein and Yiannis Polychronakis

Introduction

This research provides an overview of the difficulties experienced by a group of schools in South East England which were selected to participate in this research because they were struggling to implement the Universal Infant Free School Meals (UIFSM) initiative. Evidence of this was indicated by the schools' low take-up of government-provided free meals.

An unintended consequence of the widening of access to free school meals was a large spike in school food waste. England's experience when UIFSM was introduced into schools in 2015 is a cautionary tale and important to share given recent decisions taken by other governments to introduce or widen access to free school meals.

In May 2021, the Scottish National Party government announced that it would proceed to introduce free school meals to all primary school children in Scotland, replacing the previous system whereby only children from the lowest income families were entitled to free school meals (Foad 2021). A similar policy was announced for Wales in December 2021 (Welsh Government 2021). Up to the present time only a few English councils provide free school meals to all primary school children. Elsewhere in Europe there are long-established free school meal policies in Sweden, Finland and Estonia. Other countries which have announced the introduction of free school meals are Norway and the Russian Federation (Europe-cities 2021; Magasin Maltid 2021). However, concerns were expressed during 2021 that widening access to free school meals in Scottish school dining rooms could lead to an increase in food waste. This would be particularly unwelcome at a time of financial stringency, exacerbated by the COVID pandemic (Nourish 2021).

DOI: 10.4324/9781003294962-12

In September 2013, the UK government announced that children aged 5 to 7 would receive free school meals from September 2014 and allocated over £1 billion of new funding to the UIFSM initiative during 2014 to 2016, including £150 million of capital funding for new kitchens. The initiative meant a very substantial increase in the volume of school meal production. English authorities implemented this initiative and Scottish and Welsh devolved governments followed suit. Schools in England with low lunch take-up received a grant of £4.8 million from the Department for Education to increase take-up in the 2,000 schools where this was lowest. The grant funded the Soil Association and Children's Food Trust (CFT) to employ catering advisers to visit schools to assess why children were refusing to eat school lunches and recommend changes. This chapter discusses what one of the authors, as an independent consultant, found during her visits to 30 schools in South East England between May and November 2015.

Methodology

This chapter draws on reports written by the second author as part of an advice project for school caterers, carried out by the CFT and funded by the Department for Education (UK). An unpublished conference paper presented at the International Food Systems conference at Harper Adams University in July 2016 summarised the reports. The information provided in this chapter is based on 30 schools that were involved in the advice project.

The consultant would visit the school and talk to kitchen staff, children and head teachers. She would taste the food and observe the kitchens, servery and dining rooms at meal times. Waste bins were also examined to assess which categories of food were discarded. She would evaluate key reasons behind food refusal by students in each school and produce written recommendations to schools on how best to reduce food waste and increase the uptake of free school meals. During school visits, data was collected from staff and students through informal discussions. Data was analysed through an inductive thematic approach that identified categories and themes.

Background literature

Food waste is a significant problem within school food systems, with high cost and environmental implications in terms of pollution, biodiversity and carbon emissions (García-Herrero et al. 2019; Malefors et al. 2022). Reducing food waste is one way in which the global food system can be kept within planetary boundaries that define a safe operating space for humanity (Springmann et al. 2018).

Factors which contribute to greater or lesser amounts of food waste in school meals are evidenced across various academic studies. For example,

Tuorila et al. (2015) report on a survey of Finnish school children's attitudes to school meals, describing which dishes students preferred. It was important that caterers evaluate children's perceptions of actual dishes so they could understand and predict children's perception of food in an authentic eating context. Caterers need to be aware of children rejecting unfamiliar foods, referred to as 'food neophobia', and find ways of encouraging children to try new culinary experiences.

The usefulness of cafeteria-based tasting programs for introducing fruit and vegetables to pupils has been demonstrated by several studies (Charlton et al. 2021; Lakkalula et al. 2010). In the USA there has been recent research highlighting the large amounts of food wasted in school lunch rooms after the implementation of the School Nutrition Program which required the provision of healthier foods that were not necessarily popular with pupils (Byker et al. 2014; Gase et al. 2014).

A focus group qualitative study undertaken in an English school by Day et al. (2015) revealed that pupil and staff perceptions about school meals included a desire for more menu variety particularly regarding vegetables and fruit. Additionally, the presence of teachers in the dining room improved children's eating behaviours. Hart (2016) examined pupil's perceptions of school food service in 20 Sheffield schools. Her research describes how dining hall organisation influenced what children ate:

> Occasionally supervisors were observed …encouraging individuals to eat more. Pupil monitors also helped to clear plates and in one school they were observed issuing stickers when pupils had eaten well, tried new foods and shown good manners. In many schools pupils were observed discarding vast amounts of food and this process was largely unsupervised.
>
> *(p.14)*

Moore et al. (2010) also acknowledged the important role of dining hall staff for encouraging children to eat the school meals. It is important to point out that the nature of the physical cafeteria environment may encourage or inhibit children's consumption of school meals (Gross et al. 2019; Lalli 2021). Day et al. (2015) questioned whether children who brought packed lunches to school should be segregated from those eating the school meals. Ensaff et al. (2018) concur that nutritional concerns have been raised regarding packed lunches. Parental support is critical for both the promotion of healthier school meals and improving the standards of lunch boxes provided by parents.

The Food for Life (FFL) Partnership promotes healthy and sustainable food in UK schools. It aims to teach children about healthy and sustainable food through such means as setting up school gardens and cookery classes and organising farm visits (Weitkamp et al. 2013). The FFL is expanded on in the following section.

Results and discussion

School site visits collected information regarding aspects of catering management and practice. For example:

1)   Catering service providers;
2)   School and caterer relationships;
3)   FFL Partnership and Catering Mark accreditation at the school (if any);
4)   Food waste;
5)   The dining environment such as:

- server layout
- noise
- equipment
- adult supervision
- seating arrangements

6)   Cookery and food growing activities for children;
7)   School communications with children and parents about school meals;
8)   Packed lunch policies.

Individual schools were coded as follows:
   Schools: SC1– SC30
   Local authorities: LA1– LA4
   Food service contractors: CON1– CON10

The FFL Catering Mark advocates healthy and sustainable food and it is awarded to catering organisations by the FFL Partnership if they meet certain criteria (Food For Life 2022). Seventeen out of the thirty schools (56.6%) had implemented the FFL Catering Mark, with eight of these (just under half) having excellent results that produced a menu acceptable to school staff, parents and pupils. However other schools encountered problems implementing the FFL menu.

Out of the three supplier categories, one school had brought catering in house, which worked well with no problems. Of the 11 schools who accessed local authority catering services, 7 (63.4%) experienced problematic relationships, and this arrangement only worked well at 4 schools. While 18 schools used food service contractors, 7 schools were happy with this service whereas 11 (61.1%) experienced problematic relationships.

School feedback on catering providers

In house catering

For the one school, who provided meals 'in house' the catering arrangement was highly successful. The school was happy with the suitability of the food provided and food waste was low. Serving and dining room staff encouraged the pupils to try the food, even if they did not finish it. The dining room was not too noisy, perhaps due to the Head and Deputy visiting the dining room on a regular basis. The input by all the staff was commendable.

Local Authority Catering Service

Schools 1, 11, 16, 22

During the past year, the school and the catering team have been successful in increasing the meal uptake…the catering team have been very proactive in adjusting the service to meet the needs of the school. They have introduced a simplified menu to help meet the tastes of the pupils. The flexibility to work towards a bespoke service for the school should be commended.

The food produced looked excellent and was of high quality…well flavoured. This high standard was reflected in the fairly low quantity of waste food. The catering staff at the school should be highly commended… Their dynamic approach to the requirements of the pupils and to attract the children away from packed lunches appears to be tireless. Both the caterers and the school not communicating as well as they could and therefore not fully capitalising on the opportunity provided by UIFSM

Food service contractor

Schools 12, 27, 30

The catering team have been very proactive in adjusting the service to meet the needs of the school. They…have a programme of featured ingredients, promoted on a calendar in the dining room

The school catering service have been successful in increasing the meal uptake. This work should be highly commended. The school is in an affluent, multi-cultural area with a high vegetarian/vegan/halal take up. Parents are very keen on healthy eating.

The school is very unhappy with the food and service and are seriously looking at having a new kitchen, a different type of food preparation and to retender for a new contractor. The school feels that the menu is more geared to adult tastes. There are many items on it that are new to the parents and the pupils. So much so, that some of the parents chose not to have their child have a meal because, they do not recognise its description.

The contractor continued to serve dishes after being told that pupils did not like them

There was a serious dilemma regarding the menu. The contractor…must be commended in their efforts to achieve a high standard but … the children do not like many of the dishes or recipes the actual food was good "but unfortunately, because of the poor facilities, there will always be a limited menu. [The contractor] should be encouraged to formulate a menu and ingredients that particularly suit the facilities available".

Reducing food waste

Low food waste was evident at three schools but in other schools waste levels appeared to be high. However, one school that had significant food waste had a composter on site as an effective way of disposing of it. It was found that many schools were not separating waste, or measuring the level of waste. Consequently, it was recommended for those cases that schools separate food waste from other waste and explore recycling options. It was also recommended that the catering staff should weigh the food waste daily and monitor trends over a number of weeks. In this way, they could check patterns and formulate ways to further reduce it. Once achieved, the lowering of levels of food waste could be publicised and pupils could be rewarded for reducing food waste by giving house points or a similar reward, for pupils who finish their food. This was undertaken across a number of schools, and dining room staff at these schools were praised for their efforts to persuade children to eat the food. However, this was not the case at other schools where dining room supervisors needed to make more effort to encourage pupils to finish eating their food. Consequently, there was significant waste, mostly vegetables, with one dining room staff member criticised for being unhelpful with a negative attitude to eating healthy vegetables saying that they *"had never seen a child eat broccoli"* and therefore could not understand why it was on the menu. Portion sizes proved to be a problem with adjustment needed depending on the age of the child *"the portion sizes are too large for the youngest pupils particularly in their first term but I was told often, too small for the older children"*. Several schools mentioned that portion sizes were too large for the younger children.

Food waste varied considerably between schools. For example, sweet and sour turkey and noodles were not popular at one school with new potatoes and courgettes also rejected. At another school excessive food portions were a problem. Across other schools, varied examples of food waste were evident where the same choice for meat and non-meat meals were offered i.e. meat cottage pie and vegetarian cottage pie or where sweet potato topping a vegetarian cottage pie was tried by only a few. A school which offered a quorn-based dish found that *"nobody would even try it"*. At several schools much of the food was not eaten or hardly tried. At these schools some pupils started with nicely-presented bread and thereafter were too full to eat their meal. Moreover, the fact that pupils had their pudding in front of them, with their main meal, may not be conducive for them to try their main course first. At one school, there was a tremendous amount of untouched sliced orange and a surprising amount of chocolate pudding – possibly due to the excessive portion sizes for young children.

The kitchen and dining room environment

Most school kitchens had adequate space and equipment, reflecting the substantial capital expenditure on school kitchens which had taken place over the previous ten years but two schools had no kitchens so they had to have food brought in from a food contractor and re-heated by microwave. The servery layout needed improvement for 14 out of 30 schools with the most common fault being that counters were too high – the food was poorly displayed and could not be seen by most of the pupils, particularly the younger ones. The suggested remedy was to have sample meals on a plate, placed so that pupils could see it when they entered the dining room, to help them make a choice.

While noisy dining halls were mentioned as a distraction for eating by 13 schools (43%), the installation of acoustic boards in dining rooms and the playing of soothing music were noted as possible solutions which could improve the dining room environment. Another practice which could reduce food waste was using china plates and bowls to serve food rather than airline trays that the majority of schools used and which encouraged children to eat their dessert first and then not want to finish the main course. Proper supervision in the dining rooms was another key factor to encourage students to eat the food provided to them at school. The visit reports recommended that 14 of the 30 schools (46%) needed to improve the number of teaching staff sitting in at meal times. It was suggested that teachers should be offered a free meal to encourage them to eat in the dining rooms with the students. At one school the staff took time to interact with the children and the positive benefits of this were evident: the calm atmosphere of the dining room, the amount of food that the children ate, the lack of waste food and the lack of mess at the end of mealtime. At another school by contrast, the researcher witnessed no teaching staff in the dining hall and the pupils were not encouraged to appreciate the food, to finish the food they had taken on their plates or to try to eat items new to them.

In 9 of the 30 schools (30%) children who were eating school meals were not allowed to sit with friends who had brought packed lunches. This discouraged some children from consuming school meals.

Communication between the school, children and parents

Communication about nutritious food and food waste in three schools was highly commended by the researchers. This communication took a variety of forms: twitter messages to parents, website information, briefing parents about school food during home visits to new pupils and inviting parents to have lunch in the school dining room. For all other schools it was recommended that steps be taken to improve communication about school food with parents and children, using websites, notice boards and all school literature. Parents should be invited to visit the dining room. Parents and children should be involved in food decisions. They should be given the opportunity to taste and give their verdict on new dishes and revised recipes for familiar dishes. There should be regular opinion surveys.

Four out of the thirty schools involved in the research were making an effort to improve packed lunches. This involved the dining room staff looking at lunch boxes and where nutritional aspects were of concern, an excellent, positive, leaflet was provided to encourage the provision of more nutritious foods. The researchers recommended that schools should put in place a healthy lunch box policy and that schools put leaflets into lunch boxes containing unhealthy food, explaining what a healthy packed lunch might look like. Similar advice should be displayed on the dining room wall. It was also recommended that good quality packed lunches should be recognised through regular competitions and pupils be encouraged to eat their packed lunch from a plate – which provided a better eating experience and allowed the contents to be more easily seen.

Conclusion and recommendations

It is important to understand that the subset of schools described in this chapter is not representative of the overall national picture in terms of UIFSM take-up or food waste. The research showed that in most of the schools visited there were considerable levels of food waste because the food being offered was not necessarily palatable for the children. Notwithstanding this, a minority of the schools visited were actually performing well. For some schools the catering managers had adapted their menus to meet the requirements of the FFL Catering Mark and only in some cases was the menu popular with the children. In schools where the catering manager communicated with the children about their food preferences food waste was generally low. In other schools many children rejected the food, resulting in high levels of food waste. Several catering managers had made radical alterations to school menus to promote healthy eating but this had resulted in many children rejecting the revised menu, which increased food waste. There were other problems that involved the spaces in which eating took place in schools. Some serveries were poorly designed; dining rooms excessively noisy, and where the children were given a main meal and dessert together, the children often neglected to eat much of the latter. In some instances, inadequate adult supervision meant that children were not encouraged to try new dishes or finish the food they had taken on their plates. If children were bringing in packed lunches, they were not allowed to sit with their friends who had bought school meals, which might discourage some children from buying the school meal.

A key recommendation from this research was for caterers to modify the menu gradually, rather than suddenly introduce a large number of unfamiliar new items. At the beginning of every academic year the catering manager should re-examine the menu, particularly for those children who are in the initial year of primary school so as to gradually introduce elements of the food that the children may not be used to. Special provision needed to be made for children identified as "fussy eaters" to encourage them to try new foods – such as by setting up a "fussy eaters club". Taster pots were also recommended so that pupils can be given an opportunity to try new sample dishes which the catering manager was considering adding to the menu. This would provide a mechanism to identify if these dishes would be accepted by the pupils. Another recommendation was to liaise with parents in order to encourage them to support school meals for their children and to implement a school lunch box policy that may persuade some parents to provide healthier food. The researchers recommended implementing school gardens and garden activities (only 4 schools out of 30 already had school gardens in place). Research studies have suggested there is potential to encourage children to eat the school lunches when they have grown the food themselves (DeCosta et al. 2017; Hoover et al. 2021; Weitkamp et al. 2013). A cookery club was suggested to try out scaled-down versions of the school lunch recipes and at the conclusion of the research project with the 30 schools, 17 (56%) planned to commence this type of activity.

Acknowledgement and funding

In memory of Penny Beauchamp who loved good food and through her work in catering management and consultancy promoted better meals in hospitals, schools and restaurants.

The research project discussed in this book chapter was funded by £4.8 million from the Department for Education.

References

Byker, C. J., Farris, A. R., Marcenelle, M., Davis, G. C., and Serrano, E. L., 2014. Food waste in a school nutrition program after implementation of new lunch program guidelines. *Journal of nutrition education and behavior* [online], 46 (5). Available from: https://doi.org/10.1016/j.jneb.2014.03.009.

Charlton, K., Comerford, T., Deavin, N., and Walton, K., 2021. Characteristics of successful primary school-based experiential nutrition programmes: a systematic literature review. *Public Health Nutrition* [online], 24 (14). Available from: https://doi.org/10.1017/S1368980020004024.

Day, R. E., Sahota, P., Christian, M. S., and Cocks, K., 2015. A qualitative study exploring pupil and school staff perceptions of school meal provision in England. *British Journal of Nutrition* [online], 114 (09). Available from: https://doi.org/10.1017/S0007114515002834.

DeCosta, P., Møller, P., Frøst, M. B., and Olsen, A., 2017. Changing children's eating behaviour-A review of experimental research. *Appetite* [online], 113. Available from: https://doi.org/10.1016/j.appet.2017.03.004.

Ensaff, H., Bunting, E., and O'Mahony, S., 2018. That's his choice not mine! Parents' perspectives on providing a packed lunch for their children in primary school. *Journal of Nutrition Education and Behavior* [online], 50 (4). Available from: https://doi.org/10.1016/j.jneb.2017.12.008.

Europe-cities, 2021. *United Russia" began checking the quality of school lunches in the Chechen Republic* [online]. Available from: https://europe-cities.com/2022/09/05/united-russia-began-checking-the-quality-of-school-lunches-in-the-chechen-republic/; https://www.dnsv.eu/russland-kostenfreies-mittagessen-an-allen-grundschulen [Accessed 9 September 2022].

Foad, D., 2021. *Scotland set to extend free school meals to all primary-age children* [online]. Available from: https://www.publicsectorcatering.co.uk/news/scotland-set-to-extend-free-school-meals-all-primary-age-children [Accessed 17 March 2021].

Food For Life, 2022. *Food for Life Catering Mark award criteria* [online]. Available from: https://www.sustainweb.org/sustainablefishcity/inspired_food_for_life/ [Accessed 24 July 2022].

García-Herrero, L., De Menna, F., and Vittuari, M., 2019. Food waste at school: the environmental and cost impact of a canteen meal. *Waste Management* [online], 100. Available from: https://doi.org/10.1016/j.wasman.2019.09.027.

Gase, L. N., McCarthy, W. J., Robles, B., and Kuo, T., 2014. Student receptivity to new school meal offerings: assessing fruit and vegetable waste among middle school students in the Los Angeles Unified School District. *Preventive Medicine* [online], 67. Available from: https://doi.org/10.1016/j.ypmed.2014.04.013.

Gross, S. M., Biehl, E., Marshall, B., Paige, D. M., and Mmari, K., 2019. Role of the elementary school cafeteria environment in fruit, vegetable, and whole-grain consumption by 6-to 8-year-old students. *Journal of nutrition education and behavior* [online], 51 (1). Available from: https://doi.org/10.1016/j.jneb.2018.07.002.

Hart, C. S., 2016. The School Food Plan and the social context of food in schools. *Cambridge Journal of Education* [online], 46 (2). Available from: https://doi.org/10.1080/0305764X.2016.1158783.

Hoover, A., Vandyousefi, S., Martin, B., Nikah, K., Cooper, M. H., Muller, A., Muller., A., Marty, E., Duswalt-Epstein, M., Burgermaster, M., Waugh, L., Linkenhoker, B., and Davis, J., 2021. Barriers, strategies, and resources to thriving school gardens. *Journal of Nutrition Education and Behavior* [online], 53 (7). Available from: https://doi.org/10.1016/j.jneb.2021.02.011.

Lakkakula, A., Geaghan, J. P., Wong, W. P., Zanovec, M., Pierce, S. H., and Tuuri, G., 2011. A cafeteria-based tasting program increased liking of fruits and vegetables by lower, middle and upper elementary school-age children. *Appetite* [online], 57 (1), Available from: https://doi.org/10.1016/j.appet.2011.04.010.

Lalli, G. S., 2021. A review of the English school meal: progress or a recipe for disaster? *Cambridge Journal of Education* [online], 51 (5). Available from: https://doi.org/10.1080/0305764X.2021.1893658.

Magasin Maltid, 2021. *Norway receives free school meals* [online]. Available from: https://www-magasinmaltid-se.translate.goog/norge-far-gratis-skolmat/?_x_tr_sl=sv&_x_tr_tl=en&_x_tr_hl=en&_x_tr_pto=sc [Accessed 17 October 2021].

Malefors, C., Sundin, N., Tromp, M., and Eriksson, M., 2022. Testing interventions to reduce food waste in school catering. *Resources, Conservation and Recycling* [online], 177, 105997. Available from: https://doi.org/10.1016/j.resconrec.2021.105997.

Moore, S. N., Tapper, K., and Murphy, S., 2010. Feeding strategies used by primary school meal staff and their impact on children's eating. *Journal of Human Nutrition and Dietetics* [online], 23 (1). Available from: https://doi.org/10.1111/j.1365-277X.2009.01009.x.

Springmann, M., Clark, M., Mason-D'Croz, D., Wiebe, K., Bodirsky, B. L., Lassaletta, L., ... and Willett, W., 2018. Options for keeping the food system within environmental limits. *Nature* [online], 562. Available from: https://doi.org/10.1038/s41586-018-0594-0.

Tuorila, H., Palmujoki, I., Kytö, E., Törnwall, O., and Vehkalahti, K., 2015. School meal acceptance depends on the dish, student, and context. *Food Quality and Preference* [online], 46. Available from: https://doi.org/10.1016/j.foodqual.2015.07.013.

Weitkamp, E., Jones, M., Salmon, D., Kimberlee, R., and Orme, J., 2013. Creating a learning environment to promote food sustainability issues in primary schools? Staff perceptions of implementing the food for life partnership programme. *Sustainability* [online], 5 (3). Available from: https://doi.org/10.3390/su5031128.

Welsh Government, 2021. *Extending free school meal entitlement to all primary school children.* Available from: https://gov.wales/written-statement-extending-free-school-meal-entitlement-all-primary-school-children [Accessed 17 December 2021].

10

BELONGING, IDENTITY, INCLUSION, AND TOGETHERNESS

The lesser-known social benefits of food for children and young people

Kelly-Ann Allen, Deana Leahy, Lefteris Patlamazoglou, Claire Bristow, Caomhan McGlinchey and Christopher Boyle

Introduction

The art of connecting and socialising together with others has totally changed over the last few years and maybe even decades. People of all ages have developed certain approaches for connecting and communicating, and many young people today have a particular set of skills that has evolved in a completely digital age (Allen et al. 2014; Ryan et al. 2017). This has become the default approach for many as digital connection has been around for as long as they have. There has been a shift in family working patterns, living arrangements, and technology, and these have all been blamed (whether empirically substantiated or not) for rising rates of loneliness, mental health concerns, and other negative outcomes (Allen 2020a; Allen and Furlong 2021). What is not clear is why these social cultural shifts have taken place. Research has not been able to pinpoint definitively what this means for people and society.

Digital technology has, without doubt, afforded people more opportunities to connect digitally, and this can sometimes lead to physical connectivity (McCahey et al. 2021). Digital belonging has become more possible through advances in social media and digital communication so that the tyranny of distance has become less stark than has been the case in the past. However, digital connection and belonging does not mean that people feel they belong in the wider sense.

Despite the lack of clarity of these shifts, what is clear is that there is potential for food to play a role in meeting the fundamental human need to belong (Baumeister and Leary 1995). A sense of belonging is defined as feeling like one is an integral part of their surrounding systems, including their family, friends, school, work environment, community, and physical places (Allen 2020a; Allen et al. 2021; Hagerty et al. 1992). Food is particularly appealing to children and

DOI: 10.4324/9781003294962-13

young people who are often keen for lunch time where they can have their meals. This period also provides a break from classroom learning as well as the opportunity to interact with friends, with occasional meal sharing further strengthening social bonds. Although not limited to schools, food's potential in fostering belongingness remains particularly important in school settings, especially since a sense of belonging is critical for positive educational outcomes.

The role of food in fostering a feeling of belonging has been well established in many cultures. However, though there has been a focus across various disciplines, there has been no specific consideration in the research field of *belonging*. It is necessary to create an understanding of the importance of food for fostering a sense of belonging at school through multidisciplinary perspectives. These will include research drawn from educational psychology, sociology, psychology, education, and food sciences. This narrative synthesis will seek to explore the literature on the importance of belonging and food, especially in the school domain. This chapter also intends to explore where food may disrupt a student's sense of belonging and discusses the available research considering special populations.

A shift in how we think about and interact with food, belonging

Changes to the working patterns of parents, including dual working households, diminishing multigenerational households, and busy work lives with long work hours have been partially to blame by some for the disruptions to mealtimes and rituals observed pre-2019 (Allen et al. 2021; Jones 2018), although these mealtime rituals have arguably had a limited history. Family food practices are complex, often gendered, stereo-typed, and classed (Tanner et al. 2019; Warin et al. 2014). Although the complexity existed prior to 2019, it took a global pandemic to really mix things up and add to what is already a complex foodscape.

Food and mealtimes can be a predictable source of routine, ritual, and habit, although it is important to acknowledge this is not across the board, especially for some families where food insecurity exists or where parents engage in shift work. Yet, food can still potentially unite people around their common need to fuel their body. During lockdowns and social distancing, when other social engagements were halted, food rituals continued to provide social connectivity and people found ways to organise remote lunches, virtual parties, and meet-ups over Zoom (Ginanneschi 2020). In Chinese and US households, Dou et al. (2020) found that families spent more time cooking and eating meals together. Despite the major disruptions of COVID, food provided social benefits for many children and adolescents around social connections that had declined during lockdowns and home-learning and such benefits existed for a long time before COVID. The social benefits of food for school are well established and summarised in Table 10.1.

Food, as discussed in the above literature, is considered to provide major benefits in terms of social connectivity and social ritual, but this can be particularly relevant for children and young people at school. Lunch times and break times

TABLE 10.1 Social benefits of food

Author and Date	Result and Findings
Rearick (2009)	Food performs a major role in developing social contact and bringing society together.
Whitt (2011)	Food not only reflects personal identity but also builds cultural boundaries while expressing cultural identity.
Koc and Welsh (2001)	Food can be related to everything in life, and it plays a major role in socialisation.
Muhammad et al. (2013)	Food plays a significant role during celebrations and in encouraging togetherness, social bonding, and feelings of appreciation.
Neely et al. (2016)	Food rituals allow young people to manage their social relationships. Rituals such as lunch walks, food sharing, and gifting of food on different occasions help to strengthen social bonding. Lunch walks encourage social interactions and provide a means for being integrated into a new group while food sharing can define friendship boundaries.
Lupton (1994)	Food is sometimes significantly associated with memories and social relationships. An event or occasion might not be remembered only for the uniqueness of the food which was served but also for the people with whom the food was consumed.
Rydell et al. (2008)	One of the main reasons for eating fast food is that it is considered a means for bonding with families and friends.
Rokach (2020)	Eating does not simply involve food consumption as eating with loved ones can be a ritual. Food represents belonging to a large social group, and symbolises being part of a celebration or condolence. It unites people during different events of their lives.
Ratcliffe et al. (2019)	One thing common to different rituals is food, and it can provide psychological benefits such as enhanced social bonding. Food is not only important for sustaining physiological factors, but it may also have spiritual and social meanings in human life. Most business meetings are usually conducted during lunches while drinking alcohol can be a ritualistic conduct among peers.
Wei et al. (2014)	Food is not just a means of survival, but it can even represent a way to communicate. Food can be used for conveying a message that promotes social bonding. Unlike other means of communication, such as paper and electronic media, food messages not only engage a recipient's sense of touch and feel but the recipient can also smell and taste the message. Thus, the richness and impressiveness of the message can be enhanced through sensory stimulation by food. This, in turn, will enhance social bonding between the parties involved in the communication. Food messaging is already commonly practiced for events such as sending a cake as a birthday greeting.

built around the school timetable can provide an opportunity to socially connect, but it can be through a lunch box that food can provide school children with a feeling of comfort and identity. There is a lot of nostalgia about lunchboxes, and research has found that kids are fond of their lunchbox—but once a lunchbox is taken to school they become a site of contestation as much as anything (Leahy et al. 2022). This is because lunch boxes have become a key target of public health and intervention which has meant that teachers, for example, are surveilling lunchboxes and pointing out potential problems with certain foods often in notes sent home to parents (especially Mums) (Pike and Leahy 2012; Pluim et al. 2018).

Culture, comfort, and identity

Food practices and habits represent foundational aspects of culture. International students, for example, reconstruct food consumption habits and acquire new food production skills while forming connections to the local culture and strengthening their cultural identity and attachment to their place of origin (Gram et al. 2015). This population associates home food with family unity, nostalgia, and cultural belonging. Home country food provides reassurance, nurturing, a sense of safety, emotional and physical sustenance and stability, and helps alleviate stress and loneliness (Brown et al. 2010). Although language and pre-existing friendship networks impose barriers to international students' acculturation, receptiveness to other cultures and sharing food help develop a sense of connectedness and belonging (Rienties et al. 2013). Many events organised by or for international students place particular emphasis on the production, sharing, and consumption of meals (Karimi and Matous 2018). Food exchange and culinary events offer students a common ground to explore new cultures and promote their own emotional comfort and opportunities to construct and maintain social relationships. Therefore, as a symbol of cultural identity, food not only helps to sustain a sense of belonging or connectedness with one's home country but also becomes a means of establishing new social connections and feelings of belongingness within educational settings.

Students with special educational needs and disabilities

Students with special educational needs and disabilities (SEND) can experience the relationship between food and belonging in more unexpected ways than their peers, and more studies exploring this relationship are needed. Nevertheless, in the experience of this author, children's SEND can have an impact on their diet, which can in turn have implications for their sense of belonging.

In many parts of the world, mental health needs are considered under the rubric of SEND (sources), and we have already reviewed some of the evidence linking belongingness with clinically diagnosable eating disorders. There are, however, patterns of food consumption that we might not characterise as a 'disorder' but which do have a mental health component, such as 'comfort' or 'emotional' eating. Indeed, a number of authors have suggested that some foods become 'comforting' because they are associated with positive social interactions (Troise and Gabriel 2011; Troise et al. 2015), such as, "people reach for the comfort foods because they feel lonely" (Spence 2017, p.108). Those supporting young people engaged in emotional eating might therefore look at ways of increasing their sense of belonging, perhaps by deliberately creating opportunities for young people to meet, interact, and share food together at school.

After all, food also has an emotional and a belongingness aspect for children who do not have many opportunities to experience success at school. Many educators use a strength-based approach, which might involve asking young people what's the best part of school (Marks et al. 2017 and additional sources). In retrospect, many educators are not surprised when the reply is often, 'lunch time'. This is because, for many children, lunch time provides a welcome break from the challenges of classroom learning. However, the children and young people themselves more often highlight that lunch time is a chance to socialise with their friends, i.e., to feel like they belong, and we have no doubt that sharing a meal together is an important part of the reason why lunch time is valued so highly. This is particularly important for students with SEND who may feel segregated and for these students fostering feelings of inclusion (feelings of being 'equal' or having similar opportunities to be part of a physical or social environment) may help to feel part of mainstream social networks in schools. In this context, coming together to share food is likely to create a hospitable atmosphere which is conducive to social bonding, thereby helping them to feel included, although this may not be limited to students with SEND only.

Another important group of students whose SEND can impact both their diet and their sense of belonging in school are autistic students. For many of these students, snack time and lunch time can also involve food neophobia, preference for sameness, ritualistic eating, excessive eating or avoidance, pica, and aggressive behaviour towards self and others while eating (Gray et al. 2018; Hyman et al. 2020; Rogers et al. 2012; Sharp et al. 2013; Zimmer et al. 2012).

Naturally, some of these eating problems must be tackled to ensure a child's physical health. However, we have also noted that these eating problems put children at increased risk of becoming isolated, in much the same way that their communication and interaction needs do. Indeed, in those settings where opportunities for training and guidance around SEND are thin on the ground, these needs can increase feelings of helplessness and apprehension among the adults supporting these children. It is for this reason that raising awareness of these needs and how they can be supported is an essential part of ensuring that the most vulnerable children are made to feel like they belong.

It is clear, therefore, that food has an important role to play in promoting belongingness. However, in school settings at least, the interplay between food and belongingness can be more complex, especially for children with SEND. To support these children, a greater awareness of their needs is required; not only in education settings but in our culture more broadly. It is for this reason that a section of this chapter was dedicated to this discussion.

When food alienates and ostracises at school

Now that we have a greater understanding of the potential that food has to foster belonging, it is important to consider how it can also be a source of isolation and exclusion for some young people. This may further lead them to feel alienated or ostracised from their peers who do not experience difficulties around food. This is especially true for those with eating disorders (EDs). Eating disorders, including anorexia nervosa (AN), bulimia nervosa (BN), binge eating disorder (BED), and other specified feeding and eating disorders (OSFED) (American Psychiatric Association 2013). These are complex mental illnesses often characterised by negative body image, restrictive, abnormal, or extreme weight control practices (starvation, laxative abuse), a strong preoccupation with food and body weight, and an intense fear of weight gain (Peckmezian et al. 2017). As such, food can be a source of great fear and anxiety for this population group. In interviews with individuals diagnosed with AN, patients have described feeling uncomfortable and, at times, physically sick during meal times, explaining that this time brings about feelings of fear and panic (Long et al. 2012). In extreme cases of refeeding via gastric nasal tubes, patients have described the experience as distressing and traumatic (Fox and Diab 2015). Even simulated meal environments where food is not actually present can incite anxiety in ED populations (Gorini et al. 2010).

Schools are also a setting in which individuals with EDs may feel ostracised or alienated. Given schools are a common setting in which eating takes place, it can be difficult to hide behaviours pertinent to the ED. Restrictive eating behaviours may be very present and noticed by other peers, such as skipping meals or avoiding eating situations (Hellings and Bowles 2007). Treatment recommendations for outpatients may further contribute to feelings of isolation. Some experts have recommended the use of a 'minder' who ensures meals are eaten or eating away from others such as in a separate room (Treasure and Alexander 2013). This may lead to the student feeling further isolated from their peers. In addition, meal times in the home setting have also been described as stressful for both the family and sufferer, in cases where the sufferer does not want to eat or won't eat sufficient quantities, bringing distress to parents and ultimately leaving both parties feeling helpless (Jaffa et al. 2002).

In addition to EDs, avoidant and restrictive food intake disorder (ARFID) is another condition that may lead to feelings of isolation and exclusion. Most prevalent in childhood and adolescence (Norris et al. 2016), ARFID is not due to a desire for thinness but a strong aversion to food and its characteristics (smell, texture, etc.) or a fear of the potential consequences of eating (for example, vomiting or choking). As such, eating times may be stressful for those who suffer from the condition.

Finally, the impact of weight stigma and bullying in young people must be considered. Evidence suggests that children and adolescents of higher weights are more likely to be bullied than their peers (Brixval et al. 2012; Jendrzyca and Warschburger 2016), and weight-based bullying is one of the most commonly reported forms of bullying in the school setting (Pont et al. 2017). This can lead to social isolation and victims choosing to undertake activities alone (Hayden-Wade et al. 2005). In particular, this may include secretive eating. Secretive eating is common in children and adolescents and is usually more prevalent in those with higher BMIs (Knatz et al. 2011). This is often to avoid being seen due to eating or body shame (Kass et al. 2017), ultimately resulting in further feelings of exclusion and isolation.

It can be seen that there are instances in which food is a source of great fear, anxiety, and isolation for some young people. It is important that each of these situations and the underlying conditions are factored into discussions about food and belonging in children and adolescents. Understanding some of the triggers of food anxiety can help to form appropriate treatment solutions that do not further alienate sufferers.

The promise of school food programs in times of crisis

School food as a potential site for cultivating belonging is without question an appealing proposition. However, research over time indicates that it may well be a difficult goal to realise given the way school food operates as a platform for addressing public health crises and imperatives (see Gard and Pluim 2014). These entanglements are not new. Public health, schools, and food have a very long history, and the relationship has a significant impact on shaping school food programs (Gard and Pluim 2014). For example, in 1996 when WHO announced that the world was in the midst of an obesity epidemic, school food became an important vehicle for intervention (Gard and Pluim 2014; Leahy et al. 2022). Critical scholars from Australia, New Zealand, the UK, Canada, and the United States have mapped the different contours of the obesity epidemic and its impact on school food since the late 1990s. Over time, research has reported that school food programs have incorporated weighing children and asking children to keep food diaries (Burrows et al. 2002; Gard and Wright 2001; Leahy and Harrison 2004; Wright and Burrows 2004). Additionally, research from Australia, New Zealand, the United States (Pluim et al. 2018), and the UK (Harman and Cappelini 2015) has revealed that teachers are engaged in policing children's lunchboxes. For example, Pike and Leahy (2012) in their ethnographic research in primary schools in the UK and Australia found that teachers were being encouraged to publicly shame lunch boxes that they considered to be unhealthy. Other research has revealed that teachers, after inspecting children's lunchboxes, have sent home notes to parents to draw attention to the poor state of their child's lunchbox with some teachers even sending home the offending food item/s (Burrows and Wright 2020; Harman and Cappelini 2015;

Pike and Leahy 2012). The various food pedagogies identified across this body of research, whilst well intentioned, have served to alienate children and their families by both marginalising and stigmatising particular kinds of bodies (overweight/fat) and/or food practices (Flowers and Swan 2015; Maher et al. 2020; Tanner et al. 2019).

The obesity epidemic has also contributed to the (re) shaping of broader school foodscapes. School canteens in Australia, dining rooms across Europe and the UK, and canteens in the US have all been targeted by policies that seek to regulate what foods are available at school. As part of the broader shift towards regulating school food, birthday celebrations have also been targeted. In a study that included interviews with 50 families about school food practices, 34 families reported that birthday celebrations were a part of schooling; however, there were certain rules about what children could bring to the celebration (see Leahy et al. 2022). For example, families reported that in their local schools, birthday cakes and lollies had been replaced by sushi or hummus and carrot sticks. Other families reported that their kids were only allowed to take stationary (for example, staplers, pencils) to the birthday party (no food was permitted but stationary could be given as a gift). In some schools, teachers had stopped allowing birthday parties altogether (in settings where they had once been permitted).

This highly regulatory approach to school food has been driven by obesity prevention imperatives. There are, of course, other reasons as to why schools regulate food (for example, allergies). More recently we have also witnessed the emergence of school food programs that are attempting to respond to the climate crisis (Leahy et al. 2015). Schools, in response, are implementing a suite of new programs in attempts to intervene. For example, Nude Food Movers has become popular in schools given the initiative is aimed at both healthy lifestyles and a healthy planet. The initiative targets children's lunchboxes and adds an additional layer to what teachers and other students police. In addition to making judgements about whether or not a lunchbox is nutritionally sound or not, lunchboxes now need to be 'rubbish free'. The emphasis on rubbish-free healthy lunchboxes in schools has at times resulted in problematic implementation. Research has revealed that kids report feeling anxious about whether their lunchbox will pass the test with one young girl going so far as hiding her muesli bars (still in their store-bought wrapping) in the school garden rather than be subjected to her teacher's negative response and/or the public shaming (Leahy et al. 2022).

The regulation of school food, whether it be via intervening in birthday parties, policing lunchboxes, or weighing kids and asking kids to keep food diaries are practices that mean that we either miss opportunities for kids to genuinely use food as an opportunity to connect with peers, engage in their cultural heritages, and bond over rituals that involve interpersonal relations.

There are of course a range of other school food programs and practices that operate in schools around the globe. These include breakfast programs, recipe clubs, community/school cookbooks, and kitchen garden programs to name a few. These programs are potentially sites where a sense of belonging and identity could well be cultivated. However, these programs often run alongside initiatives that are fuelled by crisis imperatives. What this can mean for children and their families is that they can receive contradictory messages about food.

In thinking about ways to shore up the promise of school food as a catalyst for belonging, it is clear we need to find new ways to address school food. To do this we need to be attentive to what it means for food to be called on to respond to a crisis. Berlant (2011) reminds us that the temporalities of crisis limit possibilities for how we might imagine and reap the benefits of, in this case, school food programs.

References

Allen, K. A., 2020a. *The psychology of belonging*. London, UK: Routledge.

Allen, K. A., 2020b. Commentary of Lim, M., Eres, R., Gleeson, J., Long, K., Penn, D., and Rodebaugh, T., 2019. A pilot digital intervention targeting loneliness in youth mental health. *Frontiers in Psychiatry* [online]. Available from: https://doi.org/10.3389/fpsyt.2019.00959.

Allen, K. A., 2021. Belonging in an age of technology. *In*: C. McMahon, ed. *Psychological insights for understanding COVID-19 and media and technology*. Abingdon, UK: Routledge, 72–85.

Allen, K. A., and Furlong, M., 2021. Leveraging belonging in response to global loneliness special issue: belonging and loneliness. *Australian Journal of Psychology* [online]. Available from: https://doi.org/10.1080/00049530.2021.1875532.

Allen, K. A., Gray, D., Baumeister, R., and Leary, M., 2021. The need to belong: a deep dive into the origins, implications, and future of a foundational construct. *Educational Psychology Review* [online]. Available from: https://doi.org/10.1007/s10648-021-09633-6.

Allen, K. A., Kern, M. L., Rozek, C. S., McInereney, D., and Slavich, G. M., 2021. Belonging: a review of conceptual issues, an integrative framework, and directions for future research. *Australian Journal of Psychology* [online], 73 (1). Available from: https://doi.org/10.1080/00049530.2021.1883409.

Allen, K. A., Ryan, T., Gray, D. L., McInerney, D., and Waters, L., 2014. Social media use and social connectedness in adolescents: the positives and the potential pitfalls. *The Australian Educational and Developmental Psychologist* [online], 31 (1). Available from: https://doi.org/10.1017/edp.2014.2.

American Psychiatric Association, 2013. *Diagnostic and statistical manual of mental disorders (DSM-5®)*. *American Psychiatric Pub* [online]. Available from: https://doi.org/10.1176/appi.books.9780890425596.

Baumeister, R. F., and Leary, M. R., 1995. The need to belong: desire for interpersonal attachments as a fundamental human motivation. *Psychological Bulletin* [online], 117 (3). Available from: https://doi.org/10.1037/0033-2909.117.3.497.

Berlant, L., 2011. *Cruel optimism*. Durham, NC: Duke University Press.

Brixval, C. S., Rayce, S. L., Rasmussen, M., Holstein, B. E., and Due, P., 2012. Overweight, body image and bullying—an epidemiological study of 11-to 15-years olds. *The European Journal of Public Health* [online], 22 (1). Available from: https://doi.org/10.1093/eurpub/ckr010.

Brown, L., Edwards, J., and Hartwell, H., 2010. A taste of the unfamiliar: understanding the meanings attached to food by international postgraduate students in England. *Appetite* [online], 54 (1). Available from: https://doi.org/10.1016/j.appet. 2009.11.001.

Burrows, L., and Wright, J., 2020. Biopedagogies and family life: a social class perspective. *In*: D. Leahy, K. Fitzpatrick and J. Wright, eds. *Thinking with theory in health education*. London, UK: Routledge, 19–32.

Burrows, L., Wright, J., and Jurgensen, J., 2002. Measure your belly: New Zealand children's constructions of health and fitness. *Journal of Teaching in Physical Education*, 22 (1), 39–48.

Dou, Z., Stefanovski, D., Galligan, D., Lindem, M., Rozin, P., Chen, T., and Chao, A. M., 2020. The COVID-19 pandemic impacting household food dynamics: A cross-national comparison of China and the US. *Center for Open Science* [online]. Available from: https://docs.google.com/document/d/10Kbi8LAenQsNlCmaMbv3r-GtNIhe81c3/ edit#.

Flowers, R., and Swan, E., 2015. *Food pedagogies*. Surrey, UK: Ashgate.

Fox, J. R., and Diab, P., 2015. An exploration of the perceptions and experiences of living with chronic anorexia nervosa while an inpatient on an eating disorders unit: an Interpretative Phenomenological Analysis study. *Journal of Health Psychology* [online], 20 (1). Available from: https://doi.org/10.1177/1359105313497526.

Gard, M., and Pluim, C., 2014. *Schools and public health: past, present, future*. Lanham, MD: Lexington Books.

Ginanneschi, M., 2020. The future of food after COVID-19 through the lens of anthropology. *Journal of Agriculture, Food Systems, and Community Development* [online], 9 (4). Available from: https://doi.org/10.5304/jafscd.2020.094.027.

Gorini, A., Griez, E., Petrova, A., and Riva, G., 2010. Assessment of the emotional responses produced by exposure to real food, virtual food and photographs of food in patients affected by eating disorders. *Annals of General Psychiatry* [online], 9 (1). Available from: https://doi.org/10.1186/1744-859X-9-30.

Gram, M., Hogg, M., Blichfeldt, B. S., and MacLaran, P., 2015. Intergenerational relationships and food consumption: the stories of young adults leaving home. *Young Consumers* [online], 16 (1). Available from: https://doi.org/10.1108/YC-01-2014-00422.

Hagerty, B. M., K., Lynch-Sauer, J., Patusky, K. L., Bouwseman, M., and Collier, P., 1992. Sense of belonging: a vital mental health concept. *Archives of Psychiatric Nursing* [online], 6. Available from: https://doi.org/10.1016/0883-9417(92)90028-H.

Hammons, A. J., and Robart, R., 2021. Family food environment during the COVID-19 Pandemic: a qualitative Study. *Children*, 8 (5), 354.

Harman, V., and Cappelini, B., 2015. Mothers on display: lunchboxes, social class and moral accountability, *Sociology*, 49 (4), 764–781.

Hayden-Wade, H. A., Stein, R. I., Ghaderi, A., Saelens, B. E., Zabinski, M. F., and Wilfley, D. E., 2005. Prevalence, characteristics, and correlates of teasing experiences among overweight children vs. non-overweight peers. *Obesity Research* [online], 13 (8). Available from: https://doi.org/10.1038/oby.2005.167.

Hellings, B., and Bowles, T., 2007. Understanding and managing eating disorders in the school setting. *Journal of Psychologists and Counsellors in Schools* [online], 17 (1). Available from: https://doi.org/10.1375/ajgc.17.1.60.

Jaffa, T., Honig, P., Farmer, S., and Dilley, J., 2002. Family meals in the treatment of adolescent anorexia nervosa. *European Eating Disorders Review* [online], 10 (3). Available from: https://doi.org/10.1002/erv.464.

Jendrzyca, A., and Warschburger, P., 2016. Weight stigma and eating behaviours in elementary school children: a prospective population-based study. *Appetite* [online], 102. Available from: https://doi.org/10.1016/j.appet.2016.02.005.

Jones, B. L., 2018. Making time for family meals: parental influences, home eating environments, barriers and protective factors. *Physiology & Behavior*, 193, 248–251.

Karimi, F., and Matous, P., 2018. Mapping diversity and inclusion in student societies: a social network perspective. *Computers in Human Behavior* [online], 88. Available from: https://doi.org/10.1016/j.chb.2018.07.001.

Kass, A. E., Wilfley, D. E., Eddy, K. T., Boutelle, K. N., Zucker, N., Peterson, C. B., Le Grange, D., Celio-Doyle, A., and Goldschmidt, A. B., 2017. Secretive eating among youth with overweight or obesity. *Appetite* [online], 114. Available from: https://doi.org/10.1016/j.appet.2017.03.042.

Knatz, S., Maginot, T., Story, M., Neumark-Sztainer, D., and Boutelle, K., 2011. Prevalence rates and psychological predictors of secretive eating in overweight and obese adolescents. *Childhood Obesity* [online], 7 (1). Available from: https://doi.org/10.1089/chi.2011.0515.Knatz.

Koc, M., and Welsh, J., 2001. Food, food ways and immigrant experience. *Toronto: Centre for Studies in Food Security*, 2, 46–48.

Leahy, D., Gray, E., Cutter-Mackenzie, A., and Eames, C., 2015. Schooling food in contemporary times: taking stock. *Australian Journal of Environmental Education* [online], 31 (1). Available from: https://doi.org/10.1017/aee.2015.26.

Leahy, D., and Harrison, L., 2004. Health and physical education and the production of the 'at risk self'. *In*: J. Evans, B. Davies and J. Wright, eds. *Body knowledge and control: studies in the sociology of physical education and health*. London, UK: Routledge, 130–139.

Leahy, D., Wright, J., Lindsay, J., Tanner, C., Maher, J. M., and Supski, S., 2022. School food in Australia: a dog's breakfast? *In*: M. Gard, D. Powell and J. Tenorio, eds. *Routledge handbook of critical obesity studies*. Oxfordshire, UK: Routledge, 101–105.

Long, S., Wallis, D., Leung, N., and Meyer, C., 2012. All eyes are on you: anorexia nervosa patient perspectives of in-patient mealtimes. *Journal of Health Psychology* [online], 17 (3). Available from: https://doi.org/10.1177/1359105311419270.

Lupton, D., 1994. Food, memory and meaning: the symbolic and social nature of food events. *The Sociological Review*, 42 (4), 664–685.

Maher, J., Supski, S., Wright, J., Leahy, D., Lindsay, L., and Tanner, C., 2020. Children, healthy food, school and family: the '[n]ot really' outcome of school food messages. *Children's Geographies*, 18 (1) [online]. Available from: https://doi.org/10.1080/14733285.2019.1598546.

McCahey, A., Allen, K. A., and Arslan, G., 2021. Information communication technology use and school belonging in Australian high school students. *Psychology in the Schools* [online]. Available from: https://doi.org/10.1002/pits.22600.

Muhammad, R., Zahari, M. S. M., Ramly, A. S. M., and Ahmad, R., 2013. The roles and symbolism of foods in Malay wedding ceremony. *Procedia-Social and Behavioral Sciences*, 101, 268–276.

Neely, E., Walton, M., and Stephens, C., 2016. Fostering social relationships through food rituals in a New Zealand school. *Health Education* [online], 116 (5). Available from: https://doi.org/10.1108/HE-03-2015-0012.

Norris, M. L., Spettigue, W. J., and Katzman, D. K., 2016. Update on eating disorders: current perspectives on avoidant/restrictive food intake disorder in children and youth. *Neuropsychiatric Disease and Treatment* [online], 12. Available from: https://doi.org/10.2147/NDT.S82538.

Peckmezian, T., Cook, F., and Watson, H., 2017. *Eating disorders prevention, treatment and management. an updated evidence review.* National Eating Disorders Collaboration. Available from: https://nedc.com.au/assets/Uploads/Evidence-Reviewelectronic-complete-FINAL-compressed.pdf [Accessed 21 June 2021].

Pike, J., and Leahy, D., 2012. School food and the pedagogies of parents. *Australian Journal of Adult Learning*, 52 (3), 434–459.

Pont, S. J., Puhl, R., Cook, S. R., and Slusser, W., 2017. Stigma experienced by children and adolescents with obesity. *Pediatrics* [online], 140 (6). Available from: https://doi.org/10.1542/peds.2017-3034.

Ratcliffe, E., Baxter, W. L., and Martin, N., 2019. Consumption rituals relating to food and drink: a review and research agenda. *Appetite*, 134, 86–93.

Rearick, N. A., 2009. *Food is something that we gather around: foodway practices among Arab Americans in Columbus, Ohio.* Thesis (PhD). The Ohio State University.

Rienties, B., Héliot, Y., and Jindal-Snape, D., 2013. Understanding social learning relations of international students in a large classroom using social network analysis. *Higher Education* [online], 66 (4). Available from: https://doi.org/10.1007/s10734-013-9617-9.

Rokach, A., 2020. Belonging, togetherness and food rituals. *Open Journal of Depression*, 9 (04), 77.

Ryan, T., Allen, K. A., Gray, D. L., and McInerney, D. M., 2017. How social are social media? a review of online social behaviour and connectedness. *Journal of Relationships Research* [online], 8. Available from: https://doi.org/10.1017/jrr.2017.13.

Rydell, S. A., Harnack, L. J., Oakes, J. M., Story, M., Jeffery, R. W., and French, S. A., 2008. Why eat at fast-food restaurants: reported reasons among frequent consumers. *Journal of the American Dietetic Association*, 108 (12), 2066–2070.

Sonneville, K. R., Rifas-Shiman, S. L., Haines, J., Gortmaker, S., Mitchell, K. F., Gillman, M. W., and Taveras, E. M., 2013. Associations of parental control of feeding with eating in the absence of hunger and food sneaking, hiding, and hoarding. *Childhood Obesity* [online], 9 (4). Available from: https://doi.org/10.1089/chi.2012.0149.

Tanner, C., Maher, J. M., Leahy, D., Lindsay, J., Supski, S., and Wright, J., 2019. 'Sticky' foods: how school practices produce negative emotions for mothers and children. *Emotion, Space and Society* [online], 33. Available from: https://doi.org/10.1016/j.emospa.2019.100626.

Treasure, J., and Alexander, J., 2013. *Anorexia nervosa: a recovery guide for sufferers, families and friends.* Oxfordshire, UK: Routledge.

Warin, M., Zivkovic, T., Moore, V., and Davies, M., 2014. Mothers as smoking guns: fetal overnutrition and the reproduction of obesity. *In*: Karin Eli and Stanley Ulijasze, eds. *Obesity, eating disorders and the media.* 1st ed. London: Routledge, 73–89.

Wei, J., Ma, X., and Zhao, S., 2014. Food messaging: using edible medium for social messaging. *In*: M. Jones and P. Palanque, eds. 14th *SIGCHI conference on human factors in computing systems*, 26 April–1 May 2014. New York: Association for Computing Machinery, 2873–2882.

Whitt, J. B., 2011. *An appetite for metaphor: food imagery and cultural identity in Indian fiction* [online]. The ScholarShip: East Carolina Universities' Institutional Repository. Available from: https://thescholarship.ecu.edu/handle/10342/3535.

11

IS THE ABILITY TO COOK ENOUGH TO FOSTER GOOD EATING HABITS IN THE FUTURE? INVESTIGATING HOW SCHOOLS CAN EMPOWER POSITIVE FOOD CHOICES IN ADOLESCENTS

Donna Owen

The role of school and peers

A school is a place where adolescents spend a large portion of their time and is identified as an important influence on adolescence food decisions (De Rosis et al. 2019; Kubik et al. 2003; Ronto 2016a; Utter et al. 2008). This is further supported by the research reviewed by Adair and Popkin (2005) who analysed survey data conducted in Cebu, China, Russia and America to further understand the global trends in children and adolescence snacking and eating behaviours. From the review of survey data, it was highlighted that adolescence in particular consumed one third of their daily calories away from their homes. From the food and beverage choices offered at schools Kubik et al. (2003) outlined in their study the negative impacts in the school environment and the effect of snack vending machines, deep-fried menu items including the range of choice on al a carte programs on students in the school. Interestingly if the students would select high-caloric snacks in a vending machine this would decrease the chances of the students choosing to eat fruit or vegetable snacking options. Reilly et al. (2016) propose that regular audits such as the quick menu audit of the food and beverages made available in schools as an important strategy evaluate the food options available in conjunction with interventions and initiatives. It would also be imperative to ensure that the food options made available can educate students to make better food choices and for this to be the normative behaviour fostered at school.

This is further substantiated that schools are in the important position to restrict nutrient-lacking foods and beverages and include a range of healthy lunch options from which the students can make positive choices for food they select to eat. The researchers based their study on investigating the eating behaviours of students at school. It is important for schools to evaluate the options made available to students and should also look to initiatives for those students bringing

DOI: 10.4324/9781003294962-14

lunch from home and to encourage healthy lunch alternatives as a part of their school wide policy and additionally supported in the curriculum. The study suggests that there is a reduction in students purchasing foods containing high levels of sugar and fats if these options are limited in schools. Alternate healthy sources of food choices for lunches purchased from school should be affordable, easy to access and assist in supporting the students making positive choices for the food they choose to eat. It is further highlighted from this research that school-wide initiatives should support the needs of older students as well as younger children. Particular when older students have the option to leave the campus to purchase their lunch outside the school (Neumark-Sztainer et al. 2005). Further consideration needs to be taken to understand the eating patterns of adolescents and to ensure students are able to critically draw from their healthy toolkit to make positive eating choices and across a range of different situations and contexts.

Hill et al. (1998) conducted parent and student interviews in Auckland, New Zealand in various circumstances such as geographic location, cultural background and socio-economic status to better understand adolescence food attitudes when consuming fruits and vegetables to encourage healthier choices. A sample of the parents described the powerful influence of peers on their teenager. Stating the tastes and choices were influenced by what their friends are eating and what they thought was trendy to eat and that comments from peers could influence them if they would eat their packed lunch or not. As to sharing food with friends at school, fruit was viewed as a lesser option as the more attractively presented and easy-to-eat options like chocolate and chips were easily divided and shared amongst the group (Hill et al. 1998). Teaching adolescents about healthy choices is not enough for any initiative or opportunities in a school to be successful; it must also consider adolescent identity and the need to belong amongst their peers. A key theme noted that it was socially risky to choose healthy options due to some of the young participants feeling sensitive to the reactions of their peers to their food choices. It was further explained that the perception of healthy eating was linked by the participants as being unconventional and only for those that had low social standing and persona. There are potential barriers to consider when sourcing strategies that will have an impact on young people and their food choices that also takes into consideration their need for acceptance and belonging whilst also ensuring their nutritional requirements are being met (Stead et al. 2011).

To better understand adolescence food choices and the link to the social influences surrounding the young people to prevent health issues. Adolescents were surveyed to learn more about their daily food habits, their choice of communication channels and the influence of these media channels on food choice and selection. The final section of the survey looked at how adolescents see themselves individually and at the greater societal level. At a broader level teenagers acknowledge that family is the main avenue for advice but from the researched information from one of the cluster groups it was discovered that adolescents are heavily influenced by social media need to have further intervention and should be encouraged to pull from a broader base of influences to ensure positive food choices are made. Furthermore it was found that adolescents only recognised teachers as a minor influence in terms of their decision around food choice. The researchers attest that this is an important finding in light of the interventions and messages delivered in schools and by teachers. Highlighting the significance of building positive relationships between students and teachers to ensure interventions and health promotion in schools are accepted as key sources of information and support (De Rosis et al. 2019). When teachers develop positive relationships with their students this increases student engagement and learning (Corso et al. 2013). This is also supported by Patton et al. (2016) who draw valuable links to positive school messaging regarding health and healthy choices as being more successful when students feel a sense of connection to their teachers and their school. Adolescents that identified a broad base of influence were open to more of the enabling influences such as learning to make healthier food choices from their teachers (De Rosis et al. 2019).

The role of education

To generate transformative change, Food literacy education is a potential health strategy to influence food choices. Food literacy is defined as the range of skills, knowledge and choices required each day when striving to achieve dietary recommendations that support good health. (Vidgen et al. 2014). In a qualitative study conducted across 22 high schools home economic teachers' perspectives of food literacy were ascertained through a series of interviewing questions. This was to gain a deeper understanding of the teachers' knowledge of food literacy and improve adolescent awareness of their dietary choices. From the data collected it was revealed that a combination of both nutrition and food skills is necessary. Firstly, a comprehensive understanding is required of the teachers educating students to become confident in their understanding of food health literacy. The teachers also linked the dietary patterns of behaviour and obesity to limited food skills and lacking food nutrition knowledge. The teachers stated that the crucial elements to equip adolescents are food skills combined with high order and critical thinking. Combined with positive role models who can guide and improve food nutrition and knowledge (Ronto et al. 2016a,b). As such, this makes including food literacy education in schools an important intervention to ensure informed choices are made by adolescents.

Schools can play a role in further improving food knowledge in cooking classes and in the school canteens. Facilitating a deeper understanding of the role of ultra-processing and links to nutrition knowledge required when making decisions of what food to consume. Food preparation was recorded by many of the teenagers in the study by Hill et al. (1998) where they felt they had inadequate skills and knowledge to prepare a meal and how to prepare vegetable dishes. The majority of the teenagers were confident to prepare simple and ready-to-eat foods. A larger number of the teenagers commented that their main sources to learn how to cook were by watching or cooking with a family member or in a cooking class at school (Hill et al. 1998). From the adolescent perspective the teacher and cooking in schools present students with an opportunity to expand their understanding of how to prepare a nutritious lunch that can be safely transported to school whilst maintaining food appeal. Additionally it is imperative for adolescents to also develop their critical thinking skills alongside this knowledge. Schafersman (1998) defines critical thinking as the cognitive thought processes required to source accurate and relevant information about the world. For any change in food choices to occur critical thinking strategies need to be explicitly taught to students so that they are equipped with the knowledge to question and challenge their current thinking about the food they consume.

To support the development of nutritional interventions further research is required to better understand the factors that can generate transformative behavioural change in the dietary patterns of adolescents. Researchers in a study sought to find a correlation between factors that effect change in behaviour over a two year period when consuming energy-dense snacks, fruit and vegetables at the individual, environmental and social levels. It was discovered that the gender and age of the adolescent should be sex-specific when promoting healthy eating interventions. Another important point to consider when promoting health interventions is to consider self-efficacy of the adolescent. For Australian teenagers when self-efficacy is high the consumption of fruits, vegetables and the intention to make positive choices that support health increases in success rate. An additional benefit recorded was a reduction in the consumption of energy-dense snacks can also be seen when self-efficacy is high to reduce junk foods in the diet (Neumark-Sztainer et al. 2005). Shifting adolescence mindsets in terms of their self-awareness of the food choices they make every day is an important aspect to consider according to Buchan and Grieg (2021).

The global study by Adair and Popkin (2005) critically highlights the need for programs and policies to target and foster eating for health especially when there is much choice in regards to high caloric low nutrient dense lunch choices in the form of fast food worldwide with the aim to reduce childhood health problems such as obesity. Monteiro et al. (2013) link from research the risk of food choices including ultra-high processed foods due to the low nutrient density and high calories from these foods. Ultra-high processed foods are those that are processed to create a convenient, durable and appealing ready-to-eat convenience food and beverages. Monteiro (2009) draws implications to the current and traditional teaching of nutrition and health which places an emphasis on the awareness of the nutrients in food and beverages. Stating that education is lacking in knowledge surrounding food processing and the health implications from choices made from heavily processed foods. Education about ultra-processed foods and ingredients needs to also be included in the curriculum. Monterio (2009) states that ultra-processed foods are highly profitable to food manufacturers and are heavily marketed towards children. For change to be transformative it needs to be two-fold that young people are educated about the convenience foods they eat and are empowered to make positive food choices. The US guide Pyramid urges the consumption of healthy foods but lacks information on food processing and ultra-processed foods to be aware of. From an Australian perspective the Australian Dietary Guidelines make reference to patterns in diets to food and beverages and not to nutrients. It is stated that it is the quality and quantity of the food and beverages eaten on a regular basis that can have an impact on health. Further detail regarding the Australian Guidelines for healthy eating should be used in conjunction with this visual and should not be the only source of guidance to inform food and beverage decisions. Retaining students' nutritional knowledge is another area of concern. Students interviewed in a study by Hill et al. (1998) revealed that teenagers understood that fruit and vegetables were a healthy choice. However, they could not recall more detailed information on nutrition they had learnt in class. One girl aged 14 who was interviewed stated she learnt something about the food pyramid, the human body and if you ate too much of some foods it would be bad for your body. She openly stated she could not remember anything else. Interestingly the negative comments surrounding eating the wrong things were what was remembered, not the benefits of selecting healthier options as being protective for their health and wellbeing. Changing the way that adolescents view the concept of fast foods or quick and convenient foods needs to be further addressed when delivering lessons that can influence food choices in the short and long term.

Savige et al. (2007) conducted a study to investigate adolescence dietary patterns against the recommendations from the Australian Dietary Guidelines and the implications to their health in the long term. Additionally the researchers also considered the gender, geographical location where the adolescents live as well as their age. It was discovered that about two thirds of the adolescents were not eating the daily recommendations across the five food groups. Half of the participants were noted to eat across the five food groups most days. Although, a high percentage of the adolescents in this study consumed fast foods and rarely ate fruit each day. Regional adolescents were also recorded to eat more vegetables and only consumed fast foods infrequently as compared to those living in metropolitan who were noted to eat fast food more frequently. The researchers link one possible explanation for the higher intake of fast foods in these regions due to the accessibility and availability of these foods. According to the Australian Dietary Guidelines the following general statement is made in the introduction "... most of us need to choose foods and drinks more wisely to protect our health" (National Health and Medical Research Council 2013, p.1). With obesity on the rise Fayet-Moore et al. (2017b) reviewed three national surveys spanning over 16 years to better understand the evolving Australian adolescent weekly snacking patterns. An increase in snacking behaviours was revealed with the researchers highlighting 24% energy increase from snacking in 1995 to 30.5% in 2011 to 2012. The researchers made a link between the quality of adolescent diet and snacking. This is altered depending on how often snacking is occurring, portion size and more importantly the snack being chosen to eat. It is recommended that intervention programs target nutritious snacking choices based on the core food groups due to the increase in snacking patterns amongst adolescents. Supporting the research from Hill et al. (1998) when given the choice between fruit and a sugary snack adolescents will more than likely select the less nutrient-dense option. It would be important to also ensure that adolescents are aware of this and choose to make sound decisions regarding the food and beverages they choose to eat every day.

Adolescent voice and agency

When student voices are incorporated into these interventions this places the adolescent in an active role. It is recommended that utilising self-reflection visualisation tools and adolescence input to influence other young people positively about their health is a way that students are empowered in their food choices. It was also discovered that adolescents enjoyed working with other young people when playing sports and preparing meals. Through this process of working with more experienced students regarding healthy choices other adolescent partners working alongside these students became more aware of how to prepare healthy meals and make better choices about their health. The adolescents who participated in this study mentioned that it was an opportunity to connect with other students outside their immediate friendship group. One of the participants recorded that she could focus better on the task at hand when working with others she had not chosen herself. Other participants enjoyed the active nature of learning about healthy choices by doing rather than just listening about how to make better lifestyle choices. The teachers that were also included in this study expressed that the active nature of learning to make healthy food choices was more engaging and beneficial for transformative learning by adopting healthy choices in everyday practice. Another participant was recorded stating that they had not realised they could follow a recipe and prepare vegetarian meals, surprised that this type of food could be as tasty as fast food. Using digital modes of communication was also a beneficial method to aid self-reflection and to learn more about themselves in terms of making proactive choices. It is important to reinforce the importance of adolescence having a say and input in their health as a way to empower young people looking ahead to decisions and choices they make about their health in the future (Holmberg et al. 2018).

Patton et al. (2016) state that compared with adults adolescents make different decisions regarding their health one of these factors is the influence of peers and decision-making processes. Furthermore, recommending that the focus should be on adolescents becoming advocates and promoting healthy choices to other young people which has been found in the health sector to be the most empowering strategy. According to Stok et al. (2016) there is an imperative need to adopt strategies that enable adolescents to make better choices regarding their health. It is argued that Australian adolescents have inadequate dietary intake and are at risk for future health complications due to not consuming enough micronutrients. Food and beverages being selected that are low in nutrient density are of also concern. A study looked to specific food occasions to elucidate how to improve dietary intake of teenagers. It was discovered that more teenagers need to make sure they have breakfast every day, the quality of lunches needs to be improved, expanding the quantity of fruits and vegetables eaten for the lunch and dinner meal needs to also be considered. Further enhancements to the dietary patterns should limit the consumption of sweetened beverages, consume more dairy milk and foods containing more magnesium need to be targeted (Fayet-Moore et al. 2017a).

The researchers highlight a gap in adolescent voices in regards to this issue through this research they detail strategies that can be adopted to assist adolescents making healthy choices. As a result a study was conducted which included 2764 adolescents aged 10–17 from European countries who were asked to answer a series of questions to gauge their knowledge of healthy and unhealthy food and their thoughts on ten intervention strategies mentioned in the survey questions. The outcome of the study revealed that the strategies could be broadly segmented into two groups preventing unhealthy eating and encouraging healthy eating. The researcher described the adolescence from this study as open to the strategies that focused on them making healthy choices rather than those strategies that sought to minimise unhealthy decision making regarding their food choices. It was also outlined in this study as key findings that adolescents who were overweight, some adolescents from different cultural backgrounds and younger adolescents were more open to strategies encouraging healthy eating as compared to older adolescents in this study. Noteworthy from this study when surveyed regarding strategies that deter adolescents from unhealthy eating it was discovered that the participants in this study were less open to strategies discouraging healthy eating outside their home and school context and were more open to the interventions delivered by their teachers and parents. It would therefore be important to consider future strategies that incorporate student agency that focuses on the promotion of healthy eating habits if adolescents are to accept these strategies delivered at school and at home.

Greene (2013) further supports this by using the Theory of Active Involvement as a lens to explain how interventions that place the adolescent in an active role can influence their decision-making processes especially in regards to important issues relating to their health. Self-reflection is highlighted as a critical component in ensuring adolescent agency to enable a change in behaviour that is feasible in the long term. Another layer that should be incorporated is the ability for adolescents to have opportunities to relate to their fellow peers in terms of creating the important health messages. An approach to assist with communicating effectively important health messages to adolescents is to include adolescent involvement in the planning and generation of these messages for other adolescents. Utter et al. also support this argument that it is important for adolescents to have opportunities to exercise their agency and generate their own health messages incorporating their own perspectives, reflect and apply this knowledge to their own lives increasing the success of the approach to achieving the change in behaviour patterns in the future. Green further elaborates on the key elements that need to be considered when developing active involvement strategies that target adolescent health education. Firstly the careful selection of engaging adolescence engagement from the onset. This is also supported by Utter et al. (2011) whereby if programmes and interventions are to be effective and resonating with adolescents the educational activities at school must be suitable for the developmental level and age. Incorporating the use of small groups to enable adolescents to interact with their peers to increase the self-reflection opportunities in a public forum to present perspectives which also takes into consideration age and developmental suitability and experience with content related to further encouraging a positive change in attitude and behaviour regarding their health. Some specific examples of initiatives include the establishment of breakfast clubs and health-focus weeks. It is imperative that adolescents take responsibility for their health and develop an understanding of how they perceive their food choices to ensure positive food habits can flourish (Hill et al. 1998).

Food perception and mindset around food choices also need to be considered when educating adolescents about their food choices in present times and in the future. Wahl et al. (2017) in a study researched and assessed the benefits of eating from a range of food groups across eight days. The participants were asked to use their smartphones to record the type of food and their level of happiness they felt directly after eating. The researchers predicted that both unhealthy and healthy choices including vegetables and fruits would mark a high level of happiness in the participant directly after eating these food types. The study revealed indeed that vegetables attained the highest result score followed by sugary treats, dairy and bread-based food items. When combining food groups it was discovered that fruit and vegetables were the highest scoring, followed by grain food items and finally as the third highest scored by the participants were unhealthy foods. The researchers state that the results from their study will be beneficial for informing future healthy eating strategies regarding the benefits to adolescents when making positive food choices. The researchers also reinforce that healthy choices can be associated with happiness which should challenge the notion that unhealthy food choices are more flavoursome and more enjoyable to eat. Essentially this research calls for a shift in mindset from food needing to be consumed for health to "food as well-being" (Wahl et al. 2017, p.6). There is still a need in schools to develop interventions that empower, educate and generate opportunities for adolescents to think critically about their food choices now and in the future.

References

Adair, L. S., and Popkin, B. M., 2005. Are child eating patterns being transformed globally? *Obesity Research* [online], 13. Available from: https://doi.org/10.1038/oby.2005.153.
Corso, M. J., Bundick, M. J., Quaglia, R. J., and Haywood, D. E., 2013. Where student, teacher, and content meet: student engagement in the secondary school classroom. *American Secondary Education*, 41, 50–61.

De Rosis, S., Pennucci, F., and Seghieri, C., 2019. Segmenting adolescents around social influences on their eating behavior: findings from Italy. *Social Marketing Quarterly* [online], 25 (4). Available from: https://doi.org/10.1177/1524500419882059.

Fayet-Moore, F., McConnell, A., Kim, J., and Mathias, K. C., 2017a. Identifying eating occasion-based opportunities to improve the overall diets of Australian adolescents. *Nutrients* [online], 9 (6). Available from: https://doi.org/10.3390/nu9060608.

Fayet-Moore, F., Peters, V., McConnell, A., Petocz, P., and Eldridge, A. L., 2017b. Weekday snacking prevalence, frequency, and energy contribution have increased while foods consumed during snacking have shifted among Australian children and adolescents: 1995, 2007 and 2011–12 National Nutrition Surveys. *Nutrition Journal* [online], 16 (1). Available from: https://doi.org/10.1186/s12937-017-0288-8.

Greene, K., 2013. The theory of active involvement: processes underlying interventions that engage adolescents in message planning and/or production. *Health Communication* [online], 28 (7). Available from: https://pubmed.ncbi.nlm.nih.gov/23980581/.

Hill, L., Casswell, S., Maskill, C., Jones, S., and Wyllie, A., 1998. Fruit and vegetables as adolescent food choices in New Zealand. *Health Promotion International* [online], 13 (1). Available from: https://doi.org/10.1093/heapro/13.1.55.

Holmberg, C., Larsson, C., Korp, P., Lindgren, E. C., Jonsson, L., Fröberg, A., Chaplin, J. E., and Berg, C., 2018. Empowering aspects for healthy food and physical activity habits: adolescents' experiences of a school-based intervention in a disadvantaged urban community. *International Journal of Qualitative Studies on Health and Well-being* [online], 13. Available from: https://doi.org/ 10.1080/17482631.2018.1487759.

Kubik, M. Y., Lytle, L. A., Hannan, P. J., Perry, C. L., and Story, M., 2003. The association of the school food environment with dietary behaviors of young adolescents. *American Journal of Public Health* [online], 93 (7). Available from: https://doi.org/10.2105/ajph.93.7.1168.

Monteiro, C., 2009. Nutrition and health: the issue is not food, nor nutrients, so much as processing. *Public Health Nutrition*, 12 (5), 729–731.

Monteiro, C. A., Moubarac, J. C., Cannon, G., Ng, S. W., and Popkin, B., 2013. Ultra-processed products are becoming dominant in the global food system. *Obesity Reviews: An Official Journal of the International Association for the Study of Obesity*, 14 (Suppl 2). Available from: https://doi.org/10.1111/obr.12107.

National Health and Medical Research Council, 2013. *Australian dietary guidelines summary* [online]. Canberra: National Health and Medical Research Council. Available from: https://www.eatforhealth.gov.au/ [Accessed 12 June 2021].

Neumark-Sztainer, D., French, S. A., Hannan, P. J., Story, M., and Fulkerson, J. A., 2005. School lunch and snacking patterns among high school students: associations with school food environment and policies. *The International Journal of Behavioral Nutrition and Physical Activity* [online], 2 (1), 14. Available from: https://doi.org/10.1186/1479-5868-2-14.

Patton, G. C., Sawyer, S. M., Santelli, J. S., Ross, D. A., Afifi, R., Allen, N. B., ... Viner, R. M., 2016. Our future: A lancet commission on adolescent health and wellbeing. *The Lancet*, 387, 2423–2478.

Reilly, K., Nathan, N., Wolfenden, L., Wiggers, J., Sutherland, R., Wyse, R., and Yoong, S. L., 2016. Validity of four measures in assessing school canteen menu compliance with state-based healthy canteen policy. *Health Promotion Journal of Australia: Official Journal of Australian Association of Health Promotion Professionals* [online], 27 (3). Available from: https://doi.org/10.1071/HE16053.

Ronto, R., Ball, L., Pendergast, D., and Harris, N., 2016a. Adolescents' perspectives on food literacy and its impact on their dietary behaviours. *Appetite*, 107, 549–557.

Ronto, R., Ball, L., Pendergast, D., and Harris, N., 2016b. The role of home economics teachers in enhancing adolescents' food literacy to develop healthy dietary behaviours. *Journal of the Home Economics Institute of Australia* [online], (23). Available from: https://research-repository.griffith.edu.au/handle/10072/134158.

Savige, G. S., Ball, K., Worsley, A., and Crawford, D., 2007. Food intake patterns among Australian adolescents. *Asia Pacific Journal of Clinical Nutrition*, 16 (4), 738–747.

Stead, M., McDermott, L., Mackintosh, A. M., and Adamson, A., 2011. Why healthy eating is bad for young people's health: identity, belonging and food. *Social Science & Medicine (1982)*, 72 (7), 1131–1139.

Stok, F. M., de Ridder, D. T., de Vet, E., Nureeva, L., Luszczynska, A., Wardle, J., Gaspar, T., and de Wit, J. B., 2016. Hungry for an intervention? Adolescents' ratings of acceptability of eating-related intervention strategies. *BMC Public Health* [online], 16 (5). Available from: https://doi.org/10.1186/s12889-015-2665-6.

Utter, J., Scragg, R., Robinson, E., Warbrick, J., Faeamani, G., Foroughian, S., Dewes, O., Moodie, M., and Swinburn, B. A., 2011. Evaluation of the Living 4 Life project: a youth-led, school-based obesity prevention study. *Obesity reviews: An Official Journal of the International Association for the Study of Obesity* [online], 12 (Suppl 2), 51–60. Available from: https://doi.org/10.1111/j.1467-789X.2011.00905.x.

Wahl, D. R., Villinger, K., König, L. M., Ziesemer, K., Schupp, H. T., & Renner, B. (2017). Healthy food choices are happy food choices: Evidence from a real life sample using smartphone based assessments. *Scientific Reports*, 7(1), 17069. https://doi.org/10.1038/s41598-017-17262-9.

PART IV

Sociology of food

12

SOCIAL MEDIA PLATFORMS AND ADOLESCENTS' NUTRITIONAL CAREERS

Upcoming development tasks and required literacies

Tina Bartelmeß

Introduction

Those who currently count as adolescents are in a critical phase of life that can significantly influence their future relationship with food and can prescribe certain future action paths. In adolescence parents become less important and the number of people from outside the family who take a stake in secondary food socialisation increases (Beardsworth and Keil 2002). Regarding everyday food decisions and actions, the phase of the transition from childhood to adolescence involves an increase in autonomy and independence from the parental home (Glover and Sumberg 2020). During adolescence young people face a variety of developmental tasks, in which specific action-guiding norms and values are formed and identities are (re-)negotiated and become more firmly established (Erikson 1968; Havighurst 1972). In today's world, many of the adolescent developmental tasks are transferred to digital spaces and co-determined by several secondary socialisation agents emerging and becoming more present in these spheres (Paus-Hasebrink et al. 2019). Through social media platforms values and norms that often relate particularly to the topics of food and health are conveyed. The actors communicating about food and health topics on such platforms are usually not professional actors, but peers and everyday actors. These actors are given the status of lay experts through digitally supported social rating systems, such as likes and shares, through which their self-created content is evaluated and further disseminated by their readership respectively followers. The content created by those lay experts, who are also called 'influencers' when they reach a certain number of followers, is mostly based on personal experiences and less on scientific and verified knowledge (Bartelmeß 2021). Critically engaging with this content and actively considering whether and which of these communicators should be included as agents of secondary socialisation in the adolescent's developmental process seems urgent, especially in view of the amount of misinformation

DOI: 10.4324/9781003294962-16

in the social media realm. However, coping with developmental tasks in adolescence is usually not consciously controlled, but rather an unconscious process (Hurrelmann and Bauer 2018). Competences are therefore needed to enable young people not only to critically evaluate the content they are confronted with, but also to assess the role of social media at this life stage. This chapter discusses the relevance of different literacy areas for the critical and conscious use of social media food communication by adolescents against the background of their upcoming developmental tasks.

First, the chapter highlights the process of secondary food socialisation and the specific developmental tasks in adolescence as deemed important to healthy and sustainable relationships with food. Thereafter, the social media use of adolescents is examined, and different social media usage practices related to the developmental tasks are presented. Then, an overview of the current state of research on food- and health-related social media usage of adolescents and its impact on coping with developmental tasks is presented. Following that, components of food, health, and media literacy that emerge as particularly significant to adolescents' development are discussed. The chapter concludes with an outlook in which implications for future research and practice are derived.

Secondary food socialisation and food-relevant developmental tasks in adolescence

Adolescence is a stage of life with specific developmental needs and tasks and a period that is crucial for the acquisition of characteristics and behaviours that are important for young people's relationship with food and health (Havighurst 1972). The life stage of adolescence is characterised by offering opportunities for awareness-raising, as young people are generally more open to exploration, behavioural change, and transitions (Hargreaves et al. 2022). This openness to transformation also makes adolescents more susceptible to potentially harmful influences, especially of other agents of secondary socialisation, which can have long-lasting consequences for their relationship with food and health.

Following the period of primary food socialisation in the family young people enter the process of secondary food socialisation that continues to the end of an individual's life. It involves learning new skills, norms, values, and attitudes towards food, and modifying existing behaviours (Hurrelmann and Bauer 2018). Agents of secondary food socialisation at the stage of adolescence include among other friends, peer groups, teachers and historically the media (Fieldhouse 1995). The media environment and technologies are constantly and rapidly changing. Adolescents promptly adopt new applications into their daily routines, leading to significant changes in the way media can act as an agent of secondary food socialisation (Baumgartner and Kühne 2018). This new digital secondary food socialisation environment requires young people to develop specific competences to successfully master the upcoming developmental tasks at this life stage. Developmental tasks arise at certain age-specific stages and must be mastered to avoid unhappiness, disapproval by society, and challenges in tackling tasks arising at later life stages. The following developmental tasks at the stage of adolescence deem to be important relative to building a healthy and sustainable relationship to food (Havighurst 1972):

Achieving emotional independence from parents and other adults,
developing a social role,
participating in and achieving new and more mature relations with peer-groups,
accepting one's physique and keeping it healthy,
acquiring a set of values and an ethical system as a guide to behaviour, and
desiring and achieving socially responsible behaviour.

Closely related to the listed developmental tasks is the development of a personal identity in adolescence (Erikson 1968). Identity formation occurs through the evaluation, social comparison, and distinction of one's own positive and negative qualities and the exploration of different roles and engagement in different spheres of life and interaction. Social media platforms today can be understood as such spheres, which contribute to the clarification of one's own self-concept (Sebre and Miltuze 2021). In adolescence, individuals may undergo significant changes in their former socially formulated appetites and attitudes or may experience important transformations in the meanings which they attach to food and health. Individuals can be seen as having what can be termed a 'nutritional career' (Beardsworth and Keil 2002), which is closely related to the life cycle socialisation. Individual food preferences, attitudes, values, and concrete nutritional practices change according to changing bodily needs, developmental tasks and shifting social and cultural expectations, many of which are today constructed and communicated via social media.

Adolescents' social media usage practices

In 2019 almost 94% of adolescents in the European Union use the internet daily. In a comparison of age groups, adolescents are also the most frequent users of social media platforms, in 2019 the user share was 84% (Eurostat 2020). Social media platforms enable numerous users to enter communicative relationships after prior registration through a common software infrastructure. An important subgroup of social media platforms is user-generated content platforms (UGC platforms), which focus on publishing or receiving UGC. Each social media platform has specifics on how food and health are talked about and how content is presented and received, such as videos on YouTube and images on Instagram or Pinterest (Bartelmeß 2021). What all social media platforms have in common is that the topics of food and health occupy a prominent position and that the content is mostly produced by laypeople instead of food or health experts (Brandwatch 2019).

With a media sociological, practice-theoretical approach the use of social media platforms can be understood as supporting social life practices of adolescents that are related to coping with central developmental tasks (Paus-Hasebrink et al. 2019). Accordingly, social media use facilitates the three social practices of information, identity, and relationship management (Schmidt and Taddicken 2016). Information management refers to the supportive function of social media platforms for adolescents in factual engagement with information on food- and health-related topics (How do I orient myself in the world?). It encompasses the ways in which adolescents create, filter, select, manage, edit, share, and disseminate information and that help them navigate the wealth of information available. Identity management encompasses the practices of self-presentation to others by making public certain aspects of one's personality, interests, and expertise, which assists adolescents in their self-presentation (who am I?). It refers not only to the creation and publication of personal information, but also to the expression of opinions, preferences, and experiences, for example, by commenting on others' posts. Relationship management refers to the functionalities of social media platforms that support adolescents in articulating, building, and maintaining social relationships, thus encouraging them in their social interaction. By making social relationships selectable and explicitly articulable, traditional forms of social organisation are replaced by more individualised, freely configurable forms (Where is my place in society?) (Schmidt and Taddicken 2016). This media-sociological approach makes it possible to understand young people's use of social media platforms as closely related to these three social practices, which are carried out with and on social media platforms to cope with the developmental tasks outlined above. It highlights the fact that young people today no longer only seek information about food and health in the media for specific purposes, but also act with and through the media in ways that are relevant to real-life practices. This is because through the selection of information, the choice and maintenance of digital relationships, identities are always indirectly managed, which in turn guide daily actions (Hepp 2020). With social media platforms, new actors and forms of orientation and knowledge transfer emerge, which are particularly relevant when coping with developmental tasks in adolescence.

Methods

This chapter is based on desk research. In January 2022, the Web of Science database was queried for articles that thematically and theoretically fall within the scope of the chapter. Using key terms that refer to the age group of adolescents (e.g., 'adolescents', 'youth'), food (e.g., 'food', 'diet', or 'nutrition'), and social media (e.g., 'TikTok', 'Facebook', or 'Snapchat'), 34 peer-reviewed journal articles were identified. These articles were screened and analysed in terms of their findings on the impact of social media usage on adolescents' coping with developmental tasks related to food and health.

Uncertain food futures: social media platforms' role in adolescents' nutritional careers

The current state of research on adolescents' use of social media platforms in relation to food and health and its impact on coping with developmental tasks is not very advanced. Some psychological studies focus on investigating the influence of communication about food and health on social media platforms on individual behavioural variables. Several studies investigate the impact of social media usage on perceptions of body image (e.g., Goodyear et al. 2021; Jebeile et al. 2021; Rounsefell et al. 2020), followed by impact on self-esteem (Bevelander et al. 2013) and disordered eating (Herrick et al. 2021; Walker et al. 2015). Study findings provide considerable evidence that social media platforms and the communication and portrayal of food and health issues by everyday actors have a negative impact on body image concerns and self-esteem and can subsequently lead to the promotion of eating disorders among, mostly female, adolescents. The studies underline nowadays social media platforms represent an important socio-cultural context in which developmental tasks such as acceptance of one's own body are questioned, as idealised body images are often presented and associated with supposedly healthy eating.

Another strand of research highlights the influence of social media platforms on forming peer relationships to share food-related information and socially validate certain food and health behaviours. Striking is that these studies refer mostly to adolescents with specific information requirements, for example in the case of illnesses such as diabetes (Yi-Frazier et al. 2015) or cancer (Aggarwal et al. 2020), or to particular social roles caused by pregnancy and early parenthood (Marshall et al. 2019). In the context of health intervention studies, it has also been shown that interaction and communication with fellow peers with similar health concerns on social media platforms can be motivating to adopt health-promoting behaviour (Watanabe-Ito et al. 2020).

In healthy adolescents, research points out that social media platforms enable different forms of cultural interaction, especially in relation to gender and the formation and finding of a social role. In global cross-border social media interaction, various social and cultural differences such as norms, roles, and relationships between sexes, for instance, regarding food responsibility and meal preparation as well as diets, are conveyed. Through food-related communication and engagement on social media platforms, adolescents are enabled not only to understand socio-cultural aspects and differences in relation to food and health, but also to challenge and modify existing ones learned in primary food socialisation (Rambaree et al. 2020).

Research shows that social media platforms represent a digital space which young people 'know better' than their parents (Paulo and Casarin 2021) and in which they can obtain new norms, values, and orientations independently of their primary food socialisation. Adolescents value social media for expanding food choices through access to a variety of recipes and providing a venue to show what young people eat and prepare (Vaterlaus et al. 2015). However, it has been repeatedly found that exposure to and engagement with food-related social media content overwhelmingly leads to unhealthy dietary behaviours and food choice outcomes, such as dieting, restricting food, or overeating (Rounsefell et al. 2020; Vaterlaus et al. 2015). The underlying processes are complex and cannot be clearly assigned and explained. Phenomenological and interpretative studies shed light on how food- and health-related norms are constructed and communicated on social media platforms (Carrotte et al. 2015). It turns out that mainly objectifying and inaccurate food and health messages are conveyed that lack scientific validity. Problematic features include stigmatising language around weight, portrayals of guilt around food and idealising and overemphasising desirable thin bodies (Carrotte et al. 2015). The construction of new food- and health-related norms and the communication of values and how to deal with them, especially through so-called influencers who can serve as role models, has an impact on adolescents' identity constructions and might shape their actions in relation to food and health in the long term.

In contrast to the other strands of research, an emerging research area concerned with civic food engagement shows how the use of social media in adolescence can support and promote the development of the desire for socially responsible behaviour. It is demonstrated, for example, that social media platforms help adolescents to engage in civic initiatives such as food recycling programs in their communities (Ahmed and Gibreel 2021). Especially in relation to sustainability initiatives and youth movements, such as Fridays for Future or solidarity farming, it is important to get a clear understanding of the role of social media for the mobilisation and development of socially responsible food and health behaviour.

Overall, the state of research illustrates that adolescents use social media for food- and health-related information, relationship, and identity management. However, most studies to date have been experimental, in which adolescents are exposed to social media food communication stimuli in artificial environments, or they are correlational studies in which adolescents are asked to retrospectively report their behavioural tendencies as influenced by social media. Even the phenomenological and interpretative studies only conclude from the analysis of food communication on social media platforms on possible impacts on adolescents' thoughts and actions (Bartelmeß and Godemann 2022). Although these approaches are informative, they are mostly snapshots that cannot accurately describe and explain the role of adolescents' use of social media platforms in addressing their developmental tasks, nor how they shape adolescents' nutritional careers in the long term. There is thus a need for long-term studies that focus on the influence of social media use on adolescents' coping with developmental tasks that are relevant to food- and health-related behaviour.

A call to promote adolescents' food, health, or media literacy?

Secondary food socialisation in the digital space requires specific competences. Therefore, significant elements of food, health and media literacy are discussed in their relevance for adolescent users. Food literacy mainly refers to the skills and practices of planning, selecting, preparing, and eating food (Vidgen and Gallegos 2014), health literacy to the management and handling of health-related information (Nutbeam 2000; Sørensen et al. 2012) and media literacy to the ability to communicate and critically interact in and with media technologies (Aufderheide 1993; Rosenbaum et al. 2008).

Food literacy provides the tools that are "needed for a healthy lifelong relationship with food" (Vidgen and Gallegos 2014, p.54). Research has shown that the portrayal and staging of food on social media platforms can have negative impacts on psychological variables in adolescents, especially females. In food literacy, a key component is self-awareness that food intake needs to be balanced. This component includes knowledge of which foods should be consumed for good health, which should be restricted, and appropriate portion sizes and frequencies. It has been shown that many norms related to these aspects are idealised on social media platforms. They tend to have a negative impact on young people's body image and can reproduce surreal ideals of health maintenance, which can lead to distorted and unhealthy outcomes in the long run. Even though the concept of food literacy includes eating appropriately, the ability to manage food is not further questioned and concretised in digital contexts. In the context of adolescents' developmental tasks of building mature relationships with peers and developing a social role, not enough attention is paid to the aspect of social comparison, although it seems to play a major role in socialising and building relationships with and through communication about food in social media. Social comparison and, in this context, role models are also of utmost importance for the formation of a personal identity. Norms regarding good and bad food, right and wrong diets, and portion sizes can be explicit or implicit messages from secondary food socialisation agents on social media and require critical questioning and reflection by young people in relation to their personal physical needs, diet and in achieving personal health (Cullen et al. 2015).

Health literacy can be divided into functional, interactive, and critical health literacy. In this context, critical health literacy is the missing link to what is absent in the food literacy concept. Critical health literacy is about the evaluation and application of health information to make judgements and decisions to promote personal health (Sørensen et al. 2012). It requires the motivation and development of cognitive skills of the adolescent. Especially when adolescents want to become independent from their parents and make their own decisions, critically questioning certain nutrition norms conveyed in social media that are 'new' and perhaps rather 'unconventional' is of utmost importance. Precisely because such dietary patterns can be adopted unquestioningly to imitate certain diet-related identities or to express belonging to a certain peer group, the most scientifically unsubstantiated dietary messages must be examined to see whether they are merely substantiated by the communicators' personal experiences or even only serve to stage certain desirable lifestyles.

Like health literacy, media literacy is defined as the ability to access, analyse, evaluate, and create messages in various forms (Aufderheide 1993). In addition to the important ability to use media for interaction and communication to establish and maintain digital relationships with peers in the first place (Aufderheide 1993), awareness of media content creation (Rosenbaum et al. 2008) and understanding its influence on the way values and meanings are created and shared in today's society (Potter 2010) are of particular importance. Nowadays, social media not only provides individuals with information at all stages of their lives, but also shapes their values and perspectives. This is particularly evident among young people when it comes to the topic of food. This can be seen in more negative directions when it comes to values and their interpretation, for example, in relation to food changing the body, but also in positive directions when it comes to civic engagement to avoid food waste. The concept of media literacy highlights the importance of young people's awareness of the influence of media on them as users, but also on the role of producers, i.e., the agents of secondary food socialisation, and their intentions to present food and health issues according to the modalities and conventions typically presented on specific platforms. A media-literate young person is one who understands how the modalities of text and image influence the way food- and health-related meanings are constructed on social media platforms (Potter 2010). Media literate young people can assign value and meaning to both media use and media messages, which they need to critically engage with information.

It seems clear that individual literacy skills, in the context of ubiquitous social media use in adolescence, are not sufficient to successfully address developmental tasks and their implications for healthy and sustainable future nutritional careers. Different combinations, types and levels of literacy gradually enable adolescents to achieve greater autonomy and personal development and empowerment (Nutbeam 2000), and the skills discussed can be considered essential in the context presented here.

Conclusion

Adolescents are in a phase of life in which experiences and the successful accomplishment of developmental tasks can be decisive for their future relationship to food and health. In an increasing pluralism of societal norms and values and new digital environments in which divergent social and cultural expectations are conveyed (Lupton 2018), the relevance of food, health and media literacy increases and should therefore be given special consideration in educational contexts. The decision of adolescents as to which of the norms and values conveyed on social media platforms will be adopted as a guide for action and serve to cope with developmental tasks depends to a large extent on which competences have already been developed and which levels the adolescents have reached before food- and health-related identities are (re)negotiated on these platforms and thus solidify.

As shown in this chapter, there are no studies to date that explicitly address the long-term impact of adolescents' food- and health-related communication and interaction with secondary food socialisation agents on social media platforms. There is a clear need for research, as it is not yet obvious how these new socialisation contexts and new cross-national and cross-cultural relationships will affect the future nutritional careers of today's adolescents. There are also few studies on the positive aspects of secondary food socialisation in social media, for example, in relation to sustainability-related food and health movements. How, in addressing developmental tasks through social media interactions, a value system and ethics are acquired that guide future adolescent behaviour and promote socially responsible behaviour is a previously neglected topic in research.

References

Aggarwal, R., Hueniken, K., Eng, L., et al., 2020. Health-related social media use and preferences of adolescent and young adult cancer patients for virtual programming. *Supportive Care in Cancer* [online], 28 (10). Available from: https://doi.org/10.1177/1049732315583282.

Ahmed, A., and Gibreel, O., 2021. The role of social media in strengthening civic engagement in the Middle East and North Africa. *World Journal of Entrepreneurship Management and Sustainable Development* [online], 17 (3), 309–317.

Aufderheide, P., 1993. Forum report Media literacy: a report of the national leadership Conference on Media Literacy, 7–9, December 1992. Washington, DC: The Aspen Institute Wye Centre, 1–44.

Bartelmeß, T., 2021. Möglichkeiten der analyse von social-media-daten für die ernährungskommunikation. *In:* J. Godemann and T. Bartelmeß, eds. *Ernährungskommunikation:* Wiesbaden: Springer Fachmedien Wiesbaden, 291–315. Available from: https://doi.org/10.1007/978-3-658-27315-6_28-1.

Bartelmeß, T., and Godemann, J., 2022. Exploring the linkages of digital food communication and analog food behaviour: a scoping review. *International Journal of Environmental Research and Public Health* [online], 19 (15). Available from: https://doi.org/10.3390/ijerph19158990.

Baumgartner, S. E., and Kühne, R., 2018. Youth and media – An outline of key developments. *In:* S. E. Baumgartner, M. Hofer, T. Koch and R. Kühne, eds. *Youth and Media: current perspectives on media use and effects.* Baden-Baden, Germany: Nomos, 7–18.

Beardsworth, A., and Keil, T., 2002. *Sociology on the menu: an invitation to the study of food and society.* New York: Routledge.

Bevelander, K. E., Anschutz, D. J., Creemers, D. H., et al., 2013. The role of explicit and implicit self-esteem in peer modeling of palatable food intake: a study on social media interaction among youngsters. *Plos One* [online], 8 (8). Available from: https://doi.org/10.1371/journal.pone.0072481.

Brandwatch, 2019. *Food trends report 2019.* Available from: https://www.brandwatch.com/de/reports/food-trends/view/ [Accessed 20 December 2021].

Carrotte, E. R., Vella, A. R., and Lim, M. S., 2015. Predictors of liking three types of health and fitness-related content on social media: a cross-sectional study. *Journal of Medical Internet Research* [online], 17 (8). Available from: https://doi.org/10.2196/jmir.4803.

Cullen, T., Hatch, J., Martin, W., et al., 2015. Food literacy: definition and framework for action. *Canadian Journal of Dietetic Practice and Research* [online], 76 (3). Available from: https://doi.org/10.3148/cjdpr-2015-010.

Erikson, E. H., 1968. *Identity: youth and crisis.* New York: Norton.

Eurostat, 2020. *Being young in Europe today* [online]. Available from: https://ec.europa. eu/eurostat/statistics-explained/index.php?title=Being_young_in_Europe_today [Accessed 20 January 2022].

Fieldhouse, P., 1995. *Food and nutrition: customs and culture.* 2nd ed. Boston, MA: Nelson Thornes Ltd.

Glover, D., and Sumberg, J., 2020. Youth and food systems transformation. *Frontiers in Sustainable Food Systems* [online], 4. Available from: https://doi.org/10.3389/ fsufs.2020.00101 [Accessed: 30 September 2020].

Goodyear, V., Andersson, J., Quennerstedt, M., et al., 2021 #Skinny girls: young girls' learning processes and health-related social media. *Qualitative Research in Sport, Exercise and Health* [online], 14 (1). Available from: https://doi.org/10.1080/21596 76X.2021.1888152.

Hargreaves, D., Mates, E., Menon, P., et al., 2022. Strategies and interventions for healthy adolescent growth, nutrition, and development. *The Lancet* [online], 399 (10320). Available from: https://doi.org/10.1016/S0140-6736(21)01593-2.

Havighurst, R. J., 1972. *Development tasks and education.* New York: Longmans Green.

Hepp, A., 2020. *Deep mediatization.* London, UK: Routledge.

Herrick, S. S., Hallward, L., and Duncan, L. R., 2021. This is just how I cope: an inductive thematic analysis of eating disorder recovery content created and shared on TikTok using #EDrecovery. *International Journal of Eating Disorders* [online], 54 (4). Available from: https://doi.org/10.1002/eat.23463.

Hurrelmann, K., and Bauer, U., 2018. *Socialisation during the life course.* New York: Routledge.

Jebeile, H., Partridge, S. R., Gow, M. L., et al., 2021. Adolescent exposure to weight loss imagery on Instagram: a content analysis of top images. *Childhood Obesity* [online], 17 (4). Available from: https://doi.org/10.1089/chi.2020.0351.

Lupton, D., 2018. Cooking, eating, uploading: digital food cultures. *In:* K. LeBesco and P. Naccarato, eds. *The Bloomsbury handbook of food and popular culture.* London, UK: Bloomsbury Publishing, 66–79.

Marshall, E., Moon, M. A., Mirchandani, A., et al., 2019. Baby wants Tacos: analysis of health-related Facebook posts from young pregnant women. *Maternal and Child Health Journal* [online], 23 (10). Available from: https://doi.org/10.1007/s10995-019-02776-7.

Nutbeam, D., 2000. Health literacy as a public health goal: a challenge for contemporary health education and communication strategies into the 21st century. *Health Promotion International* [online], 15 (3) Available from: https://doi.org/10.1093/heapro/15.3.259.

Paulo, R. B., and Casarin, H. D., 2021. Using and sharing information on social media by high school students: a case study of a private school in Sao Paulo state. *Revista Ibero-Americana de Ciencia da Informacao* [online], 14 (1). Available from: http://doi. org/10.26512/rici.v14.n1.2021.29929.

Paus-Hasebrink, I., Kulterer, J., and Sinner, P., 2019. Socialisation in different socialisation contexts. *In:* I. Paus-Hasebrink., J. Kulterer and P. Sinner, eds. *Social inequality, childhood and the media:* Cham, Switzerland: Palgrave Macmillan. Available from: https:// doi.org/10.1007/978-3-030-02653-0_6.

Potter, W. J., 2010. The state of media literacy. *Journal of Broadcasting & Electronic Media* [online], 54 (4). Available from: https://doi.org/10.1080/08838151.2011.521462.

Rambaree, K., Mousavi, F., Magnusson, P., et al., 2020. Youth health, gender, and social media: Mauritius as a glocal place. *Cogent Social Sciences* [online], 6 (1). Available from: https://doi.org/10.1080/23311886.2020.1774140.

Rosenbaum, J. E., Beentjes, J. W. J., and Konig, R. P., 2008. Mapping media literacy: key concepts and future directions. *Communication Yearbook*, 32 (1), 313–353. Available from: https://doi.org/10.1080/23808985.2008.11679081.

Rounsefell, K., Gibson, S., McLean, S., et al., 2020. Social media, body image and food choices in healthy young adults: a mixed methods systematic review. *Nutrition & Dietetics: The Journal of the Dietitians Association of Australia* [online], 77 (1). Available from: https://doi.org/10.1111/1747-0080.12581.

Schmidt, J. H., and Taddicken, M., 2016. Soziale medien: funktionen, praktiken, formationen. *In:* J. H. Schmidt and M. Taddicken, eds. *Handbuch soziale medien.* Wiesbaden: Springer Fachmedien Wiesbaden, 1–15. Available from: https://doi. org/10.1007/978-3-658-03895-3_2-2.

Sebre, S. B., and Miltuze, A., 2021. Digital media as a medium for adolescent identity development. *Technology, Knowledge and Learning* [online], 26 (4). Available from: https://doi.org/10.1007/s10758-021-09499-1.

Sørensen, K., van den Broucke, S., Fullam, J., et al., 2012. Health literacy and public health: a systematic review and integration of definitions and models. *BMC Public Health* [online], 12. Available from: https://doi.org/10.1186/1471-2458-12-80.

Vaterlaus, J. M., Patten, E. V., Roche, C., et al., 2015. #Gettinghealthy: the perceived influence of social media on young adult health behaviors. *Computers in Human Behaviour* [online], 45. Available from: https://doi.org/10.1016/j.chb.2014.12.013.

Vidgen, H. A., and Gallegos, D., 2014. Defining food literacy and its components. *Appetite* [online], 76. Available from: https://doi.org/10.1016/j.appet.2014.01.010.

Walker, M., Thornton, L., De Choudhury, M., et al., 2015. Facebook use and disordered eating in college-aged women. *Journal of Adolescent Health* [online], 57 (2). Available from: https://doi.org/10.1016/j.jadohealth.2015.04.026.

Watanabe-Ito, M., Kishi, E., and Shimizu, Y. 2020. Promoting healthy eating habits for college students through creating dietary diaries via a smartphone app and social media interaction: Online survey study. *JMIR Mhealth Uhealth* [online], 8 (3). Available from: https://doi.org/10.2196/17613.

Yi-Frazier, J. P., Cochrane, K., Mitrovich, C., et al., 2015. Using Instagram as a modified application of photovoice for storytelling and sharing in adolescents with Type 1 Diabetes. *Qualitative Health Research* [online], 25 (10). Available from: https://doi. org/10.1177/1049732315583282.

13

FOOD POVERTY AND HOW IT AFFECTS UK CHILDREN IN THE LONG TERM

Ruth Seabrook and Marion Rutland

Introduction

Food poverty means that children have access to lower quality and a restricted range of foods and often go hungry, with their only access to food via free school meals (FSM) vouchers. Teachers regularly report that pupils are fatigued, have poor concentration and are regularly ill, due to poor nutrition and hunger. Children who get FSM are less likely to get A★–C grades at General Certificate of Secondary Education (GCSE) than wealthier peers (The Children's Society 2022). Food security on the other hand is where an individual is considered food secure when they are able to access sufficient, safe and nutritious food at all times in order to maintain an active and healthy lifestyle (Food and Agriculture Organisation 2006).

'Food creates communities and social cohesion and the benefits go way beyond its nutritional value. It brings people together, combats poor mental health, fights loneliness, increases self-worth and esteem' (Fareshare 2022). There has always been hunger and poverty in the world but as societies have grown and become prosperous, there is a perception that the majority live securely and have access to the basic necessities. Yet, millions of people are currently struggling to get by with the poorest of living standards. Around 14 million people are living in poverty in the UK; 4 million are of working age, 4 million are children and 2 million are retired (Joseph Rowntree Foundation 2020). In the State of Hunger Report (The Trussell Trust 2021) it was found that those more susceptible to food insecurity were higher in lower-income households, the unemployed, younger age groups, single parents, social housing renters and those with disabilities or ill health. It is important to highlight food poverty has been at the forefront of many UK Government manifestos over the last 150 years and little has improved.

DOI: 10.4324/9781003294962-17

Methodology

This chapter adopts a qualitative approach based on desktop research. It compares and contrasts historical, socio-economic, political and contemporary issues of child food poverty in the UK. The literature is drawn from journal articles, report findings and expert opinions from charitable bodies, who collectively work in unison to address child food poverty and the inevitable health inequalities that need to be corrected.

Historical developments

The implementation of compulsory education in the 1870 Education Act (United Kingdom Parliament 2022) directed that all children aged 3–11 were to attend school. In Bradford, Margaret McMillan argued if the state insisted on compulsory education, it must take responsibility for the proper nourishment of school children (Smith 2016). Many children were undernourished and through philanthropic measures by organisations, only the most in need were fed. Prominent philanthropists in the late 19th Century, such as Booth and Rowntree reported on the poverty of the nation indicating approximately 30% of the population lived below the poverty line and were unable to pull themselves out of destitution. These reports stunned the public and assisted in shifting opinion about the causes of poverty and a new type of liberalism emerged (Thane 2018).

1900–1942

In 1902, the School Boards Joint Committee reported over 20,000 children were receiving meals in London, and was representative across the nation (Thane 2018). The UK Parliament (1906) passed The Education (Provision of Meals) Act allowing, but not enforcing, Local Education Authorities (LEAs) to provide FSMs for the poorest children. This was as a response to children arriving at school undernourished and fatigued, unable to take advantage of their education. In 1908, 113 LEAs out of 328 were supplying free meals and milk to those in most need and supplying meals to all those who were capable of paying (Finch 2019). A diminished level of poverty followed but it was until William Beveridge, a Liberal politician drafted the *Social Insurance and Allied Services Report* (Beverage Report 1942) which spoke of 'cradle to grave' security for the populace. The main recommendations were for a Welfare State giving consideration to employment, a National Health Service, free education for all children and suitable housing (Wilde 2019).

In the lead-up to the Second World War the numbers of children receiving FSMs rose to 160,000 (approximately 3% of school children), which then rose to 500,000 during the war (approximately 8% provided free). Those city areas or Boroughs that did implement meal provision programmes had elementary education rates as high as twice those of Boroughs that did not engage (Finch

2019). In addition, under the *Milk in Schools Scheme* during 1934, the Board of Education started a scheme that provided a third of a pint of milk for a halfpenny (The Health Foundation, 2022). By 1939, 55% of children had access to milk, 20% being free. In 1937, Scottish MP James Brown argued that if a child is not properly fed, it is almost impossible for them to absorb the education that is offered to them in schools (Smith 2016). The 1944 Education Act (The National Archives 1944) required LEAs to provide meals and milk for all school children, but there was a charge for the majority with the meals provided free for only to the most deprived. By 1950, 48% of children were provided school meals with 92% provided free milk. Since then, Labour Governments have considered providing all school meals free but these proposals were either turned down by their own treasury departments or overturned before introduction by Conservative Governments (Finch 2019). In 1955, the UK government concerns about the nutritional value of school lunches introduced a guideline that meals provide 650–1,000 Kilocalories, 20 g of first-class protein (meat or fish) and 25–30 g of fat with fruit served at least once a week (Smith 2016). Up until 1980, school lunches were meant to provide at least a third of the daily requirement for energy and between a third and a half of that for protein.

1980–1998

However, with the introduction of the Education Act in 1980 (Education in England 2022) free school milk was revoked and together the requirement to deliver a meal service for any other than those on FSM. Spending on school meal budgets was reduced for economic reasons and the previous minimum nutritional standards were abolished. This led to LEAs choosing the cheapest suppliers under a new competitive tendering procedure to reduce costs. External companies were introduced and took over school kitchens to become 'free-choice' cafeterias, which were run to maximise profit and reduce waste. The result, according to the Coronary Prevention Group, was the easy option of providing popular fast-food items such as burgers and chips (Blythman 1999).

Wealth inequality grew rapidly during the 1980s and it can be argued that Britain became one of the most unequal societies in the developed world. Thane (2018) points out that by 1992, 34% of children were growing up in households below the official poverty line, and by 1998 when the new Social Security Act (The National Archives 1989) was introduced, thousands of children lost their FSM entitlement as parents were given a new family tax credit benefit. They were paid 67 pence per day to compensate for this, but it meant parents couldn't afford to provide school lunches for their children. In comparison to post war diets (protein rich foods, calcium, iron and minimal sugar), the 1990s experienced an influx of commercially produced food; i.e. processed, long-life foods (Blythman 1999) which meant children were eating savoury and processed snacks and highly refined foods instead of those with a slow release of nutrients that a balanced diet provides. One aspect of this new 'junk' food era was the levelling of the classes. It didn't matter if you were poor or disadvantaged or from an affluent background, children were united in their attachment to junk food.

The National Healthy Schools Programme (1998) was introduced by the Department of Health and Department for Children, Schools and Families. The intention was to enhance school lunch provision, reduce health inequalities, raise academic attainment, develop children's understanding of how to make healthy choices and promote a holistic school approach to health and wellbeing to improve community facilities as a whole. It introduced healthier food choices for pupils in the form of breakfast clubs, which were no longer allowed to serve pizza and the removal of snack and drink machines, and where fried foods were only allowed to be served twice a week with the introduction of a wider range of fruits, vegetables and salads

2000–2011

The *Annual Health Survey for England 2006: Latest Trends* (The Information Centre 2006) statistics showed that the levels of obesity for children had risen sharply, with 16% of children (aged 2–15) classed as obese. In 2005, Jamie Oliver highlighted the nutritional value of school lunches and started a campaign against junk food, especially the 'Turkey Twizzler'. His campaign gained significant support leading to improvements in lunchtime menus for children, although some were less happy to have their choices curtailed. At the time the daily budget for lunch was between 37p and 50p per child and this was raised by a further 10p, which some felt was not enough to cover the shortfall in lower nutritional value foodstuffs. The average budget in 2011 for a child's lunch was approximately 67p (Worrall 2011) and still is today.

The Labour government launched *The Children's Plan* (Department for Children, Schools and Families 2007) incorporating five outcomes including be healthy, stay safe, enjoy and achieve, make a positive contribution and achieve economic wellbeing. Later, the *Eatwell Plate* (Department of Health 2012) gave schools and consumers a clear guide of what food and in what proportions should be eaten. There have been numerous initiatives from governments, all of which speak of food education improvements, provision of meals and minimising children's food insecurity, but what impact has this made up to today?

Underlying issues of food poverty and why it matters

Many children around the world are living with food insecurity; yet over 4 million in one of the richest countries in the world are growing up in poverty, their access to adequate nutrition compromised. This number is due to rise to 5 million by the end of 2022 (Child Poverty Action Group 2021). There are other issues that families face in relation to food consumption. Cooking requires knowledge and skills of low- and high-level technologies. There are currently an estimated 1.9 million people in the UK living without a cooker, 2.8 million people without a freezer and 900,000 people without a fridge. Some households have the relevant 'white goods' or equipment, but not enough money to use them (National Food Strategy 2021).

Relationship between nutritional food, growth and development

The way the brain develops during gestation and the first two years of life are crucial for nerve growth and constructing the body's systems. This affects sensory development, learning, memory, and concentration, processing speed, mood and even the ability to multi-task (McCarthy 2018). The recommendation for adequate kilocalories is about 2,200 per person, with slightly more for males than females. However that figure is considerably higher in wealthier and more industrialised countries where the average is around 3,000. Though many people consume adequate calories, the important issue is that not all foods eaten provide the nutrition levels necessary for health and growth. There is widespread belief that a healthy diet supports healthy brain growth because they require a variety of essential nutrients that include zinc, iron, selenium, protein and iodine. Other nutrients necessary include Vitamin D which is essential for calcium absorption, bone growth, protection against illness and more recently, protection against respiratory disease (Public Health England 2013). In the UK it is estimated that 16% of children do not have adequate levels of Vitamin D in their diet (National Food Strategy 2021). Mothers who have poor nutrition are more likely to have lower birth weight babies, which are less likely to thrive, have developmental problems and a higher chance of being unhealthy children and teenagers (Public Health England 2020). Additionally, nutrient deficiencies, such as iron insufficiency, are known to impair learning and cause decreased productivity in school-age children.

Breakfast is perceived as the most important meal of the day, which purportedly improves cognition and working memory. Similarly, children who regularly eat breakfast have a tendency to have a lower Body Mass Index and are less likely to be overweight than those who often skip breakfast. Studies also suggest eating breakfast is more likely to meet daily recommended nutrient intakes (Hoyland et al. 2009). About 14% of children skip or do not regularly consume breakfast with the majority of these being teenagers or those constrained by food insecurity. The consumption of carbohydrate and protein-rich breakfasts with unrefined cereals, eggs, nuts and seeds leads to the release of neurotransmitters in the brain and provide higher levels of blood glucose. These factors control communication between the neurons, provide energy for good brain function and aid the regulation of mood, concentration and motivation, which in turn are likely to influence academic outcomes (Centre for Educational Neuroscience 2022).

Analysis of the annual National Diet and Nutrition Survey (Public Health England 2020) shows that children from the least well-off 20% of families consume around 29% less fruits and vegetables, 75% less oily fish, and 17% less fibre per day than children from the most well off 20%. People living in the most deprived households are almost twice as likely to die from preventable conditions like heart disease and cancers, whilst children are three times as likely to have severe tooth decay at age five and twice as likely to be overweight or obese and also shorter by age 13 (National Food Strategy 2021).

The ability for children to concentrate and fully participate in a lesson is a key issue in classrooms. Hunger not only has a biological impact, there is a psychological impact on children as well. In addition to not sleeping well, hungry children are less prepared for the day and mood inhibited, which can lead to mental health issues. A stigma exists about FSMs which affects children's relationships within friendship groups and can lead to harassment and bullying of those (Child Poverty Action Group 2021). The embarrassment of producing tokens for food and where parents feel unable to provide for their children, and the difficulty of filling out the forms, are reasons two-fifths of low socioeconomic parents never apply for FSM (Department for Education and Employment 2001). While cashless systems help to alleviate embarrassment for pupils, one issue is that one in seven children's FSM allowance does not cover the cost of a full meal for primary (£2.30) and secondary (£2.42) schools (Child Poverty Action Group 2021). There are only 14% of English schools that offer breakfast clubs, compared to 20.7% in Scotland and 64.1% in Wales (The Association for Public Services Excellence 2019), even though research shows that this improves children's academic performance. Parents in receipt of working tax credits are often not eligible for claiming FSMs which can result in having less money by paying upwards of three times as much on school meals than they gain in tax credits (Child Poverty Action Group 2021). They add that 36% of all school-aged children in the UK, approximately 1 million children, are living in poverty, yet not entitled to FSMs. Parents who receive FSM say they value the provision and it makes a huge difference to their family life.

A number of sectors have indicated all children from families in receipt of benefits up to the age of 16 be provided with a school meal (National Food Strategy 2021) but this proposal was not been taken up by the Government, as it was deemed too costly. Sweden and Finland provided free meals to all pupils in compulsory education regardless of their ability to pay. Later, the UK Government put a *Food Plan* (National Food Strategy 2021) in place to provide FSMs for all children in years one and two in England and Scotland. Yet, more families were struggling financially with only one parent working and 49% of children in lone-parent families in poverty (Child Poverty Action Group 2022). This is due in part to low-paid jobs, low contract hours and the rising costs of food, household bills and housing. No parent should have to choose between feeding their child and paying a bill. In 2020, there was a 107% increase in the amount of children receiving emergency food (The Children's Society 2022).

What can be put in place to alleviate this today?

Food Education has a tumultuous past. From its earliest inclusion in 19th Century education to teach girls how to cook, provide healthy meals and prepare for a life in service to its inclusion in the school curriculum firstly as cookery, domestic Science, Home Economics and recently food technology and food and nutrition. Today, school provision is varied in both quality and quantity and depends on how important it is viewed by the schools' Senior Leadership Team. The *Report of the Food Education Learning Landscape* by the Jamie Oliver Foundation (AKO Foundation 2017) noted many concerns. These include pupils' knowledge of healthy eating is incomplete, the delivery of all aspects of food education is patchy and many children are unable to develop their cooking skills. There is limited evidence of pupils being taught how to apply the principles of a healthy diet in their food choices. Teachers are often held back by a lack of time, resources and facilities with insufficient professional development to improve these skills.

A very important issue is that as a nation 50% of UK household food purchases are 'ultra-processed'. This is due in part to rising incomes by some making it possible for them to buy such food and more effective farming techniques making food products cheaper relative to household income. The food industry is responsible for producing highly refined, cheap foods and has had a large impact on the diets of many. A modern diet of cheap 'junk' food has the damaging quality that it can cause weight gain and poor nutritional value, a truly sad indictment for our society. It is currently projected by 2035 there will be more spent on Type 2 Diabetes than we are currently spending on all cancer treatments. However some mandatory interventions have been introduced. In an independent review commissioned by the UK government (National Food Strategy 2021), the 'soft drinks industry levy' has led to a 29% reduction in the average sugar content of soft drinks within three years.

Food banks have taken on a much more vital role in the last ten years and even more so with the pandemic years with 913,138 people receiving three days of emergency food from Trussell Trust food banks in 2013–14 (The Trussell Trust 2013). Ninety-five percent of people referred to Trussell Trust food banks were destitute, meaning they were unable to afford to eat or stay warm and dry, 18% of the households were single parents, more than twice the rate of the general population and 62% were disabled (The Trussell Trust 2021).

Online news forums (The Conversation 2020) and social media football celebrities such as Marcus Rashford, who formed the Child Food Poverty Task Force in 2020, called for the government to provide FSM not only through the pandemic, when children were taught online, but also now through school holidays (The Food Foundation 2021). Rashford also supported the three main demands of the National Food Strategy (2021) by Henry Dimbleby to widen the FSMs programme to all families who receive benefits and those who have no recourse to public funds. The situation has become worse over the last two years, largely due to the pandemic and the cost-of-living crisis. In 2021 20.8% of pupils were eligible for FSM, now increasing to 22.5% in June 2022 (Education Statistics Service 2022). With the removal of the £20 uplift in universal credit, and 8% inflation rate, parents are finding it difficult to manage their household budget, with many missing meals to ensure their children are fed (Child Poverty

Lowest price of selected 30 everyday groceries, item-level price changes, April 2022 compared with April 2021

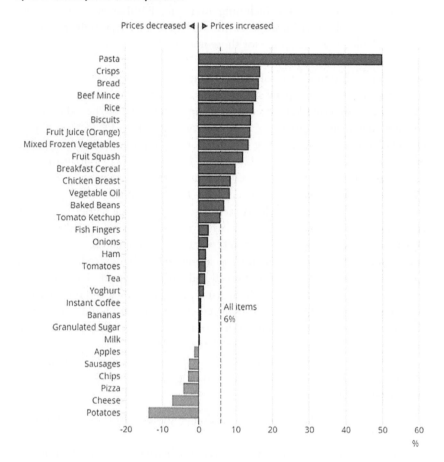

FIGURE 13.1   Tracking the increasing price of the lowest-cost grocery items, UK (Office for National Statistics 2022)

Action Group 2021). Prices of some budget foods have risen by upwards of 15% and pasta has seen price rises of 50%. Figure 13.1 shows the average price rises in certain food items in 2021.

Conclusion

The future: National Food Strategy Plan

The UK government has acted on some of the recommendations from the National Food Strategy, (2021). For example, the Holiday Activities and Food programme in all areas of England were extended in 2021 and hopefully will be extended in 2022. These clubs provide a four-day-a-week FSM programme for four weeks over the summer break. Children receive hot food, cooking lessons and sports activities, including advice for families on how to source, prepare and cook nutritious low-cost food. Some City Boroughs are making these available for a small price for those not on FSM as they can see the benefits for children and increasing the value for *'Healthy Start'* vouchers from £3.10 to £4.25 p/w. Parents with babies less than 12 months will be entitled to two vouchers each week to spend on vitamins, fruit, vegetables and milk. Some of the largest supermarkets are now willing to supplement the value of these vouchers between £1.30 and £2. A charity called 'Peas Please' has started a UK-wide initiative encouraging organisations to improve vegetable consumption (The Food Foundation 2017). Other UK government policy initiatives include programmes such as 'Excellence in Cities', 'Connexions', 'Education Maintenance Allowance', 'Extended Schools Programmes', 'Healthy Schools Initiative' and the 'Every Child Matters' agenda. The issue facing policy makers is how to combine multiple initiatives into a coherent social service and how to prioritise the most effective interventions. Although the majority of aid must come from the government there are neighbourhoods and communities that can provide different levels of social and cultural support. These interventions can help alleviate some of the worst aspects of poverty and improve prospects and educational success for children. Food can help build communities and social cohesion and the value of this stretches much further than nutritional benefits alone (Joseph Rowntree Foundation 2020).

However, recent events in the UK and around the world, together with political instability in the UK are making progress difficult when dealing with child poverty. These include:

i   The UK inflation rate has hit double digits – 10.1% – the Office for National Statistics says

ii It's a higher rate than analysts were predicting – the last time price rises were in double digits was in February 1982

iii Rising food and drink prices made the biggest contribution to the change in the inflation rate between June and July

iv Bread, cereals, milk, cheese and eggs had a particular impact on rising prices

v   But the cost of living is rising across the board, driven partly by energy costs and the Ukraine war but also factors such as the cost of raw materials

vi Meanwhile, average wage increases are falling behind, with the average salary buying 3% fewer goods and services than a year before

vii Inflation is expected to continue rising this year, with the Bank of England predicting it won't go down to the target 2% for about two years.

(British Broadcasting Corporation [BBC News Services, 2022])

It must be emphasised that children living in poverty in the UK will have a significant impact on their future health, both in terms of nutritional deficiency affecting growth, mental health and wellbeing but also long-term health problems. Poor health associated with food poverty severely limits children's future potential and future life chances (Wickham et al. 2016).

References

AKO Foundation, 2017. *A report on the Food Education Learning Landscape.* The Jamie Oliver Foundation [online]. Available from: https://www.akofoundation.org/wp-content/uploads/2017/11/2_0_fell-report-final.pdf [Accessed 21 August 2022].

BBC News Services, 2022. *Cost of food and drink pushes UK inflation to 10.1%* [online]. Available from: https://www.bbc.com/news/live/business-62566828 [Accessed 19 August 2022].

Beverage, W., 1942. *The Beverage Report: report of social insurance and allied services* [online]. Available from: https://www.bbc.co.uk/bitesize/guides/z6ctyrd/revision/6 [Accessed 21 August 2022].

Blythman, J., 1999. *The food our children eat: how to get children to like good food.* London, UK: Harper Press.

Centre for Educational Neuroscience, 2022. *Diet makes a difference to learning available* [online]. Available from: http://www.educationalneuroscience.org.uk/resources/neuromyth-or-neurofact/diet-makes-a-difference-to-learning/ [Accessed 18 August 2022].

Child Poverty Action Group, 2021. *Fixing lunch: the case for expanding free school meals* [online]. Available from: https://cpag.org.uk/sites/default/files/files/policypost/Fixing_Lunch.pdf [Accessed 7 August 2022].

Child Poverty Action Group, 2022. *Who is at risk of poverty?* [online]. Available from: https://cpag.org.uk/child-poverty/who-risk-poverty [Accessed 22 August 2022].

Department for Children, Schools and Families, 2007 [online]. *The children's plan: building bright futures.* Available from: https://assets.publishing.service.gov.uk/government/uploads/system/uploads/attachment_data/file/325111/2007-childrens-plan.pdf [Accessed 11 August 2022].

Department for Education and Employment, 2001. *Improving the take up of free school meals* [online]. Available from: https://dera.ioe.ac.uk/4657/1/RR270.pdf [Accessed 17 August 2022].

Department of Health, 2012. *Eatwell plate* [online]. Available from: https://www.forumhealthcentre.nhs.uk/your-health/the-eatwell-plate [Accessed 17 August 2022].

Education in England, 2022. *Education Act 1980* [online]. Available from: http://www.educationengland.org.uk/documents/acts/1980-education-act.html [Accessed 16 August 2022].

Education Statistics Service, 2022. *Schools, pupils and their characteristics, Academic Year 2021/22* [online]. Available from: https://explore-education-statistics.service.gov.uk/find-statistics/school-pupils-and-their-characteristics [Accessed 17 August 2022].

Fareshare, 2022. *Fighting hunger, tackling food waste* [online]. Available from: https://fareshare.org.uk/ [Accessed 16 August 2022].

Finch, A., 2019. *The provision of school meals since 1906: progress or a recipe for disaster?* [online]. Available from: https://www.historyandpolicy.org/policy-papers/papers/the-provision-of-school-meals-since-1906-progress-or-a-recipe-for-disaster#:~:text=In%201906%20the%20British%%2020parliament, out%20of%20the%20local%

20rates.&text=per%20meal%20while%20still%20providing%20some%20meals%20 free%20to%20disadvantaged%20schoolchildren [Accessed 12 August 2022].

Food and Agriculture Organisation, 2006. *Policy briefing on food security issue 2* [online]. Available from: https://www.fao.org/fileadmin/templates/faoitaly/documents/pdf/ pdf_Food_Security_Cocept_Note.pdf [Accessed 11 August 20220].

Hoyland, A., Dye, L., and Lawton, C., 2009. A systematic review of the effect of breakfast on the cognitive performance of children and adolescent. *Nutritional Research Reviews*, 22 (2), 220–243.

Joseph Rowntree Foundation, 2020. *UK poverty 2019–20* [online]. Available from: https://www.jrf.org.uk/report/uk-poverty-2019-20 [Accessed 16 March 2022].

McCarthy, C., 2018. *The crucial brain foods all children need.* New York: Harvard Health Publishing.

National Food Strategy, 2021. *The plan* [online]. Available from: file:///Users/aturner/ Downloads/25585_1669_NFS_The_Plan_July21_S12_New-1%20(1).pdf [Accessed 17 August 2022].

National Healthy Schools Programme, 1998. *Introduction to the national healthy schools programme* [online]. Available from: https://dera.ioe.ac.uk/6798/7/Introduction_ Redacted.pdf [Accessed 16 August 2022].

Office for National Statistics, 2022. *Tracking the price of the lowest-cost grocery items, UK, experimental analysis: April 2021 to April 2022* [online]. Available from: https://www. ons.gov.uk/releases/trackingthelowestcostgroceryitemsanexperimentalanalysis ukapril2021toapril2022 [Accessed 17 August 2022].

Public Health England, 2013. *School Food and Attainment- review of the literature* [online]. Available from: https://assets.publishing.service.gov.uk/government/uploads/system/ uploads/attachment_data/file/245113/School_food_and_attainment_-_review_of_ literature.pdf [Accessed 21 August 2022].

Public Health England, 2020. NDNS: results from years 9 to 11 (2016 to 2017 and 2018 to 2019) [online]. *Food consumptions, nutrient intakes and nutritional status.* Available from: https://www.gov.uk/government/statistics/ndns-results-from-years-9-to-11-2016-to-2017-and-2018-to-2019 [Accessed 17 August 2022].

Smith, J., 2016. *Key questions in education: historical and contemporary perspectives.* London, UK: Bloomsbury Publishing.

Thane, P., 2018. *Poverty in the divided kingdom – history and policy* [online]. Available from: https://www.historyandpolicy.org/policy-papers/papers/poverty-in-the-divided-kingdom [Accessed 17 August 2022].

The Association for Public Services Excellence, 2019. *Education catering: trend analysis 2017/18* [online]. Available from: https://www.apse.org.uk/index.cfm/apse/ members-area/briefings/2019/19-03-education-catering-trend-analysis-201718/ [Accessed 17 August 2022].

The Children's Society, 2022. *What are the effects of child poverty?* [online]. Available from: https://www.childrenssociety.org.uk/what-we-do/our-work/ending-child-poverty/ effects-of-living-in-poverty [Accessed 20 August 2022].

The Conversation, 2020. *Free school meals: the lifelong impact of childhood food poverty* [online]. Available from: https://theconversation.com/free-school-meals-the-lifelong-impact-of-childhood-food-poverty-148660?gclid=CjwKCAiA7IGcBhA8EiwAFfUDsSn Zzi6X3RmVjuduzrGcPweXmkADZi81ZoC7xn9MnYaDaHA2uEBZmRoCP-IQAvD_BwE [Accessed 17 August 2022].

The Food Foundation, 2017. *Peas please: making a pledge for more veg* [online]. Available from: https://foodfoundation.org.uk/initiatives/peas-please [Accessed 17 August 2022].

The Food Foundation, 2021. *Marcus Rashford MBE and Jamie Oliver MBE write to government calling for urgent review of free school meals* [online]. Available from: https://foodfoundation.org.uk/press-release/marcus-rashford-mbe-and-jamie-oliver-mbe-write-government-calling-urgent-review-free [Accessed 17 August 2022].

The Health Foundation, 2022. *Milk in schools scheme* [online]. Available from: https://navigator.health.org.uk/theme/milk-schools-scheme [Accessed 21 August 2022].

The Information Centre, 2008. *Health survey for England -2006: latest trends* [online]. Available from: https://digital.nhs.uk/data-and-information/publications/statistical/health-survey-for-england/health-survey-for-england-2006-latest-trends#:~:text=In%202006%2C%2016%20per%20cent, cent%20to%2015%20per%20cent [Accessed 16 August 2022].

The National Archives, 1989. *Social Security Act 1989* [online]. Available from: https://www.legislation.gov.uk/ukpga/1998/14/contents/enacted [Accessed 20 August 2022].

The Trussell Trust, 2013. *Highlights of the year 2013–2014* [online]. Available from: http://www.trusselltrust.org/wp-content/uploads/sites/2/2015/06/Financial-Summary-2013-2014.pdf [Accessed 20 August 2022].

The Trussell Trust, 2021. *State of hunger: building the evidence on poverty, destitution, and food insecurity in the UK* [online]. Available from: https://www.trusselltrust.org/wp-content/uploads/sites/2/2021/05/State-of-Hunger-2021-Report-Final.pdf [Accessed 8 August 2022].

United Kingdom Parliament, 1906. *The Education (Provision of Meals) Act* [online]. Available from: https://www.legislation.gov.uk/ukpga/1906/57/enacted [Accessed 16 August 2022].

United Kingdom Parliament, 2022. The 1870 *Education Act* [online]. Available from: https://www.parliament.uk/about/living-heritage/transformingsociety/living learning/school/overview/1870educationact/ [Accessed 12 April 2022].

Wilde, R., 2019. *The creation of Britain's welfare state* [online]. Available from: https://www.thoughtco.com/creation-of-britains-welfare-state-1221967 [Accessed 20 December 2021].

Wickham, S, Anwar, E., Barr, B., et al., 2006. *Poverty and child health in the UK: using evidence for action*, 101, 759–766. Available from: untitled (bmj.com) [Accessed: 15 August 2022].

World Health Organisation, 2003. *Diet, nutrition and the prevention of chronic diseases* [online]. Available from: https://apps.who.int/iris/bitstream/handle/10665/42665/WHO_TRS_916.pdf;jsessionid=CF8671BCCF0DE0FCB6AE5309B93709B0?sequence=1.

Worrall, P., 2011. *Making a dog's dinner of school meals?* [online]. Available from: https://www.channel4.com/news/factcheck/factcheck-making-a-dogs-dinner-of-school-meals [Accessed 20 December 2021].

14

SCHOOL FOOD LIFEWORLDS

Children's relational experience of school food and its importance in their early primary school years

Marianne O'Kane Boal

Introduction

In the early years of school, children have many new experiences, not least their practice of eating with peers at two demarcated food events in the school day. Their relational involvement in these food proceedings aids their initiation into this time-compressed routine in school. Employing the lens of a school food lifeworld is a constructive means of exploring children's food practices in the classroom and how these are informed by their early peer relationships. The concept of the lifeworld comes from the phenomenological tradition of philosophy and sociology. It is defined as a subjective perception of the world (Schutz 1967) and manifested through values, beliefs, attitudes and ideas (Vargas 2020). It is the realm of lived participation and includes our pre-reflective experience (Husserl 1970). The lifeworld is the space of intersubjectivity; 'the nexus or connection between all people' (Vargas 2020, p.421). This is a dynamic and vital concept that allows us to study children's social relationships and experiences in their everyday lives. In this chapter journey 'lines' through home and school lifeworlds and the relational 'knots' between these are discussed. The journey lines are the children's individual lifeworld paths and the knots are the points of intersection/ overlap that signal their connection with others. The impact of transitioning from home and preschool to primary school draws on my fieldwork study undertaken at an Irish primary school.

This exploration of the centrality of food at this school is mindful of the importance of 'belonging' for children in their early months at school and that the transition from preschool to primary school is one of the major adjustments in a child's life. Following Antonsich's (2010) concept of belonging centred on place-belongingness, this chapter explores how children feel 'at home' in a given place through interpersonal and relational experiences, and politics of

DOI: 10.4324/9781003294962-18

belongingness in school, where the institution's dialogical processes create or resist socio-spatial inclusion and exclusion. Antonsich (2010) describes 'belonging' in both micro and macro terms. It is personal, intimate and connected with immediate surroundings yet references a wider discursive space in the society politics of belonging. Children gauge belonging primarily according to micro friendships yet they demonstrate cognisance of macro influences; what is happening in the wider classroom, how friendships are configured in school and in their peer network beyond school. This represents a community of belonging and the children's desire to be part of this. It relates to personal feelings of being 'at home' in a place where there is a sense of comfort. Children normally obtain this feeling from family but how do they transition to achieving this with friends in school? Are family replaced by friends in the school setting? Is there an acknowledgement of friends and family or does a preference for family persist? The children's drawings demonstrate a range of perspectives: (1) the ongoing importance of familial relationships and transition to peer friendships, (2) peer friendships as central in school lifeworlds, (3) overlap of the contextual environments of home and school informing friendship and (4) an appreciation of school food events as embedded relationships.

Background literature

While the transition from preschool to primary school is recognised nationally and internationally as a crucial time in children's lives, it is not acknowledged in national educational policy, but instead informal 'on the ground support' is delivered in an ad hoc manner (O'Kane 2016; O'Kane and Murphy 2016). Ireland falls behind many international countries in terms of transition and school readiness research. More recently this has been addressed through three primary channels; a focused initiative (2018), government strategy (2019–2028) and tailored guidance publications (2020).[1] Ackesjö (2013) describes the transition process as a 'time of reconstruction' for children in terms of identity in the new school setting. In relation to time and place, children interpret and reconstruct old and new aspects of their identities according to their evolving understandings of their new school experience. A fundamental dimension of transition for young children is developing a sense of belonging in the school setting. These transitions are demanding of children, creating both challenges and opportunities, and the level of success experienced can have various impacts on them (O'Kane 2016). Positive early transitions inform future educational transitions in a child's life (Dockett and Perry 2007; Fabian 2002; O'Kane 2016). Children must quickly adapt to their new status and environment. It can be confusing for children given they are among the youngest and smallest in the school and their confidence can be affected (Fabian 2002).

In articulating children's experiences of moving from home to school, the work of Tim Ingold (2011, 2015) is opposite. Navigation and 'wayfinding' are useful concepts for considering the child's journey from home through school;

both mutable contexts. We follow a line, or lines, of experience perceptible as a trail that is interwoven with the trails of others:

> ...every such trail discloses a relation, this trail is not a straightforward translation of person to place, however, it is rather a trail along which life is lived [...] each such trail is one strand in a tissue of trails that together comprise the lifeworld.
>
> *(Ingold 2011, pp.69–70)*

This interconnectedness is very much part of our place-belongingness with others in that it is embedded and contextual (Antonsich 2010). Life is woven from knots (Ingold 2011), connective relational points of entanglement with others. The overlap in relationships is considered a "joining with" not a "joining up" and the sympathy of human relationships is "living with" others (Ingold 2015, p.24). Reference is made to the "memory" of the knot and experiences leave an imprint on life trails (Ingold 2015, p.26). The rope retains an impression of past knots, a subjective legacy of impression in the lifeline of the individual. In the context of this chapter, when a child moves from one context to another, they cast off an aspect of their previous role but dynamically integrate an impression of this into their new role.[2] This enduring familial relationship and the lasting knots echo the expression 'the ties that bind'.[3] It can be an ongoing association but it is one that continues as a link throughout an individual's lifetime.

Ingold's knot concept can be extended to the child's transition from home to school and the connected interplay between these environments. Here there is an untying and retying of knots enacted on a daily basis. There is a degree of 'casting off' on the first day to provide liberty for the child to begin their school journey, but built into this is on the provision that the child will return home after school. Each day is an opportunity for further integration into school informed by slow temporal progress in the lifeworld. "As our direct experience is formed in the lifeworld, the past sediments it, the present takes form in it, and the future is molded from it. Therefore we cannot understand social interaction without the lifeworld" (Vargas 2020, p.420).

This reinforces Ingold's concept of the memory of knots; impressions left by experiences, and how relationships inform the child's evolving journey as they move from home to school. A fundamental dimension of a child's school lifeworld is manifest in repetition and routine. This is important to successful transition for children and central in place-belongingness; feeling 'at home'. Children find reassurance of routine in daily school food events (morning break and lunch); these define a comforting ritual that echoes the routines of many homes. Place-belongingness then, is provided for children in school against the backdrop of 'politics of belongingness' in the institutional timetable framework. These important experiential knots are evident in the children's food and friendship drawings, foodscapes[4] and modelling clay representations. There were a number of thematic strands identified in the fieldwork; importance of family, food representing children's lifeworlds, shared perspectives, time and space for friendship and relating the experience of another. In the next section following research methods these concepts are explored.

Research methods

The data referenced in this chapter is sourced from fieldwork exploring the links between children, food and friendship undertaken in 2018 with 19 children (aged 4–6), conducted through Irish language in a primary school class-room.[5] Children participated in a series of facilitated activities using arts-based methods. Such methods encourage alternative modes of knowledge through research with children and they can affect fuller communication of children's opinions (Spyrou 2011). As "some knowings cannot be conveyed through language" (Ellsworth 2005 p.156), the arts engage the sensory dimension of children's experience and create a more meaningful understanding of what they observe and process in their interactions (Valentine 1999). Arts-based methods connect with the sensory and symbolic dimension of food while linking constructively with children's pre-reflective lifeworld experience. It has been argued that art is a way of "obtaining complex information about children's lifeworlds, while also recognising them as agentic[6] and deserving of respect" (Hickey-Moody et al. 2021, p.2). It is the often undiluted spontaneity of art that enhances the research value of appreciating children's lifeworlds through employing arts-based methods.

Findings and discussion

Importance of family

The importance of home was particularly evident in the children's first year of primary school. When asked to produce a drawing of food and friendship, some chose to represent family, sometimes without reference to food. One girl (aged 5), in her first six weeks of primary school drew a picture of her family (Figure 14.1). She is at the centre of her composition alongside her mother; both wear stripy dresses. Her father and three siblings are included, with her youngest brother as smallest. Her depiction is an articulation of Ingold's (2015) memorable 'knots' of connection, where the stripy dresses create a central association between mother and daughter from her lifeworld perspective. It can also be viewed as a relational 'tie that binds' because she demonstrates place-belongingness through familial interconnection rather than the school environment.

The use of an outdoor setting for her drawing underlines the importance of neutral territory for articulating changing roles which avoids the specificity of a family home depiction. She is actively 'reconstructing her identity' (Ackesjö 2013), providing an insight into prior and existing roles as a family member before illustrating her new role of making friends in school. This girl is one of the

FIGURE 14.1 Group family portrait girl aged 5 (photographed by the author)

youngest and smallest children in school, so she demonstrates her position in her family, where she is taller than two of her siblings and presumably older. This is an assertion strategy to affirm her familial agency and increase her confidence in school (Fabian 2002). She is at the beginning of her primary school journey and focuses on familial friendship at this stage, demonstrating family's fundamental importance to her at this transitional point.

Food representing children's lifeworlds

Children's food and friendship practices are negotiated through an "ongoing flux of their school lives" (Devine et al. 2008, p.370) that demonstrates awareness of the symbolic potential of food in their everyday relationships. All people, places and things within practices are "considered as constituent parts of an overall jigsaw puzzle" (Wills et al. 2015, p.4), with elements visible in children's journey lines as experiential 'knots' or meaningful events (Ingold 2011, 2015). Food is imbued with meaning and is symbolic and sensory. Wills (2011) makes the case that the sociology of food revolves around representations and meanings that indicate and reflect social change. This can be seen in children's relational use of food in their friendships to make sense of transitioning from preschool to primary school. They cannot share food itself at school due to lunch rules so relationality is limited to sharing food preferences or experiences in the classroom. Neely et al. (2014, p.50) have observed that "food practices are embedded in everyday life and social relationships", they are actively employed by children to "show their agency and manage relationships". This was evident in the fieldwork as food events at school are less managed by adults and children have increased relational autonomy.

Play is equally as symbolic as food and there are multiple benefits of a play-based approach to learning in early years classrooms (Lillemyr et al. 2013; Nolan and Paatsch 2018). Building on the inherent value and symbolism of play, children were invited to create a clay model relief of their ideal lunch. These representations demonstrated two main tendencies, depiction of small lunches as consumed in the short daily food breaks (Figure 14.2) or large-scale lunches that represented children's wider lifeworld preferences (Figure 14.3). The majority of boys depicted smaller lunches with four items or less; reflecting the physical school lunch they brought. The girls (Figure 14.2) produced larger depictions containing a range of foods with one constant: a fried egg as a food that did not feature in the children's physical lunches but appeared fun to create. This suggests an entwining of their home and school food lifeworlds to create a sense of belonging and feeling of being 'at home' (Antonisch 2010), with certain foods having a symbolic transitional status that can be included relationally.

Children's food preferences are clearly inspired by their peers in their ideal lunches. Food was used relationally to reflect actual school lunch items and those from home. Children habitually use their food practices for wayfinding their way from home to school and back again. Their trails are often interconnected, influencing each other and strengthening friendships through shared food experiences.

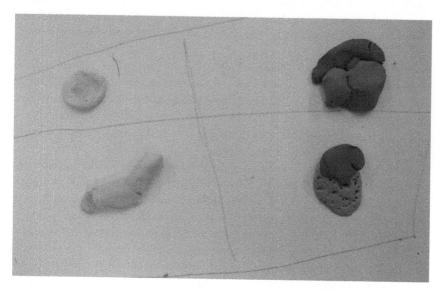

FIGURE 14.2   Ideal lunch by boy aged 5 (photographed by the author)

FIGURE 14.3 Ideal lunch by girl aged 5 (photographed by the author)

Shared perspectives

There were two boys in the first six weeks of school that drew near-identical scenes in their foodscapes, demonstrating extensive overlap in their school lifeworlds (Figures 14.4 and 14.5). The first foodscape features a boat, car, orange, banana and my friend. The second includes a boat, orange, car and park to play football with my friend. They feature each other in their drawings and the sequence demonstrates their attachment to material objects of shared importance to them: boat and car. Their toys are strongly defined whereas figures are lighter. In both drawings they are pictured alongside an orange as their shared food preference. In the second case, its large scale suggests a table between them echoing the classroom table for their school lunch.

They constructively use their favourite food to understand their recent transition from preschool to primary school. It is part of their daily food event and embedded in their awareness. For these children, shared interests and preferences in their lifeworlds are paramount. They are in the initial stages of play practices in school and lifeworld co-constructors hence the extensive overlap in their food, toy and game preferences. Their experiential life trails are fully interwoven at this stage in their school journey and they embrace momentary 'knots' of connection in their lifelines. Their toys underline the ongoing importance of home and a feeling of belonging.

FIGURE 14.4 Foodscape, boy 5 (photographed by the author)

FIGURE 14.5 Foodscape, boy 4 (photographed by the author)

Time and space for friendship

Children constructively use food in their peer relationships to understand their recent transition to primary school, as this is a key time in their lives (O'Kane 2016). Carter and Nutbrown (2016) underline the sociocultural dimension of children's friendship particularly, imaginary friends; losing friends; protecting time and space to develop friendships; and children's routines as they form and maintain friendships (Moustakas 1994). These dimensions of making and keeping friends are represented in a range of the children's artworks, where they often utilise everyday food practices to represent their peer interactions.

Two best friends drew similar pictures of their experience of school lunchtime highlighting their overlapping viewpoints on their friendships around food. The first drawing (Figure 14.6 – the taller girl drew the picture) features the girls surrounded by an abundance of healthy food. It references shared ownership of food preferences in the lifeworld and school food practices. The girls wear their school uniform and the food reflecting the contents of their daily lunches (carrot, strawberries, cucumber, red pepper, orange, plum, banana and apple) is arranged in a circle around them. They reside alongside each other in their individual lifeworlds but share commonality in their uniform, food and smiling faces. It is joyful with favourite foods floating around the girls to select and enjoy. I asked the girl about the featured foods and she said "we are best friends and we like the same foods" and I asked if best friends always like the same foods, she replied "not always but it is nice when we do". The shared foods demonstrate a sense of belonging, togetherness and understanding for them.

FIGURE 14.6 Lunchtime in school, girl 6 (photographed by the author)

FIGURE 14.7 Two best friends by girl aged 5 (photographed by the author)

This depiction of herself with one friend was the same drawing approach adopted by her featured friend, a five-year-old girl in her second year of primary school. She stands with her best friend outdoors (Figure 14.7) surrounded by their favourite school foods; strawberries, apples, oranges and bananas. The girls stand within their own framed food circles that meet and overlap, symbolising lunchtime at school. These circles are akin to a protective common barrier against outside influence and the food frames their friendship. It is equally distributed and appears in motion as if it is being juggled playfully by each of the girls.

The girls developed and maintained a strong friendship in school; they sit and eat together in the classroom, play in the school yard and socialise beyond school. They took every opportunity to incorporate food into their drawings as a symbolic dimension of their two-person friendship. They were also delighted in discussing and drawing their shared food preferences. This depiction can be seen as a representation of one of the two worlds of school; the informal playful child world as opposed to the formal controlled adult world (Valentine 2000), where the girls represent themselves surrounded by floating food outdoors away from the otherwise controlled setting of the classroom.

Their constructive use of school food, aids the girls' sense-making process of their recent transition to school. They are 'reconstructing their identities' (Ackesjö 2013) around their everyday food practices, using 'place-belongingness' (Antonsich 2010) to feel 'at home' through relational and interpersonal connections. To create a sense of belonging school food has been used as mini-enclosures; small protective units for each of the girls and their friendship to feel 'at home' in their shared agency, preferences and common understanding. This depiction is in line with the findings of Carter and Nutbrown (2016) working with children aged 5 to 6 who underlined the importance of protecting time and space to develop friendships and how practices inform ongoing peer relationships.

Relating the experience of another

One fieldwork activity invited children to produce a 'pair picture' where children articulate key food and friendship scenes on behalf of a companion they sit beside in class. This helped children to consider the experience of another and relate it visually. In Figure 14.8, a four-year-old girl has illustrated the preferences of a boy of the same age that she sits beside. She includes them both and the sky is full of the boy's favourite foods; strawberries and blueberries. Both the children have their mouths wide open to catch some of the fruit as it falls. The boy is also holding a gun to shoot the fruit if there is too much to eat. The gunfire is shown on the right of the page above the door to the house. Within this picture we see the child's imaginative portrayal of the boy's preferences where fruit can fall from the sky like snow. She is illustrating their converging lifeworlds and features both children as protagonists in the action. She includes a dimension of 'childhood symbolic culture' (Cosaro 2003); the computer game,

FIGURE 14.8 Pair picture by girl (4) showing friend's preferences (photographed by the author)

where the children's imaginative experience is transformed into a different play dimension. Both these children were in their first six weeks of their primary school journey and this picture demonstrates the ongoing importance of home in the school lifeworld, where imagination and play dominate.

One possible interpretation is that this abundance of food illustrates the child's awareness that there can be too much food to eat in the short lunchtime frame, yet within the drawing children's lifeworlds can be articulated according to their own wishes. The children inhabit *their* world of food and this picture captures a sensory dimension and surprise in experiencing food falling from the sky. The boy was delighted with the representation and when I asked if he liked the picture he replied; "yes I love it". The girl demonstrates an awareness of the power of imaginative storytelling where children can make the everyday world adapt to their own designs (Wolf and Heath 1992), and children as active agents in their school food practices with capacity to use food imaginatively in friendship from a young age. It further emphasises that objects for play are diverse (Sutton-Smith 1986) and food can be animated to become a central part of children's play. Arts-based methods have the potential to connect diverse elements of children's play culture – peer-to-peer imaginative play, video games and food-based scenarios.

Conclusion

Following the initial transition to school, children demonstrate a connection with home through their emphasis on family; shared perspectives on material objects and favourite foods and a clear understanding of the preferences of another peer. As their school experience continues, children show how food can represent intersections between their home and school lifeworlds, exhibiting a time and space priority for friendship. The depictions in this chapter emphasise the individuality of friendship in the early years of school. Friendship can be explorative, combining real and imagined scenarios as seen in play and children have their own approaches to communicating relationality. This research illustrates that friendship is central to the successful transition from preschool to school (Carter and Nutbrown 2016) and provides a 'blueprint' for future transitions (Dockett and Perry 1999). School was considered a good place if children were provided with friendship opportunities (Dockett and Perry 2002) and for the boys who share a preference for oranges and special toys, or the girls who love all the same foods, it is clear that food itself can provide this prospect for friendship. The four-year-old girl demonstrates an appreciation of a companion's experience that shows empathetic understanding of his school food lifeworld. There are relational lines between food and friendship manifested in important moments or 'knots' where lifeworlds converge and overlap in shared experiences. This concept extends to the metaphor of lifelines where children's lives move along lines that are interwoven with those of family and friends. They are impacted by the child's situated experience in everyday places informing the tapestry of entangled lifeworlds. When children imaginatively share the food preferences of a friend, their lifeworlds converge in mutual appreciation. This is particularly important in children's school food lifeworlds where daily food events contribute to a developing sense of belonging, helping children adjust to their recent school transition. Through creatively articulating their perspectives, it is evident that children are aware of the relational potential of food in their friendships within and beyond school.

Notes

1 The National Council for Curriculum and Assessment (NCCA) Preschool to Primary Transition Initiative (2018); includes a more focused approach to developing, piloting and evaluating reporting templates, First Five 2019–2028: whole of government strategy to improve lives of babies, children and their families, and the Insights – Transitions publications from the Department of Education for early years, parents and primary school teachers.
2 Ingold's use of the word 'dispersal' is interesting in this context as it is a synonym for 'diaspora', referencing the scattered geographic distribution of individuals beyond their locale of origin.
3 The words come from the title of a Christian hymn written in 1782 by John Fawcett, "Blest be the ties that bind".
4 Within the fieldwork, children were asked to draw foodscapes that reflected their experiences of eating (Brembeck et al. 2013). Foodscape is informed by the relational use of food in children's lives. The four scene format provides an opportunity for children to create lifeworld mini-narratives and provide an extended window on their perspectives and everyday experiences.
5 The study was granted full ethical approval from IT Sligo and the IT Sligo Ethics Committee. It follows the IT Sligo Research Ethics Procedure (2018). Written consent was obtained from the parents/guardians of children participants and from the children themselves, along with ongoing verbal consent as the fieldwork was conducted.
6 'Children's perception of agency is related to their experience of the efficacy of their actions. Defining children as agentic is to grant them a mind of their own and with their own will and thereby acknowledge their self-efficacy and personal control' (Gurdal and Sorbing, 2019).

References

Ackesjö, H., 2013. Transitions: times of reconstruction. *International Journal of Transitions in Childhood* [online], 6. Available from: https://education.unimelb.edu.au/__data/assets/pdf_file/0012/3549873/journal6_-ackesjo.pdf.

Antonsich, M., 2010. Searching for belonging: an analytical framework. *Geography Compass* [online], 4 (6). Available from: https://doi.org/10.1111/j.1749-8198.2009.00317.x.

Brembeck, H., Johansson, B., Bergstrom, K., Engelbrektsson, P., Hillen, S., Jonsson, L., Karlsson, M., Ossiansson, E., and Shanahn, H., 2013. Exploring children's foodscapes. *Children's Geographies* [online], 11 (1). Available from: https://doi.org/10.1080/14733285.2013.743282.

Carter, C., and Nutbrown, C., 2016. A pedagogy of friendship: young children's friendships and how schools can support them? *The Journal of Early Years Education* [online], 24 (4). Available from: https://doi.org/10.1080/09669760.2016.1189813.

Cosaro, W. A., 2003. *We're friends right? inside kids' culture.* Washington, DC: Joseph Henry Press.

Devine, D., Kenny, M., and Macneela, E., 2008. Naming the 'other': children's construction and experience of racisms in Irish primary schools. *Race Ethnicity and Education* [online], 11 (4). Available from: https://doi.org/10.1080/13613320802478879.

Dockett, S., and Perry, B., 1999. Starting school: what do the children say? *Early Child Development and Care* [online], 159 (1). Available from: https://doi.org/10.1080/0300443991590109.

Dockett, S., and Perry, B., 2002. 'Who's ready for what? Young children starting school. *Contemporary Issues in Early Childhood* [online], 3 (1). Available from: https://doi.org/10.2304/ciec.2002.3.1.9.

Dockett, S., and Perry, B., 2007. *Transitions to school: perceptions, expectations., experiences.* Sydney, Australia: UNSW Press.

Ellsworth, E., 2005. *Place of learning: media, architecture, pedagogy.* New York: Routledge.

Fabian, H., 2002. Empowering children for transitions. *In*: H. Fabian and A. W. Dunlop, eds. *Transitions in the early years.* London: Routledge, 123–134.

Gurdal, S., and Sorbring, E., 2019. Children's agency in parent-child, teacher-pupil and peer relationship contexts. *International Journal of Qualitative Studies on Health and Well-being* [online], 13. Available from: https://www.tandfonline.com/doi/full/10.1080/17482631.2019.1565239.

Hickey-Moody, A., Horn, C., Willcox, M., and Florence, E., 2021. *Arts-based methods for research with children.* Cham, Switzerland: Palgrave Macmillan.

Husserl, E., 1970. *The crisis of European sciences and transcendental phenomenology: an introduction to phenomenological philosophy.* New Brunswick: Ateost Press.

Ingold, T., 2011. *Being alive.* London, UK: Routledge.

Ingold, T., 2015. *The life of lines.* London, UK: Routledge.

Lillemyr, O. F., Dockett, S., and Perry, B., 2013. *Varied perspectives on play and learning: Theory and research on early years education.* Charlotte, NC: Information Age Publishing.

Moustakas, C., 1994. *Phenomenological research methods.* London, UK: Sage.

Neely, E., Walton, M., and Stephens, C., 2014. Young people's food practices: a thematic synthesis. *Appetite* [online], 82. Available from: https://doi.org/10.1016/j.appet.2014.07.005.

Nolan, A., and Paatsch, L., 2018. (Re)affirming identities: implementing a play-based approach to learning in the early years of schooling, *International Journal of Early Years Education* 26 (1). Available from: https://doi.org/10.1080/09669760.2017.1369397.

O'Kane, M., 2016. Transition from preschool to primary school, Research Report No. 19, Dublin: NCCA. Available from: https://ncca.ie/media/1504/transition_to_primary_research_report_19.pdf.

O'Kane, M., and Murphy, R., 2016. *Transition from preschool to school: Audit of policy in 14 jurisdictions.* Dublin: National Council for Curriculum and Assessment. Available from: https://ncca.ie/media/3194/international-audit-draft-11.pdf.

Schutz, A., 1967. *Collected papers.* 2nd ed. Hague: Martinus Nijhoff.

Spyrou, S., 2011. The limits of children's voices: from authenticity to critical, reflective representation. *Childhood* [online], 18. Available from: https://doi.org/10.1177/0907568210387834.

Sutton-Smith, B., 1986. *Toys as culture.* New York: Gardner Press.

Valentine, G., 1999. Being seen and heard? The ethical complexities of working with children and young people at home and at school. *Philosophy and Geography* [online], 2 (2). Available from: https://doi.org/10.1080/13668799908573667.

Valentine, G., 2000. Exploring children and young people's narratives of identity. *Geoforum* [online], 31 (2). Available from: https://doi.org/10.1016/S0016-7185(99)00047-0.

Vargas, G., 2020. Alfred Schutz's life-world and intersubjectivity. *Open Journal of Social Sciences* [online], 8, 417–425. Available from: https://doi.org/10.4236/jss.2020.812033.

Wills, W. J., 2011. Introduction to food: representations and meanings. *Sociological Research Online* [online], 16 (2). Available from: https://doi.org/10.5153/sro.2345.

Wills, W. J., Dickinson, A. M., Meah, H., and Short, F., 2015. Reflections on the use of visual methods in a qualitative study of domestic kitchen practices. *Journal of Sociology* [online], 50 (3). Available from: https://doi.org/10.1177/0038038515587651.

Wolf, S., and Heath, S., 1992. *The braid of literature: children's worlds of reading*. Cambridge, MA: Harvard University Press.

15

'I LIKE IT WHEN I CAN SIT WITH MY BEST FRIENDS'

Exploration of children's agency to achieve commensality in school mealtimes

Samantha Stone and Kyoko Murakami

Introduction

Educational institutions are fundamental to transmitting the values of society. Research has shown how the organisation of society is continually negotiated through food practices in everyday and mundane forms (DeVault 1991; Ochs and Shohet 2006; Valentine 1999). Mealtimes are considered as complex socialising situations that transmit important sociocultural norms imposed by adult authorities. In this chapter, we will argue that rather than children being passive recipients of those sociocultural mealtime norms, they act agentically, working around the norms, modifying and transforming their own frames for thinking, feeling and acting in the world (Ochs and Shohet 2006). We will illustrate how children use non-verbal communication to socially and spatially organise and negotiate material and moral complexities to achieve commensality in school mealtimes together.

Commensality and children's mealtime research

Commensality is the act of eating together and is often considered important for social communion, underpinning the core value of mealtime practices. It literally means eating at the same table and, more broadly, describes eating a meal together in a social setting (Kerner et al. 2015). Commensal practices are essential for conveying social and cultural norms and values in society, which involves creating and reinforcing social relations, nourishing the symbolic and material connections between those involved (Fischler 2011; Kerner et al. 2015; Sobal and Nelson 2003). Everyday mealtimes consist of the sharing of food, conversation, exchanging of body language and eating meals in the company of commensal partners. School mealtimes are an example of such commensal practice

DOI: 10.4324/9781003294962-19

in which children, regardless of school, family or other social situations, are in a socialisation process (Stone 2020). They are inducted into societal norms, learning to conform and negotiate the norms of institutions by forming social relations and learning to collaborate to achieve the goal of commensality. Our research on commensality in school mealtimes focuses on the very process of children's socialisation and explores the notion of their emerging sense of agency as they take part and act in the mealtime practices.

In the context of school mealtimes, Lalli's research (2017) explores the school dining room as a significant space for commensality that fosters children's social learning. Moreover, several studies have identified the tension between the children's priority to spend time with friends and the school's priority to feed many children in a short timeframe (Daniel and Gustafsson 2010; Pike 2010; Valentine 1999). Metcalfe and colleagues' research (2011) considers how school mealtimes govern what children eat as a way of civilising them. Moreover, they provide a detailed account of how children actively shape their own lunchtimes and spaces, revealing that they perform civility in their own social worlds. For example, children practice commensality by putting themselves into smaller groups and sitting down together with their friends to eat their meals. To achieve commensality in school mealtimes, children face time-pressured decisions about where they will sit in relation to others. This illustrates how they develop friendships and create boundaries of friendship patterns (Sobal and Nelson 2003; Stone and Murakami *In Press*; Valentine 1999).

Everyday mealtime routine, including school mealtimes, is practised in a stable group of commensal partners, which are bound by trust and reciprocity (Stone and Murakami *In Press*). The social and moral order in which children work towards commensality gives cohesion to the group and sets the spatial boundaries (Goodwin 1990; Kyratzis 2004). However, if the implicitly agreed commensal goals are broken, for example, if regular companions decide to eat with other peers or do not protect the interactive space from intruders, the group formation is dynamically changed (Corsaro 1992). Our argument for this chapter aligns with the view that commensality is considered essential to children developing sociality and morality, whereby they are socialised into local situated knowledge (Ochs and Shohet 2006). Children's social skills develop through strategically acting in, and reorganising, their social worlds, which can at times result in disagreements or disputes. Kerner and Chou argue 'exclusion from and inclusion in commensal events need not be absolute categories, that is to say, it does not necessarily mean total exclusion or total inclusion per se' (2015, p.6). This idea of inclusion–exclusion is a matter of membership being flexibly and dynamically organised and reorganised by those involved in the commensality practice. For example, Corsaro (1985) may argue that inclusion or exclusion in mealtime shows the fragile and shifting nature of friendship. However, children may choose to be partially included or excluded from group dynamics. This can be analysed by focusing on the ways they configure the material space, which allows children to be a part of the group and maintain connection for friendship and interaction from the periphery. Rather than viewing these children as silent, passive members of the group, or assuming that they have been subjected to exclusion; we consider exclusion–inclusion of group membership as an emergent phenomenon, where we can observe children's learning and agency emerging within the constraints of social norms in the mealtime space, in particular, the way they work with space and coordinate through non-verbal communication to achieve commensality.

Children's tacit learning has been documented by Rogoff (2003). In her cognitive apprenticeship model, Rogoff suggests that children listen in and observe others to expand on their prior knowledge, developing familiar repertories of cultural practices through their immersion in everyday events and routines in which they participate. Children learn new skills by a process of changing knowledge in action, in which the apprentice combines knowledge from the more knowledgeable other with implicit knowledge that is all part of the activity (Lave and Wenger 1991; Rogoff 2003). In the school mealtime children use tacit and non-verbal communication, such as gazes, gestures, posture, facial expression, as symbolic resources to instruct others and to collaborate and mobilise their actions, often against the mealtime rules. Our analysis of the interview with the children shows their social interaction in the mealtimes, including the tacit communication that is aided by those non-verbals in order to achieve commensality. The findings address how children interact with other children in complex demands of the rules and norms of the school mealtime and achieve commensality with mealtime friends. The analysis supports a broader argument that children's communicative actions transform material spaces and create social boundaries which set the limits around how they imagine whose space it is and construct their sense of self and other (Stone 2020; Valentine 1999).

Methodological approach

To illustrate our argument, we draw on empirical material taken from the first author's doctoral research of children's school mealtime socialisation from a child-centred perspective (Stone 2020). The ethnographic research was situated in a Catholic state-funded primary school in Southwest England. At the time of the research, the school had approximately 197 pupils (97 boys and 100 girls) on the roll aged 4–11 years. The first author conducted ethnographic observations in a dinner-lady role and assisted in menial school dinner tasks between 2013 and 2017. Prior to any data collection, we ensured to follow the research ethics guidelines by the Economic and Social Research Council and the University of Bath. Pseudonyms have been used throughout the research to replace the names of the school and all participants.

The data featured in this chapter were taken from 1 of 5 semi-structured group interviews, with 23 children in total. The children, who regularly ate together during the school mealtime, were invited to participate in the interviews. The interviews were conducted in the infant library, adjacent to the meal hall, immediately after the children had eaten their lunch. Each interview lasted approximately 30 minutes. The purpose of the group interviews was to gain a deeper insight into how children socially and spatially locate themselves together and claim a lunch table with friends. We used open-ended interview questions in order to elicit a range of responses from the children. In the interviews, they challenged and expanded on each other's ideas and provided different versions of events, detailing, for instance, how they sat at the dining table and who they wanted to sit next to. Following the child perspective research approach (Hedegaard et al. 2012), we ensured that all the children were given an equal opportunity to speak about their mealtime experiences. The interview interaction was lively.

Group interviews with young children can be challenging because they often talk very quickly, talk over each other, finish each other's sentences, rapidly change topics in conversation and can be easily distracted. To keep them talking on the topic of how they sit during the mealtime, we asked the children to draw pictures of their mealtime experiences, as if they were explaining to their granny or someone who has never been to their school mealtime. Interview questions include who they normally sit with at lunchtime; if there is anything they do so that they can sit with their friends. To illustrate the argument for children's commensality, we conducted the thematic analysis (Braun and Clarke 2006) of the interviews with the children to address how children locate each other, dealt with material and moral complexities and use non-verbal communication to achieve eating together at the same table.

Analysis

The children interviewed place great importance on their seating arrangements at the school lunch table and how sitting next to someone (or not) seems to represent *doing friendship* (Hey 1997), with its associated moral pressures. It is important to understand the intricacies of children's socialisation during the mealtime in terms of how children negotiate their mealtime relationships, which are shared between groups of children, individual children, and unwanted mealtime peers (according to the children's own views). The following extract is taken from a group interview with six female participants from Year Group Four. The interviews were analysed thematically, according to the themes that emerged from the ethnographic field-work of the first author (for a full account, see Stone 2020, Stone and Murakami 2021a and 2021b). For example, the themes include how children worked around the mealtime structure and rules; how they relate to one another and negotiate seating arrangements for achieving commensality (Table 15.1).

The first step in our analysis is to illustrate the importance of children's relationships with each other by highlighting why children make such an effort in the mealtime. In this extract, the children say they sit with their friends (Turns 2 and 5). Except one child, Pippa, all children's responses include the word 'friend' and it is mentioned eight times, among which 'best friend(s)' was mentioned by Darla (Turn 5) and Jenny (Turn 10). It goes to show how important it is for the children to 'sit with friends' or 'best friend(s)' in the school mealtimes. The

TABLE 15.1 A dataset from fieldnotes taken from the research

Turn No	Speaker	Utterance
1	SS	So, are there any seats at the table that you usually sit in or do you just sit anywhere you can find a seat?
2	Poppy	With friends, I like to sit together with friends and do stuff.
3	Pippa	It's cold by the door. I sit on this one ((pointing to her drawing)). It's calm at the sides.
4	Danny	Yeah it's calm at the sides but cold by the door. I like sitting here ((pointing to her drawing)). I don't know why I always sit on this table but I either sit in this chair or that chair
5	Darla	The best seat is opposite my best friend and then after that the second best seat is next to my friend. If I can't, I sit somewhere else near my friends, either next to or opposite or somewhere, anywhere on the table.
6	Kim	I want to sit next to you and you and you and you (pointing to others in the group interview).
7	Dann	Eve promised to sit with me and then she didn't.
8	Pippa	Yeah, once Flo did that to me and then blamed me.
9	Kim	I get my food and then I wait for them to get their food and then we sit down together.
10	Jenny	I like it when I can sit with my best friends but sometimes there might not be a seat for me.
11	SS	Do you all queue up together then?
12	Kim	No, in the playground everybody pushing in but when we go inside we're not allowed to do that because the dinner ladies watch us. When I am in the queue inside [the dining hall] I watch to see where my friends are going and think about what food I will ask the dinner lady [cook] for when it's my turn and then get a seat.
13	Darla	If I get to the table first I can choose and pick friends to sit with.
14	SS	What do you mean?
15	Darla	I look at em weirdly and they sit somewhere else but then we'll be friends when we go to the playground.

Six female participants, Year Group Four, group interview 3, 24/02/2017

importance of sitting with their friends is elaborated around the topic of the seating arrangement, where they sit in relation to their friends. Darla reveals her order of preference for the seating arrangement of her friends (see Turn 5 'opposite to', 'next to', 'near' and 'anywhere on the table'). Some children express their preference in other ways. In Turn 2, Poppy says 'I like to sit together with friends'. It is not just that they eat and 'do stuff', whereas Pippa, who does not mention the word 'friend' in her response, refers to her preferred place to be calm. The children explain their different material preferences, ranging from the practical temperature and noise experienced in a seating position (Turn 3) to the value and significance of social relationships between friends (Turns 4, 5).

Children use gestures and other non-verbal communication as a means to achieve commensality. For example, Darla says she uses a gaze to communicate with non-members to guard the table space for her friends (Turn 15). Children's expressive gestures are displays of their affective stances (Aronsson and Gottzén 2011). They are used in place of, or in conjunction with, speech and can subtly communicate a variety of thoughts and feelings to embrace, disregard or reject others. Children are good at understanding tacit communication, such as glances, winces, and direction of gaze (Rogoff 1990). Non-verbal communication may not always be a means to instruct but it is a powerful means for in-group members to communicate (Rogoff 2003) and helps the children achieve the commensality goal.

The extract highlights another feature of children's commensality practice, that is, a fluidity in commensality relationships, which are formed, rehearsed and remade in response to discursive practice and social interaction (Sikes 2006). Continually changing plans of seating arrangement can be partially pre-defined, but they are fragile and open to change when intentions are in flux. For example, Dann talks about Pippa promising to sit with her and then sitting with someone else (Turns 7 and 8). Interactions such as these are imbued with morality where, for example, Pippa was blamed by Flo for not having an available seat for her to sit in, close to her (Turns 7 and 8). What is right and wrong in a given situation, or what it means to be with friends at school dinner tables, is significant for the children. Furthermore, affective alignments and stances (Aronsson and Gottzén 2011) are observable in this extract. The children say they become upset when unable to sit with their friends, particularly when plans and promises are made prior to the mealtime (Turn 8). Those plans and promises seem to work as a powerful hinge for the children's socialisation. Corsaro's research (2018) is relevant here. He argues that children demonstrate reciprocal if not necessarily intentional regulation of each other's behaviour. Aside from being socialised into the institutional rituals of mealtime, children act toward the commensality goal and socialise with each other through socially and experientially asymmetrical relationships in their peer-produced worlds (Corsaro 2018; Lave and Wenger 1991; Ochs and Shohet 2006; Rogoff 1990). The extract illustrates the children's socio-spatial organisation of commensality in their fluid social relationships as they navigate the mealtime space aided by their social competence, resilience and understanding of mealtime organisation.

Awareness of the organisational structure of the mealtime is observed in Kim's utterance (in the meal hall 'dinner ladies watch us' (Turn 12). She employs a strategy to delay sitting down, which potentially avoids blame from friends if she is unable to save a seat (seat saving is generally prohibited in this school) until they have their lunch. This is, again, to achieve commensality – the children find seats and eat together. Kim articulates her strategy, which is to know what she wants to eat before she gets to the cook, so that she can pass through the food servery quickly to meet up with friends and ensure success in sitting together. Daniel and Gustafsson note that 'being able to sit with your friends was something that required considerable effort and planning for most of the children' (2010, p.271). For Kim, getting her food quickly and maintaining awareness of others is part of making commensality happen.

Finally, children construct and contest for themselves whose space it is on a daily basis, depending on what is temporally, spatially and relationally significant to each child or small group. As undesirable peers (depending on the interests of the children involved) approach the table, sameness and otherness are constructed and contested, which 'produce(s) very real material consequences in terms of social exclusion or discrimination' (Valentine 1999, p.58).

In Turn 15, for example, Darla establishes and maintains her discrete territorial space by sitting down and staking a claim to the other seats at the table (represented by looking at non-desired peers weirdly to discourage them from sitting down) for her friends (who have not arrived yet); she creates an imagined boundary. It is imagined because Darla's mental construct endows the materiality of eight chairs around the table with meaning, constructing a sense of 'self' and 'otherness' (Valentine 1999). However, a 'look' can only be powerful if it is understood by the recipient and may be dependent on the child's status in relation to others. The ability to read, understand and communicate with gesture and tacit knowledge can play a pivotal role in children's commensality, enabling the desire to eat with their 'best friend' or 'friends'. In turn, these informal communications are internalised, which create peer group alliances that may very subtly change over time.

Discussion

The analysis of the extract shows that commensality is vitally important to the children, and they do not take for granted that they can sit together at school mealtimes every day. They use non-verbal communication to orientate themselves (frown, nod, gaze) and coordinate their actions and seating arrangements so that they can not only sit together but sit in their preferred seat next to their ideal friend. In so doing, they negotiate material and moral complexities during their continuously changing co-constructed plans, working within the mealtime rules and responding to factors that they cannot control on a given day. The children are agentic when it comes to moving around the table with friends either by sitting down together in a mealtime space or guarding it from non-members to occupy. 'Both direct and indirect strategies can co-occur in the same mealtime' (Ochs and Shohet 2006, p.36).

Children use various communication strategies for locating each other in the mealtime and exert pre-planned actions of managing and negotiating the territory of their assigned year group tables (Valentine 2000). The concept of imagined boundaries is relevant as they exist in a complex web of relations where other children may be compelled to sit down or they may have imagined boundaries that conflict with their own. Social boundaries require constant enactment from children to maintain their interactive territory within the fast-paced changing landscape of the school mealtime. From the children's active involvement, with both collaborators and competitors, experience is gained in organising their interactions according to the situational and relational demands. Their 'imagined boundaries' allow us to see their planned actions and strategies for achieving commensality. This can be interpreted as a negative aspect of commensality practice, especially, when dinner ladies and researchers alike are quick to perceive children as selfish or resistant to the rules of the mealtime practice or blinded to the dynamics within peer-produced worlds. From the child's perspective, however, it can be argued that children often protect their interactive space from the intrusion of others so that they can maintain control over shared activities, and they are intensely involved in defending and creating a space for sharing (Corsaro 2018). Moreover, children often use non-verbal communication to maintain connection from the periphery when unable to achieve a central ideal seating position (Stone and Murakami *In Press*).

Through these seemingly innocuous everyday practices, children gain opportunities to learn about moral sensibilities within their peer relations. Meanings emerge from children's situated activities and the analysis highlighted how children protect a particular space by giving unwanted peers a 'weird' look or by directing or redirecting non-desirable peers (based on their preferences) to another table. In terms of morality and moral sensibilities, we have touched on how children may feel a sense of responsibility and guilt if they are unable to save a seat for friends who cannot compete with stronger peers or the fast-paced social dynamics. Children's emergent and recursive mealtime practices are imbued with moral expectations (Ochs and Kremer-Sadlik 2007) as they negotiate who they are in relation to others, examining and critiquing the moral basis of their social bonds. The outcome of some alliances and collaborations includes some children at the expense of others, which may lead to unpleasant experiences and social conflict. As a result, school mealtimes may provide unwanted conditions where children may be socialised into marginalisation or other unfavourable and problematic positions (Karrebæk 2011).

Conclusion

In this chapter we have illustrated how children achieve commensality at school mealtime. They exhibit interactional skills, how to communicate and collaborate in noisy multifarious social contexts, gaining social skills that can be transferable well beyond the meal hall. Significantly, such tacit and unscripted experiences require control, a degree of shared knowledge and an element of power within subtle non-verbal communication. Our argument and discussions in this chapter come with limitations. One limitation is the gender imbalance within the sample group in the interview extract. A mixed gender interview might provide further nuances about how friendship groups interact together. It might also be pertinent to explore narratives of marginalised children within the mealtime in terms of commensality. Finally, children's drawings were not included in our analysis.

Due to the scope of this chapter, only the thematic analysis of an extract has been presented. For future works, analysing children's drawings in conjunction with the interviews may provide further insight into other aspects of their peer-led socialisation processes.

More research is needed to further explore children's use of space in relation to their socialisation in school mealtime practice. Such research may stimulate interest in re-conceptualising children's agency. School mealtimes do more than enliven the school day. They give children a break from the mental exertion of classwork and nourish the physical body; when children freely interact, they reveal much about themselves and their social worlds (Sharp and Blatchford 1994). Due to the limited space in this chapter, however, we could not fully account for children's agency emerging from the commensality practice in school mealtimes. There are important opportunities and insights to be gained from educational researchers who conceptualise school mealtimes as an integral component of the ecology of education (Weaver-Hightower 2011). School mealtimes are an important context in which to learn something new about children's socialisation in the commensality practice and employ children's disruptions as a source of critical examination of our normative understandings of children's socialisation process.

Acknowledgement

We wish to thank Alison Douthwaite and a reviewer for their valuable feedback on an early version of the manuscript.

References

Aronsson, K., and Gottzén, L., 2011. Generational positions at a family dinner: food morality and social order. *Language in Society*, 40, 405–427.

Braun, V., and Clarke, V., 2006. Using thematic analysis in psychology. *Qualitative Research in Psychology*, 3 (2), 77–101.

Corsaro, W., 1985. *Friendship and peer culture in the early years*. Norwood, NJ: Ablex.

Corsaro, W., 1992. Interpretive reproduction in children's peer cultures. *Social Psychology Quarterly*, 55 (2), 160–177.

Corsaro, W., 2018. *The sociology of childhood*. 5th ed. Thousand Oaks, CA: Pine Forge.

Daniel, P., and Gustafsson, U., 2010. School lunches: children's services or children's spaces? *Children's Geographies*, 8 (3), 265–274.

DeVault, M., 1991. *Feeding the family: the social organization of caring as gendered work: women in culture and society*. Chicago, IL: University of Chicago Press.

Fischler, C., 2011. Commensality, society and culture. *Social Science Information*, 50 (3–4), 528–548.

Goodwin, M. H., 1990. Tactical uses of stories: participation framework within girls' and boys' disputes. *Discourse Processes*, 13, 35–71.

Hedegaard, M., Aronsson, K., Højholt, C., and Skjar Ulvik, O., 2012. *Children, childhood, and everyday life: children's perspectives*. Charlotte, NC: Information Age Publishing Inc.

Hey, V., 1997. *The company she keeps: an ethnography of girls' friendships*. Buckingham, UK: Open University Press.

Karrebæk, M., 2011. It farts: the situated management of social organization in a kindergarten peer group. *Journal of Pragmatics*, 43 (12), 2911–2931.

Kerner, S., Chou, C., and Warmind, M., 2015. *Commensality: from everyday food to feast*. London, UK: Bloomsbury Publishing.

Kyratzis, A., 2004. Talk and interaction among children and the co-construction of peer groups and peer culture. *Annual Review of Anthropology*, 33 (1), 625–649.

Lalli, G., 2017. An investigation into Commensality in the 'School Restaurant'. *British Education Studies Association: Educational Futures*, 8 (2), 69–88.

Lave, J., and Wenger, E., 1991. *Situated learning: legitimate peripheral participation*. Cambridge, UK: Cambridge University Press.

Metcalfe, A., Owen, J., Dryden, C., and Shipton, G., 2011. Concrete chips and soggy semolina: the contested spaces of the school dinner hall. *Population, Space and Place*, 17 (4), 377–389.

Ochs, E., and Kremer-Sadlik., 2007. Introduction: morality as family practice. *Discourse and Society*, 18 (1), 5–10.

Ochs, E., and Shohet, M., 2006. The cultural structuring of mealtime socialization. *New Directions for Child and Adolescents Developments*, 111, 35–49.

Pike, J., 2010. 'I Don't Have to Listen to You! You're Just a Dinner Lady!': power and resistance at lunchtime in primary schools. *Children's Geographies*, 8 (3), 275–287.

Rogoff, B., 1990. *Apprenticeship in thinking: cognitive development in social context*. New York: Oxford University Press.

Rogoff, B., 2003. *The cultural nature of human development*. Oxford, UK: Oxford University Press.

Sharp, S., and Blatchford, P., 1994. Understanding and changing school break time behaviour: themes and conclusions. *In:* P. Blatchford and S. Sharp, eds. *Breaktime and the school: understanding and changing playground behaviour*. London, UK: Routledge, 118–133.

Sikes, P., 2006. On dodgy ground? Problematics and ethics in educational research. *International Journal of Research and Method in Education*, 29 (1), 105–117.

Sobal, J., and Nelson, M., 2003. Commensal eating patterns: a community study. *Appetite*, 41, 181–190.

Stone, S., 2020. An investigation of children's mealtime socialisation in a primary school in Southwest England. *Unpublished PhD Thesis*, University of Bath, UK.

Stone, S., and Murakami, K., 2021a. Children's subversive interactions in the school mealtime. *Culture and Psychology*, 27 (4), 1–16.

Stone, S., and Murakami, K., 2021b. Humour and the grotesque pleasures of children's school mealtime socialisation. *Children and Society* [online]. Available from: https://doi.org/10.1111/chso.12451.

Stone, S., and Murakami, K., School mealtimes and children's spatial agency, *Children's Geographies* (in progress).

Valentine, G., 1999. Imagined geographies: geographical knowledges of self and other in everyday life. *In:* D. Massey, J. Allen and P. Sarre, eds. *Human geography today*. Cambridge, UK: Polity Press, 47–61.

Valentine, G., 2000. Exploring children and young people's narratives of identity. *Geoforum*, 31 (2), 257–267.

Weaver-Hightower, M. B., 2011. Why researchers should take school food seriously. *Educational Researcher*, 40 (1), 15–21.

16

FRIENDS, NOT FOOD

How inclusive is education for young vegans in Scotland?

Lynda M. Korimboccus

Introduction

This chapter draws on desk-based research from literature-based information, empirical studies, legislation and reports and reflects on the significance of findings. It opens with an example that highlights the difference and division created by a lack of understanding of full curricular inclusion, veganism more generally, and the specific educational experience of many young vegans. For example, recently the author learned of a 7-year-old vegan child's lesson with a teacher who had created a class counting activity using marshmallows. Despite the availability of vegan marshmallows at local supermarkets, the child was given Lego instead, then had to watch other classmates enjoy eating their projects before home time. That 7-year-old felt a lack of fairness and sense of exclusion that day (not for the first time) that education is supposed to counter in the lives of young children.

In this chapter, 'young vegans' are referred to as vegan children undertaking Primary School in Scotland, aged between 4–5 (Primary 1) and 11–12 (Primary 7). These children number approximately 393,300 of the estimated 5.5 million residents of Scotland (Clark 2021; Scotland's Census 2021). Even though a small minority of United Kingdom (UK) schoolchildren are vegan (Vegan Inclusive Education [VIE] 2020), veganism is increasing exponentially (Veganuary 2022). It is worth noting that many individuals who prefer 'plant-based' foods adhere to veganism in terms of dietary consumption, but this may not include *ethical* vegan consumption, which extends to all areas of life from clothing and household products to hobbies and interests. This chapter provides a brief overview of the Scottish education system, policy drivers, teaching pedagogy (with examples of curriculum delivery where animal use is commonplace and speciesism evident), and recommends several means by which full inclusion may be delivered.

DOI: 10.4324/9781003294962-20

To be or not to be vegan...that is the question

Veganism is essentially:

> a philosophy and way of living which seeks to excluded—as far as is possible and practicable—all forms of exploitation of, and cruelty to, animals for food, clothing or any other purpose; and by extension, promotes the development and use of animal-free alternatives for the benefit of animals, humans and the environment.
>
> *(The Vegan Society 2014)*

Even though veganism maintains important links with social justice and resistance (White 2018), some believe it as simplified 'material practice' rather than it being recognised as a belief system (Dutkiewicz and Dickstein 2021). What is socially and culturally consumed is just as significant as what is physically consumed – TV programming and other media, shared social values and normative praxis, including everyday language and practical action, are traditionally speciesist (Dunayer 2001). It is important to realise that navigating a nonvegan world remains tricky for young vegan children, in addition to learning about themselves and finding their way in life.

A recent report by an independent health charity, The Nuffield Trust, showed a deterioration in obesity, infant and early childhood mortality, and life expectancy for UK children compared to 14 other countries overall (Cheung 2018). The public support a strategy to make healthier choices easier, particularly as childhood obesity risk is around one in six (Public Health Scotland 2021). With clear correlations consistently made between consumption of nonhuman animals and various human diseases (Physicians' Committee for Responsible Medicine n.d. World Health Organisation (2015), and the detrimental impact particular forms of consumption are having on the environment (Xu et al. 2021), it is perplexing why plant-based foods remain so elusive in everyday life, including (and perhaps specifically) in educational settings. Recent data shows that 5–11 year-old children tend to morally consider nonhuman and human life as equal (McGuire et al. 2022; Wilks et al. 2021), suggesting speciesism is a learned, social constructed value. Many children say they love animals, yet many of those children also regularly eat animal body parts. This 'meat paradox' phenomenon since 2010 (Loughnan et al. 2010) has been extensively explored, reviewed (Gradidge et al. 2021) and applied (Korimboccus 2020). The education and reinforcement of paradoxical socialised norms and values by wider society can cause early socialisation in adopting eating patterns for certain animal species (Cole and Stewart 2014). Whatever the folkways, it remains puzzling why the consistent position of 'friends, not food' adhered to by vegan children is met with at best confusion, and at worst, derision or discrimination against this "benign yet social-norm challenging" belief system (MacInnis and Hodson 2017, p.721). These children show compassion for fellow beings, but can be met with contempt for so doing, even from trusted adults.

Whilst this research grows, it tends to deal with individual cognitive processes and dissonance, yet less so regarding veganism as identity or praxis. Some literature exists focusing on veganism as embodied self-identity in adults (Greenebaum 2012; Wrenn and Lizardi 2021), 'vegaphobia' or other vegan stigma (Cole and Morgan 2011; Markowski and Roxburgh 2019), and adult experiences of raising a vegan child (Barwick 2016; Torres and Torres 2010). Evidence key to this chapter is thus far notably absent, however, much has been written about children's social identities in general (Bennett 2011), and the motivations of *vegetarian* children, or vegan *teenagers* have also been investigated (Cherry 2014; Hussar and Harris 2010). At the time of writing, evidence remains mostly anecdotal of how young vegan children experience life in education and the other social institutions within which they live, and hope to thrive. This chapter is one step towards gaining an understanding of their lived experiences within a setting in which they are finding their place, and how it can be made more welcoming… for everyone.

Scottish education as curriculum for excellence

> Scotland's 'needs led' and rights based educational system is designed to be an inclusive one for all children and young people in Scottish schools.
>
> *(Education Scotland 2022, para 1)*

Inclusion is the fanfare of most public sector organisations as the 21st Century advances, and with education so vital to the socialisation of future generations, it should be at the helm of such positive change. In 1496, Scotland became the first country in the world to mandate education (McEnaney 2021), and has retained its learning and teaching independence from the other UK home nations since. Children in Scotland receive structured early learning from age 3, then more formal education from 4 or 5, birthdate dependent. They receive 7 years of primary education followed by 4–6 years of secondary education from ages 11–12 through to 16–18. Children spend 36–40 hours per week on school grounds, 38 weeks per year. It is therefore essential their interactions within the system, its representatives (and theirs) are positive and inclusive. This is eminently possible, as evidenced in the following overview of Scotland's 'Curriculum for Excellence' and associated policy drivers of 'Getting It Right For Every Child' (GIRFEC) and 'SHANARRI': that every child should be Safe, Healthy, Achieving, Nurtured, Active, Respected, Responsible and Included.

A commitment to inclusive education is heralded by Education Scotland (2017b) in its *Curriculum for Excellence* implemented in 2010. It incorporates eight curriculum areas, and four central capacities taught across all subjects to ensure Scottish children and young people develop essential knowledge, skills, and attributes to succeed in life, learning, work and societal roles. Each capacity has attributes and capabilities to be evidenced through Experiences and Outcomes (E&Os). Whilst good teaching should always have included these important elements, it is now mandatory to fully consider how learning and teaching enable the development of these skills and abilities.

Education Scotland Benchmarks for Early Level Food and Health *"[r]ecognises and respects that others' food choices may be different from their own"* (2017a, p.28) and *"[describe] which foods come from plants and which come from animals when working with and tasting foods"* (2017a, p.29). That food and animals are conflated, exemplifies speciesist linguistic associations, asserting the (exclusive) status quo, and has potential to make any challenge to teachers' authority particularly difficult for vegans in the classroom. Nevertheless, language is powerful, and speciesist norms are maintained by such "habitual patterns of language [that] make meat-eating and factory farming seem natural" (Moore 2014, p.59). On the other hand, testing, assessment and examination are regulated by the Scottish Qualifications Authority (SQA) and, unlike its other UK counterparts, has no direct competition in Scotland regarding formal Scottish education yet governs all formal Scottish qualifications other than those awarded by Scottish Universities. Although independent, the SQA works closely with the Scottish Government through Education Scotland, charged with ensuring learners receive the best possible educational experience. The success of this curriculum remains a contested topic, worthy of further research (Organisation for Economic Cooperation and Development 2021).

Local, national and international guidance

The UK Human Rights Act 1998, is based on the European Convention on Human Rights (ECHR), and The Equality Act 2010. The aim is to ensure fairness, inclusion and consideration for all. The ECHR details ten protected characteristics prohibited from discrimination, including sex, race, religion and political opinion (Council of Europe 2021). The United Nation Convention on the Rights of the Child (UNCRC) is promoted extensively throughout primary education, providing young people with awareness of their rights and responsibilities throughout childhood. The seven-year-old mentioned earlier can recite each of the rights of the child at any fortuitous point in time: I have the right to relax and play!. The 45+ UNCRC articles also include the right to (1) freedom of expression, (2) have views considered and taken seriously (to be heard), (3) think and believe what they choose and (4) access reliable information from a variety of sources (United Nations Children's Fund UK 1990). It is unsurprising then, that children recognise the feeling of being left out or mocked for their beliefs, or when presented with one-sided representations of nonhumans. In loco parentis[1] is a position of trust that should not be broken, yet sometimes school staff are the very source of these feelings.

Case law

In early 2020, an employment tribunal established veganism as a legally protected characteristic (Her Majesty's Courts and Tribunals Service) akin to religious belief in terms of equality and human rights, and changed the landscape of employment law on equality and diversity. The Vegan Society swiftly issued a guide for employers of vegan staff (2020) and the National Association of Head Teachers (NAHT) has encouraged its 45,000 members (excluding Scotland) to take a first step of establishing how many vegan staff and pupils they have, and appear to be taking seriously the implications of VIE's survey on vegan students (2021).

Children health and wellbeing (SHANARRI)

A policy driver, GIRFEC, aims to improve the wellbeing of all children through a holistic approach for each child. Their position is for children to *"grow up feeling loved, safe and respected and can realise their full potential. At home, in school or the wider community, every child and young person should be: Safe; Healthy; Achieving; Nurtured; Active; Respected; Responsible; [and] Included (SHANARRI)"* (Scottish Government n.d.).

However, a recent survey suggests in practice, only one in ten vegan children feel valued and supported in their beliefs, three-quarters have been teased or bullied for having them, and 85% felt discriminated against at school (Vegan Inclusive Education 2020). This is unacceptable and unsustainable, although it takes nothing away from the potential of policy drivers to become a route to a more acceptable and inclusive educational experience for everyone.

School food and beverage contexts

Faught et al. (2017) emphasise good childhood health is vital, not just for academic achievement, but for lifelong health. In Scotland, free school meals are available to all Primary one to five pupils (means-tested thereafter), and many are eligible for free (or subsidised) school milk. The *Milk and Healthy Snack Scheme (Scotland) Regulations 2021* replaced an earlier, dairy-only system and now under-5s are offered free, unsweetened, fortified soya milk where there are medical, ethical or religious requirements (Scottish Government 2021). In contrast, the accompanying guidance makes the claim: *"it is noted that these alternatives do not offer the same nutritional benefit as cow's milk and should not therefore be regarded as equivalent."* With this contradiction in mind it is does not make sense to include such declarations. From an environmental perspective, oat milk is significantly less harmful to the planet than dairy (Poore and Nemecek 2018), yet is excluded from school milk guidance in favour of soy, despite soy being in the top 14 UK food allergens alongside dairy (Allergy UK 2022). The health benefits of oats and other wholegrains are clear (Harvard College 2022), as well as their sustainability as local produce, with oats having long been a healthy staple of the Scottish diet since early Medieval times (National Geographic 2021). Nutritional requirements set by food standards and agencies, discriminate and contradict. For example, the Scottish Food Standards Agency categorise 'dairy' as a specific food group yet the 'Eatwell Guide' produced by four UK standards agencies state "dairy and alternatives" (Food Standards Scotland 2019). Parents of older vegan children must send plant milk to school because children over five 'alternatives' are not sourced by local authorities.

Practical activities

Pedersen (2019) identifies the use of the nonhuman animal as being 'deeply embedded' within the education system, evidence through the following statements:

> displayed, classified, studied, and represented, as well as confined, manipulated, consumed, and killed, in a multitude of forms in education […] students are […] taught to utilize, dominate, or control other species as […] scientific objects […or in…] visits to zoos (where their captivity is often normalized and rarely rendered problematic.
>
> *(pp.1–2)*

While Scottish schoolchildren are not introduced to experimentation or dissection in science at primary school level, separating a vegan child during baking activities magnifies 'difference', when vegan spread or oil could replace hen's eggs for the whole class recipe. Having a 'zoo' or 'farm' topic is easily replaced through a focus on endangered species, or a local animal sanctuary. Removing feathers from craft boxes requires minimal effort. Advance notice of activities is merely one short communication away, so vegan marshmallows become possible, and 7-year-old children do not find themselves in a space feeling awkward, humiliated, or excluded. Another key point is that industrial targeting supports learning outcomes through free materials or sponsorship, including pedagogical plans and teaching resources, that also promote and expand their products' reach (Gillard 2003). In sociological terms, the systems and structures within which children find themselves are merely a state facilitative apparatus, which in turn does the bidding of capitalist corporations similar to 'farming to pharmaceuticals' (Nibert 2002).

Sustainability and ethical consumption

The Eco-Schools green flag scheme is supported by the Foundation for Environmental Education (FEE) and the United Nations Educational, Scientific and Cultural Organization (UNESCO), and rewards suitably successful attempts to promote environmental awareness and sustainability within an extensive framework (Keep Britain Tidy, n.d.). It is argued a vegan-friendly curriculum would benefit all students, regardless of moral, religious or ethical beliefs because it would provide a more ethically inclusive system. Springmann et al. recently concluded that:

> national guidelines could be both healthier and more sustainable. Providing clearer advice on limiting […] the consumption of animal source foods,

in particular beef and dairy, was found to have the greatest potential for increasing the environmental sustainability of dietary guidelines.

(2020, p.1)

UK-founded Veganuary captured a record 629,000 people sign-up to go vegan in January 2022, from many countries globally (Veganuary 2022). It would be reasonable to suggest that ethical consumption is here to stay because veganism supports social responsibility and individuals in minority groups through healthy choices. In 2021, US-based Vegan Outreach (2022) had 460,000 sign-ups to their *10 Weeks to Vegan* program, which operates in 43 countries. The stigma that once surrounded veganism is abating as major supermarkets and restaurants add vegan items to their portfolios and menus. One English primary school recently implemented meat-free menus and encouraged meat-free packed lunches largely due to the headteacher citing environmental concerns over factory farming, and a need for commitment to action for the planet and pupils' futures. Despite anger from some parents, uptake of school meals increased following the changes (Collis 2022) and evidences that initiatives can create positive results (Garnett and Balmford 2022).

Hidden barriers

Previously, providers could be forgiven for not realising the extent to which veganism extends to everyday custom and practice, but with the recent increase in awareness of veganism and guides provided to employers and educators, for example, The Vegan Society, change is progressing. In any case, ignorance is no defence in law, and the law is now clear regarding the rights of vegan beliefs to be recognised as worthy of protection (Her Majesty's Courts and Tribunals Service 2020). Regardless of any tendency to resist progressive legal moves, barriers are being dismantled and there is at least a legal obligation to walk through the newly created space. Minority groups not so long ago faced the same situation with little guidance from uneducated educators. There was a certain level of normalisation of discrimination that many people were completely unaware of. In any case, if the law or system requires consideration for all protected groups, vegans should be included as well. In spite of this, barriers to progress remain hidden, and the complex nature of childhood can further disguise what can be an incredibly alienating experience on a daily basis.

Comparatively, secondary and tertiary education also have their challenges. For example, (1) the expectation that students handle pieces of a dead animal or live animal emissions (eggs) as mandatory ingredient categories in practical cookery qualifications (Scottish Qualifications Authority 2019), (2) being asked to accept that a certain level of nonhuman animal use is necessary in nutrition or dietetics training (Sallaway-Costello et al. 2021) and (3) being expected to use animal-tested or derived products in hairdressing or beauty courses where training salons are corporate-sponsored, or where affordability restricts student options. In other study areas, despite long-standing availability of alternatives promoted by organisations such as InterNICHE (Jukes and Chiuia 2003), students must either dissect and study the body parts of dead animals in biology, or alienate themselves by conscientiously objecting; or be subjected to the grim details of behavioural psychology experiments such as Pavlov's dogs, Skinner's mice, or Harlow's monkeys. Whilst the ethics of such experimental approaches form part of their evaluation, any critique seems incongruent when neuroscientific and psychological experiments on the 'nonhuman' continue, supported by professional organisations (Bedwell 2016). Even charity choices raise ethical difficulties for vegan learners, who might oppose charitable giving to Cancer Research UK, the British Heart Foundation or other pro-vivisection organisations (Animal Aid 2022), and then be unjustly accused of being uncharitable, or not caring about human health. There are numerous human health charities undertaking humane medical research without nonhuman animals. Their selection would avoid such terrible accusations. Animal use is not inevitable, nor necessary: it is simply a symptom of continual reinforcement of normative values that overlook the needs of the animal themselves, and the humans who choose not to be part of their downfall.

Conclusion

The social dynamics of childhood are complex and fraught with anxiety, as children and young people discover and develop their personal and social identities. School is a significant site of this growth and it is imperative (morally, as well as legally) that barriers are removed for every child. Equality, diversity and inclusivity are important within 21st-century social institutions, and veganism is now a protected characteristic in law. There is much more to investigate here than this chapter can cover: the responsibility of vested industry interests in maintaining the status quo within education (and the latter system allowing it); or differences between state and fee-paying schools in terms of control, choice, availability, and inclusion. Social class inequality is an ongoing national problem that spills into classrooms (McEnany 2021), and that Scotland has struggled to rectify, so whether the intersectional nature of inequality across the system results in certain groups of vegan children being more overlooked than others may also be relevant. Vegan inclusion is equally difficult for adults in various settings, though the commitment society claims to raising children well should lay the foundations for a more inclusive future for everyone. The Vegan Society has long provided guidance on good nutrition and health at all life stages, including childhood, in pregnancy, and older adults (1944–2022).

Inequalities are not mutually exclusive: inclusion is inclusion. Kindness to all beings necessitates kindness to each other. Veganism can help alleviate global hunger and food poverty (United Nations Environment Program 2010) and create a healthier society (Tuso et al. 2013). Plant-based pedagogy and fully-rounded, all-inclusive education can create a conscious awareness in practitioners that can benefit all children in their care. To sum up, individuals seeking change shall persevere with writing such as this, and alongside organisations such as ProVeg UK and VIE, continue to strive for an education system within which vegan learners can feel valued, included, heard and respected. We can surely want no less for our youngsters, as they want no less for their nonhuman kin.

Note

1 With reference to a teacher or other adult responsible for children in the place of a parent.

References

Allergy UK, 2022. *Food allergy* [online]. Available from: https://www.allergyuk.org/types-of-allergies/food-allergy/ [Accessed 31 May 2022].

Animal Aid, 2022. *Which charities fund animal experiments?* [online]. Available from: https://www.animalaid.org.uk/the-issues/our-campaigns/animal-experiments/victims-charity-campaign/charities-fund-animal-experiments/ [Accessed 31 May 2022].

Barwick, E. M., 2016. *Are vegan kids social outcasts? parents answer* [online]. Available from: http://www.bitesizevegan.org./bite-size-vegan-nuggets/qa/are-vegan-kids-social-outcasts-parents-answer/ [Accessed 31 May 2022].

Bedwell, S. A., 2016. Opinion: why research using animals is important in psychology. *The Psychologist* [online], 29 (8). Available from: https://www.bps.org.uk/psychologist/opinion-why-research-using-animals-important-psychology.

Bennett, M., 2011. Children's social identities. *Infant and Child Development* [online], 20 (4), Available from: https://doi.org/10.1002/icd.741.

Cherry, E., 2014. I was a teenage vegan: motivation and maintenance of lifestyle movements. *Sociological Inquiry* [online], 85 (1). Available from: https://doi.org/10.1111/soin.12061.

Cheung, R., 2018. *International comparisons of health and wellbeing in early childhood*. London, UK: Nuffield Trust.

Clark, D., 2021. *Number of pupils attending schools in Scotland from 2013 to 2020, by school type* [online]. Available from: https://www.statista.com/statistics/715853/number-of-pupils-in-scotland-by-school-type/ [Accessed 31 May 2022].

Cole, M., and Morgan, K., 2011. Vegaphobia: derogatory discourses of veganism and the reproduction of speciesism in UK national newspapers [online]. *The British Journal of Sociology*, 62 (1). Available from: https://doi.org/10.1111/j.1468-4446.2010.01348.x.

Cole, M., and Stewart, K., 2014. *Our children and other animals: the cultural construction of human-animal relations in childhood*. Surrey, UK: Ashgate Publishing Ltd.

Collis, D., 2022. *Barrowford headteacher defends 'environmentally friendly meat free' school menu* [online]. Available from: https://www.burnleyexpress.net/education/barrowford-headteacher-defends-environmentally-friendly-meat-free-school-menu-3562962 [Accessed 31 May 2022].

Council of Europe, 2021. *Guide on article 14 of the European convention on human rights and on article 1 of protocol No. 12 to the convention* [online]. Available from: https://www.echr.coe.int/Documents/Guide_Art_14_Art_1_Protocol_12_ENG.pdf.

Dunayer, J., 2001. *Animal equality: language and liberation*. Derwood, MD: Ryce Publishing.

Dutkiewicz, J., and Dickstein, J., 2021. The Ism in veganism: the case for a minimal practice-based definition. *Food Ethics* [online], 6 (2). Available from: https://doi.org/10.1007/s41055-020-00081-6.

Education Scotland, 2017a. *Benchmarks: early level, all curriculum areas.* Livingston, Scotland: Education Scotland.

Education Scotland, 2017b. *Equality policy* [online]. Available from: https://education.gov. scot/Documents/Education-Scotland-Equality-Policy-October-2017.pdf [Accessed 31 May 2022].

Education Scotland, 2022. *Embedding inclusion, wellbeing and equality* [online]. Available from: https://education.gov.scot/education-scotland/what-we-do/embedding-inclusion-wellbeing-and-equality/ [Accessed 31 May 2022].

Faught, E. L., Gleddie, D., Storey, K. E., Davison, C. M., and Veugelers, P. J., 2017. Healthy lifestyle behaviours are positively and independently associated with academic achievement: an analysis of self-reported data from a nationally representative sample of Canadian early adolescents. *PLoS ONE* [online], 12 (7). Available from: https://doi.org/10.1371/journal.pone.0181938.

Food Standards Scotland, 2019. *The eatwell guide* [online]. Available from: https://www. foodstandards.gov.scot/downloads/Eatwell_Guide_Booklet_-_new.pdf [Accessed 31 May 2022].

Garnett, E. E., and Balmford, A., 2022. The vital role of organizations in protecting climate and nature. *Nature Human Behaviour* [online], 6. Available from: https://doi. org/10.1038/s41562-021-01260-z.

Gillard, D., 2003. *Food for thought: child nutrition, the school dinner and the food industry* [online]. Available from: www.educationengland.org.uk/articles/22food.html [Accessed 31 May 2022].

Gradidge, S., Zawisza, M., Harvey, A. J., and McDermott, D. T., 2021. A structured literature review of the meat paradox. *Social Psychological Bulletin* [online], 16 (3). Available from: https://doi.org/10.32872/spb.5953.

Greenebaum, J., 2012. Veganism, identity and the quest for authenticity. *Food, Culture & Society* [online], 15 (1). Available from: https://www.tandfonline.com/doi/abs/10.275 2/175174412X13190510222101.

Harvard College, 2022. *Oats and health* [online]. Available from: https://www.hsph .harvard.edu/nutritionsource/food-features/oats/ [Accessed 31 May 2022].

Her Majesty's Courts and Tribunals Service, 2020. Mr J Casamitjana Costa v The League against cruel sports [online]. 3331129/2018, Employment Tribunal decision. Available from: https://assets.publishing.service.gov.uk/media/5e3419ece5274a08dc828fdd/ Mr_J_Casamitjana_Costa_v_The_League_Against_Cruel_Sports_-_3331129-18_-_ Open_Preliminary_Hearing_Judgment___Reasons.pdf [Accessed 31 May 2022].

Hussar, K. M., and Harris, P. L., 2010. Children who choose not to eat meat: a study of early moral decision-making. *Social Development* [online], 19 (3). Available from: https://doi.org/10.1111/j.1467-9507.2009.00547.x.

Jukes, N., and Chiuia, M., 2003. *From guinea pig to computer mouse: alternative methods for a progressive, humane education* [online]. Available from: https://www.interniche.org/ru/ system/files/public/Resources/Book/jukes_and_chiuia_-_2003_-_from_guinea_ pig_to_computer_mouse_interniche_2nd_ed_en.pdf; https://www.interniche.org/ ru/system/files/public/Resources/Book/jukes_and_chiuia_-_2003_-_from_guinea_ pig_to_computer_mouse_interniche_2nd_ed_en.pdf [Accessed 31 May 2022].

Keep Britain Tidy, no date. *Empowering young people to protect our planet since 1994* [online]. Available at: https://www.eco-schools.org.uk/ [Accessed 31 May 2022].

Korimboccus, L. M., 2020. Pig-ignorant: The Peppa Pig paradox: contradictory consumption in childhood. *Journal for Critical Animal Studies* [online], 17 (5). Available from: http://journalforcriticalanimalstudies.org/wp-content/uploads/2020/10/ JCAS-Vol-17-Iss-5-October-2020-1-FINAL.pdf.

Loughnan, S., Haslam, N., and Bastian, B., 2010. The role of meat consumption in the denial of moral status and mind to meat animals. *Appetite*, 55 (1), 156–159.

MacInnis, C. C., and Hodson, G., 2017. It ain't easy eating greens: evidence of bias toward vegetarians and vegans from both source and target. *Group Processes & Intergroup Relations* [online], 20 (6). Available from: https://doi.org/10.1177/1368430215618253.

Markowski, K. L., and Roxburgh, S., 2019. If I became a vegan, my family and friends would hate me: anticipating vegan stigma as a barrier to plant-based diets. *Appetite*, 135, 1–9.

McEnaney, J., 2021. *Class rules: the truth about Scottish schools*. Edinburgh, Scotland: Luath Press.

McGuire, L., Palmer, S. B., and Faber, N. S., 2022. The development of speciesism: age-related differences in the moral view of animals. *Social Psychological and Personality Science* [online]. Available from: https://doi.org/10.1177/19485506221086182.

Moore, A. R., 2014. That could be me: Identity and identification in discourses about food, meat, and animal welfare. *Linguistics and the Human Sciences* [online], 9 (1). Available from: https://journal.equinoxpub.com/LHS/article/view/12814.

National Association of Head Teachers, 2021. *Veganism in schools* [online]. Available from: https://naht.org.uk/Advice-Support/Topics/Management/ArtMID/755/ArticleID/1072/Veganism-in-schools [Accessed 31 May 2022].

National Geographic, 2021. *Journey through the history of porridge, from Scotland's rugged landscapes to the alpine world of Switzerland* [online]. Available from: https://www.nationalgeographic.co.uk/travel/2021/09/the-journey-of-the-oat-grain-from-the-rugged-landscapes-of-scotland-to-the-alpine-world-of-switzerland [Accessed 31 May 2022].

Nibert, D., 2002. *Animal rights/human rights: entanglements of oppression and liberation*. Oxford, UK: Rowman and Littlefield.

Organisation for Economic Cooperation and Development, 2021. *Scotland's curriculum for excellence: into the future, implementing education policies*. Paris, France: OECD Publishing.

Pedersen, H., 2019. The contested space of animals in education: a response to the 'Animal Turn' in education for sustainable development. *Education Sciences* [online], 9 (3). Available from: https://doi.org/10.3390/educsci9030211 [Accessed 31 May 2022].

Physicians' Committee for Responsible Medicine, no date. *Fact sheet: health concerns about dairy* [online]. Available from: https://www.pcrm.org/good-nutrition/nutrition-information/health-concerns-about-dairy [Accessed 31 May 2022].

Poore, J., and Nemecek, T., 2018. Reducing food's environmental impacts through producers and consumers. *Science* 360 [online]. Available from: https://www.science.org/doi/10.1126/science.aaq0216 [Accessed 31 May 2022].

Public Health Scotland, 2021. *Diet and health weight*. Available from: https://www.health-scotland.scot/health-topics/diet-and-healthy-weight/food-and-diet (Accessed 31 May 2022).

Sallaway-Costello, J., Corbett, M., Larkin, A., Mellard, A., Murray, L., and Sellins, K., 2021. Vegan faces in anthroparchal spaces: student reflections on educational experiences of veganism in nutritional sciences. *Student Journal of Vegan Sociology* [online], 1. Available from: https://www.vegansociology.com/wp-content/uploads/2021/10/SJVS-2021-1-Sallaway-Costello-et-al-FINAL.pdf [Accessed 31 May 2022].

Scotland's Census, 2021. *Population* [online]. Available from: https://www.scotlandscensus.gov.uk/census-results/at-a-glance/population/ [Accessed 31 May 2022].

Scottish Government, no date. *Getting it right for every child* [online]. Available from: https://www.gov.scot/policies/girfec/wellbeing-indicators-shanarri/ [Accessed 31 May 2022].

Scottish Government, 2021. *The milk and health snack scheme (Scotland) Regulations 2021.* Available from: https://www.legislation.gov.uk/ssi/2021/82/contents/made [Accessed 31 May 2022].

Scottish Qualifications Authority, 2019. *The Annual Statistical Report 2019* [online]. Available from: https://www.sqa.org.uk/sqa/91419.html

Springmann, M., Spajic, L., Clark, M. A., Poore, J., Herforth, A., Webb, P., Rayner, M., and Scarborough, P., 2020. The healthiness and sustainability of national and global food based dietary guidelines: modelling study. *BMJ* [online], 2322 (8254). Available from: https://doi.org/10.1136/bmj.m2322.

The Vegan Society, 1944–2022. *Life stages* [online]. Available from: https://www.vegansociety.com/resources/nutrition-and-health/life-stages [Accessed 31 May 2022].

The Vegan Society, 2014. *Ripened by human determination: 70 years of the Vegan Society* [online]. Available from: https://www.vegansociety.com/sites/default/files/uploads/Ripened%20by%20human%20determination.pdf [Accessed 31 May 2022].

Torres, B., and Torres, J., 2010. *Vegan freak: being vegan in a non-vegan world.* Oakland, CA: PM Press.

Tuso, P. J., Ismail, M. H., Ha, B. P., and Bartolotto, C., 2013. Special report: nutritional update for physicians: plant-based diets. *The Permanente Journal* [online], 17 (2). Available from: https://doi.org/10.7812/TPP/12-085 [Accessed 31 May 2022].

United Nations Children's Fund's UK, 1990. *The United Nations convention on the rights of the child.* London, UK: UNICEF.

United Nations Environment Program, 2010. *Assessing the environmental impacts of consumption and production: priority products and materials* [online]. Available from: https://wedocs.unep.org/handle/20.500.11822/8572.

Vegan Inclusive Education, 2020. *Improving vegan support in UK Schools!* [online]. Available from: https://vieducation.co.uk/ [Accessed 31 May 2022].

Vegan Outreach, 2022. *About us.* [online]. Available from: https://veganoutreach.org/about/ [Accessed 31 May 2022].

Veganuary, 2022. *Veganuary takes world by storm with participants in nearly every country* [online]. Available from: https://veganuary.com/veganuary-2022-takes-world-by-storm/ [Accessed 31 May 2022].

White, R. J., 2018. Looking backward/moving forward. Articulating a "Yes, BUT...!" response to lifestyle veganism, and outlining post-capitalist futures in critical veganic agriculture, *EuropeNow* [online], (20). Available from: http://shura.shu.ac.uk/22661/4/White%20Looking%20backward%20.

Wilks, M., Caviola, L., Cahane, G., and Bloom, P., 2021. Children prioritize humans over animals less than adults do [online]. *Psychological Science* [online], 32 (1). Available from: https://doi.org/10.1177/0956797620960398 [Accessed 31 May 2022].

World Health Organisation, 2015. *Cancer: carcinogenicity of the consumption of red meat and processed meat* [online]. Available from: https://www.who.int/news-room/questions-and-answers/item/cancer-carcinogenicity-of-the-consumption-of-red-meat-and-processed-meat [Accessed 31 May 2022].

Wrenn, C. L., 2017. Toward a vegan feminist theory of the state. *In:* D. Nibert, ed. *Animal Oppression and Capitalism.* Santa Barbara, CA: Praeger Press, 201–230.

Wrenn, C. L., and Lizardi, A., 2021. Older, greener, and wiser: charting the experiences of older women in the American vegan movement. *Journal of Women & Ageing* [online], 33 (6). Available from: https://doi.org/10.1080/08952841.2020.1749501.

Xu, X., Sharma, P., and Shu, S., 2021. Global greenhouse gas emissions from animal-based foods are twice those of plant-based foods. *Nature Food* [online], 2. Available from: https://doi.org/10.1038/s43016-021-00358-x.

17

FOOD PATHWAYS TO COMMUNITY SUCCESS

Rounaq Nayak

Introduction

Hunger is defined as "an uncomfortable or painful physical sensation caused by insufficient consumption of dietary energy" (Food and Agriculture Organization 2022, para. 3). It is a term often used to define periods when populations are unable to eat due to lack of money, access to food, fuel and/or other resources. The United Nations' list of Sustainable Development Goals (SDGs) defines 'Zero Hunger' as one of its goals with the aim of ending hunger, achieving food security, improved nutrition and promotion of sustainable agriculture (The General Assembly 2015). Although hunger and food insecurity are closely related in terms of impact on public health and wellbeing, they are distinct concepts. While the former refers to a personal physical sensation of discomfort, the latter refers to a lack of *regular* (physical and economic) access to safe and nutritious food required for normal growth and development (Food and Agriculture Organization 1996).

The Food Foundation survey (2022) estimated approximately 4.7 million households in the UK were food insecure. Even though severe food insecurity is at the extreme end of the hunger spectrum, a person experiencing moderate food insecurity may have to prioritise meals and/or sacrifice other basic needs to overcome hunger for a short period of time (Figure 17.1).

Some individuals may only have access to cheap and/or readily available foods that are more energy dense (processed foods high in saturated fats, sugars and salt) rather than nutrient dense. Consumption of such food groups may provide some daily caloric needs but consumption of essential nutrients is significantly reduced (Food and Agriculture Organisation 2022; Lindberg et al. 2015). In 2008, the Food and Agriculture Organization identified four dimensions of food security: (1) physical availability of food; (2) economic and physical access to food; (3) food utilization and (4) food stability (Food and Agriculture Organization 2008) (Table 17.1).

DOI: 10.4324/9781003294962-21

FIGURE 17.1   Significant levels of food insecurity

TABLE 17.1   Four dimensions of food security

Dimension	Description
Food availability	Addresses the *supply chain* aspect of food security. Focus: Degree of production, stock levels (surplus) and net trade.
Food access	Concerned with economic and physical access to food (post creation of adequate food supply at the national and regional levels). Focus: Influence policy emphasis on the following to achieve food security: • Incomes • Expenditure • Markets • Prices
Food utilisation	Utilisation: The way the body makes the most of various nutrients in the food. Nutritional availability provides sufficient energy and is the consequence of good care and feeding practices, food preparation, diet diversity and intra-household distribution of food. Focus: Nutritional status of individuals
Food stability	People are food insecure if they have inadequate access to food on a periodic basis leading to a risk of deterioration of their nutritional status. Focus: Consistency of availability, access and utilisation of food.

Source: Adapted from FAO (2008, p.1)

In 2014, the Committee on World Food Security concerning the impact of over-reliance on globalised supply chains initiated discussion concerning nutrition and food accessibility for people in the lower socioeconomic strata. Further, food access and stability haven't received enough attention despite their link to food security and public health, which is an important topic in geographies with high household essential expenditures. Food and fuel prices have soared due to global inflation caused by the Covid-19 pandemic (Haldane 2021) and the Ukraine war (Molina et al. 2022), therefore fuel poverty, economic and physical access to food are essential for further exploration of rising utility costs.

A household in fuel poverty is one that cannot afford adequate heating at home for 10% of its income, as described by Bradshaw and Hutton in 1983. Although there are multiple definitions for fuel poverty, collectively most definitions are similar: (1) fuel and energy consumption; (2) threshold income; (3) household; (4) spending and expenditure and (5) warmth. Since fuel poverty has a wider impact on public health and wellbeing, it has been classified as a "highly complex social problem" (Baker et al. 2018, p.610).

Past research highlighted the negative impact fuel poverty has on public health outcomes. The London School of Hygiene and Tropical Medicine (2014) and the National Institute for Health and Care Excellence (2015a) investigated the impact of inadequately heated homes in the UK. Cardiovascular, cerebrovascular and respiratory disorders in vulnerable populations were identified, in tandem with mental health issues due to the inability to keep warm. Previously, Bhattacharya et al. (2003) suggested cold weather adversely impacts family budgets and nutritional outcomes for low-socioeconomic families – the amount of *extra* money spent on fuel decreases food spending, leading to a decrease in caloric intake during the winter/colder months. Further concerns have been raised about the impact of fuel poverty on child development by O'Meara (2016) where they put forward infant children require higher calorific consumption during growth spurts and the need to keep warm and grow normally during winter compared to children living in cooler homes. It is argued this trade-off between basic human rights has a lasting impact on quality of life.

Although fuel poverty has been a highly discussed topic, studies have seldom explored the impact of fuel poverty on food security, specifically food utilisation and stability in the UK. To address this gap, this chapter explores the impact of UK state-sponsored and private entity-sponsored food assistance programs through a 'fuel poverty' lens and for the purpose of this chapter, the term 'food assistance program' refers to any set up which aims to reduce food poverty, whether private or state-sponsored.

Methodology

Desktop research was used to identify relevant literature on food assistance programmes and to develop an understanding of current policy and social needs in the UK. The following 13 integrated digital databases covering heterogeneous disciplines were used to collect articles, Doctoral theses, book chapters, white papers, grey literature and business reports: Web of Science, Food Science Source, British Library Catalogue, Emerald, Ethos, Google Scholar, Research Gate, CAB Abstracts, EBSCO, Academic Complete, Access to Research, Wiley Online and Science Direct. Furthermore, search engines and portals were used to find additional information on the use of food assistance programmes: www.google.com, www.bing.com, www.linkedin.com, www.fareshare.org.uk, www.foodaidnetwork.org.uk, www.feedingbritain.org and www.trusseltrust.org.

Specific search term combinations with Boolean search operators were entered into online databases to capture primarily available published, catalogued and relevant documents through a comprehensive and an un-biased search process. All keywords and synonyms searched were based on existing literature in the domains of *food assistance and community feeding programmes* in the UK. Search terms were established as defined in the protocol (James et al. 2016).

State-sponsored food assistance programs in the UK

During the Great Depression (1929–1939), people lined up to receive soup, bread and other handouts. Many governments in more economically developed countries, started state-sponsored food assistance programs to deal with the queues and food insecurity issues. Inspired by the United States *Food Stamp Program* (established in 1939), the UK's *Welfare Food Scheme* (WFS) was introduced in 1941 (Martin et al. 2003; Ministry of Food and Ministry of Health 1959). Both schemes supplemented wartime rations for vulnerable populations. The UK scheme evolved from utilising wartime rationing systems to post office tokens that provided a social safety net for low-income individuals (Martin et al. 2003) (Figure 17.2).

The 1934 *Milk in Schools Scheme* provided school children with milk and during the 1940s, the WFS supplemented this scheme. Developed as a rationing tool, dried milk was provided to mothers and children during the post-war period, and by 1954, was labelled a 'benefit in kind' under the *Family Allowance Scheme*. These schemes were the responsibility of the Board of Education, then the Ministry of Health, the Ministry of Agriculture, Fisheries, and Food, Ministry of Health, and eventually, the Ministry of Agriculture, Fisheries and Food managed procurement (Ministry of Food and Ministry of Health 1959). While revisions to eligibility criteria limited eligibility to lower-income families, cod liver oil, concentrated orange juice, and vitamin tablets were added to the list in 1975 (Machell 2014). In 2006, the WFS was replaced by the '*Healthy Start*' scheme, yet people from higher low socioeconomic families perceived it as a flawed system believing it was a lifestyle option by lower-income families (Asthana et al. 2010).

Launched in 2006, the *Healthy Start Scheme* aimed to offer state-funded nutritional welfare for UK families on low incomes (National Institute for Health and

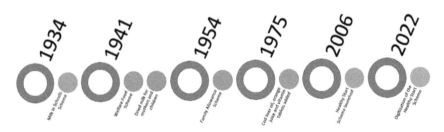

FIGURE 17.2 Evolution of the state-sponsored food assistance program in the UK

Care Excellence 2015b). Historically, beneficiaries were provided with vouchers for fruit, vegetables, pulses, milk and/or infant formula, including vitamin supplements coupons for women and children (Machell 2014). The vouchers have now been replaced by prepaid cards, automatically topped up every four weeks. Currently, prepaid cards are used by over 100,000 people.

Beneficiaries include women who are 20 weeks pregnant or individuals (parents and carers) that have children under the age of four and on low incomes. They have access to nutritional supplements pre and post pregnancy, yet access to nutritional food items because the list of products available to purchase via the scheme (fresh fruits and some fresh vegetables) is limited. For other food products, regular access to fuel (gas and/or electricity) would be required either for storage or to cook a meal, thus there is a need to focus on (1) ensuring strategies to reduce fuel poverty, and (2) balancing the food provided.

Beneficiaries are sent a 'Healthy Start card' with money on it which can be used in some shops in the UK (National Institute for Health and Care Excellence 2015b). The card can be used to purchase: (1) cow's milk; (2) fresh, frozen and tinned fruits and vegetables; (3) fresh, dried and tinned pulses and (4) infant formula milk based on cow's milk (National Health Service 2022) (Table 17.2).

Today, a growing concern in the UK is the low uptake of the Healthy Start Scheme, partly due to the complex application process. According to Landon (2021), local uptake of the scheme decreased from 67% of eligible families in January 2017 to 56% in January 2020. Key contributory factors involved poor communication and inadequate promotion of the scheme. A report by Defeyter et al. (2022) highlighted the issues of prepaid cards where shop assistants were unfamiliar with cards and subsequently being declined, causing humiliation, anxiety and embarrassment for the user, compounded with difficulties contacting government helplines. It is important to note that uptake data is estimated due to inadequate mechanisms for capturing data once families access the scheme. Hence, it is critical to develop a system to better understand the systemic factors contributing to the poor uptake of the Healthy Start Scheme (Lucas et al. 2013). One way of identifying these factors is by carrying out a 'Hierarchical Task

TABLE 17.2 Overview of healthy start vouchers – voucher values

Product	Term	Value/Week
Milk, fruits, vegetables, pulses	From tenth week of pregnancy	£4.25
	From birth to the age of 1	£8.50
	Between ages 1 and 4	£4.25
Vitamins	Between Week 10 of pregnancy and breastfeeding periods	56 tables for eight weeks (one tablet/day)
	Between the ages of 0 and 4	280 drops for eight weeks (five drops/day)

Source: Adapted from NHS (2022) (Last updated 23rd February 2022.)

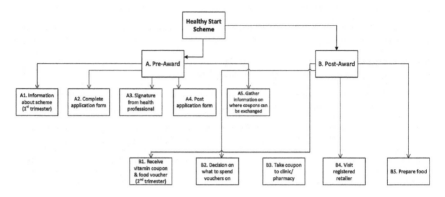

FIGURE 17.3 Skeleton Hierarchical Task Analysis to evaluate the challenges of accessing the Healthy Start Scheme

Analysis' (HTA), which describes hierarchical goals, sub-goals, operations and plans for activities or workflow analysis (Stanton et al. 2013). Often used in the healthcare sector, adopting this methodology may help identify systemic 'barrier' factors for the Healthy Start scheme (Figure 17.3).

Private entity-sponsored food assistance programs in the UK

The UK has a much higher rate of food poverty than other countries. Food prices have increased 4.2% since 2020 due to inflation which has pushed a larger portion of UK households into food and fuel poverty since 2020. Approximately 4.7 million adults and 2.5 million children have experienced household food insecurity (Goudie and McIntyre 2021). In the UK, approximately 2.5 million people relied on private entity-sponsored food assistance programs in 2020/2021 (The Trussell Trust 2022). These numbers only represent beneficiaries of approximately 1,400 food banks from approximately 2,572. Nearly two decades before this report, similar factors motivated the launch of the first private entity-sponsored food assistance program in the UK. Founded in Salisbury in 2000, The Trussell Trust was born out of the poverty, deprivation and unequal distribution of wealth that led to a hunger crisis (Williams and May 2022). The Covid-19 pandemic and recession only exacerbate the situation. Food assistance programs like food banks, soup vans and subsidised community markets have been established to bridge the food security gap (Bazerghi et al. 2016). The purpose, operation method and limitations of three commonly occurring private entity-sponsored food assistance programs in the UK will be discussed in the following sections (Figure 17.4).

In addition to The Trussell Trust food banks, the UK also has independent food banks, approximately 1,172 of which are registered with the Independent Food Aid Network (IFAN), established in 2017. A survey by the Independent Food Aid Network (2022) stated that 93% of independent food banks reported an increase in the need for their services in 2022, with more than 80% reporting that they have

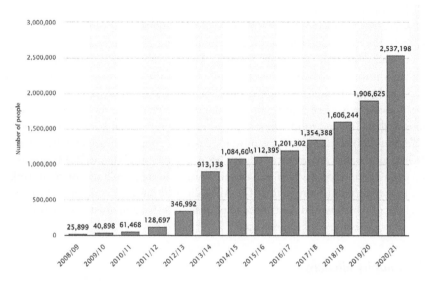

FIGURE 17.4   Number of people receiving emergency food from Trussell Trust food-banks in the UK

struggled with food supply issues since February 2022, while 78% reported a reduction in food and/or financial donations due to a cost-of-living crisis in the UK.

Food banks

Often confused with pantries and larders, food banks collect, store, and distribute donated and/or purchased food to food insecure families (Sunuwar et al. 2020). Food assistance programs in high-income countries tend to not meet the needs of their citizens (Lambie-Mumford 2013; Loopstra and Tarasuk 2012). People/families who are economically, geographically or socially disadvantaged can use food banks as temporary measures to bridge the food security gap, however, food banks cannot provide permanent food security (Handforth et al. 2013; Middleton et al. 2018; Renzaho and Mellor 2010).

Food banks cater to people in two ways: (1) by providing cooked/uncooked food directly to beneficiaries (e.g., IFAN food banks), and (2) by redistributing food to charities that provide groceries and other essential household items (e.g., Trussell Trust food banks). Additionally, large warehouses and some food banks are run by churches or community service centres. It is important to note that not all projects are guided by religious principles because every food bank operates on a similar model as they rely on donations and oversupply from industry. However, the option to purchase food is not available to all food banks due to limited resources (Riches 2002; Tarasuk et al. 2014).

Volunteers at food banks prepare pre-packaged parcels or run pseudo-supermarkets where beneficiaries can select food items. Since food poverty is closely linked with transient and persistent financial poverty (Mahadevan and Hoang 2016; Omotayo et al. 2018), many food banks provide more than just food parcels; they provide other services including debt management, skill development and education on budget cooking. Despite the differences in operational logistics among food banks, their purpose remains the same: to provide nutritious food and other household essentials to those in need (Middleton et al. 2018), yet fresh produce is often lacking in food donations. Processed foods' lower prices, longer shelf-life and food safety are reasons why most food banks prefer not to offer fresh foods. Consequently, most food parcels contain tinned and dried food. While food banks are meant to act as a 'stop-gap measure' (Iafrati 2018), anecdotal evidence and reports by The Trussell Trust indicate people rely on food banks for longer periods (Perry et al. 2014). An additional cause for concern is the rising fuel prices which would contribute to poor food utilisation due to restrictions on the use of existing cooking methods.

Community kitchens

Communities own and operate these kitchens with the hope of becoming self-sufficient after a period of community support (Iacovou et al. 2013; Loopstra and Tarasuk 2013) and reducing food poverty and social isolation (Mundel and Chapman 2010). As opposed to creating a dependency on emergency food parcels, community kitchens focus on building beneficiary resilience through skills training and community development endeavours (Loopstra and Tarasuk 2013). Budgeting, menu planning, food safety, cooking and nutrition training are often provided to stakeholders where meal preparation is a regular function of community kitchens. As a result, food is shared among participants and other food insecure members of the community. In addition to improving social interaction, community kitchens reduce social isolation (Iacovou et al. 2013), provide skills involving active participation and reduces the need to access charitable food sources (food banks). Community kitchens improve beneficiaries' dignity and self-worth. Examples of Community kitchens in the UK are displayed below.

A community kitchen's operational model incorporates skills training that improves food choice and helps to alleviate some of the food insecurity issues related to food poverty (Engler-Stringer and Berenbaum 2006). Following the training, beneficiaries increased their fruit and vegetable purchases. However, nutrition awareness alone will not improve food stability. By adopting a systems thinking approach, the program can return to being an emergency stop-gap measure (Lang 2022; Monroe 2022) (Table 17.3).

Social supermarkets (SS)

Founded in the late 1990s, SS's receive used consumable products (often donated by manufacturers and retailers) and resell them at heavily subsidised prices (due to wrong labels, slight physical damage). The goods are sold to poor or at-risk

TABLE 17.3 Example of community kitchens in the UK, the beneficiaries, services provided, advantages and methods of ensuring economic sustainability

Community Kitchen	Location	Beneficiaries	Services Provided	Advantages	Cost Management
Grassmarket Community Project	Edinburgh	People dealing with complex issues such as: 1. Homelessness 2. Mental health problems 3. Physical health problems 4. Learning difficulties 5. Poverty 6. Substance misuse 7. Physical abuse	*Social Enterprise* 1. Café jobs 2. Events management 3. Catering service 4. Furniture-making 5. Tartan textiles making *Education/Training* 1. Literacy workshops 2. Gardening 3. IT skills 4. Sewing *Activities* 1. Hill-walking 2. Mindfulness 3. Drama 4. Art 5. Choir 6. Book group 7. Creative writing 8. Meditation 9. Film-chat *Community service (free)* 1. Open-door meals 2. Vet clinics 3. Hairdressing 4. Benefit support	1. Employment opportunities 2. Skills & confidence development 3. Relationships within communities 4. Improved health and wellbeing	Customers and supporters can buy £5 meal vouchers via the café counter or online shop. The voucher is provided to someone in need.

(Continued)

TABLE 17.3 (Continued)

Community Kitchen	Location	Beneficiaries	Services Provided	Advantages	Cost Management
Cracking Good Food	Manchester	People dealing with complex issues such as: 1. Homelessness 2. Poverty	*Education/Training* 1. Pantry Pod (cooking skills using ingredients from food assistance programs) 2. Education on food waste reduction, nutrition and sustainability 3. CookBank: Reducing food insecurity in local communities (budgeting and accessing nutritious food) 4. Food hygiene and allergen awareness Level 2 training *Activities* 1. Online cooking classes	1. Skills & confidence development 2. Improved health and wellbeing	Gift vouchers Donations Business membership (CSR opportunities for businesses)
Community Chef – Lewes Community Kitchen	Lewes, Sussex	1. Carers 2. Families 3. Communities	*Education/Training* 1. Cookery and bakery classes 2. Cooker leader training 3. Food hygiene training *Activities* 1. Workshops *Social Enterprise* 1. Running community events (hosting supper and lunch clubs; food and film nights)	1. Skills & confidence development 2. Caters to all individuals irrespective of their socioeconomic status 3. Aims to create a community spirit by passing on information on: (1) sharing and eating food with other people; and (2) responsible sourcing and consumption	Provides food safety and hygiene training to commercial organisations and private individuals, and other services such as 'for hire smoothie bikes'.

| **Food Cycle** | Nationwide | People ('guests') from all walks of life, including those dealing with complex issues such as:
1. Homelessness
2. Poverty | *Education/Training*
1. Education about nutrition
2. Cooking with surplus ingredients | 1. Connect communities through food – volunteers and guests eat the meal together leading to conversation flows, break down of barriers and forming of new friendships
2. Support mental health, wellbeing and reduce loneliness
3. Nourish the hungry
4. Promote sustainability
5. Inspire change through a *community dining model* and *storytelling* to engage the wider audience
6. Guests become volunteers to give back to society | Volunteers collect surplus food and cook it into meals which are served to guests from the local community. |

(Continued)

TABLE 17.3 (Continued)

Community Kitchen	Location	Beneficiaries	Services Provided	Advantages	Cost Management
Loaf	Birmingham	1. Homeless 2. Charities	*Education/Training* 1. Cookery/Bakery classes	1. Connect communities through food 2. Nourish the hungry 3. Provide bread to multiple local charities	1. Subscribers pay a monthly sum which is invested in equipment and ingredients, in return for regular delivery of bread. Unsold bread at the end of the day is given to the homeless and/or charities. 2. Profits raised through community/pop-up events is directed towards furthering social objectives. 3. Cookery school courses, sales of heritage grains and other sweetmeats.

Source: Adapted from *The Guardian* (2014)

consumers (Holweg et al. 2010). SS is a social innovation that promotes social solidarity where food supply chains and social needs are interconnected through SS (Klindzic et al. 2016). Donors, volunteers, philanthropists and corporations contribute time, resources and/or services to these non-profit supermarkets and thus allows people in lower socioeconomic positions (SEP) to choose and purchase goods at affordable prices. This allows them to preserve their dignity as well as meet their material needs (Maric and Knezevic 2014). Furthermore, SS can only offer a limited selection since they rely on donations, but are normally consumables that would otherwise be thrown away. Holweg et al. (2010) state that access is limited to those at risk of poverty yet there has been little academic research on SS since the 1990s despite their growth.

'Community Shop' is the UK's largest surplus distributor, and by educating people on poverty, hunger and food waste, the Community Shop aims to not only help people in SEP circumstances, but also change mindsets. Their SS is distributed nationwide through retailers, manufacturers, food service providers and logistics companies. Also, surplus products from well-known brands are donated at reduced prices through the network of donors. Two entities make up their operating model: (1) Company Shops (which are available at market value to members), and (2) Community Shops (SS). Directly donated food and other products can be sold at reduced prices at the SS. Members purchase food at market value at Company Shops, and the proceeds go to Community Shops when food cannot be sent directly to SS. As a result, Community Shops make additional purchases to update their stock. In addition to donated goods, Community Shops can make their own purchases. When the quantity of products donated exceeds the storage capacity of Community Shops, or when large batches are discarded due to factors like incorrect labelling, products are sent to Company Shops. The 'Community Shop Model' provides diverse products to a wider group of people in need, reduces waste and returns surplus to retailers and manufacturers.

By giving beneficiaries freedom of choice in the SS model, they could potentially purchase more food without consuming fuel. The assumption is that non-processed food products will be readily available and beneficiaries will have a good understanding of nutrition. Moreover, SS are sparsely distributed across the UK, which is a limitation. Consequently, some potential beneficiaries will become dependent upon food banks due to this barrier.

Conclusion

Most community food assistance programs provide assistance to people suffering from poverty, but their definitions are often based on household income and ability to afford food and other essentials. The frequent issuance of food requiring fuel often takes a back seat to fuel poverty. Furthermore, the requirement for longer shelf-life may facilitate the donation and distribution of food that requires fuel. Hence, limitations at the beneficiaries' end need to be explored further.

A recommendation to improve what is seemingly a complex system is to not only identify and work with those currently experiencing fuel poverty, but also those households who have become vulnerable to fuel poverty due to external factors. Therefore, food and related social policies ought to be designed with all stakeholders, including beneficiaries and it is crucial that the interconnections between social and food issues at macro (community/government), micro (individual) and meso (group) levels are acknowledged to achieve optimal food sustainability outcomes. As opposed to utilising a system where only citizens higher up the socioeconomic strata are food and financially secure, more needs to be done to ensure food and economic justice for everyone. Similarly, the need to adopt a model and implementation plan towards a mature global food system, i.e., one in which every citizen can have access to healthy food while not having to compromise on their access to fuel, is crucial.

References

Asthana, A., Helm, T., and Harris, P., 2010. How Britain's new welfare state was born in the USA, *The Guardian* [online]. Available from: https://www.theguardian.com/politics/2010/nov/07/britain-welfare-state-born-usa [Accessed 6 February 2022].

Baker, K. J., Mould, R., and Restrick, S., 2018. Rethink fuel poverty as a complex problem. *Nature Energy* [online], 3 (8). Available from: https://doi.org/10.1038/s41560-018-0204-2 [Accessed 5 October 2022].

Bazerghi, C., McKay, F. H., and Dunn, M., 2016. The role of food banks in addressing food insecurity: a systematic review. *Journal of Community Health* [online], 41 (4), pp. 732–740. Available from: https://doi.org/10.1007/s10900-015-0147-5 [Accessed 1 July 2022].

Bhattacharya, J., et al., 2003. Heat or eat? cold weather shock and nutrition in poor American families. *American Journal of Public Health* [online], 93 (7). Available from: https://doi.org/10.2105/ajph.93.7.1149 [Accessed 3 March 2022].

Bradshaw, J., and Hutton, S., 1983. Social policy options and fuel poverty. *Journal of Economic Psychology* [online], 3. Available from: https://doi.org/10.1016/0167-4870(83)90005-3 [Accessed 5 January 2022].

Defeyter, G., et al., 2022. *Families' early experiences of prepaid cards under Healthy Start: yet another barrier to entitlement?* Available from: https://feedingbritain.org/wp-content/uploads/2022/02/Families-early-experiences-of-prepaid-cards-under-Healthy-Start-February-2022.pdf [Accessed 3 September 2022].

Food and Agriculture Organization, 1996. *The State of Food and Agriculture, 1996* [online]. Available from: https://www.fao.org/documents/card/en/c/640b875a-92f0-56df-b4e4-c99fbfe2483d.

Food and Agriculture Organization, 2008. *An introduction to the basic concepts of food security* [online]. Available from: https://www.fao.org/3/al936e/al936e00.pdf [Accessed 5 October 2022].

Food and Agriculture Organization, 2022. *Hunger and food insecurity* [online]. Available from: https://www.fao.org/hunger/en/ [Accessed 7 February 2022].

Food and Agriculture Organization et al., 2020. *The state of food security and nutrition in the world 2020: transforming food systems for affordable healthy diets* [online]. Available from: https://www.fao.org/3/ca9692en/online/ca9692en.html [Accessed 28 February 2022].

Food pathways to community success **243**

Goudie, S., and McIntyre, Z., 2021. *A crisis within a crisis: the impact of Covid-19 on household food insecurity* [online]. Available from: https://foodfoundation.org.uk/sites/default/files/2021-10/FF_Impact-of-Covid_FINAL.pdf [Accessed 4 Oct 2022]

Haldane, A., 2021. *Inflation: a tiger by the tail* [online]. Available from: https://www.bankofengland.co.uk/-/media/boe/files/speech/2021/february/inflation-a-tiger-by-the-tail-speech-by-andy-haldane.pdf [Accessed: 5 October 2022].

Handforth, B., Hennik, M., and Schwartz, M., 2013. A qualitative study of nutrition-based initiatives at selected food banks in the feeding America network. *Journal of the Academy of Nutrition and Dietetics* [online], 113 (3). Available from: https://doi.org/10.1016/j.jand.2012.11.001 [Accessed 17 May 2022].

Holweg, C., Lienbacher, E., and Schnedlitz, P., 2010. Social supermarkets: typology within the spectrum of social enterprises [online]. Available from: https://www.anzmac2010.org/proceedings/pdf/ANZMAC10Final00244.pdf [Accessed 7 July 2022].

Holweg, C., Lienbacher, E., and Zinn, W., 2010. Social supermarkets: a new challenge in supply chain management and sustainability. *Supply Chain Forum: An International Journal* [online], 11 (4). Available from: https://doi.org/10.1080/16258312.2010.11517246 [Accessed 18 March 2022].

Iacovou, M., et al., 2013. Social health and nutrition impacts of community kitchens: a systematic review. *Public Health Nutrition* [online], 16 (3). Available from: https://doi.org/10.1017/S1368980012002753 [Accessed 19 May 2022].

Iafrati, S., 2018. We're not a bottomless pit: food banks' capacity to sustainably meet increasing demand. *Voluntary Sector Review* [online], 9 (1). Available from: https://doi.org/10.1332/204080518X15149744201978 [Accessed 19 June 2022].

Independent Food Aid Network, 2022. *Survey of members of the Independent Food Aid Network (IFAN)* [online]. Available from: https://uploads.strikinglycdn.com/files/67e54044-3371-4112-a8af-8b0860e6a309/IFAN%20independent%20food%20bank%20survey_PRESSRELEASE_18.5.22._1.30pm.pdf?id=3904129 [Accessed 2 October 2022].

James, K. L., Randall, N. P., and Haddaway, N. R., 2016. A methodology for systematic mapping in environmental sciences. *Environmental Evidence* [online], 5 (70). Available from: https://doi.org/10.1186/s13750-016-0059-6 [Accessed 8 September 2022].

Klindzic, M., Knezevic, B., and Maric, I., 2016. Stakeholder analysis of social supermarkets. *Poslovna izvrsnost* [online], 10 (1). Available from: https://hrcak.srce.hr/file/236647 [Accessed 5 October 2022].

Lambie-Mumford, H., 2013. Every town should have one: emergency food banking in the UK. *Journal of Social Policy* [online], 42(1). Available from: http://doi.org/10.1017/S004727941200075X [Accessed 9 February 2022].

Landon, G., 2021. Improving uptake of healthy start vouchers during the COVID-19 pandemic. *Archives of Disease in Childhood* [online], 106. Available from: https://www.tnlcommunityfund.org.uk/funding/publications/a-better-start/increasing-the-uptake-of-healthy-start-food-vouchers [Accessed 14 February 2022].

Lang, T., 2022. Food poverty of plain inequality? [Online] Available from: https://foodresearch.org.uk/blogs/tim-langs-field-notes-food-poverty-or-plain-inequality/ [Accessed 12 March 2022].

Lindberg, R., et al., 2015. Food insecurity in Australia: implications for general practitioners. *Australian Family Physician* [online], 44(11), Available from: https://pubmed.ncbi.nlm.nih.gov/26590630/ [Accessed 16 July 2022].

London School of Hygiene and Tropical Medicine, 2014. *Evidence review and economic analysis of excess winter deaths: factors determining vulnerability to winter and cold-related mortality/morbidity for the national institute for health and care excellence* [online]. Available from: https://www.nice.org.uk/guidance/ng6/evidence/evidence-review-1-factors-determining-vulnerability-to-winter-and-coldrelated-mortalitymorbidity-pdf-544621933 [Accessed 15 February 2022].

Loopstra, R., and Tarasuk, V., 2012. The relationship between food banks and household food insecurity among low-income Toronto families. *Canadian Public Policy* [online], 38 (4). Available from: https://www.jstor.org/stable/41756766 [Accessed 19 January 2022].

Loopstra, R., and Tarasuk, V., 2013. Perspectives on community gardens, community kitchens and the Good Food Box program in a community-based sample of low-income families. *Canadian Journal of Public Health* [online], 104 (1). Available from: https://doi.org/10.1007/BF03405655 [Accessed 1 January 2022].

Lucas, P., et al., 2013. *Healthy Start vouchers study: the views and experiences of parents, professionals and small retailers in England.* Available from: http://www.bris.ac.uk/sps/research/projects/completed/2013/rk7149/index.html [Accessed 11 January 2022].

Lucia L. Kaiser, Hugo Melgar-Quiñonez, Marilyn S. Townsend, Yvonne Nicholson, Mary Lavender Fujii, Anna C. Martin, Cathi L. Lamp. 2003. Food insecurity and food supplies in Latino households with young children. *Journal of Nutrition Education and Behavior*, 35 (3), 148–153, ISSN 1499-4046. Available from: https://doi.org/10.1016/S1499-4046(06)60199-1. (https://www.sciencedirect.com/science/article/pii/S1499404606601991).

Machell, G. M., 2014. *Food welfare for low-income women and children in the UK: a policy of analysis of the Healthy Start scheme* [online]. Available from: https://openaccess.city.ac.uk/id/eprint/15159/ [Accessed 7 February 2022].

Mahadevan, R., and Hoang, V., 2016. Is there a link between poverty and food security? *Social Indicators Research* [online], 128. Available from: https://doi.org/10.1007/s11205-015-1025-3 [Accessed 1 April 2022].

Maric, I., and Knezevic, B., 2014. Social supermarkets as a new retail format driven by social needs and philanthropy: case of Croatia. *In*: D. Kantarelis, ed. *24th International Conference Business and Economics Society International*, 6–9 July 2014. Florence: Business and Economics Society International, 278–286.

Middleton, G., et al., 2018. The experiences and perceptions of food banks amongst users in high-income countries: an international scoping review, *Appetite* [online], 120. Available from: https://doi.org/10.1016/j.appet.2017.10.029 [Accessed 25 March 2022].

Ministry of Food and Ministry of Health, 1959. *Ministry of food and successors: welfare food scheme, registered files (WF and WFP Series), The National's Archive's Catalogue.* Available from: https://discovery.nationalarchives.gov.uk/details/r/C10953#:~:text=The Welfare Food Scheme was, and also certain elderly people.&text=During the post-war period, whilst rationing was in force [Accessed 16 February 2022].

Molina, G., Montoya-Aguirre, M., and Ortiz-Juarez, E., 2022. *Addressing the cost-of-living crisis in developing countries: poverty and vulnerability projections and policy responses.* [online]. Available from: https://www.undp.org/nepal/publications/addressing-cost-living-crisis-developing-countries-poverty-and-vulnerability-projections-and-policy-responses? [Accessed 4 February 2022].

Monroe, J., 2022. We're pricing the poor out of food in the UK: that's why I'm launching my own price index. *The Guardian*, 22 January, p. 1. [Online]. Available from: https://www.theguardian.com/society/2022/jan/22/were-pricing-the-poor-out-of-food-in-the-uk-thats-why-im-launching-my-own-price-index [Accessed 12 January 2022].

Moore, R., 2012. Definitions of fuel poverty: implications for policy. *Energy Policy* [online], 49. Available from: https://doi.org/10.1016/j.enpol.2012.01.057 [Accessed 11 June 2022].

Mundel, E., and Chapman, G., 2010. A decolonizing approach to health promotion in Canada: the case of the urban Aboriginal Community kitchen garden project. *Health Promotion International* [online], 25. Available from: https://doi.org/10.1093/heapro/daq016 [Accessed 5 October 2022].

National Health Service, 2022. *Get help to buy food and milk: the Healthy Start Scheme* [online]. Available from: https://www.healthystart.nhs.uk/ [Accessed 23 February 2022].

National Institute for Health and Care Excellence, 2015a. *Excess winter deaths and illness and the health risks associated with cold homes* [online]. Available from: https://www. nice.org.uk/guidance/ng6/resources/excess-winter-deaths-and-morbidity-and-the-health-risks-associated-with-cold-homes-51043484869 [Accessed 11 July 2022].

National Institute for Health and Care Excellence, 2015b. *Nutrition: improving maternal and child nutrition* [online]. Available from: https://www.nice.org.uk/guidance/qs98/chapter/Quality-statement-3-Healthy-Start-scheme [Accessed 10 July 2022].

O'Meara, G., 2016. A review of the literature on fuel poverty with a focus on Ireland. *Social Indicators Research* [online], 128. Available from: https://doi.org/10.1353/jda.2018.0034 [Accessed 15 March 2022].

Omotayo, A., et al., 2018. Understanding the link between households' poverty and food security in South West Nigeria. *The Journal of Developing Areas* [online], 52 (3). Available from: https://doi.org/10.1353/jda.2018.0034 [Accessed 22 March 2022].

Perry, J. et al., 2014. *Emergency use only: understanding and reducing the use of food banks in the UK* [online]. Available from: https://www.trusselltrust.org/wp-content/uploads/sites/2/2016/01/foodbank-report.pdf [Accessed 18 March 2022].

Renzaho, A., and Mellor, D., 2010. Food security measurement in cultural pluralism: missing the point or conceptual misunderstanding? *Nutrition* [online], 26 (1). Available from: https://doi.org/10.1016/j.nut.2009.05.001 [Accessed: 18 March 2022].

Riches, G., 2002. Food banks and food security: welfare reform, human rights and social policy: lessons from Canada? *Social Policy & Administration* [online], 36 (6). Available from: https://www.historyofsocialwork.org/1967_food_banks/2002%20Riches%20food%20banks.pdf [Accessed 2 October 2022].

Stanton, N., et al., 2013. *Human factors methods: a practical guide to engineering design*. 2nd ed. Farnham, England: Ashgate Publishing Limited.

Sunuwar, D. R., Singh, D. R., and Pradhan, P. M. S., 2020. Prevalence and factors associated with double and triple burden of malnutrition among mothers and children in Nepal: evidence from 2016 Nepal demographic and health survey. *BMC Public Health* [online], 20 (1). Available from: https://doi.org/10.1186/s12889-020-8356-y [Accessed 4 January 2022].

Tarasuk, V., et al., 2014. A survey of food bank operations in five Canadian cities. *BMC Public Health* [online], 14. Available from: https://doi.org/10.1186/1471-2458-14-1234 [Accessed 17 March 2022].

The Food Foundation, 2022. Food insecurity tracking [online]. Available from: https://foodfoundation.org.uk/initiatives/food-insecurity-tracking [Accessed 19 March 2022].

The Guardian 2014. *Find your local community kitchen* [online]. Available from: https://www.theguardian.com/lifeandstyle/2014/mar/22/find-local-community-kitchen-do-something.

The General Assembly, 2015. *Transforming our world: the 2030 agenda for sustainable development, United Nations General Assembly* [online]. Available from: https://sustainabledevelopment.un.org/post2015/transformingourworld/publication [Accessed 17 July 2022].

The Trussell Trust, 2022. *Trussell Trust data briefing on end-of-year statistics relating to use of food banks: April 2020 – March 2021* [online]. Available from: https://www.trusselltrust.org/wp-content/uploads/sites/2/2021/04/Trusell-Trust-End-of-Year-stats-data-briefing_2020_21.pdf [Accessed 20 September 2022].

Williams, A., and May, J., 2022. A genealogy of the food bank: historicising the rise of food charity in the UK. *Transactions of the Institute of British Geographers* [online], 47 (3). Available from: https://doi.org/10.1111/tran.12535 [Accessed 29 September 2022].

18

A RENEWED PEDAGOGY FOR HEALTH CO-BENEFIT

Combining nutrition and sustainability education in school food learnings and practices

Neha K. Lalchandani, Danielle Proud and Suzanne Suggs

Concept introduction – nutrition, environment, and the combination in school education

The school food environment has influential roles on children's consumption patterns and dietary outcomes (Pineda et al. 2021). Depending on the school type and geographical context, children can consume at least one-third of their daily energy intake during school hours (Bollella et al. 1999; Manson et al. 2021; Nelson 2006). This can reach 40% in schools with breakfast programs and/or after-school care. Consistent exposure to the school environment, where school lunches are consumed at least five days a week, means that children not only gain education, but also develop food preferences and habits. Good nutrition helps form dietary behaviours during children's school years supporting their growth and development, academic performance, health and wellbeing.

Schools also have a key role to play in environmental education. The impact of awareness of climate change on child and youth mental health is gaining prominence (Hickman et al. 2021; Sciberras and Fernando 2022). Environmental education in the early years will support children's mental, social, and emotional development (Ardoin and Bowers 2020). This will also translate to pro-environmental behaviours that will carry forward into adolescence and beyond (Rosa et al. 2018) not only benefitting long-term health but also the environment. Therefore, planetary education and sustainability practices are necessary learning attributes in school settings.

Kosáros et al. (2009) suggested approaching sustainability and health education concurrently, noting that the former cannot be regarded without the other. The dichotomisation of nutrition and environment is witnessed in schools globally through food waste audits (Antón-Peset et al. 2021; Shanks et al. 2017), decreased consumption of packaged foods (Folta et al. 2018; Goldberg et al.

DOI: 10.4324/9781003294962-22

2015), multi-component school programs involving experiential food growing and cooking activities (Black et al. 2015; Karpouzis et al. 2021), and greenhouse gas output measures of school meals and lunches from home (Wickramasinghe et al. 2016). Consideration of both aspects in synergy can create bidirectional benefits for dietary and planetary health outcomes when education is tailored for children to understand the importance and connections of both.

Context – School food environment

School meal provision models vary across countries. School lunches are provided for free in countries like Brazil, Finland, and Sweden, while in countries such as France, Hong Kong, Italy, Japan, Spain, the United Kingdom (UK), and the United States of America (USA) meals are partly subsidised by the government. Sources of catering also vary, from schools cooking all meals such as in Italy and Japan; mixed services in Brazil, Finland, France, and the UK, to an externally sourced privatised model found in Australia, Hong Kong, Spain, Sweden, and the USA. In Australia, New Zealand (NZ), Canada, and Norway, a vast majority of children bring their lunch from home although some purchase their food from school canteens, tuck shops, or vending machines. Children typically go home for lunch in most of Austria and Switzerland and breakfast programs are common in Australia, Canada, and the UK. Other food types in schools include mid-morning snacks whereby brain foods such as fruits and vegetables are encouraged (Benton and Jarvis 2007; Zeinstra et al. 2021), food provided during out-of-school hours care (Crowe et al. 2020; Thompson et al. 2006), and 'nude food' days that involves a litter free lunch initiative in Australia where school lunchboxes are encouraged to contain nutritious and package-free foods (Nude Food Movers 2019). Environmental practices are also a key component of the school day, and they can exist independently or have some associations with the school food environment.

Context – Food and sustainability education policies

Various models of school food consumption have been assessed for their nutritional characteristics and quality. For instance, school menus against nutritional guidelines (Aliyar et al. 2015) and viability of school meals for improved health and sustainability outcomes (Briefel et al. 2009; Oostindjer et al. 2017) are often investigated. Studies on the influence of school policy and environments to reduce consumption of sugar-sweetened beverages are ample (Briefel et al. 2009; Rahman et al. 2018). However, there is an ongoing scarcity of evidence of policy impacts on parameters such as obesity and metabolic factors, especially those translating to long-term health benefits (Jaime and Lock 2009). Moreover, despite health improvement potential, school nutrition policies often lack monitoring and investment in quality evaluation.

Australia, home to different jurisdictions, tends to implement varying policies and nutrient criteria which further accentuates the challenge of poor policy implementation and uptake (Rosewarne et al. 2020). This situation is worrying when students find the school food environment not conducive to healthy food choices (Ronto et al. 2021). Despite the presence of dietary guidelines and intervention strategies, global food consumption patterns do not meet recommendations and there is an overconsumption of discretionary foods in schools (Grieger et al. 2016). But just providing a healthy school food environment does not result in healthier eating habits of students, as seen in an initiative in Dutch secondary schools (Evenhuis et al. 2020). This illustrates the complexities of changing dietary behaviour and the need to recognise the influence of other factors. Financial, structural, and social barriers were reported for school food policy implementation while the need for funding, improved policy communication and management, and positive attitudes of various school stakeholders are drivers (Ronto et al. 2020). Predictably, these same structural boundaries would apply to any environmental policy aspirations.

The necessity of sustainability education within the early years curriculum was introduced over a decade ago (Duhn 2012; Price 2010) and called for interventional, experimental, and holistic approaches to early childhood education (Yıldız et al. 2021). However, in schools, environmental and sustainability education policies are often developed reactively to specific environmental issues such as climate change or environmental degradation. Due to their specificity or a siloed approach to development, they are frequently considered in isolation from other topics such as food or health. Two decades ago, evidence demonstrated the effectiveness of environmental education programs in engaging students to learn and think about environmental issues, but longitudinal studies of sustained behavioural change are required (Ballantyne et al. 2001; Gralton et al. 2004). Hence, ongoing calls to approach the educational process differently and comprehensively continue (Pihkala 2017; Walsh 1984). International policy initiatives, such as the United Nations Sustainable Development Goals which articulate the symbiotic link between health, diet, and climate into clear objectives are useful for driving this long-needed call to action and could drive renewed educational perspectives (United Nations 2016).

Context – School curriculum

Food and health education

In the Australian Curriculum (Australian Curriculum Assessment and Reporting Authority [ACARA] 2022a), food, by middle senior school, diverge into two subjects: (1) Health and Physical Education and the optional (2) Design and Technologies subject and then further specialise into (optional) Physical Education; Nutrition; Health or Design Technologies in the final two years of school (Stage 1 and 2 Certificate of Education). This is not dissimilar to other countries, such as the US, NZ, Sweden, and Scotland (ACARA 2022a; Smith et al. 2022). The focus of Health and Physical Education is to understand healthy choices and the influences of these choices, focusing on applied knowledge and skill development as it relates to food, safety, physical activity, and other personal and community wellbeing targets. Food specialisation occurs in Design and Technologies, where food production and food properties are studied, food systems linkages are made, and creative solutions are designed to solve ecological food issues. Students by nature of their schooling pathway, may cease health- or food-related education by 15 years of age. This presents a crowded agenda and there is limited time, duration, or realised learning outcomes to transform children into health, food, or environmentally literate citizens. Notably, food education is also occurring informally in classrooms, eating areas, school gardens and after-school care settings, involving different stakeholders such as peers, caterers, teachers, and volunteers. Given the multiple and varied stakeholders that influence a student's interest in food, participatory planning should be considered to develop and communicate desired food and sustainability education targets across formal and informal channels. Programmatic approaches include Farm-to-School, growing food in school gardens, and cafeterias that transform into food learning labs.

Current pre-determined learning outcomes, as described in curricula learning standards, often lead to interpretation of foods being labelled or grouped as 'healthy' or 'unhealthy' (Lobstein and Davies 2009) with an insinuation of 'good' or 'bad' – alias for nutrient-dense and nutrient-poor foods. Informal education opportunities are heavily influenced by complex external factors such as food availability, production/processing methods, food standards and guidelines, lobbying industries, marketing tactics, economic arguments, cultural and sociopolitical norms, and social inequalities. The influence of digital media advertising and pop-culture on children's interests and resultant food consumption patterns adds additional complexities (Kraak and Story 2015). Building on these facets, nutrition education can be narrowly focused on health outcomes, and thus lack genuine enjoyment or skill-building that draws on food environment realities (Welch and Leahy 2018). A change in educational purpose that addresses children's thinking and feelings towards food is much needed, so positive relationships with nutritious and sustainable foods can be developed.

Environment and sustainability education

In the Australian curriculum, optional sustainability elaborations within Health and Physical Education focus on environmental preservation that supports health and physical wellbeing, outdoor recreation, and learnings tied to nature (ACARA 2012). The addition of sustainability as a cross-curriculum priority suggests that sustainability should be included in subjects like English, Mathematics, Science, Humanities and Social Sciences, Arts, Technologies, Health and Physical Education, Languages, and Work Studies, although the degree to which this occurs remains to be seen. Suggestibly, where sustainability education remains a cross-curricular approach, and largely optional, students will not receive sufficient sustainability education. Moreover, the failure of integration of sustainability education into the curriculum as part of an interdisciplinary approach was a key finding of the systematic review conducted by Aikens and colleagues (2016). This dependence on cross-curricular approaches (Scott and Reid 1998) would often result in a diluted version of environmental education when embedded into core subjects like English, Mathematics, History, and Science and is solely reliant on the desire and capacity of school community members (Kennelly et al. 2011). Moreover, given the long-standing existence and intense focus on NAPLAN (National Assessment Program Literacy and Numeracy) in Australia, the scant focus on sustainability education is due to its exclusion as a distinct educational outcome the way numeracy and literacy was and continues to be today (Barnes et al. 2019; Kennelly et al. 2011). Suggestibly, where sustainability education remains a cross-curricular approach, and largely optional, students will not achieve lasting knowledge and skills in sustainability. This approach should be revamped, where the significance of environmental education should be magnified when integrated across various curriculum subjects.

Context – Pedagogy

Food and health pedagogies

School food and health pedagogies have been reactively influenced by the obesity epidemic (Leahy and Wright 2016). Moreover, teachers can bring their own views and beliefs to the topics they teach. These views, like anyone's in society, are generated by external influences such as media, marketing, general interest and upbringing. This may be problematic in some courses with a focus on personal or social outcomes, such as health and nutrition. A 2015 Australian study found that pre-service Health and Physical Education teachers had a strong implicit and moderate explicit anti-fat bias, as well as significantly lower expectations for obese children (Lynagh et al. 2015). However, regardless of bias or entrenched values, teachers, through the limitation of the current curriculum, may not acknowledge or be able to articulate the impact determinants outside of the school that influence children's health decisions and thus behaviours, such as social, cultural, and financial situation. These limitations produce challenges to the learner, who is unable to translate a purist approach to their everyday reality (Boyd 2015). This calls for a new directive in curriculum development, which considers the complexities of the socio-ecological systems outside of the school, moving away from mainstream dogmas of healthism and medicalised tenets, where personal responsibility to make the right decisions is expected to minimise health risks.

Sustainability pedagogies

Using the concept of sustainability to make cross-disciplinary connections is imperative to societal change, but weaving sustainability into the Australian curriculum requires willingness to embrace the urgency of this topic. Whether teachers have ecocentric or anthropocentric views towards the environment and practice pro-environmental behaviours themselves or not, is neglected in curriculum development. Educators' ecological identity when unrecognised prevents successful policy uptake, which means that even a well-designed curriculum is less effective when teachers themselves lack strong environmental beliefs (Almeida et al. 2018).

Although educators' perspectives in the context of environment and sustainability education are now being studied to develop educational resources (Morris et al. 2018), limited teacher understanding and capability have been recognised (Hill and Dyment 2016). This is a limiting factor to effective inclusion of sustainability education in the Australian school context. Minimal expectation to infuse environmental learning into teaching and lack of educational training in this domain when teachers pursue higher education has led teachers to learn environmental education concepts in an ad hoc fashion, drawing on their own experiences and interests over the years (Almeida 2015). Hence, renewed pedagogical stances are required.

The way forward

Defining and combining food and sustainability literacy

Food and sustainability literacy might hold some answers by weaving environmental education with food knowledge and skills as a core competency. The definition of food literacy from Canada, who are at the forefront of a food literacy evolution, considers food literacy as:

> the ability of an individual to understand food in a way that they develop a positive relationship with it, including food skills and practices across the lifespan in order to navigate, engage, and participate within a complex food system. It's the ability to make decisions to support the achievement of personal health and a sustainable food system considering environmental, social, economic, cultural, and political components.
>
> *(Cullen et al. 2015)*

The United Nations defines sustainability literacy as "the knowledge, skills and mindsets that allow individuals to become deeply committed to building a sustainable future and assisting in making informed and effective decisions to this end" (United Nations 2020). Both definitions uplift the learner to confidently navigate their environments, contribute to them productively, and become engaged and participatory citizens.

Recognising key stakeholders

Educational targets, school regulations, and study plans should be prepared involving every member of the educational community. Our main recommendations in this chapter's context revolve around the inclusion of teachers, children and parents, who can be supported to drive meaningful shifts in classroom education. Using a systems approach, it is important to draw on the values and attitudes of school community stakeholders and find connection with the larger system (Buchanan 2012). These stakeholders need to move away from the idea that they have an inconsequential role to play in the larger picture of planetary health and sustainability (Barnes et al. 2019).

Strengthening the knowledge base and eco-values and confidence of teachers will foster better knowledge transfer to children as confidence and enthusiasm are weaved into curriculum outputs. Regardless of framework and political influence, teachers must be engaged in leading the work. To empower children to apply a strengths-based approach to their health, and their environment, teachers themselves must be offered theoretical and skills-based training in these topics, as well as dedicated ongoing support. Where emotion is so closely intertwined with learning, as it is in food- and climate-related education, it is critical that teachers are supported to confidently apply a neutral, evidence-informed stance whilst nurturing enthusiasm and ownership. The challenges of this call to action are recognised.

Hedefalk et al. (2015) suggested that instead of teaching children factual information to connect them to nature, a better approach would be tapping into their understanding of environmental issues through critical thinking and acknowledging them as agents of change. As environmental stakeholders, children have the potential to connect with the community and create social action (Barratt Hacking et al. 2007; Percy-Smith and Burns 2013). Knowledge and skill building for children while centring them as change agents may appear controversial, but it could overcome the harsh reality of judgmental scrutiny and nutritive regulation of school children's food choices (Pluim et al. 2018; Tanner et al. 2019). We also need to be cognisant of children's autonomy and needs and their social environment within and beyond the school. The lack of freedom and space in the context of children's school lunch has been identified, whereby children would wish that their lunch meal would be separated from school learning and activities, and devoid of governance and supervision (Fossgard et al. 2019). As a result, participatory research with children in holistic approaches where healthy eating behaviours are not expected via the route of rules and meals and are instead viewed as an opportunity for enjoyment is needed.

Participatory approaches should also move beyond the school into the home. Ideas raised in the classroom could provide scaffolding to inquiry-based learning at home, creating an enhanced learning experience. Contradictory to current practice, this would acknowledge that home environments exert the greatest influence on food choices (Mahmood et al. 2021; Scaglioni et al. 2018). Knowledge obtained at school can be considered and unpacked alongside nutrition and sustainability concepts and practices at home.

Recommendations

Children being informed about what to do and what not to do in relation to food choices does not necessarily translate into improved nutrition and health outcomes. Similarly, teaching theoretical dogmas of 'reduce, reuse, recycle' and stirring fear and anxiety around climate change will not yield sustainable behaviour change. A recent review of 11 countries suggested that whilst each country had a dedicated food education pathway, there is no consensus as to the topics and makeup of food education (Smith et al. 2022). Because school education competencies involving sustainability and food literacy are weak, a conceptual shift is required to change the way food and health education in school is approached, taught, and legitimised. We resonate with Hensley's 'localizing', 'experiantilizing', and 'ecologizing' recommendations and suggest a few case examples of food and sustainability literacy and skill development.

A shifting narrative calls for an educative basis of critical enquiry and strengths-based skills development, for students to understand and apply reasoned thinking to personal decision making (ACARA 2022b). Dudley and colleagues (2015) showed that experiential learning strategies have the greatest impacts on food consumption changes and improved nutrition knowledge, especially in the instance of increased fruit and vegetable intake through garden-based learning strategies. The successes of the kitchen or community garden learning come to light when children are engaged in food and health in a fun and practical manner. Unwittingly, skills in food system and production awareness, core ingredients of food and sustainability literacy are developed. Their willingness to develop a palette for new foods that are unprocessed, along with increased confidence and social skills are all equally positive (Block et al. 2012).

Organisations promoting healthy school approaches in Canada have defined food literacy competencies on the back of a supportive National Food Guide embedding it into whole of school interventions (Alberta Health Services 2022). This framework is yet to reach the curriculum but lends itself well to doing so. Slater et al. (2018) created a list of food literacy competencies under the headings of functional (confidence and empowerment with food), relational (joy and meaning through food), and systems (equity and sustainability for food systems) for young people (see Figure 18.1); this could inform senior schooling curriculum development. Ansari and Stibbe (2009) have a similar literacy model for sustainability, with notable similarity of skill attainment between the two models. Suggestibly these frameworks could be further developed into curriculum topics using a co-creation approach with children and young people driving learning outcomes.

Example of canteen-driven intervention

We propose educational pedagogies that connect children positively to food, develop their skills and practices, and ultimately support their health and environmental sustainability. Current perceptions portray school lunch merely as a component of the school's daily schedule, a midday meal at home as a lunchtime chore or routine, and school food education as an 'inconvenient necessity' (Rud and Gleason 2018). This dispersion and disconnection can be a problem when implementing health-related and environmental initiatives in schools. Canteen-based interventions can create connections to various school objectives such as hospitality, retail ventures, school gardens and agriculture (Jones et al.

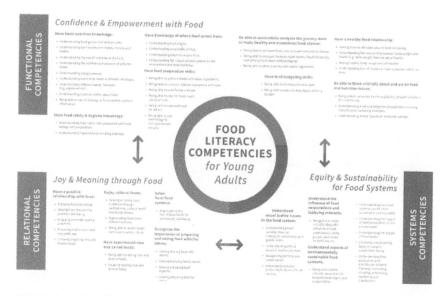

FIGURE 18.1   Food literacy competencies for young adults (Slater et al. 2018)

2012). Leveraging on the successes and strengths of school meal provision models where canteen-based interventions teach health and sustainability concepts to children is an avenue that would lend itself easily to the Australian schooling system, just as in countries such as Japan and Italy (Dunbabin 2018). When planning, canteens can align food and sustainability activities such as kitchen gardens, cooking and plate waste collections, and waste sorting. The perk of this type of intervention is the pragmatism that it provides, the way the culture of school food eating is seen not just as eating time intertwined with health expectations, but also as an interactive learning opportunity where eco-agendas can be fulfilled.

Examples of curriculum integration

Our final recommendation is to carve out time in the existing curriculum for food, health, and sustainability education by making simple but pivotal connections, especially in the primary years. This can be achieved by opportunistically embedding health and sustainability education across the curriculum in various subjects, in lieu of a distinct subject. Through illustrative case studies from the UK and Australia, below we present three examples of integrating food, health, and sustainability learning into pre-existing classes.

Taste education and sensory science

The TasteEd program in the UK (Taste Education 2022) supports and trains teachers to teach children to use their senses to talk and write about food. In turn, this empowers children to make self-determined choices, instead of imposing what is deemed right by nutritionists, the government, school authorities, and

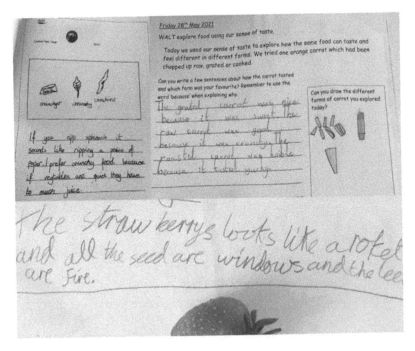

FIGURE 18.2 Examples of children's portrayal of their experience with fruits and vegetables as part of the TastEd program

Source of images: Twitter @tastedfeed

parents. As Bee Wilson aptly said in her book *First Bite* (Wilson 2015), "When children are exposed through 'sensory education' to a wider range of flavours they start to love complexity and be bored by simplicity". Some of the examples of children describing fruits and vegetables (see Figure 18.2) are testimony to the creative way they can embrace new foods and develop willingness to try fruits and vegetables. Its importance has also been recognised in the UK's latest National Food Strategy (2021) where it is advised that sensory food education should be added to the early years curriculum. A similar evidence-based program called the CSIRO Taste & Learn™ for Australian primary schools supports uptake and enjoyment of vegetables (Poelman et al. 2020). It is aligned to the Australian curriculum as a cross-curricular unit and involves sensory and flavour attributes alongside children's exposure to and preference for a vegetable.

1. Linking nutrition and packaging waste:

A STEM activity developed by the NSW Department of Education called "Waste in our classroom" (NSW Government 2020) leveraged on sustainability to drive nutritious food consumption (see Figure 18.3). Five phases of learning were included: Empathy, Definition, Ideation, Prototype, and Test and Share. The comprehensiveness of this activity and the clarity of objectives to be achieved is commendable, yet we recommend to first link food

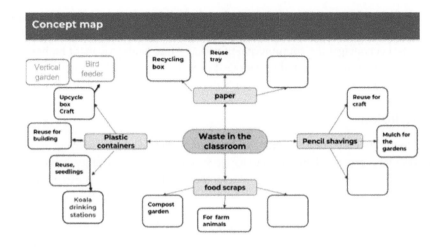

FIGURE 18.3   NSW Department of Education's STEM activity: Waste in our classroom

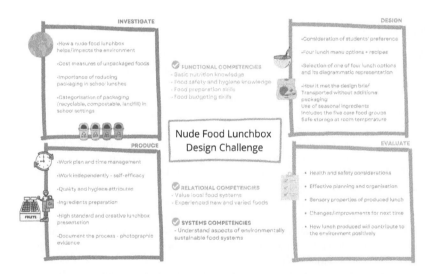

FIGURE 18.4   Nude food lunch design challenge by Home Economics Victoria

(packaging, consumption) choice and health implications whilst uncovering waste behaviours, given the first principle of waste reduction being 'Refuse'.

2. **Teach about food through active learning that leads to a healthy lifestyle:**

This case study outlines a lesson plan developed as part of the Food Design Challenge 2015 by Home Economics Victoria (Home Economics Victoria 2015). Linking to Design and Technologies within the Australian Curriculum, 'Nude Food Lunch' Design Challenge involved investigating, designing, producing, and evaluating a waste-free lunchbox (see Figure 18.4). It promotes sustainability awareness among school community stakeholders about over-packaging, benefits the environment by reducing packaging waste, and encourages the consumption of package-free foods that are of higher nutritional value compared to packaged processed foods (Monteiro et al. 2019). Food literacy competencies as per Slater et al. (2018) are also addressed.

Conclusion

Lifelong learning begins and habits develop in schools. Existing school-curriculars to create behavioural change in food and sustainability habits need revisions. Pragmatic and experimental methods of teaching are required, instead of relying on ad hoc 'healthy' and 'unhealthy' pedagogies that are ineffective. We recommend more empowerment of teachers so they can drive health and sustainability education while keeping the target population at the forefront and centre. It is time to pack creativity in school learning, create space for pragmatic experiences and experiments, and involve children so they value, demand, and consume healthy and sustainable foods.

References

Aikens, K., McKenzie, M., and Vaughter, P., 2016. Environmental and sustainability education policy research: a systematic review of methodological and thematic trends. *Environmental Education Research*, 22 (3), 333–359.

Alberta Health Services, 2022. *The comprehensive school health framework* [online]. Available from: https://education.alberta.ca/comprehensive-school-health/what-is-comprehensive-school-health/ [Accessed 4 June 2021].

Aliyar, R., Gelli, A., and Hamdani, S. H., 2015. A review of nutritional guidelines and menu compositions for school feeding programs in 12 countries. *Frontiers in Public Health* [online], 3, 148. Available from: https://doi.org/10.3389/fpubh.2015.00148 [Accessed 6 June 2021].

Almeida, S. C., 2015. *Environmental education in a climate of reform: understanding teacher educators' perspectives*. Amsterdam, The Netherlands: Brill - Sense.

Almeida, S. C., Moore, D., and Barnes, M., 2018. Teacher identities as key to environmental education for sustainability implementation: a study from Australia. *Australian Journal of Environmental Education*, 34 (3), 228–243.

Ansari, W. E., and Stibbe, A., 2009. Public health and the environment: what skills for sustainability literacy – and why? *Sustainability*, 1 (3), 425–440.

Antón-Peset, A., Fernandez-Zamudio, M., and Pina, T., 2021. Promoting food waste reduction at primary schools: a case study. *Sustainability* [online], 13 (2), 600. Available from: https://doi.org/10.3390/su13020600 [Accessed 6 June 2021].

Ardoin, N. M., and Bowers, A. W., 2020. Early childhood environmental education: a systematic review of the research literature. *Educational Research Review*, 31, 100353.

Australian Curriculum Assessment and Reporting Authority, 2012. *The shape of the Australian Curriculum: health and physical education* [online]. Available from: https://docs.acara.edu.au/resources/Shape_of_the_Australian_Curriculum_Health_and_Physical_Education.pdf [Accessed 26 February 2022].

Australian Curriculum Assessment and Reporting Authority, 2022a. *Food and wellbeing* [online]. Available from: https://australiancurriculum.edu.au/resources/curriculum-connections/portfolios/food-and-wellbeing/ [Accessed 26 February 2022].

Australian Curriculum Assessment and Reporting Authority, 2022b. *Key ideas - health and physical education propositions* [online]. Available from: https://www.australiancurriculum. edu.au/f-10-curriculum/health-and-physical-education/key-ideas/[Accessed 26 February 2022].

Ballantyne, R., Fien, J., and Packer, J., 2001. School environmental education programme impacts upon student and family learning: a case study analysis. *Environmental Education Research*, 7 (1), 23–37.

Barnes, M., Moore, D., and Almeida, S., 2019. Sustainability in Australian schools: a cross-curriculum priority? *Prospects*, 47 (4), 377–392.

Barratt Hacking, E., Barratt, R., and Scott, W., 2007. Engaging children: research issues around participation and environmental learning. *Environmental Education Research*, 13 (4), 529–544.

Benton, D., and Jarvis, M., 2007. The role of breakfast and a mid-morning snack on the ability of children to concentrate at school. *Physiology & Behavior*, 90, 382–385.

Black, J. L., et al., 2015. Sustainability and public health nutrition at school: assessing the integration of healthy and environmentally sustainable food initiatives in Vancouver schools. *Public Health Nutrition*, 18 (13), 2379–2391.

Block, K., et al., 2012. Growing community: the impact of the Stephanie Alexander kitchen garden program on the social and learning environment in primary schools. *Health Education & Behavior*, 39 (4), 419–432.

Bollella, M. C., et al., 1999. Nutrient intake of Head Start children: home vs. school. *Journal of the American College of Nutrition*, 18 (2), 108–114.

Boyd, W., 2015. The tensions between food choices and sustainable practices in early childhood centres. *Australasian Journal of Early Childhood*, 40 (4), 58–65.

Briefel, R. R., et al., 2009. School food environments and practices affect dietary behaviors of US public school children. *Journal of the American Dietetic Association*, 109, 91–107.

Buchanan, J., 2012. Sustainability education and teacher education: finding a natural habitat? *Australian Journal of Environmental Education*, 28 (2), 108–124.

Crowe, R., et al., 2020. Healthy eating and physical activity environments in out-of-school hours care: an observational study protocol. *BMJ Open* [online], 10 (9). Available from: http://doi.org/10.1136/bmjopen-2019-036397 [Accessed 20 June 2022].

Cullen, T., et al., 2015. Food Literacy: definition and framework for action. *Journal of the American Dietetic Association*, 76 (3), 140–145.

Dudley, D. A., Cotton, W. G., and Peralta, L. R., 2015. Teaching approaches and strategies that promote healthy eating in primary school children: a systematic review and meta-analysis. *International Journal of Behavioral Nutrition and Physical Activity* [online], 12 (1). Available from: https://doi.org/10.1186/s12966-015-0182-8 [Accessed 12 June 2021].

Duhn, I., 2012. Making 'place' for ecological sustainability in early childhood education. *Environmental Education Research*, 18 (1), 19–29.

Dunbabin, J., 2018. *Investigate the factors that enable school lunch programs to impact positively on student health and wellbeing -Julie's school lunch journey.* Available from: https:// www.churchilltrust.com.au/project/the-elvie-munday-churchill-fellowship-to-investigate-factors-that-enable-school-lunch-programs-to-impact-positively-on-student-health-and-wellbeing/ [Accessed 2 June 2022].

Evenhuis, I. J., et al., 2020. The effect of supportive implementation of healthier canteen guidelines on changes in Dutch school canteens and student purchase behaviour. *Nutrients*, 12 (8), 2419.

Folta, S. C., et al., 2018. Branding a school-based campaign combining healthy eating and eco-friendliness. *Journal of Nutrition Education and Behavior*, 50 (2), 180–189.

Fossgard, E., et al., 2019. School lunch — children's space or teachers' governmentality? A study of 11 year olds' experiences with and perceptions of packed lunches and lunch breaks in Norwegian primary schools. *International Journal of Consumer Studies*, 43 (2), 218–226.

Goldberg, J. P., et al., 2015. Great taste, less waste: a cluster-randomized trial using a communications campaign to improve the quality of foods brought from home to school by elementary school children. *Preventive Medicine*, 74, 103–110.

Gralton, A., Sinclair, M., and Purnell, K., 2004. Changes in attitudes, beliefs and behaviour: a critical review of research into the impacts of environmental education initiatives. *Australian Journal of Environmental Education*, 20 (2), 41–52.

Grieger, J. A., et al., 2016. Discrete strategies to reduce intake of discretionary food choices: a scoping review. *International Journal of Behavioral Nutrition and Physical Activity*, 13 (1), 57.

Hedefalk, M., Almqvist, J., and Östman, L., 2015. Education for sustainable development in early childhood education: a review of the research literature. *Environmental Education Research*, 21 (7), 975–990.

Hickman, C., et al., 2021. Climate anxiety in children and young people and their beliefs about government responses to climate change: a global survey. *The Lancet Planetary Health*, 5 (12). Available from: https://doi.org/10.1016/S2542-5196(21)00278-3 [Accessed 15 January 2022].

Hill, A., and Dyment, J. E., 2016. Hopes and prospects for the sustainability cross-curriculum priority: provocations from a state-wide case study. *Australian Journal of Environmental Education*, 32 (3), 225–242.

Home Economics Victoria, 2015. Food Design Challenge 2015- Empowering students to eat and live well. Available from: https://www.yumpu.com/en/document/view/52513687/food-design-challenge-2015 [Accessed 28 July 2021].

Jaime, P. C., and Lock, K., 2009. Do school based food and nutrition policies improve diet and reduce obesity? *Preventive Medicine*, 48 (1), 45–53.

Jones, M., et al., 2012. Food sustainability education as a route to healthier eating: evaluation of a multi-component school programme in English primary schools. *Health Education Research*, 27 (3), 448–458.

Karpouzis, F., et al., 2021. Evaluating OzHarvest's primary-school food education and sustainability training (FEAST) program in 10–12-year-old children in Australia: protocol for a pragmatic cluster non-randomized controlled trial. *BMC Public Health*, 21 (1). Available from: https://doi.org/10.1186/s12889-021-10302-0 [Accessed 28 July 2021].

Kennelly, J., Taylor, N., and Serow, P., 2011. Education for sustainability and the Australian curriculum. *Australian Journal of Environmental Education*, 27 (2), 209–218.

Kosáros, A., Ildikó, K., and Lakatos, G., 2009. Sustainability pedagogy in practice: an example from health education. *Journal of Teacher Education for Sustainability*, 7, 79–87.

Kraak, V. I., and Story, M., 2015. Influence of food companies' brand mascots and entertainment companies' cartoon media characters on children's diet and health: a systematic review and research needs. *Obesity Reviews*, 16 (2), 107–126.

Leahy, D., and Wright, J., 2016. Governing food choices: a critical analysis of school food pedagogies and young people's responses in contemporary times. *Cambridge Journal of Education*, 46 (2), 233–246.

Lobstein, T., and Davies, S., 2009. Defining and labelling 'healthy' and 'unhealthy' food. *Public Health Nutrition*, 12 (3), 331–340.

Lynagh, M., Cliff, K., and Morgan, P. J., 2015. Attitudes and beliefs of nonspecialist and specialist trainee health and physical education teachers toward obese children: evidence for anti-fat bias. *Journal of School Health*, 85 (9), 595–603.

Mahmood, L., et al., 2021. The influence of parental dietary behaviors and practices on children's eating habits. *Nutrients*, 13 (4). Available from: https://doi.org/10.3390/nu13041138 [Accessed 15 September 2021].

Manson, A. C., et al., 2021. The food and nutrient intake of 5 to 12 year-old Australian children during school hours: a secondary analysis of the 2011–2012 National Nutrition and Physical Activity Survey. *Public Health Nutrition*, 24 (18), 5985–5994.

Monteiro, C. A., et al., 2019. Ultra-processed foods, diet quality, and health using the NOVA classification system [online]. *Food and Agriculture Organisation*. Available from: https://www.fao.org/3/ca5644en/ca5644en.pdf [Accessed 22 June 2021].

Morris, H., et al., 2018. Evaluating the impact of teacher-designed, wellbeing and sustainability play-based learning experiences on young children's knowledge connections: a randomised trial. *Australasian Journal of Early Childhood*, 43 (4), 33–42.

National Food Strategy, 2021. *National food strategy independent review: The plan* [online]. Available from: https://www.nationalfoodstrategy.org/ [Accessed 2 March 2022].

Nelson, M. 2011. The school food trust: Transforming school lunches in England. *Nutrition Bulletin*, 36 (3), 381–389.

Nelson, M, N. J., et al., 2006. *School meals in primary schools in England*. Available from: https://www.researchgate.net/publication/240636478_School_Meals_in_Primary_Schools_in_England [Accessed 16 April 2022].

NSW Government, n.d., *How can we manage waste more effectively in our classroom?* [online]. Available from: https://education.nsw.gov.au/teaching-and-learning/curriculum/key-learning-areas/primary/stage-2-resources/how-can-we-manage-waste-more-effectively-in-our-classroom- [Accessed 20 January 2022].

NSW, 2020. *The NSW Healthy School Canteen* [online] Available from: https://www.health.nsw.gov.au/heal/Publications/food-drink-criteria.pdf.

Nude Food Movers, n.d. *Nude food day* [online]. Available from: https://www.nudefoodmovers.com.au/ [Accessed 26 February 2022].

Nude Food Movers, 2019. Website [Online]. Available from: https://www.nudefoodmovers.com.au/.

Oostindjer, M., et al., 2017. Are school meals a viable and sustainable tool to improve the healthiness and sustainability of children's diet and food consumption? a cross-national comparative perspective. *Critical Reviews in Food Science and Nutrition*, 57 (18), 3942–3958.

Percy-Smith, B., and Burns, D., 2013. Exploring the role of children and young people as agents of change in sustainable community development. *Local Environment*, 18 (3), 323–339.

Pihkala, P., 2017. Environmental education after sustainability: hope in the midst of tragedy. *Global Discourse*, 7 (1), 109–127.

Pineda, E., Bascunan, J., and Sassi, F., 2021. Improving the school food environment for the prevention of childhood obesity: what works and what doesn't. *Obesity Reviews*, 22 (2), e13176.

Pluim, C., Powell, D., and Leahy, D., 2018. Schooling lunch: health, food, and the pedagogicalization of the lunch box. *In*: S. Rice and A. G. Rud, eds. *Educational dimensions of school lunch*. Heidelberg, The Netherlands: Springer, 59–74.

Poelman, A. A. M., et al., 2020. Effect of experiential vegetable education program on mediating factors of vegetable consumption in australian primary school students: a cluster-randomized controlled trial. *Nutrients*, 12 (8), 2343.

Price, C., 2010. Sowing the seed: education for sustainability within the early years. *Curriculum European Early Childhood Education Research Journal*, 18 (3), 423–432.

Rahman, A. A., et al., 2018. Effectiveness of behavioral interventions to reduce the intake of sugar-sweetened beverages in children and adolescents: a systematic review and meta-analysis. *Nutrition Reviews*, 76 (2), 88–107.

Ronto, R., et al., 2020. Enablers and barriers to implementation of and compliance with school-based healthy food and beverage policies: a systematic literature review and meta-synthesis. *Public Health Nutrition*, 23 (15), 2840–2855.

Ronto, R., et al., 2021. Adolescents' views on high school food environments. *Health Promotion Journal of Australia*, 32 (3), 458–466.

Rosa, C. D., Profice, C. C., and Collado, S., 2018. Nature experiences and adults' self-reported pro-environmental behaviors: the role of connectedness to nature and childhood nature experiences. *Frontiers in Psychology*, 9, 1055.

Rosewarne, E., et al., 2020. A comprehensive overview and qualitative analysis of government-led nutrition policies in Australian institutions. *BMC Public Health*, 20 (1), 1–15.

Rud, A., and Gleason, S., 2018. School lunch curriculum. *Educational Dimensions of School Lunch*. Heidelberg, The Netherlands: Springer, 173–187.

Scaglioni, S., et al., 2018. Factors influencing children's eating behaviours. *Nutrients* [online], 10 (6). Available from: https://doi.org/10.3390%2Fnu10060706 [Accessed 12 June 2021].

Sciberras, E., and Fernando, J. W., 2022. Climate change related worry among Australian adolescents: an eight year longitudinal study. *Child and Adolescent Mental Health*, 27 (1), 22–29.

Scott, W., and Reid, A., 1998. The revisioning of environmental education: a critical analysis of recent policy shifts in England and Wales. *Educational Review*, 50 (3), 213–223.

Shanks, C. B., Banna, J., and Serrano, E. L., 2017. Food waste in the National School Lunch Program 1978–2015: a systematic review. *Journal of the Academy of Nutrition and Dietetics*, 117 (11), 1792–1807.

Slater, J., et al., 2018. Food literacy competencies: a conceptual framework for youth transitioning to adulthood. *International Journal of Consumer Studies*, 42 (5), 547–556.

Smith, K., Wells, R., and Hawkes, C., 2022. How primary school curriculums in 11 countries around the world deliver food education and address food literacy: a policy analysis. *International Journal of Environmental Research and Public Health* [online], 19 (4). Available from: https://doi.org/10.3390/ijerph19042019 [Accessed 5 April 2022].

Tanner, C., et al., 2019. Sticky foods: how school practices produce negative emotions for mothers and children. *Emotion, Space and Society*, 33, 100626.

Taste Education, 2022. *What is TastEd?* [online]. Available from: https://www.tasteeducation.com/what-do-we-do/ [Accessed 26 February 2022].

Thompson, E., et al., 2006. Food and activity in out of school hours care in Victoria. *Nutrition & Dietetics*, 63 (1), 21–27.

United Nations, 2016. *Transforming our world: the 2030 agenda for sustainable development* [online]. Available from: https://sdgs.un.org/2030agenda [Accessed 2 March 2022].

United Nations, 2020. *Raising awareness and assessing sustainability literacy on SDG 7* [online]. Available from: https://sustainabledevelopment.un.org/sdinaction/hesi/literacy [Accessed 2 March 2022].

Walsh, M., 1984. Environmental education: a decade of failure but some hope for the future. *Australian Journal of Environmental Education*, 1 (1), 21–24.

Welch, R., and Leahy, D., 2018. Beyond the pyramid or plate: contemporary approaches to food and nutrition education. *ACHPER Active and Healthy Magazine* [online], 25 (2/3), 22–31. Available from: https://www.achper.org.au/products/volume-25-issue-23/beyond-the-pyramid-or-plate-contemporary-approaches-to-food-and-nutrition-education [Accessed 2 March 2022].

Wickramasinghe, K. K., et al., 2016. Contribution of healthy and unhealthy primary school meals to greenhouse gas emissions in England: linking nutritional data and greenhouse gas emission data of diets. *European Journal of Clinical Nutrition*, 70 (10), 1162–1167.

Wilson, B., 2015. *First bite: how we learn to eat*. Basic Books. Available from: https://www.tasteeducation.com/what-do-we-do/ [Accessed 10 March 2022].

Yıldız, T. G., et al., 2021. Education for sustainability in early childhood education: a systematic review. *Environmental Education Research*, 27 (6), 796–820.

Zeinstra, G. G., van der Haar, S., and Haveman-Nies, A., 2021. Strategies to increase primary school children's fruit and vegetable intake during 10 AM snack time. *Appetite*, 163, 105235.

19

EXPLORING INTERSECTIONAL FEMINIST FOOD PEDAGOGIES THROUGH THE RECIPE EXCHANGE PROJECT

Barbara Parker

Introduction

Food provides a rich context for experiential learning and as Jennifer Sumner (2008) reminds us, 'eating is a pedagogical act'. Whether we provide opportunities to eat, cook, or grow food in the classroom, learning through food produces embodied food knowledge(s) constructed through individual and collective histories. Through eating, individuals embody their food practices and engage bodily senses of touch, taste, smell and feelings connected to emotions and memories (Brady 2011; Lupton 1996). We learn about foods through our socialization experiences in childhood and through our families, public health, cultural practices, migration, education and religion (Guptill et al. 2016), which are always shaped by gender, race, ethnicity, social class and abilities among other intersecting axes of identity (Parker et al. 2019; Williams-Forson and Wilkerson 2011).

Within everyday experiences, we learn to label some foods as 'healthy', or good for us, or even good for the planet (e.g. veganism), or alternatively many foods are labelled bad for us because they lack nutritional quality or their production is harmful to the environment and/or Indigenous Peoples (e.g. avocados, almonds) (Parker 2020). These good/bad food binaries are deeply problematic, but recognizing them acknowledges understanding that the relationships we have with food are complex. Food represents who we are, our identities and our subjectivities, while at the same time, our food practices embody and mark social differences. Although some people celebrate their food practices, particularly foods that hold ethnic or cultural significance or foods that are meaningful on particular holidays (Guptill et al. 2016), most everyday food practices go unquestioned, particularly as these relate to the construction and maintenance of intersectional identities and the oppression or privilege that accompany social

DOI: 10.4324/9781003294962-23

identities. For feminist food scholars, it is imperative that we not only unpack how food is experienced in relation to the local and global structures, conditions and practices of food consumption and food production, but also that we teach our students to think critically about these issues.

This paper explores community-based teaching and learning (Etmanski et al. 2014; Mooney and Edwards 2001)[1] and intersectional feminist food pedagogies through critical reflections of two post-secondary courses, a third-year undergraduate class and a graduate-level seminar course, both of which were focused on gender, health and food justice. Intersectional feminist food pedagogy is a conceptual framework, as well as a pedagogical approach that builds theoretically on critical food pedagogies, broadly understood as teaching and learning about food that is oriented towards social justice (Flowers and Swan 2015; Sumner 2013).

According to Case (2017), an effective intersectional pedagogy must,

> *conceptualize intersectionality* as a complex analysis of both privileged and oppressed social identities that simultaneously interact to create systemic inequalities and therefore, alter lived experiences of prejudice and discrimination, privilege and opportunities, and perspectives from particular social locations. Intersectional theory pushes us beyond the additive model that conceptualizes identity and structural oppression as categorical and mutually exclusive.
>
> *(p.9)*

Case (2017) suggests that intersectional pedagogy must elevate "neglected" positionalities (immigrant status, sexuality, ability, gender identities) and "uncover invisible intersections", including thinking about how privilege operates in power analyses to "push the boundaries of teaching multiculturalism, diversity, oppression and discrimination" (p.9). A key aspect of intersectional pedagogy is both student and instructor reflexivity, which enables careful consideration of the power and oppression experienced through our intersecting social identities (p.9). In setting up the courses as community-based learning (CBL), Case's (2017) model framed how I conceptualized intersectional feminist food pedagogy and developed the Recipe Exchange Project.

Each week, the Gender, Health and Food Justice students were required to cook, taste and teach themselves and their peers, making connections to course content that included required readings and assessments. Both courses ran in a 13-week term in the kitchen of our community partner, a local not-for-profit food organization. In this community space, students were offered an integrated learning experience in a lab kitchen. Students were exposed to learning across curricula as the undergraduate course in sociology was cross-listed with women's studies, while the graduate sociology seminar was cross-listed with social justice studies.

The aim of the courses was to have students explore intersectionality theory, social inequality and the socio-cultural concepts of food–body–health through cooking and tasting in the kitchen lab and the Recipe Exchange Project. The Recipe Exchange Project asked students to choose a recipe from 'home' and teach the class to make it. Following Brady (2011), cooking was presented to students as a form of embodied inquiry. Practically, this required that food was available each week in class in order for students to engage with the embodied act of cooking and eating—as a shared relational experience, mediated through their own and their peers' experiences and memories of home and identity. To integrate learning, students were also presented with information about cooking techniques, food budgeting, food safety, nutrition, sustainable food systems and the not-for-profit food sector.

There were several learning objectives for the Recipe Exchange Project and I draw into focus two of these below. First, students were to engage with intersectionality as a theory of social justice and to develop their understanding of power, privilege, oppression and social inequalities as these are constructed and maintained through individual food practices with individual and collective historical contexts. Specifically, students were asked to use intersectionality as a framework or mechanism for thinking about the co-construction of race, gender, social class among other aspects of their identity as mutually constitutive or as an "interactive structural system of oppression" (Case 2017, p.5). Second, to deepen their learning, students were asked to think beyond food as nourishment, and consider the effects and experience of culture and social structures such as gender, race, abilities, to understand their own, embodied food practices.

My pedagogical approach in both courses was also contextualized by my awareness of our increasingly diverse student population, which in the context of the institution where I teach, there are high numbers of first-generation students, Indigenous students, international, mature or returning students and high rates of student food insecurity (Silverthorn 2016). Not unlike other Canadian post-secondary institutions (Power et al. 2021), post-secondary student food insecurity is a growing social problem that affects students' ability to concentrate in class and learn because of hunger. Thus, connecting with students through food and feeding them was central to the curriculum. Below, I share my critical reflections on CBL through intersectional feminist food pedagogy. First, I briefly describe the Recipe Exchange Project as it unfolded in the graduate seminar and undergraduate course. This is followed by a discussion of the CBL context including challenges and opportunities.

The Recipe Exchange Project

Through the Recipe Exchange Project students were encouraged to think about 'home' in any way that fit their experience, and as a place constructed through their memories of food using reflexive practices.[2] To orient them, I had students share a food memory in class, thinking about what was significant for them in that memory (e.g. the taste, smell or feelings attached to the food, where they ate the food, etc.). The memory could be positive or negative, whatever the student felt comfortable sharing. This exercise facilitated deeper thinking about their material experiences of a particular food or meal and helped them to connect with peers. Students were surprised to find a common thread running through many of their individual memories—that is, their memories of various foods (or meals in some cases) contained strong emotional connections to family and friends.

Next, I prepared a set of questions to guide the students in thinking through their choice of a recipe for their project. For instance, they were told that they would be asked to describe the recipe and think about how often they prepare the dish and explain why or why not it is cooked or prepared often or infrequently; to think about the socio-cultural meanings of health and/or nutrition attached to the ingredients in their recipe, or the recipe itself (e.g. did they consider it healthy or not?); to explore the history of the recipe both within their family and within a broader social context, and also consider the political economy of the ingredients or recipe itself (think about the 'stories' of the ingredients such as where are they produced, are they readily available, who produces them). Students were reminded that they did not have to answer all of the questions, but rather use them as a guide to think through their analysis and reflections on the recipe in relation to their identity.

A key part of the assignment was to think through their own intersectional identities—not as single-axis categories but rather as multidimensional—potentially experiencing privilege and oppression simultaneously depending on the context of their interactions with others and the systems in which their experiences are framed (Collins and Bilge 2016). For example, I explained that a student might have privilege as a university student, but can also experience oppression through racialized, gendered and classed social identities, which are experienced relationally through ongoing everyday social interactions (Case 2017; Romero 2018) within their university experience with professors or peers. I encouraged them to think about their recipes not only through the material aspects of cooking or preparing the food, but also through the social interactions they engendered.

Students were given video and podcast links on intersectionality to complement their course readings and class discussion.[3] They were further encouraged to use and make connections to the required readings in food justice including how food systems have been subjected to colonization and ongoing settler colonialism (Parker *In Press*; Dennis and Robin 2020), food insecurity (Power et al. 2021), the relationships between food, health and risk, including public health nutrition (Parker 2020), critical dietetics (Hayes-Conroy and Hayes-Conroy 2013) and Health at Every Size© (HAES) (Association for Size Diversity and Health [ASDAH] 2015) among other themes.

Students were asked to develop a presentation based on their chosen recipe and sign up to share it with the class. To accompany their presentation, they were required to write up a reflexive paper to be handed in following their presentation. These requirements were the same for both classes although the page length expectations were less for the third-year class, and they were evaluated differently based on the year level.

The graduate course

From the first class, graduate students were excited about CBL in a lab kitchen, and that they would have an opportunity to cook their chosen recipe with the class in the Recipe Exchange Project. Each student signed up to facilitate one class, where they would present their recipe (giving each student a copy on a recipe card) and teach their peers to prepare it. Once the food was cooking, they would lead the class discussion on the readings, and as the dish was ready, our seminar would continue as we shared the food, eating together and cleaning up afterwards. Students were asked to let me know a week in advance what their recipe was, and prepare a budget under $50 for the ingredient list.[4] All students came in under budget and each student shopped for their own class. In addition to preparing instructions on how to cook their recipe, students also organized discussion questions based on the readings and facilitated the seminar discussion.

The recipes reflected the diversity of the class and students made many significant connections using an intersectional feminist food pedagogical framework. For instance, one mature student shared her life experiences as a single, white mother who would bring her family together through a pasta dish with homemade tomato sauce, which as she explained, she could make cheaply, but from whole ingredients; another female student shared her experiences of food as a second generation Canadian and member of the Afghani diaspora and taught us to prepare emerald rice, a traditional food that brought her comfort living away from 'home', both real and imagined; while yet another Indigenous female student shared with us a meal of moose, blueberries and bannock, traditional Indigenous foods, making connections to the land as an urban Indigenous woman and a product of the 'Sixties Scoop'.[5] The presentations were personal, yet critical as students made meaningful connections between their chosen recipe, and their food practices as these intersected with their identities.

The undergraduate course

Unlike the graduate class, where there was time to cook each student's recipe, in the undergraduate class it was not possible to cook all 30 student's recipes. Thus, all students had to present their chosen recipe in class and were required to hand in a reflection paper, however because of the larger class size, students were assigned to a small group and following all presentations, had to collectively choose one recipe to cook as a group and share with the class. Groups were given guidelines to assist with their decision-making about which recipe to prepare (i.e. budget, constraints on preparation time, availability of ingredients, and food allergies). As I did the shopping for this class, they were required to give me their grocery list one week prior to class. In the end, there were four groups and as a class, over four weeks, we cooked and ate homemade gnocchi with red sauce, eggless chocolate cake, banana bread and bannock with blueberries. Because of food allergies in this cohort, recipes were prepared both with flour and eggs, and also gluten and egg free, which as an integrated learning experience, gave us an opportunity to experiment with recipes and learn a little about the science of eggs and gluten. In the weeks leading up to cooking foods from the Recipe Exchange Project, I had students prepare foods that I selected to accompany the weekly assigned readings (e.g. one week we made soup and bread, another week we made cricket-flour cookies, while another week we prepared homemade salsa and guacamole and served these with corn chips), which we ate together while we discussed course materials, watched films and worked with the kitchen coordinator in preparing foods for our community partner's social enterprise.

Similar to the graduate students, the undergraduate students focused their presentation of recipes from home on culture, ethnicity and race, with attention to gender, religion and social class. Shorter in length than the graduate student presentations, many white students made connections between their recipe and their ethnicity (e.g. Finnish, Italian, Scottish heritage) while students of colour provided more critical analyses of how their recipe involved racialized foods (e.g. baked beans, collard greens with cornbread, bannock). Students seemed to most easily associate their food practices with their ethnic heritage, which presented opportunities for critical discussion about the racialization of foods and conversations emerged about "ethnic foods" and why some foods such as Chinese or Indian food are viewed as Other (Hooks 2014; Ray 2016).[6]

Through their intersectional analyses, students also talked about gendered domesticity (Hollows 2008) and how recipes were passed down and taught to them by their mothers and grandmothers, with a couple of students resisting traditional gendered narratives and in one case, sharing their grandfather's tomato sauce recipe that had been in their family for several generations. Less common, but also significant for understanding the intersections of religion, was the student who presented a family recipe for challah bread, a Jewish tradition for Hanukkah. Finally, social class was discussed in relation to the affordability of certain recipes and these students talked about how to cook their recipe on a budget presenting two versions of the ingredient list, explaining how they were able to continue to prepare their recipe as a post-secondary student with limited incomes. In all, students demonstrated their engagement and learning about intersectionality in the Recipe Exchange Project, as well, they learned from our community partner, who taught them canning and how to make chutney, and prepare moose jerky.

Reflections on community-based teaching and learning

These courses were initially inspired by the John Dewey Kitchen Institute, where education is viewed "as a practice of democracy" and "learning happens by doing".[7] A key aim of the courses was to explore intersectional feminist food pedagogy and cooking as inquiry, through experiential, material and embodied learning, in addition to developing further understanding of community-based teaching and learning with our community partner (Brady 2011; Michelson

1998).[8] Research relationships with community organizations are integral to community-based teaching and learning, and based on my previous work on school food environments (Parker and Koeppel 2020), the community organization responded positively to my request to bring students to their kitchen space. We shared the belief that food provides an opportune lens for learning, and I saw teaching in this space as an opportunity to promote justice-oriented and public pedagogy (Flowers and Swan 2015; Giroux 1988). Beyond the opportunities for students to learn cooking skills and better understand the work of our community partner, we were also able to learn from the employees of the organization, with staff regularly sitting down with us to talk about what we were learning in the course and help us with our weekly cooking assignments.

Our community partner was a local not-for-profit food organization that uses food to outreach in the community. Their work involves working with marginal youth to run a community-supported agriculture (CSA) and farmer's market with two urban farming sites in the summer months, farm-to-cafeteria programs in several high schools, K-12 school food workshops and gardening programs, adult education courses for credit, as well as a culture kitchen with new immigrants. In addition to their social programs, they have a newly designed large kitchen space that they rent out to small food businesses. This supplements their funding from government sources, fundraising and donations, as well as their social enterprise activities which include selling value-added foods such as granola, jams, tomato and barbeque sauce (foods my students were able to help prepare).

When I first began to think about holding university-level classes in a kitchen space and incorporating cooking as a weekly part of the curriculum, I realized quickly that there was no suitable kitchen space on campus and that I would have to figure out a community space that could accommodate my students and the activities I envisioned. As I had been working with my community partner prior through a community-based research project, I was aware of their space. I met with one of the program coordinators early on, who shared her experiences running cooking classes and helped me to strategize about how I could incorporate food and cooking into my university curriculum in a meaningful way. The biggest hurdle was from my institution's administration, who, although they want experiential learning opportunities for students, are not set up to deal with scheduling courses off-site. I also had to navigate the university's risk policy as I was requiring students to attend classes off campus. Fortunately, the kitchen coordinator of our community partner helped me arrange details such as figuring out insurance and scheduling. She also suggested that they could teach the students how to preserve food (e.g. canning) through their social enterprise activities.

Although I was excited to teach food experientially and let students cook and eat as part of the curriculum, I was also nervous about teaching in the kitchen lab—off campus. Some of my concerns centred around logistics such as student transportation (how would students travel from campus to our community partner's location), course enrolment (limited seats and a waitlist), and the costs of food. Also, I was unsure of how I would teach culinary and food skills. Although I'm an avid home cook and consider myself fairly adept in the context of my own kitchen, I have no formal culinary training and admittedly, I felt outside my comfort zone teaching in the new industrial kitchen with its four cooking stations, professional convection ovens and commercial dishwashers. Again, my community partner assisted me in instructing students on day one providing advice about hair and shoes in the kitchen, as well as teaching us how to use the kitchen equipment.

These tensions that I felt never fully went away over the course of the term. Upon reflection, I see the novelty of the learning environment and the fact that both myself and the students were operating outside traditional structures and expectations of a university classroom that led to uncertainties for all of us. For one, the courses flattened the hierarchy of power between myself and the students (Crabtree and Sapp 2003). I did not claim expertise in the kitchen and saw my role more as a facilitator or activator of experiential food knowledge including cooking and kitchen skills. This lack of experience in a teaching kitchen was in tension with my experience as a professor. Students in the classes who had chef's training and restaurant kitchen experience knew how to convert recipes to make larger quantities, substitute ingredients, use professional kitchen appliances and were demonstrably more comfortable in the space. Etmanski et al. (2014) suggest that community-based research and teaching "offers us an opportunity to deconstruct false dichotomies, and to upend rigid power relations that constrain our possibilities for learning" (p.5). By minimizing the expert/lay binary in our learning space, students were empowered to demonstrate their food knowledge and kitchen skills and take ownership of the space and in the class.

These experiences were an opportunity to question our assumptions about the university classroom and what it should be [could be], and to think about how learning happens on many levels. I set the stage for this in week one when I introduced the Head, Heart, Hand exercise (Singleton 2015) and asked students to draw each—a head, a heart and a hand, and then quietly reflect on each of the headings in relation to their experiences or knowledge of gender, health and food justice. This was followed by a second question when I then asked them to think about what they might offer the class in each of these areas. Students were encouraged to think about how they could contribute to the class, and shared their kitchen experience, specific skills, their love of food and talked about their relationships to food justice, gender and health. This reflexive exercise, and the food memory exercise discussed earlier, helped to set the tone of the courses by centring student expertise, and placing importance on reflexive practice in relation to creating a transformative learning experience.

Discussion

Similar to my course offerings, not-for-profit food organizations and health centres regularly offer learning opportunities to cook, grow and learn about food, health, nutrition and food systems. Although there are potential benefits of these programs, the critiques offered by Biltekoff (2013) and Guthman (2008) about the problematic assumptions of *"bringing good food to others"* cannot be ignored. Food literacy is often framed through food access programs and almost always, through charity. Kimura (2011) also addresses the trouble that arises from the often-cited social problem that food and cooking skills are on the wane with young adults, and thus students become the targets for food literacy programs in institutions (p.466).

One of the unintended consequences of food literacy and cooking classes is that they can operate as highly moralizing discourses, professing ideas about a 'right' way to eat. Although there is increasing awareness about nutritionism, healthism and how healthy eating discourses individualize food choices, and subsequently blame individuals for their food failings, there are equally compelling narratives about eco-nutritionism and alternative food systems that inform dominant ways of knowing food (Parker 2020). The search for the 'right way to eat' is one of the central preoccupations of our times, and some students looked to me to provide guidance on how or what to eat, which I understood to be an effect of my positionality as their instructor. In an effort to dislodge dominant discourses about healthy eating and that we can know the right way to eat, I purposively steered class discussions away from didactic advice about food, diets, health and instead, encouraged conversations about the socio-cultural aspects of food and food justice.

Conclusion

As a feminist sociologist, teaching students about the theory of intersectionality and what this means for food practices is complicated by tensions within the theory itself that make it difficult to teach (Naples 2017). Although it is a theory of social justice, intersectionality does not "remedy 'racism, classism and sexism'" (Cooper 2015, p.5 cited in Naples, p.111), and teaching students to move beyond analyses of their individual food consumption practices and to think more broadly about the wider consequences of food systems that maintain systems of privilege, inequalities and oppressions was a challenging aspect of the Recipe Exchange Project and the courses. Intersectionality is an analytical tool for understanding how power operates through social identities and the "matrix of domination" that accompanies social structures (Collins 1990; Crenshaw 1991). To varying degrees, students demonstrated their ability to use reflexivity and think about their food practices and their chosen recipe from home, and recognize that our social identities are a product of social structures such as food systems that maintain racism, sexism and classism among other oppressive systems.

Although there were challenges logistically in offering these courses, overall, the benefits of CBL and intersectional feminist food pedagogy were many.

Students shared positive feedback on their experience with many saying they wished there were more opportunities to learn by doing, in this case, cooking and eating. Through the Recipe Exchange Project, I was able to better understand the experiences and lives of my students, which facilitated a deeper engagement and promoted new ways of learning for me as well as for them. The integrated, CBL model gave students cooking skills and food literacy layered with an ability to think reflexively about their own embodiment of food. Students took an active role in their learning, cooking and sharing food. Finally, through an intersectional feminist food pedagogy, students considered the relationality of their own social positionalities as these are constructed through food practices that are shaped by wider food systems, which arguably, *is* social justice in the classroom.

Notes

1 Community-based learning (CBL) refers to a style of engaged scholarship whereby community partners are involved in the practice of teaching, learning and research. Although there are numerous ways in which CBL is taken up, it shares the two principles of being participatory (or experiential) and action-oriented (Etmanski et al. 2014, p.8).
2 'Home' is put into quotations to remind us that it is a constructed idea that varies considerably depending on one's social positionality and experiences. See: Joanne Hollows book, *Domestic Cultures* (2008), Berkshire England: Open University Press, which provides a comprehensive analysis of the many ways in which ideas about home are constructed through gender, domestic labour, and consumption; Ghassan Hage's (1997) discussion of the feelings attached to food and home for immigrants in, "At Home in the Entrails of the West: Multiculturalism, "ethnic food" and migrant home building" in *Home/World: Community, identity, and marginality in Sydney's West*, Sydney: Pluto Press; and Anne Murcott's (1982) analysis of cooking in the home in relation to masculinity and femininity in "On the social significance of the 'cooked dinner' in South Wales," *Anthropology of Food*, 21(4/5): 677–696.
3 See for example: Yasmin Jiwani, Intersectionality Research Hub at Concordia University, "What is Intersectionality?" https://soundcloud.com/user-739908629/episode-0; Akilah Obviously: On Intersectionism in Feminism and Pizza; and Peter Haskins from Newcastle University: https://vimeo.com/263719865.
4 Financial support for these courses was available through a teaching grant offered by the Faculty of Social Sciences and Humanities.
5 See Raven Sinclair (2007) "Identity Lost and Found: Lessons from the Sixties Scoop," *First Peoples Child & Family Review*, 3(1): 65–82. Retrieved December 3, 2021 from: https://fpcfr.com/index.php/FPCFR/article/view/25.
6 See: https://www.npr.org/sections/thesalt/2016/04/09/472568085/why-hunting-down-authentic-ethnic-food-is-a-loaded-proposition.
7 See: *Democracy in the kitchen: John Dewey's education through cooking and eating.* University of Vermont Professional and Continuing Education (November 4, 2021). Retrieved December 3, 2021, from https://learn.uvm.edu/program/john-dewey-kitchen-institute/.
8 This was not my first community-based course. See: Pictou, Robin, Parker and Brady, 2021. "Pestiewink/Wihokewin: Invitation to Indigenous and Intersectional Feminist Food Studies," in *Critical Perspectives in Food Studies* (pp.90–104). Don Mills, ON: Oxford University Press.

References

Association for Size Diversity and Health (ASDAH), 2015. *Poodle Science* [online]. Available from: https://www.youtube.com/watch?v=H89QQfXtc-k [Accessed 3 December 2021].

Biltekoff, C., 2013. *Eating Right in America: The Cultural Politics of Food and Health*, Duke University Press.

Brady, J., 2011. Cooking as inquiry: A method to stir up prevailing ways of knowing food, body and identity. *International Journal of Qualitative Methods* [online], 10 (4), 321–334. Available from: https://journals.sagepub.com/doi/full/10.1177/160940691101000402 [Accessed 15 April 2021].

Case, K. A., 2017. *Intersectional pedagogy: complicating identity and social justice*. New York: Routledge, Taylor and Francis Group.

Cole, E. R., 2017. Teaching intersectionality for our times. *In:* K. Case, ed. *Intersectional pedagogy: complicating identity and social justice*. New York: Routledge, Taylor and Francis Group, ix–xii.

Collins, P., and Bilge, S., 2016. *Intersectionality*. Cambridge, UK: Polity Press.

Collins, P. H., 1990. *Black feminist thought: knowledge, consciousness and the politics of power*. New York: Routledge.

Cooper, B., 2015. Intersectionality. *In:* L. Disch and M. Hawkesworth, eds. *The Oxford handbook of feminist theory*. doi:10.1093/oxfordhb/9780199328581.013.20 [Accessed 09 March 2023].

Crabtree, R. D., and Sapp, D. A., 2003. Theoretical, political, and pedagogical challenges in the feminist classroom: our struggles to walk the walk. *College Teaching*, 51 (4), 131–140.

Crenshaw, K. W., 1991. Mapping the margins: intersectionality, identity politics, and violence against women of colour. *Standford Law Review*, 43, 1241–1299.

Dennis, M. K., and Robin, T., 2020. Healthy on our own terms: indigenous wellbeing and the colonized food system. *Journal of Critical Dietetics*, Special Issue, 5 (1), 4–11.

Etmanski, C., Hall, B. L., and Dawson, T., eds., 2014. *Learning and teaching community-based research: linking pedagogy to practice*. Toronto, Canada: University of Toronto Press.

Flowers, R., and Swan, E., eds., 2015. *Food pedagogies*. Surrey, England: Ashgate Publishing Company.

Giroux, H. A., 1988. *Teachers as intellectuals: toward a critical pedagogy of learning*. Westport, CT: Greenwood Publishing group.

Guthman, J., 2008. Bringing good food to others: investigating the subjects of alternative food practice. *Cultural Geographies*, 15, 431–447.

Guptill, A., Copelton, D., and Lucal, B., 2016. *Food & society: principles and paradoxes*. 2nd ed. Cambridge, UK: Polity Press.

Hayes-Conroy, A., and Hayes-Conroy, J., 2013. *Doing nutrition differently: critical approaches to diet and dietary intervention*. Surrey, UK: Ashgate.

Hollows, J., 2008. *Domestic cultures*. Berkshire, England: Open University Press.

Hooks, b., 2014. *Black looks: race and representation*. 2nd ed. Boston, MA: South End Press.

Kimura, A., 2011. Food education as food literacy: privatized and gendered food knowledge in contemporary Japan. *Agriculture and Human Values* [online], 28, 465–482. Available from: https://doi.org/10.1007/s10460-010-9286-6 [Accessed 15 May 2021].

Lupton, D., 1996. *Food, the body and the self*. London, UK: Sage Publications.

Michelson, E., 1998. Re-membering: the return of the body to experiential learning. *Studies in Continuing Education* [online], 20 (2), 217–233. Available from: https://doi.org/10.1080/0158037980200208 [Accessed 15 May 2021].

Mooney, L. A., and Edwards, B., 2001. Experiential learning in sociology: service learning and other community-based learning initiatives. *Teaching Sociology* [online], 29 (2), 181–194 Available from: https://www.joycerain.com/uploads/2/3/2/0/23207256/experiential_learning_in_sociology__service_learning_and_other_community-based_learning.pdf [Accessed 10 April 2021].

Naples, N., 2017. Pedagogical practice and teaching intersectionality intersectionally. *In:* K. A. Case, ed. *Intersectional pedagogy: complicating identity and social justice.* New York: Routledge, Taylor and Francis Group.

Parker, B., 2020. Consuming health, negotiating risk, eating right: exploring the limits of choice through a feminist intersectional lens. *Journal of Critical Dietetics* [online], Special Issue, 5 (1). Available from: https://doi.org/10.32920/cd.v5i1.1336 [Accessed 5 March 2021].

Parker, B., Brady, J., Power, E., and Beylea, S., eds., 2019. *Feminist food studies: intersectional perspectives.* Toronto, Canada: Women's Press.

Parker, B., and Koeppel, M., 2020. Beyond health and nutrition: imagining the school food environment through an integrated approach. *Canadian Food Studies/La Revue Canadienne des études sur l'alimentation* [online], 7 (2). Available from: https://canadian-foodstudies.uwaterloo.ca/index.php/cfs/article/download/371/366/2492 [Accessed 6 April 2021].

Parker, B., In Press 2023. Anti-colonial praxis in community-based research in feminist food studies. *In:* M. Romano and R. Chapple, eds. *The research handbook on intersectionality.* Northampton, MA: Edward Elgar Publishing.

Power, E., Dietrich, J., Walter, Z., and Belyea, S., 2021. I don't want to say I'm broke: student experiences of food insecurity at Queen's University. *Canadian Food Studies/La Revue Canadienne des études sur l'alimentation*, 8 (1), 48–68.

Ray, K., 2016. *The ethnic restaurateur.* New York: Bloomsbury.

Romero, M., 2018. *Introducing intersectionality.* Cambridge, UK: Polity Press.

Silverthorn, D., 2016. *Hungry for knowledge: assessing the prevalence of student food insecurity on five Canadian campuses.* Available from: http://mealexchange.com [Accessed 28 August 2021].

Singleton, J., 2015. Head, heart and hands model for transformative learning: place as context for changing sustainability values. *The Journal of Sustainability Education* [online]. Available from: http://www.susted.com/wordpress/content/head-heart-and-hands-model-for-transformative-learning-place-as-context-for-changing-sustainability-values_2015_03/ [Accessed 22 May 2021].

Sumner, J., 2008. Eating as a pedagogical act: food as a catalyst for adult education for sustainable development. *In:* J. Groen and S. Guo, eds. 27th National Conference of the Canadian Association for the Study of Adult Education (CASAE) l'Association Canadienne pour l'Étude de l'Éducation des Adultes (ACÉÉA) *thinking beyond borders: global ideas, global values,* 4–7 June 2008 Vancouver, British Columbia. Available from: https://docplayer.net/130998782-Eating-as-a-pedagogical-act-food-as-a-catalyst-for-adult-education-for-sustainable-development.html [Accessed 5 September 2021].

Sumner, J., 2013. Eating as if it really matters: teaching the pedagogy of food in the age of globalization. *Brock Education Journal*, 22 (2), 41–55. Available from: https://doi.org/10.26522/brocked.v22i2.341 [Accessed 28 August 2021].

Williams-Forson, P., and Wilkerson, A., 2011. Intersectionality and food studies. *Food, Culture & Society: An International Journal of Multidisciplinary Research* 14 (1), 7–28. Available from: https://doi.org/10.2752/175174411X12810842291119 [Accessed 20 August 2021].

PART V
Conclusion

20

CONCLUSION

Food futures in education

Gurpinder Singh Lalli, Angela Turner and Marion Rutland

Food futures is complex, entangled yet fluid in that it embraces and celebrates a variety of contexts discussed in this book. Through food we can re-imagine a more inclusive society given how much lifestyles, home roles, food manufacturing industries and food products have changed over the past 50 years, and the variety of fresh produce now available but more often than not, unaffordable for many people. At the other extreme, food scarcity and poverty have been the catalyst for the rise of food banks and other organisations that ensure poverty ought not be a blocker for people to have access to food. Education, pedagogy and policy drivers are key to ensuring children and young people are exposed to food through playful, creative spaces and more importantly, are given a voice about what type of food meets their societal expectations and cultural preferences. These formative years determine their personal position as adults regarding cognitive, emotional, psychological and behavioural tendencies. It is further hoped that the issues and accordance put forward in this book, based on findings from reports and projects that have disseminated knowledge through scholarly research, promote sustainable and effective understandings about the meaning of food futures in a multidisciplinary context. Through a sociological lens, these various contexts have been examined at micro and macro levels.

Overall, this collection brings together a multidisciplinary set of chapters on food education from across the globe with a focus on policy, pedagogy, health, psychology and sociology. It sets out to establish evidence-based arguments that recognise the many facets of food education, and how learning through a futures lens and joined-up thinking is critical for shaping intergenerational fairness concerning food futures in education and society. It addresses several key issues and has a multidisciplinary approach. This book is distinctive through its multidisciplinary collection of chapters on food education from across the globe with a

DOI: 10.4324/9781003294962-25

focus on policy, pedagogy, health, psychology and sociology. The three sections of the book, i.e. (i) policy, curriculum and pedagogy, (ii) psychology of food and (iii) sociology of food, highlight thematic coverage across food studies, and how closely intertwined these areas of work are and have become.

It is important to appreciate that not all children today will learn how to cook in the home, though this may have been true in the past and still will be the case in some countries. Due to changes in lifestyle and roles many societies have seen a reduction in the time spent preparing food in the home. The food industry is an increasingly powerful and prosperous sector across the world, and some people rely increasingly on heavily processed, factory-produced food products that are easy to buy and store, quick to prepare. Foods that are relatively inexpensive against using fresh ingredients and take less preparation time. There are also countries and populations where there is food scarcity and food poverty with people relying on 'food banks' and other charity-based organisations to feed their families. These issues highlight that good food education in the classroom is very important, but that it will be dependent on the local environment and the expectations and requirements of a society, the culture of the area surrounding the school and the people that live there. All these aspects need to be considered when planning children's food education in the classroom and are essential to prepare and educate them for their future lives.

Food education in the classroom is much broader than just 'teaching children how to cook'. When they are handling food, they need to know and understand how, why and what they are doing. Food education should include the development and creative design of food products, combining all the skills and knowledge related to food preparation and nutrition. It would be unwise to leave this to out-of-school clubs or sideline it into less important and less valued elements of the school curriculum.

In the classroom children need to be exposed to a curriculum and pedagogy that provides a pathway into their future lives as healthy adults in a multicultural world, considering issues such as where foods come from, food availability, the environment and sustainability. Food education lessons in schools need to provide a pathway and progression for children who want to follow a career in the hospitality and food industry, teaching and the many other careers and activities that require an understanding of the issues involved in food and its relationship with a healthy body. The many food-related courses in further and higher education will broaden and expand the basic scientific and technological understanding of food taught in schools. Essentially, food education in schools should ensure that children are fully prepared and informed, from the perspective of 'food futures' for their healthy lives in the 21st century.

There is also an environment, other than the classroom discussed in this book where children can learn about food, in a safe, creative space during the school day. It is common across the world for schools to have a school feeding programme that provides an environment where children can eat either when they arrive at school and during a main break during the school day. However, this will vary considerably depending on the local policies adopted. Chapters in the book outline and describe varying situations.

There may be a government-funded school policy where children are able to access a well-developed and monitored school meals system providing nutritious and wholesome foods that the children can buy or, can access through a voucher scheme based on their individual needs. However, in a multicultural society with many differing parental and children's expectations this may not be fully effective. There must be a carefully structured system, managed by people with the appropriate professional skills and knowledge to monitor and ensure that the foods meet both the pupil's and parents' expectations and needs. In some countries in the past, there were advisers with nutritional expertise providing advice to several schools in a specific area. Food teachers may play an advisory role in this process, but their main role is related to teaching food within the school curriculum which, in itself, is a demanding task.

If the system is not fully planned and managed by a professional team there will be problems and disappointment for the children, increasing parental concern and wasted food. The foods provided should not be on a profit-making basis, for example 'what will sell well and make a profit for the tuck shop'. The system needs to be well established and carefully overseen by the school-based management team in co-operation with the parents. Packed meals for school children in many countries play an important role and children and parents should be encouraged, but not openly censored by the teachers to ensure that the packed meal provides the appropriate, culturally acceptable, and necessary requirements for growing children. Food teachers can play a role in exploring the concept of packed lunches in the context of their food lessons. Within the school there needs to be a safe, welcoming environment where children can eat their food, relax, enjoy and benefit from the social contact with their friends.

Food futures in education and society is an area of scholarship and public service which continues to thrive, through advocacy of a more equitable future. The learning starts in the home, it extends to society, and if we are to fulfil ambitions, then a joint-up approach is critical and ensuring voices are captured are critical to inform and operationalise future policy making.

INDEX

Note: **Bold** page numbers refer to tables; *italic* page numbers refer to figures and page numbers followed by "n" denote endnotes.

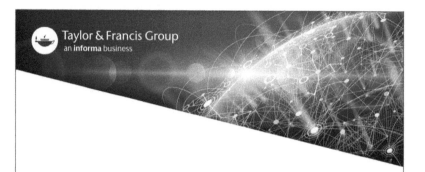